Praise for
*Kentucky Marine: Major General Logan Feland
and the Making of the Modern USMC*

"Major General Logan Feland is not a household name; David J. Bettez's work is a significant step toward rectifying that problem. Bettez has given new life to General Feland and his many accomplishments, most of which are still visible in today's modern Marine Corps. Bettez's research and writing pull together the scattered pieces of Feland's life and career at a crucial time in the Corps's history—the one-hundredth anniversary of World War I, and the downsizing of the Corps after a major war. These events still resonate, and Feland's efforts are as relevant today as they were one hundred years ago. *Kentucky Marine* is a must-read for any Marine Corps historian or enthusiast."—Annette Amerman, senior reference historian, Marine Corps History Division

"In *Kentucky Marine,* David J. Bettez opens a window on a crucial period in U.S. Marine Corps history—the first three decades of the twentieth century. Holding an architecture degree from MIT, Logan Feland was better educated than most Marine officers of his day, but proved he possessed a warrior's heart at Belleau Wood and other bloody battlefields of World War I. Bettez also shows how Feland oversaw the development of the small wars techniques in Nicaragua, which became the Marines' trademark during the interwar period and encouraged the budding amphibious warfare doctrine that permitted his Corps to come into its own during World War II."—Gregory J. W. Urwin, professor of history, Temple University

"*Kentucky Marine* follows the changes in the Marine Corps from its role as colonial infantry to amphibious assault force. David J. Bettez uses the career of Major General Logan Feland to chart this institutional change, which took Feland and the Marines to the battlefields of France. This book takes its objective."—Allan R. Millett, author of *Semper Fidelis: The History of the United States Marine Corps*

"Logan Feland is a virtually unknown Kentuckian whose story needs to be told. *Kentucky Marine* offers a wealth of research from a variety of sources to piece together the life of an important individual."—William E. Ellis, author of *A History of Education in Kentucky*

KENTUCKY MARINE

KENTUCKY MARINE

Major General Logan Feland and the Making of the Modern USMC

David J. Bettez

UNIVERSITY PRESS OF KENTUCKY

Copyright © 2014 by The University Press of Kentucky

Scholarly publisher for the Commonwealth,
serving Bellarmine University, Berea College, Centre College of Kentucky,
Eastern Kentucky University, The Filson Historical Society, Georgetown
College, Kentucky Historical Society, Kentucky State University, Morehead State
University, Murray State University, Northern Kentucky University, Transylvania
University, University of Kentucky, University of Louisville, and Western
Kentucky University.

Editorial and Sales Offices: The University Press of Kentucky
663 South Limestone Street, Lexington, Kentucky 40508-4008
www.kentuckypress.com

Unless otherwise noted, photographs are courtesy of the U.S. Marine Corps.

Library of Congress Cataloging-in-Publication Data

Bettez, David J., 1952-
  Kentucky Marine : Major General Logan Feland and the making of the modern
USMC / David J. Bettez.
     pages cm
  Includes bibliographical references and index.
  ISBN 978-0-8131-4457-3 (hardcover : alk. paper) — ISBN 978-0-8131-4482-5 (pdf)—
  ISBN 978-0-8131-4481-8 (epub)
  1. Feland, Logan, 1869-1936. 2. United States. Marine Corps—Officers—
Biography. 3. Generals—United States—Biography. 4. United States. Marine
Corps—History—20th century. 5. Belleau Wood, Battle of, France, 1918.
6. Americans—Nicaragua—Biography. 7. Nicaragua—History—1909-1937.
I. Title. II. Title: Major General Logan Feland and the making of the modern
USMC.
  VE25.F39 2014
  359.9'6092--dc23
  [B]   2013045015

This book is printed on acid-free paper meeting the requirements of the American
National Standard for Permanence in Paper for Printed Library Materials.

Manufactured in the United States of America.

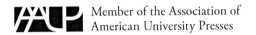 Member of the Association of
American University Presses

For my parents

Contents

Prologue

The Marine Corps general from Kentucky sat down at his desk and typed. He was sixty-one years old, brown-haired, blue-eyed, and, standing at five feet ten inches tall and weighing 160 pounds, had remained in fighting trim.

On the one hand, Logan Feland was a "Marine's Marine": tattooed, much decorated for bravery and leadership in World War I, a drinker, a smoker, and occasionally a cusser. He epitomized what the Marines called a "bushwhacker," a veteran of several expeditions overseas. On the other hand, he was an MIT graduate, an admittedly intelligent man who had married a well-respected and refined soprano. He was comfortable in New York, Philadelphia, and Washington, D.C., high society, dining with politicians, statesmen, and millionaires. He had recently commanded the Marine Corps in Nicaragua, where he had been described as "a powerful man." A Nicaraguan caricature had portrayed the general with sharp features, a pointed nose, bushy eyebrows, and closed eyes.[1]

The date was August 22, 1930. Nearing the end of a distinguished Marine Corps career spanning three decades, the general poured out his heart in lamentation. He had recently been informed that he would not achieve his goal of becoming Commandant of the U.S. Marine Corps. In a letter to his World War I commander and mentor James Harbord, the Kentucky Marine bitterly wrote: "I cannot help feeling deeply humiliated because it is true that I have been cast aside for one of the most worthless men we have ever had in the Corps. All of us know that. However, I am probably better off as it is, although I could have accomplished some good in Washington."[2]

The general had much to be proud of. Having entered the Marine Corps at the turn of the twentieth century, he had campaigned around the world, far from his birthplace in Hopkinsville, Kentucky. He had proved his bravery during World War I in the most savage battle in the history of the Marine Corps: Belleau Wood. The Kentucky Marine had risen to become one of the Corps's highest-ranked and best-regarded officers. Unfortunately, he was also approaching mandatory retirement age and had hoped to be named Commandant before ending his military career.

With his combination of field command and administrative experience, Logan Feland seemed a viable candidate for the Commandant's position when the legendary Major General John Archer Lejeune announced his retirement in 1929. At that time, however, Major General Wendell "Buck" Neville trumped his claim to the slot. Having served under Neville during World War I, Feland recognized the worthiness of the appointment. Unfortunately, Neville died only a year later, and jockeying for the Commandant's position began again. In 1930 Feland and three other officers, including his archrival Major General Smedley Darlington Butler, vied to become Commandant. Both Feland and Butler were disappointed when the secretary of the navy appointed his former Naval Academy classmate, Brigadier General Ben Fuller, to succeed Neville. Hence Feland's August 1930 lament that he had been passed over in favor of a less worthy officer. Despite his bitter disappointment, the general sent the new Commandant a congratulatory telegram.

This book is the story of that Kentucky Marine: Major General Logan Feland, USMC. Until now, his story remained largely untold, despite the fact that Feland was well known throughout Kentucky, the United States, and internationally in the 1920s. Since his death in 1936, however, Feland had been relegated to the "dustbin of history."

Much of the reason for this lack of attention rests in the man himself. Compared with his rival, Butler, Feland was a quiet figure. Butler, the son of a congressman and a two-time Medal of Honor recipient, was often the public face of Marine Corps publicity efforts in the 1920s. Feland kept a somewhat lower public profile, even though he was one of the Marine Corps's most highly decorated officers in World War I and, along with his wife, Katherine, consistently appeared in the social pages of the *Washington Post*. While Butler boosted public attention for the Marine Corps during the 1920s, Feland served in important command and administrative jobs that were at the heart of the postwar development of the Marine Corps.

In 1927 Commandant Lejeune faced a tough decision. When increasing agitation in Nicaragua and China required him to send Marine Brigades abroad, Lejeune chose then–Brigadier General Logan Feland for the most difficult and noteworthy task: commanding the hunt for Augusto Sandino in Nicaragua. In selecting Feland over Butler, Lejeune may have tacitly acknowledged which man was the more valuable Marine Corps general.

Despite failing to achieve his goal of becoming Commandant, Feland had an outstanding military career. He played a major role in the development of the modern Marine Corps—now known as the "Old Breed"—that served with distinction in World Wars I and II. During Feland's tenure, the Corps expanded exponentially in manpower, strength, and prestige. He was one of the first instructors and then a company commander in the Marines' new Advanced Base Force, which served as the forerunner of the amphibious assault force adopted before World War II. Feland's heroic actions at Belleau Wood helped make that battle one of the Corps's major successes during its illustrious twentieth-century history. Belleau Wood began the roll call of famous battles—Guadalcanal, Tarawa, Iwo Jima, Inchon, the "Frozen Chosin," Khe Sanh—that marked the USMC as a brave, effective fighting force rather than "Useless Sons Made Comfortable." In Nicaragua, Feland also played a key role in fighting the United States' "small wars," a mission that continues in the twenty-first century in Iraq and Afghanistan.

Despite Feland's active participation in the early-twentieth-century development of the Marine Corps, he remains largely unrecognized, both in his home state and in the Marine Corps that he served so faithfully. Kentuckians are familiar with other Marines, such as Presley O'Bannon, who commanded on "the shores of Tripoli" in the Barbary Wars, an event commemorated in the Marines' Hymn. Although born in Virginia, O'Bannon moved to Logan County, Kentucky, after his military service and was interred in the state capital, Frankfort. Kentuckians also remember Fleming County's Hilltop native Franklin Sousley, who helped raise the flag at Iwo Jima, an event captured in Joseph Rosenthal's iconic photograph and at the U.S. Marine Corps War Memorial outside Washington, D.C. Although Feland was included in the 1936 edition of *Who's Who in Kentucky*, the more recent *Kentucky Encyclopedia*, which lists both O'Bannon and Sousley, does not include an entry for Feland.[3] Although there is a short biography of Feland in the USMC History Division's online pantheon of personalities, the Corps has not recognized Feland by naming any bases, buildings, or roads after him, unlike his contemporaries Robert Dunlap (Dunlap Hall, Quantico), Louis McCarty Little (Little Road, Quantico), James Carson Breckinridge (Breckinridge Hall, Quantico), and Smedley Darlington Butler (Camp Butler, Okinawa).

Part of the reason Feland remains relatively unknown lies in the lack of sources, making it difficult to discover more about the man. The one-box collection of his personal papers at the Marine Corps Archives at Quantico, Virginia, is sparse, with very few personal materials. Most of the collection consists of a few official communications, such as recommendations. The collection does include a family scrapbook, most likely compiled by Feland's sister, who lived in Owensboro, Kentucky; it contains primarily newspaper accounts of Feland's career, especially its later stages. The collection also includes a fair amount of photographs; some show Feland as a young man, but most were taken in Nicaragua in the late 1920s. Unfortunately, there is no great corpus of materials such as letters to his wife of nearly forty years. Katherine and Logan Feland had no children, and there are no letters to immediate family members in the archives.

The most significant source that reveals Feland as a person is the correspondence he had with James Harbord in the 1920s and 1930s (including the previously cited letter from August 1930). During the Battle of Belleau Wood, Harbord was a U.S. Army general in charge of the Marine Brigade in which Feland served as second in command of the Fifth Regiment. Harbord was impressed with the young Kentuckian's bravery, and the two stayed in contact after the war. In 1922 Harbord retired from the U.S. Army to serve as president and then chairman of the Radio Corporation of America (RCA). The Harbord collection at the New-York Historical Society contains several letters between the two men, providing insight into Major General Logan Feland.

When these personal letters are combined with magazine and newspaper articles and Feland's official communications (such as his confidential letters to Lejeune during the Nicaraguan crisis in the late 1920s), a portrait of the general emerges. Some questions remain unanswered, but enough material exists to warrant a book devoted to this Kentuckian who became a noteworthy figure in early-twentieth-century American military history.

1

The Early Years

Logan Feland's ancestors came from Virginia, traveling over the mountains and settling in Kentucky in the early 1800s. Records indicate that his grandfather, Samuel Feland, was born in 1811 in Barren County in western Kentucky. A building contractor, he married Nancy Hammil in 1835 and was a member of the Methodist Episcopal Church. He lived to an old age, dying on January 21, 1895, in Hopkinsville, Kentucky. Samuel and Nancy Feland had two children: William, who became a physician, and Logan Feland's father, John, who became a notable lawyer and politician.[1]

John Feland was born on December 23, 1837, in Barren County, near the county seat of Glasgow. When John was a boy, the family moved farther west to Hopkinsville, the county seat of Christian County, where Samuel served as postmaster. John Feland attended Centre College in Danville, Kentucky, and then returned to Hopkinsville in 1858 to study law with James F. Buckner; he was admitted to the bar in 1860.[2]

A well-known lawyer and planter, James Buckner raised a Union infantry regiment at the outbreak of the Civil War and was elected its colonel. Like much of Kentucky, Christian County was split during the war; despite being a large slave-owning county, most of the men there became Union soldiers. Family members sometimes chose opposite sides, however. James Buckner's relative, Simon Bolivar Buckner, served as head of the Kentucky State Guard and later became a well-known general in the Confederate army. When fighting broke out, Simon Bolivar Buckner's Confederate forces attacked Christian County and captured James Buckner, whose barely organized regiment dispersed and joined other Union forces in nearby Owensboro and Henderson.[3] Some officers, including John Feland's future law partner Benjamin Bristow, joined the Union

Twenty-Fifth Kentucky Infantry; Bristow later served as a colonel with the Eighth Kentucky Cavalry. John Feland also joined the Union forces, serving as quartermaster of the Third Kentucky Cavalry. He fought with the Third Kentucky until after the Battle of Shiloh, then transferred to the Eighth Cavalry. In poor health, Feland left the army in 1863 and returned to Hopkinsville to resume his law practice.

On February 12, 1863, John Feland married Sarah (Sallie) Kennedy, great-granddaughter of Michael Kennedy, an Irish coppersmith who had immigrated to the United States in time to serve in the Revolutionary War. After the war, Kennedy moved his family to Lincoln County, Kentucky, near Stanford, one of several families that accompanied General William Logan. Eventually the Kennedy family moved farther west to Todd County. Two of Michael Kennedy's children, James and William (Sarah Kennedy's grandfather), went to Indiana to fight with General Samuel Hopkins in a campaign against the Indians at Tippecanoe and Fort Harrison. William and his wife, Ann, settled in Gibson County, Indiana, and had two sons, Seneca and William. Seneca Kennedy married Sarah Petrie; they had six children, including Sarah. Although Sarah Kennedy actually hailed from Indiana, she was descended from one of the early pioneer families of Kentucky.[4]

A year after he married Sarah, John Feland formed a law partnership with Benjamin Bristow. The partnership lasted for two years, after which Bristow decided to enter politics. He went on to serve as a Republican state senator, assistant U.S. attorney, U.S. district attorney in Louisville, the first U.S. solicitor general, and eventually secretary of the treasury under Ulysses S. Grant. John Feland also became involved in Republican politics. He served as a Kentucky state representative from 1875 to 1881 and as a senator in 1889. He ran unsuccessfully for a seat in the U.S. House of Representatives in 1880 and was considered a possible candidate for lieutenant governor in 1887.[5]

John and Sarah Feland had four children: William, John, Logan, and Mary.[6] Logan Feland was born on August 18, 1869. At the time, Christian County numbered about 23,000 inhabitants, nearly half of which were newly freed African Americans; Hopkinsville had a population of approximately 3,100. In 1870 the state legislature granted the village of Hopkinsville a charter establishing it as a city, and a board of seven councilmen was created to oversee city affairs. After the national economic depression and a severe drought in the early 1870s, Hopkinsville and Christian County began to prosper. A railroad connected the region to the outside world when Hopkinsville became a stop on the Evansville, Henderson, and Nashville line. It was still largely a farming community: a prosperous tobacco market developed, supplementing other staples such as corn, wheat, and oats. A succession of newspapers, both Democrat and Republican, covered the news.[7]

Little is known of Logan Feland's early life and education. He most likely led the typical life of a son of a successful, upper-middle-class lawyer-politician in small-town western Kentucky. Despite being a "city boy," Feland developed a love of hunting and fishing. As a young lad, he had a dog—a black and tan setter—that he loved dearly. When the animal went astray, Feland put an advertisement in the local newspaper, offering a "liberal reward" for the dog's return.[8] Following in the footsteps of his two older brothers, Logan attended Ferrell's School in Hopkinsville from 1878 to 1882. An early photograph of him shows a young boy dressed in what appears to be a Confederate uniform, in keeping with the legacy of the school's founder, Major James Overton Ferrell.[9]

Born in South Carolina, Ferrell had been a teacher before joining the Confederate army in 1861. He served throughout the South under Generals Joe Johnston and Braxton Bragg. He took part in Bragg's campaign in Kentucky, fighting at Munfordville before participating in the battles of Missionary Ridge and Chickamauga. When the war ended, Ferrell resumed teaching, first in South Carolina and then in Maryland; he relocated to Frankfort in 1869 to teach at the Kentucky Military Institute. Ferrell eventually moved to Hopkinsville in the summer of 1873 to become principal of the Christian County Military Institute, "a Military academy with a curriculum which included languages, higher mathematics, and the sciences."[10] Major Ferrell had a strong impact on his pupils. He ran Ferrell's Military Academy from 1873 to 1876; the school continued from 1876 to 1903 as Hopkinsville High School and then as Ferrell's High School. More than 600 boys passed through its doors and received a rigorous education, attending classes from 8:00 a.m. to 4:00 p.m. and studying Latin and Greek. Major Ferrell opened each day with a Bible reading.

Major Ferrell died in 1910, but his legacy would continue when a group of alumni held the first "Ferrell's Boys" reunion in 1915. Nearly

150 "boys" attended, traveling from ten states. Feland's brother John paid tribute to Ferrell in a lengthy recollection. Others spoke of his high expectations backed up by strict discipline. A Hopkinsville newspaper announcement for the 1915 reunion reproduced the 1878 "Programme of Closing Exercises" of Hopkinsville High School, revealing that each of the three Feland brothers had spoken; Logan's topic was "I'll Be a Man."[11]

After Ferrell's School, Logan Feland moved on to South Kentucky College in Hopkinsville. Originally founded in 1849 as a women's college, the school had become coeducational in 1881. In 1885 the college added a military department and a course in civil engineering. It was at South Kentucky College that Feland's technical aptitude and interest were piqued. On February 5, 1885, he was inducted into the college's Alpha Epsilon chapter of Sigma Alpha Epsilon Fraternity, along with future Kentucky governor Augustus O. Stanley. At the college's commencement exercise in June 1886, Feland received a diploma in mechanics and astronomy from the School of Mathematics, as well as a degree from the School of Engineering.[12]

In 1885 Logan Feland also began his military career when he joined Company D of the Latham Light Guards (a Hopkinsville company of the State Guard), in which his brother John served as first lieutenant. In the spring of 1886 Feland went with the Latham Light Guards to help quell disturbances at the Greenwood mine in Pulaski County, where local residents were protesting the use of prison labor in the mines. By 1888, Feland had become first sergeant of the Guards.[13]

Feland's decision to join the military can be seen as a natural outgrowth of his upbringing and environment. His ancestors had fought in the Revolutionary War and the War of 1812. Born shortly after the Civil War to a father who had fought at Shiloh, he and other Hopkinsville boys were surrounded by men who were full of stories of the war. His early education took place in what was essentially a military school, and its headmaster was a veteran of the Confederate army. He may have taken classes in the new military department at South Kentucky College. Joining the Latham Light Guards with brother John may have been viewed as a natural undertaking for a young man of his age and place in Hopkinsville society. In any case, Feland became imbued with a military spirit at an early age, and joining the Guards was just the first step toward what would eventually become a military career.

Apparently, Logan Feland also got some life experience working on the railroad as a civil engineer. Sigma Alpha Epsilon reported that "Logan Feland, C.E. '87, is an assistant on the Georgia Central Railroad, and temporarily located at Columbia, Alabama." The local newspaper also kept track of Feland, reporting that he had gone to Kuttawa, Kentucky, to "work on the O. V. road" and later noting when he returned to town for a visit.[14]

In 1889 the Feland family moved to Owensboro, Kentucky, when John Feland Sr. became a federal collector of internal revenue, a political patronage job. His son William S. Feland became deputy collector. Both men made good salaries: the collector was paid $4,500 in 1891, and the deputy collector earned $2,000.[15] Soon, however, the two Felands become embroiled in a controversy over the alleged sale of offices and other improper practices, and the scandal made the national newspapers. "Judge" Feland, as the father was known, was accused of levying assessments on Revenue Department officials and allegedly using the money to support John Jr.'s candidacy for Christian County attorney. The U.S. House of Representatives Committee on Civil Service Reform was investigating similar activities taking place throughout Kentucky. A deputy collector in Feland's office (not his son William) was eventually found guilty of violating civil service law by eliciting money to aid Republican candidates.[16] Thus Logan Feland learned about the rough-and-tumble world of politics, and he would not be afraid to use political influence in the future.

Logan Feland himself, however, avoided being caught up in the family's political difficulties. The same year his family moved to Owensboro, he enrolled at St. John's Military Academy in Manlius, New York, just outside Syracuse. Founded in 1869, St. John's had developed into a strong military school under the direction of the former adjutant general of New York, General William Verbeck, who had taken over as head of the academy in 1887. St. John's placed a special emphasis on science and engineering, serving as a preparatory school for college or the military. In light of what we know about Feland's future, a school that blended technical and military courses would have been a perfect fit for his interests.[17] At St. John's, military instruction included "practical and theoretical work in Infantry Drill Regulations, Manual of Guard Duty, map reading, duties of advance and rear guards, patrols, military law, military correspondence, organization and tactics, customs of the service and military history."[18]

Although Feland must have had a serious, studious side, he also displayed a lighter side at St. John's. During his stay there, Feland narrowly missed being caught for a prank involving an attempt to fire the sunset gun at midnight: "Feland loaded the gun with five pounds of powder, triple the normal charge, filled the muzzle with stones, and laid a kerosene soaked rope from the nozzle to a point 30 feet back and lighted it. He then ran a safe distance away to watch the fun. His prank was nipped by the housemaster, who managed to pull the burning fuse away from the nozzle before it could reach the powder. It was several years before General Verbeck learned definitely that Feland was responsible for the deed."[19]

In 1890 Logan Feland moved north to attend the Massachusetts Institute of Technology (MIT). Founded in 1861 and known informally as "Boston Tech," MIT grew exponentially from about 300 students in 1881 to more than 1,000 students in 1891 under the inspired leadership of former Union general Francis Walker. Admittance to the university was dependent on passing an examination in arithmetic, geometry, algebra, English grammar, and geography. Feland likely continued his military training in MIT's mandatory military classes for the first two years. He allegedly failed chemistry and had to take it over. Feland became a member of the Architectural Society and graduated in 1892 with a BS from the Department of Architecture after writing a senior thesis titled "An Official Residence." In later years, MIT's campus newspaper, *The Tech*, would report on Feland's notable achievements in World War I and in Nicaragua in the 1920s, and he visited the campus at least once.[20]

After graduation, Logan Feland returned to Owensboro, where he became a well-known architect. The Hopkinsville newspaper, the *Kentucky New Era*, proudly announced its receipt of a photograph of the "most complete and convenient house in Owensboro" produced by "Logan Feland, the leading architect there." Even today, standing prominently in downtown Owensboro is a restored Queen Anne–style house for which Feland served as the superintending architect.[21] In 1897 Logan Feland and contractor Robert Burch published a book, *"Southern Homes": A Collection of Designs for Residences of Modest Cost*, in which they reproduced photographs and plans of houses "in which straightforward treatment and simplicity predominate." These plans reflected a style "following the dictates of common sense," a response to what the authors excoriated as the "over-ornamented 'gingerbread' atrocities that disfigure so many of our towns and cities."[22]

With the inauguration of Democratic president Grover Cleveland in 1893, Judge Feland resigned his collector's position and resumed practicing law with John Jr. A graduate of Vanderbilt University, John Jr. had briefly been the junior member of the law firm Feland, Stipes & Feland before barely losing the 1890 election for county attorney. He then worked on the 1890 census before becoming a deputy collector of internal revenue in Louisville. With the new Democratic administration in place, he too resigned and returned to Owensboro to partner with his father. The two became well known for their role in a civil rights case: *W. H. Anderson v. Louisville and Nashville Railroad Company.*[23]

In 1892, as a follow-up to several other Jim Crow laws, the Kentucky state legislature had passed a "separate coach law" affirming railroads' right to provide "separate but equal" railroad cars for African Americans. In 1893 W. H. Anderson, an African American minister from Indiana, was traveling with his wife from Evansville on the Louisville and Nashville Railroad, having bought first-class tickets. On arriving at the train station in Henderson, Kentucky, the Andersons were forced to move to a segregated car. When Anderson sued the railroad for $15,000, John Feland Sr. served as his attorney, with John Jr. as an associate counsel. The Felands won the case in U.S. District Court in Owensboro, where Judge John Barr ruled that the Kentucky law was unconstitutional because it violated interstate commerce laws. However, a similar court case originating in Louisiana eventually led to the famous U.S. Supreme Court decision in *Plessy v. Ferguson,* affirming the legality of "separate but equal."[24]

The fact that the Felands agreed to take Anderson's case demonstrated the family's beliefs. John Sr., a staunch Republican, had served in the Union army and had lived in a county where half the population was African American. He was a champion for blacks seeking to affirm their rights in the aftermath of a war that had led to constitutional amendments granting African American slaves their freedom, making them citizens, and giving them the right to vote. The Felands fought vigorously and successfully (at least temporarily) against any abridgment of those new rights. In a state populated by numerous former slaveholders and Confederate veterans, the Felands' support of African American rights provided an important lesson in courage and strength for Logan Feland.

In his future military career, he would be much liked by his subordinates, an officer who respected his men and shared their difficulties.

In 1895 John Sr. and Sarah returned to Hopkinsville, while sons Logan and John, as well as daughter Mary, remained in Owensboro. Mary Feland had wed Owensboro businessman John Gilmour in September 1894 in what the local newspapers described as a "brilliant affair." Logan Feland served as one of the groomsmen at his sister's wedding.[25]

By age twenty-eight, Logan Feland was an established architect in Owensboro; he was an intelligent, well-educated professional with a demonstrated acumen for technical subjects. He had been brought up and trained by educated men with military backgrounds and had spent time in New York and Massachusetts, outside the restricted bounds of western Kentucky. Even as a successful professional, he retained an interest in military affairs. In June 1897 Feland helped establish a state militia company in Owensboro comprising fifty men; he was named company captain. In September 1897 Feland moved to New York City, where he worked as an architect for a college classmate, Ross F. Tucker, who had a flourishing concrete construction company.[26]

His stay in New York City would be short, however, as the Spanish-American War loomed on the horizon. The time would soon come for Logan Feland to prove his mettle as a soldier.

2

Spanish-American War Service

During the 1890s the United States looked outward: diplomacy and international relations expanded as the nation stabilized in the Gilded Age following the Civil War and Reconstruction. European powers continued to carve out spheres of influence, particularly in Africa and Asia, while also eyeing the potential for economic expansion in Latin America. Navy captain Alfred Thayer Mahan published an important book—*The Influence of Seapower upon History* (1890)—underscoring the need for a strong navy to ensure a country's power and prosperity. This prescription was reflected in Britain's worldwide naval superiority, deemed necessary to protect its far-flung empire.

The United States built a larger fleet, and political leaders became more inclined to expand U.S. influence abroad. In particular, they supported the Monroe Doctrine, under which the United States asserted its authority in the Western Hemisphere. For example, politicians and diplomats successfully resolved a serious dispute between Great Britain and Venezuela, as the United States assumed a major role in Caribbean affairs. However, a conflict with Spain over Cuba would have a different outcome.[1]

After 1895, a Cuban rebellion against Spanish control threatened extensive U.S. economic interests and citizens on the island. Mass-circulation newspapers, the so-called yellow press of William Randolph Hearst's *New York Journal* and Joseph Pulitzer's *New York World*, covered the conflict, stoking the interest and concern of many people in the United States. According to the eminent historian George Herring, "National pride, a resurgent sense of destiny, and a conviction that the United States as a rising world power must take responsibility for world events in its area of influence gave an increasing urgency to the Cuban crisis."[2]

In 1897 and into 1898, diplomatic tension grew between Spain and the United States, inexorably drawing the two countries closer to war. On February 9, 1898, Hearst's *New York Journal* published a private letter from Spain's minister in Washington, Enrique Dupuy de Lôme, that disparaged President William McKinley. A week later, on February 15, the USS *Maine* exploded in Havana Harbor. Many people blamed Spain for the deaths of more than 250 U.S. sailors and Marines and demanded war. Pushed by a jingoistic press and politicians, and pulled by the attractiveness of eliminating a persistent problem, McKinley acquiesced as Congress took the lead in seeking war. On April 19 Congress passed a joint resolution recognizing Cuban independence and approving a rider, the Teller amendment, that prohibited the United States from laying claim to the island. Spain subsequently declared war, and on April 25 Congress retroactively declared that war had existed with Spain since April 21.[3]

The United States was unprepared for battle, especially a land campaign. U.S. officials quickly determined that the onus for fighting the war would fall primarily on the U.S. Navy, which was a bit better prepared than the other armed forces to fight the Spanish. The U.S. Army was particularly weak, comprising a relatively small number of troops better suited to fighting small-scale wars against the Indians out on the Great Plains.[4] With the declaration of war, a massive effort was undertaken to expand the army for what could be a two-front war: in the Caribbean, in Cuba and Puerto Rico, and in the Pacific in the Philippine Islands. To increase troop strength, U.S. military officials decided to call on National Guard units from the states. Each state was assigned a quota for troops. In Kentucky, three infantry regiments were at first envisioned, drawn from various State Guard troops and other volunteers. In western Kentucky, the State Guard units from Hopkinsville and Owensboro would initially be led by John Feland and Logan Feland, respectively.[5]

Logan Feland was working in New York City as an architect at the time. His former classmate and future MIT professor Ross Tucker later reminisced: "At the outbreak of the Spanish War he was working in my office. Forthwith he disappeared—joined a Kentucky regiment—and served through the war, from lieutenant to major." Tucker seemed astonished: "He was the last man in the world you would ever have picked out to be a soldier—a tall, skinny, slouchy Kentuckian, who couldn't be serious three minutes at a time."[6] As the prospect of war grew, Feland sent word that he would return to Owensboro and take command of Company H as soon as war was declared. The *Owensboro Daily Messenger* looked forward to Feland's return and noted, "Logan Feland is a fine young man, refined, modest and retiring, but game as they are ever made. The affection his company bears for him is shared by all citizens who know him. He should and will have upon his arrival a hearty welcome from Company H and all Owensboro."[7]

On Sunday, April 24, the commander of the Third Kentucky Regiment, Colonel T. J. Smith, informed Captain Morton Radford that Company H would be called out on Monday. Radford instructed his men to show up in uniform at the local armory at 9:00 a.m. Monday for drill. According to Radford, they had no choice in the matter: no company member would be excused. Some of the men were surprised, believing that their service would be voluntary. The company was authorized to have 103 men, and several volunteers stepped forward to fill the ranks.[8]

Many Owensboro citizens turned out on Monday morning to watch Company H muster. Questions arose about what would happen next: Would the company be sent immediately to Louisville or Bowling Green to join other Kentucky companies? Or would Company H be sent directly to the main staging ground for militia volunteers and regular army troops at Chickamauga Battlefield Park, Georgia? After drilling for an hour, the men of Company H dispersed until later that evening, when they and an excited Owensboro citizenry greeted Captain Feland when he arrived by train from New York. The overflow crowd then moved to the courthouse yard, where several folks gave speeches. After being presented with a flag, Logan Feland thanked the citizens and "pledged himself and his company to defend the flag with their lives." Feland also thanked Captain Radford, calling him the "bravest of the brave." Radford had decided to stay home to care for his mother while Feland took command of the company. Thus, Feland diplomatically handled what could have been an awkward moment for his colleague. The *Owensboro Daily Messenger* observed: "Capt. Feland surprised his friends by his oratory."[9]

Swelled by new enlistments, Company H reached 179 members, but as Captain Feland pointed out, not everyone was qualified. He would not accept any volunteer younger than eighteen years old; the rest would be examined by Dr. Griffith, the regiment's physician, to ensure they met the physical requirements for military service. Contrary to popular expectations, Feland did not anticipate much happening in the next few days. The old army adage about "hurry up and wait" proved true. National conditions dictated the pace of preparation and mobilization. After debate, U.S. civilian and military officials changed the course of action. Instead of a small force pressed into immediate action against Cuba, a larger force would be gathered, based largely on a volunteer army of state militiamen. This decision led to serious challenges in training and equipping the army. In the meantime, U.S. Navy action would take precedence, with an immediate blockade of Cuba.[10]

On Tuesday evening, April 26, members of Company H met and formally elected Logan Feland their captain. On April 28 Feland received orders from Colonel Smith to keep in close contact with his company, which could be called up at any time, although there was speculation that the order would come the following week. As Company H languished, awaiting further orders, men from the countryside stayed in Owensboro at the campground, while men from the city went home each evening. Volunteers continued to come and go; the company's makeup shifted constantly. Then orders came from state authorities limiting each company to eighty-four men, with no one younger than eighteen or older than forty-five allowed to serve. Feland drilled the men daily, but they chafed at the delay, and by May 4 many of the rural men had gone home, while the city men returned to their normal employment. Only a dozen remained in camp, but Feland felt certain that he had a pool of ninety-six men from which to achieve the quota of eighty-four.[11]

On May 5, 1898, Logan Feland received orders that Company H should be prepared to move in two days. State authorities had wavered between Louisville and Lexington as the main staging ground for the three Kentucky regiments, but they eventually decided that Lexington had the best railroad connections to Chattanooga, where there was a major army staging ground at nearby Fort Thomas in Chickamauga. Feland and his men met at the Owensboro armory on Friday in anticipation of marching to the train station and departing at 11:00 a.m. on Saturday, fully prepared for their new adventure. Because of a surplus of volunteers, Feland put up a notice that no man younger than twenty-one could go without parental permission. Of the company's eighty-four men, thirty-two were from the original Company H, and the rest were newcomers. Their occupations ranged from architect (Feland) to banker to druggist to teacher, but the majority of the men listed their occupation as farmer.[12]

An estimated crowd of more than 3,000 people—a huge number in a county that size—turned out on Saturday, May 7, 1898, to watch Company H, along with other companies from Madisonville and Henderson, leave on the train bound for Lexington. After arriving in Lexington shortly after 5:00 p.m., Company H detrained and marched the short distance to Tattersall's Fairground, which had been designated Camp Collier, after the adjutant general of the Kentucky troops, Daniel R. Collier. The Second and Third Kentucky Regiments remained at Camp Collier, while the First Regiment went to Lexington's Woodland Park Chautauqua Grounds, where Camp Bradley, named after the governor, had been created. At Camp Collier, the men were housed in the Tattersall's Racetrack barns, with eight men assigned to each eight- by ten-foot horse stall. Captain Feland found himself quartered with seven privates. Feland and the company quartermaster went into town on Sunday and "bought beef steak, eggs, potatoes, beans, onions, etc." Feland was reportedly kept "busy night and day hustling for his men to get a comfortable place to sleep and plenty to eat."[13]

At Camp Collier, Feland's Company H drilled and underwent further physical examinations. Not all the Owensboro men were found to be qualified, so Feland sent word back home asking for more volunteers to replace them. According to initial reports, the "Kentucky boys" were somewhat undisciplined and had a liking for strong alcoholic drink, but within a couple of weeks the troops had acquired a more appropriate military bearing. Company H followed a routine: roll call at 6:00 a.m., breakfast at 7:00, drill from 9:30 to 11:30, lunch at 12:30 p.m., more drill from 3:00 to 5:30, supper at 6:30, and lights out at 9:30.

Even under this regimen, Company H chafed. Approximately a month had passed since Feland's arrival in Owensboro, and he was growing impatient. By May 20, Feland "was so disgusted with delays and rejections . . . that he thought of withdrawing his company, and seven men did go home, but he [Feland] thought better of it and remains."[14] By May 22, however, Company H had finally been officially mustered into the U.S. Volunteer Army, with sixty-five privates, twelve noncommissioned officers, and three officers. Under a new ordering system, Company H

Logan Feland as a U.S. volunteer in the Spanish-American War. (Marine Corps Archives)

became Company F, Third Kentucky Regiment, with Logan Feland as the captain.

In the meantime, brother John continued to prepare his own Company D—also known as the Latham Light Guards (because of its funding by John Latham)—as war fever gripped the small town of Hopkinsville. On April 29 Company D assembled to receive a gift of a flag presented by a gathering of 500 local citizens, and by May 10, it too had arrived in Lexington. Unfortunately, John Feland ran into far more trouble than did his younger brother Logan. On May 20 the *Hopkinsville Kentuckian* reported that Company D had begun to disintegrate as many dissatisfied men returned home, including John Feland. It is unclear whether he resigned or was terminated, but John's conduct and command of the company aroused criticism. The controversy became political when Governor Bradley refused to accept Gordon Nelson, chosen by the men of Company D, as John's successor (state guardsmen traditionally elected their own leaders). Instead, the governor appointed a Frankfort man, Noel Gaines, to be the new captain of Company D, but the majority of the Hopkinsville men refused to serve under Gaines.[15]

In response to the upheaval, Adjutant General Daniel R. Collier issued a statement explaining the situation: "The company had become disorganized and substantially disbanded, owing to its Captain's [John] having been intoxicated and incapacitated for duty." Collier noted that "at the request of Captain Feland and upon the urgent request of his father and brother, to let him down as easily as possible," he had worked out a deal with Governor Bradley to allow John Feland to return to Hopkinsville with any disaffected men and create a new company of the State Guard.[16]

A week after returning to Hopkinsville, John met with members of his old command and gave them an accounting of the money spent from John Latham's generous donation.[17] Given the governor's apparent high-handedness in appointing a political crony of dubious reputation to command Company D, John Feland emerged from this incident seemingly unscathed; he remained a prominent Hopkinsville lawyer and judge for many years. During this tumultuous period, brother Logan managed a quick trip to Hopkinsville on May 26 to deal with the family crisis. He then returned to Lexington, remaining in firm control of his own company.[18]

While the Feland brothers were trying to get their companies in order and the U.S. Volunteer Army was gradually coming together, the naval war with Spain developed quickly. On May 1, 1898, a U.S. fleet under Commodore George Dewey entered Manila Bay in the Philippines and engaged a Spanish fleet commanded by Rear Admiral Patricio Montojoy Pasaron. In a quick and decisive battle, Dewey's fleet decimated the Spanish vessels, proving the strength and effectiveness of the U.S. Navy, establishing Dewey as a national hero, and identifying the United States as a major power in the Pacific.[19]

On June 1, 1898, Captain Logan Feland's Company F and the other companies of the Third Kentucky Regiment broke camp and boarded a train for Camp George H. Thomas in Chickamauga, Georgia, just south of Chattanooga, Tennessee. New orders had been issued to increase company strength to 106 men, so Feland wrote to his former sergeant Otis Ford (sent back to Owensboro after failing the physical examination), asking him to find more men to fill the newly allocated slots. Speculation about the regiment persisted. Would it remain at Camp Thomas all summer? Or would it be sent to the Philippines?[20]

In April 1898 Camp Thomas (named for the gallant Union general at the Battle of Chickamauga) became the staging ground for regular army troops being sent to the Caribbean. After the regulars moved south in mid-May, the volunteer regiments started pouring in, swelling the camp population to nearly 60,000 men. The camp suffered as men and material came together in a somewhat haphazard fashion. The army erected supply depots and warehouses, and it provided water, sanitary, and medical facilities. All this took time and coordination. Conditions at Camp Thomas highlighted the enormous difficulties in quickly assembling more than 250,000 regular and volunteer soldiers.

Initially the war mobilization plan had called for far fewer troops, but pressure from guard members and the states had resulted in a larger call-up. The national army was therefore unprepared logistically to deal with such large numbers. As historian Graham Cosmas has noted, "the great troop concentrations presented an administrative problem that was almost insurmountable, considering the staff and resources available to the War Department at the outset. . . . In every camp a critical shortage of staff officers prevented efficient management."[21]

At Camp Thomas the Third Kentucky became part of First Corps headed by Major General John R. Brooke. Unfortunately, Brooke (the commander of Camp Thomas) had too many responsibilities and not enough experience in organizing and leading large groups of soldiers. He "all but lost control of Camp Thomas" and "neglected the sanitary condition of the camp."[22] As Feland's Company F settled into a routine at Camp Thomas, the men complained about the heat, the lack of water, and the lack of pay. The water situation proved to be a huge challenge, as Chickamauga Creek was located on the camp's eastern edge, far from where the men were bivouacked. Governor Bradley visited the Third Regiment but brought no funds. The men grew more dissatisfied, and a June 16 headline reported "Almost a Mutiny—In the Third Regiment Because of the Scarcity of Food."[23] The regimental commander, Colonel Smith, scouted out a new location and ordered Captain Feland to use his engineering skills and technical expertise to lay out the new facilities.[24] Conditions at the new camp were healthier, and order was imposed.

Still, the men of Company F needed diversions from the heat, the monotonous food, and the drilling. Despite the efforts of aid groups such as the Red Cross, the War Relief Commission, and the Women's Christian Temperance Union, the men drank and gambled to while away the hours, in addition to participating in healthier pursuits such as playing baseball, attending concerts and plays, and wandering the hallowed historical ground of Chickamauga.[25]

The two-front war continued without the Third Kentucky Regiment. On June 9, 1898, Marine Corps troops landed at Guantanamo Bay, Cuba, to set up a base to support a naval fleet operating under Admiral William Sampson. A U.S. naval force accepted the surrender of the Pacific island of Guam on June 20. Former assistant secretary of the navy Theodore Roosevelt and his "Rough Riders" charged to fame up Kettle Hill in the Battle for San Juan Heights on July 1. Two days later a U.S. fleet commanded by Commodore Winfield Scott Schley destroyed a Spanish fleet attempting to leave Santiago Bay, Cuba; on July 15 the Spanish garrison at Santiago surrendered. The Spanish soon initiated contact with the goal of suspending hostilities and negotiating an end to the war. Nevertheless, U.S. officials believed the fight in the Caribbean was not over: Puerto Rico might be next. Preparations also continued to send troops to the Philippines, where insurgents under the leadership of Emilio Aguinaldo had declared independence from Spain.[26]

At the end of July 1898 the Third and First Kentucky Regiments received orders to depart for Newport News, Virginia. Feland's Company F left Chickamauga by railroad on July 27 and arrived in Newport News two days later. At a camp named for former Union general and president Ulysses S. Grant, the regiment bivouacked along the banks of the James River and prepared to be posted to Puerto Rico. Although not as bad as Camp Thomas, conditions at Camp Grant were less than ideal because of the sandy soil, high temperatures, and bad food.[27]

The *Owensboro Daily Messenger* reported on August 3, 1898, that the Third Kentucky Regiment would sail for Puerto Rico on the transport *Yale*, along with brigade commander General Frederick Dent Grant, son of the former president. As reported by "Warrior," the newspaper's special correspondent, morale remained high in Captain Feland's unit, and the men were anxious to go to Puerto Rico. Unfortunately, the deleterious conditions at Camp Thomas finally caught up with Company F and the Third Regiment. Due to the overcrowding and lack of sanitation there, many of the men were suffering from typhoid, mumps, and measles. While elements of the First Kentucky Regiment—the "Louisville Legion"—set sail for Puerto Rico on August 4, the Third Kentucky Regiment and Company F were left behind, their places taken by an Illinois regiment.[28]

The War Department eventually addressed the food issue by ordering each regiment to hire a "competent cook." By mid-August, "confusion in Washington and in the camps gradually subsided," and "most of the regiments called out in early May were approaching battle readiness."[29]

On August 12, 1898, the United States and Spain signed a peace protocol that ended the fighting; the official end of the war would come with the signing of the Treaty of Paris in December 1898. The Third Kentucky Regiment left Newport News on August 16 and arrived two days later in Lexington, Kentucky, where it awaited its fate: it would either be disbanded or used as occupation troops in former Spanish colonies. Sent first to Wells Farm and then to Camp Hamilton, much of the regiment was still ill, and many of the men signed a petition asking that the regiment be mustered out. Feland "seemed to be very much hurt and surprised at their signing the petition in such numbers, and among other things talked of resigning and going in the ranks to show he had no ill feeling in the matter and only wanted discipline."[30]

The disaffection among Feland's troops mirrored the malaise infecting much of the volunteer army at this point. When the war began, expectations had been high, and everyone had anticipated adventure and glory in foreign lands. Given the quick nature of the Spanish defeat on sea and land, however, less than a quarter of the 200,000 U.S. volunteers had been sent abroad by the time an armistice was signed in August. Many of the volunteers remained in camps that were ill equipped to deal with the influx of troops. Finally, as Cosmas points out: "With the opening of peace talks in July and the signing of the armistice in August, discipline and morale among the Volunteers began to break down." For nearly four months they had trained but had never engaged in combat. Cosmas notes that men refused orders, mutinied, and demanded that they be allowed to return home.[31] After the armistice, President McKinley disbanded about half of the volunteer army, but the Third Kentucky Regiment would be retained for occupation duty.

Captain Feland's men reflected the volunteers' discontent. Many of them wished to be mustered out, but others wanted to stay and serve in what would apparently be an army of occupation in the Caribbean. *Owensboro Daily Messenger* correspondent "Tin Soldier" speculated that if Company F was not mustered out, the men would return temporarily to Owensboro using the "hot foot" method: "simply walking away some bright morning and staying nine days"—one day short of being termed a deserter. Somewhat tongue in cheek, "Tin Soldier" noted that the officers were "as solicitous of our welfare as any mother could be of her young baby. We are petted and caressed so that we are getting very much spoiled." As for Feland:

The most notable event in military circles last night was Capt. Feland having us march down town and giving an exhibition drill on one of the principal streets. No speeches were made nor promises to plant the flag on Cuban soil, and this was the whole performance, but we did have a glorious time, although the captain did forget himself and imagine he was at old Chickamauga once more and give half of the company "double time" for about a mile in the broiling hot sun. People can say what they please of Capt. Feland's conduct toward us at Chickamauga and Newport News, but here at Lexington, when we were about to be mustered in, and now that we are about to be mustered out and go home and settle old scores there is not a nicer captain on the grounds or one that is more devoted to his men.[32]

The *Messenger's* "Tin Soldier" had it wrong: the Third Regiment was not mustered out. When division commander Brigadier General Joseph Sanger visited Lexington, he complimented the regiment. When a petition in favor of staying in the army was circulated, it was signed by 520 of the 672 men. The Third Kentucky received notice that it would become part of the army of occupation in the Caribbean, and speculation grew that it would be posted to Puerto Rico.[33]

Despite some discontent, Feland's Company F participated in a drill competition and tied for first place with a company from the 160th Indiana. Winning the contest certainly improved morale, as noted in the *Owensboro Daily Messenger*: "When Company F, under Capt. Feland, returned to the regiment Friday night after winning the competitive drill, a most enthusiastic welcome awaited them. Cheers and shouts filled the air, and for a time pandemonium reigned at camp." In mid-October Feland's company represented the Third Regiment in a replication of the salute fired at Queen Victoria's Jubilee and at a reception for First Army Corps commander Major General Joseph C. Breckinridge, who would become the U.S. Army inspector general.[34]

After going home to Owensboro on leave from October 20 to 26, Feland and the rest of the Third Regiment entrained on November 11 for Columbus, Georgia, headed for their winter quarters at Camp Conrad. Fortunately, the army handled the reorganization and redeployment of the remaining troops better than it did the initial preparations for war. Conditions at Columbus were much better than at Camp Thomas, with a much smaller contingent and correspondingly better supplies, sanitation, and health services.[35] At Columbus, Feland became provost marshal, effective January 6, 1899. As such, he would assume greater responsibilities, such as ensuring law and order in the camp, and gain important administrative experience. The Columbus newspaper described Feland as an "efficient and capable officer" who was "very popular among the members of his company, all of whom regret to give him up from their midst." Before he could assume his duties, however, Feland rushed home to Hopkinsville, where John Feland Sr. was gravely ill. He passed away on January 8, 1899.[36]

Feland returned to Columbus just in time to leave: on January 17 his regiment departed by rail for Savannah, the main embarkation point for troops bound for Cuba. In Savannah, Feland's men boarded a transport ship, the *Minnewaska*, which arrived at Matanzas, Cuba, on January 21, 1899. In Matanzas, Feland's architectural and engineering skills proved valuable again when he was put in charge of repairing a barracks. A week later the Second Battalion, including Company F, traveled to Cardenas to set up camp. Company F remained in Cardenas until March 2, when it returned to Matanzas. During this time, Feland also went on detached duty, serving temporarily as acting army quartermaster at Colon. While in Colon, he also oversaw repair of the jail. Feland performed well, and a *Louisville Courier-Journal* correspondent concluded that he was among the best officers of the regiment.[37]

Company F and the Third Regiment's other units stayed in Cuba for two months before boarding the army transport *Kilpatrick* on April 8 for the return voyage to the United States. They stayed at a quarantine station near the mouth of the Savannah River before being sent to Dafuskie Island to be quarantined. Company F returned to Savannah on April 18 to await mustering out, which finally took place on May 16, 1899.[38]

Logan Feland had served in the U.S. Volunteer Army for a year. Although he did not see combat, he gained valuable experience as a company commander integrated into a regiment. He had been selected as provost marshal at Columbus, an acknowledgment of his leadership. He had managed his troops during a contentious period, yet his men still performed well. His technical skills also set him apart from most other officers. Feland's life changed dramatically as a result of his army experience. Instead of returning to civilian life as an architect, he contemplated further military service.

Back in Owensboro, the ladies' committee of the YMCA prepared to honor the returning men of Company F. Captain Feland had telegraphed the *Owensboro Daily Messenger* that the company would arrive home on Thursday morning, May 18, and they were greeted by a couple thousand townspeople. The company marched to the former armory, where Feland called them to attention, and the company's first sergeant gave the command to dismiss. At the YMCA banquet that evening, Captain Feland thanked the main speakers on behalf of the company. The *Daily Messenger* reported that Feland would not remain in the city but would return to Hopkinsville to visit his mother.[39]

Back in Hopkinsville, Logan Feland and a few other members of Company F were feted at the new house of his older brother John on May 25. Guests included prominent local figures such as Colonel Jouett Henry, who would soon be elected mayor of Hopkinsville and would eventually serve as adjutant general of the Kentucky State Guard, as well as members of the Latham Light Guards and others who had served in the war.[40]

Feland was not planning to stay in Hopkinsville; nor would he return to his architectural practice in New York City. His military experience had shifted, or clarified, his career interests. Supported by Senator William J. Deboe and Judge Walter Evans (his father's former law partner), Feland sought both a temporary appointment to the U.S. Volunteer Army (which was gearing up to go to the Philippines) and a permanent appointment to the U.S. Marine Corps. He received the temporary army appointment as a first lieutenant and scored exceptionally well on the Marine Corps examination, earning the highest grade: 98.75. Unfortunately, he failed the physical examination in Washington, D.C., "owing to an affection of the heart," as reported in the *Hopkinsville Kentuckian*. He would, however, be allowed to continue with the "mental" examinations and then be reexamined physically.[41]

Faced with possible rejection from the Marine Corps on medical grounds, Logan Feland called on important contacts to plead his case. Senator Deboe wrote to Secretary of the Navy John D. Long and asked that Feland's physical examination be waived, especially in view of his successful service during the Spanish-American War. In a bipartisan effort, Kentucky's other senator, Democrat William Lindsay, also wrote to President William McKinley on Feland's behalf, requesting that the medical examination be waived. Dr. Austin Bell from Hopkinsville, who had served as surgeon major of the Third Kentucky Regiment, wrote a letter attesting to Feland's excellent physical condition. Feland also received support from the current collector of internal revenue in Owensboro, E. T. Franks, and from Democratic congressman Henry Dixon Allen, who represented Kentucky's Second District, which included Hopkinsville.[42] The efforts of Feland's supporters worked. Despite the alleged heart defect that would have disqualified him from service, Feland received a permanent appointment as a Marine Corps first lieutenant, reportedly making $1,900 a year in salary plus a housing allowance of $40 a month.[43]

Smedley Darlington Butler.
Son of a Pennsylvania
congressman and two-time
recipient of the Medal of
Honor, Butler would be first
a friend and then a rival of
Feland's.

Logan Feland fit the profile of the typical Marine Corps officer of the period. From 1882 until the start of the Spanish-American War, Marine Corps officers had been graduates of the U.S. Naval Academy. This so-called naval aristocracy included future Marine Corps Commandants Wendell Neville, John Lejeune, and Ben Fuller, who would play large roles in Feland's career. These Annapolis graduates were often well connected politically, and many of their fathers had served in the armed forces. Nearly half the officers had attended private schools before enrolling at Annapolis. Most appointees were from middle- to upper-middle-class families; their fathers' professions included military officer, banker, lawyer, manufacturer, physician, government official, and merchant. These officers were white, primarily Protestant, and dedicated to "service, glory, and honor."[44]

Feland and his fellow officers in the 1899 intake were not necessarily Annapolis graduates, but they shared most of the same characteristics. The group included some men who would become Marine Corps leg-

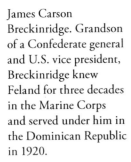

James Carson Breckinridge. Grandson of a Confederate general and U.S. vice president, Breckinridge knew Feland for three decades in the Marine Corps and served under him in the Dominican Republic in 1920.

ends and some who would serve through World War II. Smedley Darlington Butler and James Carson Breckinridge were among those who had joined the Corps during the Spanish-American War. The son of a congressman, Butler had enlisted at age sixteen and had gone to Cuba as part of Lieutenant Colonel Robert Huntington's Battalion stationed at Guantanamo. Like most other new officers, Second Lieutenant Butler had been mustered out of the Corps in February 1899, but the newly legislated increase in the Marine Corps's size enabled him to rejoin in April 1899 as a first lieutenant. Destined to become a legend and a two-time recipient of the Medal of Honor, Butler would be a friend and then a rival of Logan Feland as their Marine Corps careers developed.[45]

Despite being born in Memphis, James Carson Breckinridge was one of the famous Breckinridges of Kentucky, who counted among their number a vice president of the United States, a U.S. senator, and other distinguished members. Grandson of Vice President John Cabell Breckinridge and son of Clifton Rodes Breckinridge, a U.S. minister to Russia,

James Carson Breckinridge had been appointed a Marine Corps second lieutenant at the outbreak of the Spanish-American War. Like Butler, he had been released in March 1899, only to rejoin a month later. Breckinridge would go on to have a distinguished forty-three-year career, becoming well known for his efforts in Marine Corps education.[46]

Other officers who joined the Marine Corps in 1899 came from other backgrounds. Several had served in army units during the Spanish-American War. Many would go on to win fame in the Marine Corps. David Dixon Porter, grandson of a famous Civil War admiral of the same name, eventually received a Medal of Honor and became a major general. Hiram Bearss would earn a Medal of Honor before retiring as a colonel. Louis McCarty Little, a graduate of the well-regarded Rensselaer Polytechnic Institute, would become a major general and assistant to the Marine Corps Commandant, a position also held by Lejeune, Neville, Fuller, and Feland. Another contemporary who was released after serving in the Corps during the Spanish-American War and then recommissioned was Randolph Berkeley; he would receive a Medal of Honor, serve under Feland in Nicaragua in the late 1920s, and retire as a major general. Harry Lee would command a Marine Corps regiment in World War I, serve as military governor of Santo Domingo, and retire as a major general. Harold C. Snyder would be Feland's second in command in the Fifth Regiment during World War I and would retire as a colonel. Like Feland, Julius Turrill would receive a Distinguished Service Cross for gallantry at Belleau Wood and become a general.[47]

In sum, when he was appointed to the Marine Corps in 1899, Logan Feland joined a group of peers who would distinguish themselves. Although many of these men were well connected socially and politically, they would not enjoy the easy lives of their predecessors; they would not be "Useless Sons Made Comfortable."[48] The United States had new responsibilities, and the Marine Corps would be called on to engage in combat and peacekeeping operations throughout the new American empire and beyond.

The impact of the Spanish-American War on the Marine Corps was tremendous. Even if its combat contributions were modest, the Corps changed dramatically as a result of its involvement. In the words of Marine Corps historians analyzing the conflict 100 years later: "The modern Marine Corps owes its genesis to the Spanish-American War when the United States entered the world stage."[49]

When the USS *Maine* blew up in Havana Harbor on February 15, 1898, twenty-eight Marines died. At the end of April, the Marine Corps Commandant, Colonel Charles Heywood, assembled a battalion of 600 men drawn from Marine Corps barracks along the East Coast. Under the command of Civil War veteran Lieutenant Colonel Robert Huntington, the battalion shipped out from Brooklyn, New York, to Key West, Florida, where it went ashore in anticipation of an assignment. In the meantime, Marines on Commodore George Dewey's ships fought first, manning guns during the Battle of Manila Bay on May 1, 1898. Two days later, Marines under Lieutenant Dion Williams landed and captured the Spanish naval base at Cavite, southwest of Manila. The Marine Corps would maintain a garrison there for the next fifty years.

When the Marine Corps came under severe scrutiny a few years later, then-Admiral Dewey acknowledged that if he had had a force of 5,000 Marines in 1898, he could have captured Manila, possibly averting the subsequent Philippine insurrection. In 1898 the Marine Corps totaled just over 3,000 men, and they were divided among widespread ships and barracks. A new Naval Appropriations Act increased the Marines' manpower by 43 lieutenants and 1,500 men, but only for the duration of the war.[50]

In Cuba in mid-May, fleet Marines participated in a raid that cut underwater telegraph cables, disrupting Spanish communications. In support of an army decision to capture Santiago, the navy sought a nearby location for a coaling station. Subsequently, Huntington's Battalion sailed to Cuba to establish an advance base on Guantanamo Bay. Fleet Marines under Captain Mancil Goodrell landed first on June 7, followed by Huntington's Battalion on June 10. After facing some Spanish resistance, Huntington sent some of his Marines, under Captain George Elliott, to destroy a nearby Spanish water source, Cuzco Well. American novelist and journalist Stephen Crane accompanied Elliott's men, and his *New York World* articles highlighted the bravery they displayed during the raid. On July 3 Marines in the U.S. fleet under the command of Commodore Schley participated in the destruction of the Spanish fleet in Santiago Harbor. In the Pacific, fleet Marines also helped secure the island of Guam. With the signing of the peace protocol in August, the Marines of

Huntington's Battalion returned to Portsmouth, New Hampshire, where the citizenry greeted them like heroes. Part of the battalion also paraded before President McKinley during a rainstorm in the nation's capital.[51]

In this "splendid little war," the Marine Corps claimed to be the "first to fight," having participated in the first land action and first flag raising on enemy territory. Previously suspect, the Marine Corps greatly improved its image based on the good publicity it received during the war. Huntington's Battalion not only captured the attention of Stephen Crane but also received extensive coverage in major newspapers and periodicals such as the *Chicago Tribune* and *Harper's Weekly*. Regardless of whether the action at Guantanamo was significant, as has been debated by modern historians, the public attention and approbation garnered by Huntington's Battalion set the stage for increased attention to publicity in the future. When the United States entered World War I nearly twenty years later, the Corps would put its slogan, "First to Fight," to good use in recruitment.[52]

Historian George Herring has noted that "although it was by no means clear at the time, the War of 1898 also marked the beginning of what would come to be called the American Century." The acquisition of territories such as the Philippines, Guam, Puerto Rico, and Cuba, even if temporary, increased the need for a larger navy and an expanded Marine Corps. More Marines were needed on ships and to garrison barracks at new naval stations such as Guantanamo and Cavite.[53]

The stage was set for a new chapter in Logan Feland's life—as a career U.S. Marine Corps officer and a sea soldier of the new empire.

3

Professional and Personal Milestones, 1899–1907

In March 1899 President McKinley signed a bill doubling the size of the Marine Corps to 6,000 men and 201 line officers. The bill also authorized an increase in rank to brigadier general for the Marine Corps Commandant. In the words of Corps historian Allan Millett, "The War with Spain was a historic watershed for the Marine Corps." Given the navy's success during the war, "the twentieth century began with both the Navy and the Marine Corps in a state of high institutional prosperity."[1] Thus the Marine Corps's role in the new American empire solidified.

On July 22, 1899, newly appointed First Lieutenant Logan Feland reported to the Marine Barracks at Eighth and I Streets in Washington, D.C. It was the oldest post of the Corps, having been founded in 1801. It also contained the residence of the Marine Corps Commandant and was home to the Marine Corps Band. From its inception in 1891, the School of Application at the Marine Barracks had trained new officers, stressing infantry skills, guard duty, small-arms firing, tactics, and strategy, as well as subjects such as naval gunnery, use of mines and torpedoes, and military law. Because the school had been suspended during the war, Feland would have to learn from fellow officers stationed at the barracks, especially the war veterans. Like the veterans, Feland offered something other new officers might not possess: maturity and experience. Just a month shy of his thirtieth birthday, Feland was older than most of his contemporaries by almost a decade. For example, he was eight years older than James Carson Breckinridge, eleven years older than Smedley Darlington Butler, and nearly nine years older than Louis McCarty Little.[2]

Feland reported to Captain Francis H. Harrington, barracks com-

Logan Feland as a new Marine Corps first lieutenant. (Marine Corps Archives)

mander and a veteran of the Spanish-American War. Harrington had been captain of artillery Company F of Huntington's Battalion at Guantanamo Bay, commanding four three-inch guns. He would retire from the Marine Corps in December 1904 as a brigadier general. During his time under Harrington's command, Feland trained and served as officer of the day. In this capacity, he made periodic visits to men on watch; inspected men, quarters, and provisions; and contributed to the overall vigilance of the barracks.

On October 2 Harrington led a combined contingent of sailors and Marines in welcoming home the hero of Manila Bay, Admiral George Dewey. The Marine Corps Band marched in a grand parade, along with a Marine battalion consisting of 17 officers and 221 enlisted men drawn from Washington, Philadelphia, Annapolis, Norfolk, and several ships. On this memorable day, Feland served as battalion adjutant during the parade, managing administrative duties. Participants included two other Marine Corps officers with Kentucky connections: Captain Cyrus S. Radford, an 1899 graduate of the U.S. Naval Academy hailing from Christian County, and First Lieutenant James Carson Breckinridge. (Both Radford and Breckinridge would cross paths with Feland in the future and would eventually retire as generals.) Shortly after Dewey's parade, on October 12, Feland and Breckinridge, under the command of Captain Herbert L. Draper, led a sesquicentennial parade in Arlington, Virginia.[3] Feland would soon serve under Draper again—this time, in the Philippines.

After the war against Spain, some Filipinos, led by Emilio Aguinaldo, balked at replacing one imperialist conqueror, Spain, with another, the United States. The day after Manila fell to U.S. forces in August 1898, Major General Wesley Merritt announced the formation of a military government, and in December 1898, under the Treaty of Paris, the Spanish ceded the Philippines to the United States. In February 1899 Aguinaldo declared war on the United States—known as the Philippine insurrection—and the revolutionary government of the Philippines promulgated a constitution. Armed conflict between U.S. armed forces and the insurrectionists continued throughout 1899, with the Americans winning several pitched battles against the Filipinos. In November 1899 Aguinaldo announced that the Filipinos would conduct a guerrilla war, which compelled the United States to send more forces to the islands.[4]

As the insurgency spread, the U.S. Navy base at Cavite (site of the former Spanish naval base on the southern shore of Manila Bay) became increasingly important. In May 1899 Secretary of the Navy John D. Long sent one Marine battalion to reinforce the base's protection; a second battalion arrived in September 1899. The Marines began to expand their outposts into the surrounding area and won a small battle against insurgents at Noveleta in the beginning of October. Soon thereafter the Marine commander (and future Marine Corps Commandant), Lieutenant Colonel George F. Elliott, requested more men, and Admiral J. C. Watson, commander of the Asiatic Station, cabled Secretary Long, petitioning for another battalion of Marines. Long concurred, and Commandant Charles Heywood created a third battalion for Philippine service, drawing from Marines stationed at various East Coast barracks. Among them was First Lieutenant Logan Feland.[5]

Feland had received his first fitness report at the end of October

1899. While acknowledging that Feland had "just been appointed in the Marine Corps and lacks experience," Lieutenant Colonel Harrington gave him "excellent" marks for the manner in which he performed his duties as an "officer under instruction" and "officer of the day." Feland also received excellent marks for his "attention to duty" and "general conduct and bearing." Harrington rated Feland's health as "very good." To the standard question of whether said officer was under the influence of liquor at any time, Harrington wrote "No."[6] Feland had made a strong first impression as a Marine Corps officer in training. Next he would be challenged to prove his mettle in combat during the Philippine insurrection.

On November 1, 1899, Lieutenant Logan Feland joined the newly formed battalion headed by Major Littleton Waller Tazewell "Tony" Waller, who was already on his way to becoming a Marine Corps legend. Characterized as a "short, pugnacious, hard-drinking, and very energetic Virginian," Waller would loom large in Feland's early Marine Corps life. Despite being court-martialed for the famous incident at Samar (after Feland left the Philippines), Waller would be found innocent of atrocity charges and would continue to rise through the ranks, falling just short of the Commandant's position in 1909.[7]

On November 1, 1899, Waller's Marines boarded a train bound for the West Coast. The enlisted men were assigned to "tourist sleepers," but the officers traveled in Pullman sleeping cars. The officers included some who would become leading Marine Corps figures in the early twentieth century: Frederick "Fritz" Wise, Hiram "Hiking Hiram" Bearss, Louis McCarty Little, James Carson Breckinridge, and Logan Feland. In his memoirs, Wise described Feland during the trip to the Philippines as "very quiet. Very little to say. Older than the rest. But always listening in."[8]

The train transporting Waller's troops arrived in San Francisco after a week's journey across the continent. The battalion's 15 officers and 325 men then crammed into a converted troop transport, the USS *Solace*, which had previously served as a hospital ship. Wise noted that the *Solace* had a very narrow beam, which made it roll heavily in the slightest sea. The ship was designed to hold only 250 men, prompting Wise to declare later: "I have been in one or two hell-holes in my life. But the U.S.S. *Solace* wins the blue ribbon."[9]

The *Solace* covered about 240 miles per day. After a stopover in Hawaii, where the Marines exercised, drilled, shot target practice, and rested, the

Frederick "Fritz" Wise. Wise was a veteran Marine Corps campaigner, serving in the Philippines, China, Cuba, Mexico, Haiti, Santo Domingo, and France. (Courtesy of *Leatherneck* magazine)

Solace proceeded to Guam, where it left a small contingent after a three-day layover. The *Solace* then left Guam and arrived in the Philippines on December 15, 1899. According to Feland, there was "no excitement whatever" on the trip across the Pacific. Noting that the ship had left four lieutenants at Guam, Feland wrote that he "was certainly sorry for them, as you cannot imagine a lonelier place." In his letter, which was quoted in his hometown newspaper, Feland observed, "the news that we hear is that the insurrection is probably at an end." He predicted that "no doubt the fighting is over and I don't think we will ever even see a hostile Filipino."[10] Feland would be proved wrong, however, as the fighting would continue for several years.

After arriving in the Philippines, Feland served in Company E, under the command of Captain Herbert L. Draper. A veteran of the Spanish-American War campaign at Guantanamo, Draper had been mentioned in Stephen Crane's short story about the storming of the Cuzco Well. He had also been photographed raising the first U.S. flag to fly over Cuban territory. Draper's company settled in at Olongapo on Subic Bay, about sixty miles northwest of Manila. Draper took over command on Christmas Day 1899 from Captain John Twiggs "Handsome Jack" Myers, who had led the initial capture of Olongapo in September 1899. At Olongapo, Draper had 3 officers—Lieutenants George C. Thorpe, Logan Feland, and James W. Lynch—and 117 enlisted men at his disposal, with orders to hunt down insurgents and ensure civil order in the region.[11]

Draper and his men began conducting operations against the Filipino insurgents soon after New Year's Day. Feland played an important role in these missions. On January 6, 1900, he led a scouting party to burn down an "insurgent signal station to the northwest of Olongapo."

Small raids continued. On January 16 Feland joined Draper in setting up an ambush on the Bacbac trail, but to no avail. Forced to go some distance for water, Draper's Marines ran into Filipino guerrillas on February 16, and two Marines were killed. In retaliation, Draper led his men to Morong the next day and burned portions of the town, where they found stored ammunition. On February 23 Draper led his Marines to Benictan, which was being shelled by the USS *Nashville*; after relocating the inhabitants to Olongapo, Draper's men torched the town. On March 8 Feland led eighty men on a raid of the nearby town of Calapacuan, where the insurgents had established a warehouse. Feland's patrol found several bolos and caches of rice. Draper ordered Feland to round up the Filipino men and escort them to Olongapo; this group included the much-feared insurgent Captain Calixto Mindogorin. Draper subsequently reported to Commandant Heywood "the efficient, zealous, and courageous qualities displayed by First Lieut. Logan Feland," and Heywood included this praise in his annual report to the secretary of the navy.[12]

Draper's Marines not only pursued the Filipino guerrillas but also made several civic improvements, presaging the Marine Corps's future strategy. They established a municipal government, created a police force, opened an English-language school, and provided food and medical assistance. These pacification efforts reflected that "the army of occupation and U.S. civilian officials took seriously McKinley's charge of 'benevolent assimilation,' seeking to defuse resistance through enlightened colonial policies." Although the Marines continued to seek out insurgents, Feland's participation in these raids diminished after April 1900. Once again he was called on to take an administrative role, serving first as district and post adjutant at Olongapo, then as the First Regiment's assistant quartermaster in January and commissary officer in February 1901.[13]

Having gained valuable martial as well as administrative experience, Feland left the Philippines on March 30, 1901, to command the USS *Oregon*'s Marine contingent. Feland would not see Draper again; the captain died of heart disease in September 1901 in Hong Kong. The Kentuckian attended Draper's eventual interment in the U.S. Naval Academy Cemetery at Annapolis, and he kept in contact with the family. In 1925 Feland would stand in for his old commander, giving away Draper's daughter Royall at her marriage to U.S. Army major David Garrison.[14]

Before leaving the Philippines, Feland's final fitness report was completed by Lieutenant Colonel Mancil Goodrell, the First Regiment's commanding officer in the district of Subic and Olongapo. Another hero of the Spanish-American War, Goodrell had led the first Marines into Cuba, establishing the position near Guantanamo. Goodrell rated Feland "excellent" in all categories and remarked that "Lieutenant Feland is an officer of exceptional capacity. He has performed all the various duties required of him with zeal and intelligence."[15]

Feland's departure from the Philippines meant that he missed one of the most controversial incidents involving the early-twentieth-century Marine Corps. The insurgency had increased on the island of Samar, where a company of Ninth U.S. Army Infantry at Balangiga had been caught unawares during mealtime and massacred by Filipino fighters. When Major Waller's battalion sailed from Cavite to Samar, Brigadier General Jacob Smith allegedly instructed Waller to make the area a "howling wilderness" and that killing all Filipinos over the age of ten was justified. In a series of extensive operations, Waller's men destroyed housing, food, and transportation. Waller led one expedition into the interior under the harshest of conditions, facing starvation and exhaustion. After that expedition, in retaliation for an attack on one of his lieutenants, Waller ordered the execution of eleven Filipinos. Major General Adna Chaffee, commander of all U.S. troops in the Philippines, ordered that Waller be court-martialed. Although he was found not guilty of murder, a blemish remained on Waller's record, precluding his serving as Commandant. Several of Feland's friends were involved in the action on Samar, including Robert Dunlap, Harry Lay, and James Bootes; Hiram Bearss and David Porter eventually received Medals of Honor for their bravery in fighting the Filipinos. The horrible conditions of the Samar expedition became legendary, and in recognition of their courage, subsequent Marine Corps tradition held that veterans of Samar would be toasted with the phrase: "Stand, gentlemen, he served on Samar."[16]

Marines would remain in the Philippines for half a century, occupying areas for increasing amounts of time as they provided shock troops in the United States' new empire. Although historian Brian Linn has concluded that the Marine Corps "did not—with one notable exception—play a significant combat role in the Philippine War," the war in the Philippines revealed that the Marines could garrison conflict areas for long periods and could serve well in continuing pacification efforts.[17]

After sailing across the Pacific on the *Oregon*, Feland arrived at Mare Island, north of San Francisco, and then continued cross-country to report to Headquarters Marine Corps in Washington, D.C. Following a brief stint with the quartermaster, Feland proceeded to the U.S. Naval Academy at Annapolis in March 1902. There, he used his skills as an architect and civil engineer to oversee construction of a new Marine Barracks. The barracks, which would eventually be named Halligan Hall, proved to be a difficult, severely underbudgeted project. Feland and the building's architect, Henry Ives Cobb, had to deal with changing plans, problems procuring materials, and bad weather. Feland's task was challenging, but he had the technical skills and leadership to complete the project successfully. When it was finished, the four-story building became a model of barracks construction, with "electric lighting, a brick bake oven, a large refrigerator, and a sewer system that ran into the Severn River." Intended to hold up to 500 men, the barracks fulfilled Commandant Heywood's goal of creating a site for a school of instruction for officers and enlisted men.[18]

In addition to the Marine Barracks, Feland oversaw construction of a new firing range, for which he received recognition from Colonel George Reid, the Marine Corps adjutant and inspector. The assistant inspector, Major Charles Lauchheimer, had visited the range and reported that it was "vastly superior" to the previous range, with a "line of fire clear of all obstructions," so that "bullets in their flight can in no possible way do any harm." The report concluded that the range "reflects great credit upon Lieutenant Feland."[19]

In July 1903 First Lieutenant Logan Feland reported to a Marine Corps promotion examining board that included two future Commandants: Lieutenant Colonel William P. Biddle (1911) and Captain Wendell C. Neville (1929). Neville would also be Feland's immediate commanding officer throughout most of World War I. Hence, Feland had an early opportunity to make a good impression on two key Marine Corps officers. He did not disappoint, performing reasonably well. After passing the mandatory medical examination, Feland underwent the oral examination. On day one, board members questioned him in fifteen-minute increments on administration, drill regulations, fire discipline, naval and military law, minor tactics, military field engineering, and naval gunnery. The next day, the board put him through the paces of battalion drill, with the third day devoted to company drill. Feland received an overall average score of 87.83, scoring highest in professional efficiency (95) and lowest in drill regulations—oral (71). Consequently, the examining board concluded that Feland had "the physical, mental, moral and professional qualifications to perform efficiently all the duties of the grade to which he will next be eligible, and recommend him for promotion thereto." On July 24 Feland was promoted to captain, with a retroactive effective date of March 3, 1903. The date was important in establishing his status among Marine Corps officers, who were most often promoted based on time in rank.[20]

On November 6, 1903, Captain Feland reported to League Island in Philadelphia, where the Marine Corps was assembling a force to support the United States' latest venture into Latin America. Trouble had broken out in Colombia on November 3, when revolutionaries had declared the independence of the province of Panama. Eager to ensure the building of a canal across the Panama isthmus, President Theodore Roosevelt pushed to support the Panamanians, and the United States immediately recognized Panama's independence. Several U.S. naval ships were already stationed in the area, and Marines and sailors from the USS *Nashville*, under the command of Lieutenant Commander H. M. Witzel, went ashore at Colon to help deter the Colombians from sending in troops. Two companies of Marines under Major John A. Lejeune (another future Commandant) landed the following day. Over the next few days, more Marines landed until Lejeune had enough men for an entire battalion, and they established a camp at Empire, about thirty miles from Colon.[21]

Although no real fighting had taken place in Panama, U.S. authorities deemed a second Marine battalion necessary for support and summoned Marines stationed along the East Coast to League Island. In Philadelphia, Feland joined 10 other officers and 300 men under the command of Major Louis C. Lucas. The battalion boarded the USS *Prairie* on November 9 and sailed to Guantanamo Bay, Cuba, where it set up camp and commenced training. By then, Captain Feland was commanding a company of Marines. After a brief stay in Cuba, Feland and the other Marines reboarded the *Prairie* on December 11 and sailed to Panama. They arrived on December 21 and set up camp in Bas Obispo.

The events taking place in Panama were serious, and the atmosphere was tense. On December 18 Secretary of the Navy William Moody transmitted a message from President Roosevelt to the Marine Corps Commandant, Brigadier General Elliott, ordering him to go to Panama and take command of U.S. forces on the ground there. Not since 1836–1837, during a war against the Seminole and Creek Indians in Florida, had a Marine Corps Commandant led troops in the field. As historian Henry J. Hendrix II has noted, "The importance of this order in measuring the magnitude of President Roosevelt's engagement with the issue of Panama and his actions and intentions regarding the country in the immediate wake of its revolution cannot be understated."[22] Roosevelt meant to have his canal, and the Marine Corps would ensure that he got it.

Brigadier General Elliott and more Marines arrived on the USS *Dixie* in early January 1904. Given that a brigadier general led them, the Marines in Panama were organized as a provisional brigade consisting of two regiments. Biddle commanded the First Regiment, which included two battalions led by Lejeune and Major Eli K. Cole. The Second Regiment was led by Feland's former commander on the Philippines expedition, L. W. T. Waller, who had been acquitted of the charges resulting from the Samar expedition and had recently been promoted to colonel. Under Waller, Major J. E. Mahoney commanded the First Battalion, and Major Lucas led the Second Battalion. Feland served as captain of Company D in the Second Battalion before transferring to Company G in Mahoney's First Battalion. Altogether, Elliott had 28 officers and nearly 1,100 men at his disposal. This force proved to be a formidable deterrent to any attempt by Colombia to retake its former province of Panama.[23]

The secretary of the navy had ordered Elliott to prepare the Marines for a possible attack on the Colombian port of Cartagena, "the country's chief source of tariff revenues." Elliott therefore "instituted a training program to maintain his Marines at a high level of combat readiness. Simultaneously, he dispatched his forces on quick 'out-'n-back' expeditions that fulfilled the dual purposes of maintaining security while building his understanding of the surrounding countryside." Feland and the other men stayed busy. They "constructed weapons ranges . . . to practice their marksmanship" and "trained in assault tactics, entrenching procedures, and construction of obstructions." Reconnaissance parties mapped roads and trails "in the first comprehensive survey of the isthmus."[24]

By mid-February 1904 it became apparent that Colombia was in no position to thwart either the Panamanian independence movement or Roosevelt's determination to build a canal (construction would begin in May 1904). Although the Marines would stay in Panama until the year the canal opened—1914—Feland and the rest of Major Lucas's Second Battalion left on February 14 aboard the *Prairie*, bound for Guantanamo Bay.

Captain Logan Feland would spend the rest of the year in the Caribbean, first at Guantanamo and then as commander of the Marine Barracks in San Juan, Puerto Rico. In November 1904 he reported to Commandant Elliott in Washington, D.C., and was assigned to be an instructor at the School of Application at Annapolis.[25]

Back in the United States, Logan Feland renewed friendships with fellow officers from the Panamanian expedition—a veritable who's who of current and future Marine Corps leaders. A photograph of Waller's Second Regiment taken at Bas Obispo on January 15, 1904, portrays several officers who would play prominent roles in Feland's life and in the Corps, including Smedley Darlington Butler, Robert H. "Hal" Dunlap, George C. Reid, and Charles H. Lyman. These men, along with Waller and Feland, would all play prominent roles in the building of the Marine Corps in the early twentieth century.[26]

Butler had joined the Marine Corps at age sixteen and served in Cuba during the Spanish-American War. After duty in the Philippines, he was sent to China during the Boxer Rebellion, where he was wounded and brevetted to captain for his bravery. The son of well-known congressman Thomas Butler from Pennsylvania, Butler would go on to receive two Medals of Honor: during the occupation of Vera Cruz in 1914, and for his bravery in Haiti in 1915. Feland and Butler would become two of the most prominent Marine Corps generals of the 1920s, vying for the Commandant's position in 1930.[27]

Dunlap's career would be intertwined with Feland's: as his equal in Panama, as Feland's commanding officer at Vera Cruz in 1914, and as Feland's subordinate in Nicaragua in 1928. Envisioned as a future Marine Corps Commandant, Dunlap would die in 1931 while rescuing a woman from a cave in France.[28]

As the Marines consolidated and reorganized in Panama, Feland came

"All Quiet along the Chagres." Panama, 1904: L. W. T. Waller sits in the middle of the first row, surrounded by his officers, including Logan Feland at top right, Smedley Darlington Butler standing next to Feland, and Robert Dunlap fourth from top right.

into contact with others who would play prominent roles in the Corps. These included old friends Hiram Bearss and Fritz Wise from the Philippines and future major general Louis McCarty Little, who had joined the Marines on the same day as Feland. Many of these men would continue to interact both professionally and personally.

Over the next year, several of Feland's brother officers got married. At the end of December 1904, Feland and Butler were ushers at the wedding of First Lieutenant William Radford Coyle, who would later serve as a Pennsylvania congressman (Feland would ask for Coyle's help in obtaining another position toward the end of his career). In January 1905 Robert Dunlap married Katherine Wood, with Butler and Feland again serving as ushers; young Lieutenant Harry Lay, who would be a key staff officer in World War I, was best man. Later that month, Feland and Butler ushered at the wedding of Captain Wade Jolly, another Panama expedition colleague. Then, at the end of June, Feland, Little, and Waller were ushers at Smedley Butler's wedding to Ethel Conway Peters.[29] In sum, in the expanded but still small Marine Corps, Captain Logan Feland had become popular and well connected.

Feland took up his duties as an instructor in the School of Application in November 1904.[30] After a two-year hiatus during the Spanish-American War, Commandant Heywood had resurrected the school in November 1900; it was transferred to Annapolis in May 1903 upon completion of the Marine Barracks. A class of twenty-nine second lieutenants had enrolled in the school in September 1904, and another class of thirty-six officers soon joined them.

Although Feland had not attended the school himself (it had been suspended during his training period), his maturity and experience made him a valuable role model for young officers. He took his career as a soldier seriously. For example, soon after the U.S. Infantry Association started publishing its *Infantry Journal* in 1905, Feland subscribed. He wanted to keep up with the latest thinking about his profession by reading articles such as "Normal Attack for a Battalion of Infantry" or "Military Landing Operations"; the latter was written by fellow Marine major Dion Williams for the July 1906 issue. Feland would maintain an interest in education and training throughout his career.[31]

Instructors at the School of Application were kept busy. They oversaw a daily routine that began with reveille at 6:45 a.m. and ended with lights out at 11:00 p.m. During the day, the student-officers underwent training in subjects such as tactics, field engineering, ordnance and gunnery, law, hygiene, and signaling. The curriculum also included plenty of physical activity, such as practical military exercises in the field and lots of time in the gym. During their free time between 4:00 and 6:30 p.m. (after drill and before supper), the students could golf, sail, play tennis, ride horses, and engage in social pursuits.[32]

While at the School of Application at Annapolis, Feland served with several officers who would be important in the Corps over the next couple of decades. Charles Doyen and Franklin Moses served as school commanders and were ably assisted by future Marine Corps generals Feland, Robert Dunlap, and James Carson Breckinridge and future Marine Corps commandants Thomas Holcomb and John Russell. Feland also met and instructed several second lieutenants who would become prominent officers and would be closely allied with him, including Sam Bogan, Andrew Drum, Henry Manney, Maurice Shearer, Phil Torrey, and Ralph Stover Keyser.

Feland also served as judge advocate (prosecuting the offender) in a court-martial while at Annapolis. This was typical duty for Marine Corps officers. For example, Feland's commander in the Philippines, Herbert Draper, had served as judge advocate in 1895 in a well-publicized court-martial in which a navy captain was held responsible for a crash while docking in Southampton, England. In Feland's case, a young Marine Corps second lieutenant, Frederick A. Gardener, was charged with "intoxication and conduct to the prejudice of good order and discipline" after insulting the Naval Academy superintendent, Captain Willard Brownson, at a masked ball.[33]

In May 1905 Feland and the school's other officers were temporarily posted to the Marine Barracks at Narragansett Bay, Rhode Island, where they took a course on underwater mines at the Torpedo Station. This instruction would be instrumental to Feland, who would one day command a Marine company in charge of setting mines for the defense of captured naval ports.[34]

Feland found life at Annapolis delightful, and he participated in the many social activities that marked the school year. The highlight of the fall 1905 season came when Prince Louis of Battenburg, nephew of Britain's King Edward, visited Annapolis with a fleet of six English warships. For two days the Naval Academy superintendent, Rear Admiral James Sands, hosted festivities to mark the prince's visit, including a reception and the annual midshipmen's ball. Captain Feland attended these events, as did the legendary Lieutenant Colonel McLane Tilton, an Annapolis resident who had served in the Marine Corps from the Civil War until his retirement in 1897.[35]

Like most Marines at the time, Feland was a "soldier of the sea," so in December 1905 he reported to Captain Edward D. Taussig on the USS *Massachusetts*, where he commanded the Marine Guard aboard the ship. When the *Massachusetts* was decommissioned in January 1906, Feland and Taussig transferred to the USS *Indiana*, an old battleship that had recently been refitted with new equipment, including electric rather than steam-powered gun turrets. Though used mainly as a reserve vessel, the

Indiana participated in the presidential naval review in September 1906 in Long Island Sound, near Theodore Roosevelt's home in Oyster Bay, New York. On board the presidential yacht *Mayflower*, Roosevelt watched with delight as his ship passed through the fleet, arranged in three squadrons. The gathering of forty-five ships—including twelve battleships and eight cruisers—represented the most powerful naval force ever assembled in U.S. waters. When the *Mayflower* reached the head of the fleet, commanded by Rear Admiral Robley "Fighting Bob" Evans on the USS *Maine*, the ships fired a twenty-one-gun salute. Each vessel fired a salute as the president's yacht sailed between the squadrons, and bands played on the pennant-draped ships. A crowd estimated at nearly 100,000 people watched onshore and in boats, and they were particularly impressed when the ships turned on their festive nighttime illumination.[36]

While Feland was serving on the *Indiana*, trouble arose in Cuba. After defeating Spain in 1898, the United States had retained the right to intervene in Cuban affairs, when necessary, through the Platt Amendment of 1902. In August 1906 an insurgency arose, pitting Liberal Party opponents against forces loyal to the government of Tomas Estrada Palma. By mid-September Marines on the USS *Denver* had gone ashore and established camp at the presidential palace in Havana. Around the same time, President Roosevelt sent a peace commission, headed by Secretary of War William Howard Taft, to Cuba, whereupon the Cuban government resigned and relinquished administration of the island to U.S. representatives. Taft formed a provisional government on September 29, and the call went out for more Marines, who had already begun marshaling at League Island in Philadelphia and at Norfolk. Feland was among the more than 2,000 Marines who went ashore to posts in Havana and nearly two dozen other Cuban towns. These detachments ranged from over 1,000 men at Camp Colombia, near Havana, to a single officer and 25 men in Trinidad and Arriete. The First Provisional Brigade under L. W. T. Waller was divided into two regiments headed by Lieutenant Colonel George Barnett and Lieutenant Colonel Franklin J. Moses.[37]

The U.S. Army would eventually play the lengthiest and most important role in the pacification of Cuba, commonly known as the second Cuban intervention (the first being in 1898). Colonel Waller reported to U.S. Army brigadier general Frederick Funston, who arrived in late September to take command of all U.S. armed forces in the country. A Medal of Honor recipient, captor of Filipino insurgent Emilio Aguinaldo, and the army's youngest general, Funston had spent 1896–1897 fighting in the Cuban revolutionary army against Spain.

When Funston first arrived, many Cuban areas seemed peaceful enough, with a few exceptions. One of these was the town of Guines, about forty-five miles southeast of Havana. Guines had been a hotbed of rebel activity led by Ernesto Asbert, the former chief of police, and Faustino (Pino) Guerra, a former Liberal congressman whose uprising in the western province of Pinar del Rio had initiated the insurgency. "On August 25, Guerra with two thousand horsemen rode into the city of Guines and routed the [Rural] Guards there, killing three and wounding six."[38] By the end of September, the situation in Guines remained volatile, as Asbert's insurgents continued to threaten the area. Probably hoping for U.S. intervention, Asbert agreed to disarm and disband his men, but only if the police force in Guines was also disbanded. General Funston and Cuban general Eugenio Sanchez Agramonte of the Disarmament Commission traveled by car to sort out the situation in Guines, where Mayor Ayala refused to disarm his police. Funston negotiated for Marines to be sent in to oversee the disarmament and keep the peace.[39]

Captain Feland, along with 2 other officers and 103 enlisted men, traveled to Guines to quell the disturbances caused when the insurgents refused to give up their arms and disperse. The town was a tinderbox, as the insurgents staged a sham disarmament. General Funston "telegraphed to Captain Feland, commander of the Marines at Guines, to patrol the streets and protect life and property at all costs." Despite these instructions, the rules of engagement remained unclear. The *New York Times* reported that Taft had told Funston: "the officers of Marines stationed in various localities are advised that they are not expected to take part, in an active way, in the suppression of disorder unless an extreme emergency arises in which it is absolutely necessary for them to protect life and property. The duties of the Marines are generally limited to tendering their good offices between conflicting elements and the prevention of the friction which, in the high state of tension between the political parties, is inevitable during the present crisis."[40] Feland found himself in a complex and delicate situation: he had to use his judgment to negotiate the fine line between force and persuasion to maintain order and peace.

A delegation from Guines traveled to Havana and informed Funston that insurgents had entered the town, attacked the police with machetes, and threatened to kill the entire police force. The next day, however, Feland seemed unfazed. "Instead of several men being cut with machetes at Guines, Capt. Feland, commander of the Marines there, reported: 'Several brawls; none injured.'"[41] Nevertheless, "Guines continued to be a source of trouble for some time. Since Feland had so successfully controlled the situation from the beginning, he was left in charge at Guines by special request of responsible Cuban officials."[42]

During this time, Feland garnered national attention when he figured prominently in an article in the popular *Harper's Weekly* magazine. *Harper's* correspondent William Inglis spent several months in Cuba reporting on the revolution, and when word reached Havana that violence had broken out in Guines, he quickly made his way to the town. Instead of chaos, he found Guines much as Captain Feland had described it: peaceful enough. Inglis reported that Feland and his Marines supported the local Rural Guards primarily by marching up and down the streets of Guines smiling, but still exuding the impression that they would shoot if necessary. Inglis's article included a photograph of the Marines marching through town in column abreast, bayonet-topped rifles across their chests, looking determined. There was also a photograph of a relaxed, rail-thin Captain Feland in his Marine Corps expeditionary uniform and campaign hat, smiling broadly at a shorter Cuban man in a traditional white suit and Panama hat. The Cuban, former rebel captain Francisco Somora, had offered Feland five dollars for the return of his confiscated machete, but, according to Inglis, Feland merely patted the Cuban on the shoulder and suggested that he talk to the Rural Guards. Turning to Inglis, Feland added, "You can't blame the poor devils. They've had to give graft for generations and they can't get used to obeying some rules without graft."[43]

By the end of November, the *New York Times* could inform its readers that "a report of insurgents operating near Guines had proved false," and "the last vestige of disorder in Cuba had disappeared." In sum, the U.S. military had handled the Cuban situation well. Although the army would remain in Cuba for the next three years, Colonel Waller and most Marines had left by November. Feland remained there until December 6, 1906.[44]

Once again, Logan Feland had been given great responsibility and had performed admirably in a potentially powder-keg situation. Under his

Katherine Feland. The Felands married on Valentine's Day 1907 and remained together until his death in July 1936. (Library of Congress)

supervision, the Marines at Guines had kept the peace. As a result of his fine leadership, Feland received "excellent" marks in all categories on the fitness report completed by Lieutenant Colonel Franklin J. Moses as the Kentuckian prepared to exit Cuba.[45]

On December 7, 1906, Feland set sail from Havana on the U.S. Army transport *Sumner*, bound for Newport News, Virginia, where he rejoined the Marine Guard on the *Indiana*. A few days after Christmas, Feland went to Norfolk and prepared to take command of the Marine Guard on the USS *Minnesota*, which would be commissioned on March 9, 1907, under the command of Captain John Hubbard. But first, Feland got married.

The *Washington Post* reported on February 14, 1907, that the marriage of Captain Logan Feland, USMC, to Mrs. Katherine Cordner Heath of New York City would take place that day. After a brief wedding trip, the Felands would reside in Norfolk, where the captain was stationed. Noting that the new Mrs. Feland was originally from Columbus, Ohio, the *Washington Post* described her as "a beautiful and attractive widow, well-known in musical circles as the possessor of a highly cultivated voice."[46]

Nearly a year earlier, however, the *New York Times* had reported that Katherine Cordner Heath was seeking a divorce from her husband of ten years, Orlando Heath, from whom she had been separated for six months. The *Times* noted that Mrs. Heath was a soprano soloist at the West End Presbyterian Church and earned $1,500 a year. The *Times* also quoted her as saying, "Mr. Heath and I were married when I was a schoolgirl. . . . My friends have known for some time that I was not happy with him."[47]

Katherine Cordner Heath's father, Joseph W. Cordner, had served in the Union army during the Civil War and remained a staunch Republican. His marriage to Ann Carpenter had produced six children, four of whom—all daughters—were still living at the time of Katherine's marriage to Logan Feland. Joseph Cordner was a well-known businessman, active in veterans' organizations and in the Church of Christ.[48]

The Felands were married in New York City on Valentine's Day, which was also Katherine's birthday. Unlike the Butler and Dunlap weddings, the Feland wedding was a quiet affair. Apparently, the wedding had to be moved up quickly because of the *Minnesota's* pending departure. The *Army and Navy Journal* reported that the wedding took place at high noon, with Captain T. H. Low serving as best man. The marriage certificate noted that Katherine Cordner Heath was divorced and gave her age as twenty-eight; in fact, she was four years older. The marriage ceremony, held at Wells Memorial Presbyterian Church in Manhattan, was performed by the Reverend William Bishop Gates. James M. Gifford and Theo H. Sorr witnessed the marriage and signed the certificate. Feland's hometown newspaper, the *Hopkinsville Kentuckian*, ran this headline: "Logan Feland Weds. Bride a Beautiful and Popular Widow of New York."[49]

Contrary to newspaper reports, Katherine was a divorcée, not a widow. Her former husband died after they were divorced. In an interview with a Feland niece years later, historian Gus Paris learned that Katherine's status as a divorcée bothered the Feland family, and they opposed the marriage. According to Paris, "In later years the family gradually accepted Katherine into the family fold, and she visited the family in Owensboro, Kentucky, on several occasions."[50]

On another score, the newspapers were correct: Katherine was an accomplished musician, appearing in venues ranging from church weddings to piano recitals to Chautauqua presentations. After her marriage, she would continue to sing in public on various occasions, as duly noted by the press in Philadelphia and Washington, D.C., where the Felands would spend increasing amounts of time.[51] They would become well known in society, and the events of their professional and personal lives would be reported in the major East Coast newspapers. The marriage would last nearly thirty years, ending only with Logan Feland's death.

In sum, Logan Feland's first seven years in the Marine Corps were peripatetic, challenging, and varied. He proved his mettle in a guerrilla war in the Philippines and in a significant peacekeeping operation in Cuba. He would use these experiences in the future in more of America's "small wars." His technical skills set him apart from most other officers, and he would continue to use them to distinguish himself. Feland gained administrative, managerial, and teaching skills through his service as adjutant and judge advocate, his instructorship at the School of Application, and his command of troops in Cuba. He met lifelong friends, traveled to faraway places, and got married. The stage was set for further maturation—both personal and professional—as Logan Feland took on new duties in the Marine Corps.

4

Shuttling between the States and the Caribbean, 1907–1913

On March 9, 1907, Captain Logan Feland presided over the Marine Guard on the USS *Minnesota* as the battleship was commissioned. In April, after a shakedown cruise to New England, the *Minnesota* joined other Atlantic Fleet vessels off the coast of Virginia in celebrating the Jamestown Exposition. The exposition commemorated the 300th anniversary of the founding of the Jamestown colony. Many famous people attended, including Mark Twain, William Jennings Bryan, Booker T. Washington, William Randolph Hearst, Samuel Gompers, and President Theodore Roosevelt. A lavish affair, the exposition underscored the military and naval might of the United States, despite some objections from exposition board members about the display of "extravagant militarism."[1]

Sailing down the Potomac River on the presidential yacht *Mayflower*, Roosevelt opened the exposition on April 26 and reviewed a naval parade in Hampton Roads that included twelve international ships and thirty-eight U.S. vessels. Ships from Britain, Germany, Argentina, Brazil, and Chile participated in the parade. The Atlantic Fleet, commanded by Rear Admiral Robley "Fighting Bob" Evans, had on hand sixteen battleships, three cruisers, and an assortment of other ships. Feland and the sailors and Marines on the *Minnesota* participated in various events throughout the summer, welcoming foreign ships and dignitaries and once again sailing past Roosevelt for a presidential review on "Georgia Day" on June 10. The Jamestown Exposition festivities were marred, however, when the *Minnesota*'s steam launch sank in rainy weather and choppy seas as it was ferrying sailors back to the ship after they had attended an army and navy ball on land. Eleven men, including six Naval Academy midshipmen, died in the accident. One of the midshipmen was the brother of Lieutenant Thomas Holcomb, a future Marine Corps Commandant.[2]

In mid-August Captain Feland and his Marine detachment participated in the *Minnesota*'s final acceptance trial. Then, at the end of September, tragedy struck again. While conducting maneuvers off Cape Cod with other members of the North Atlantic Fleet, the *Minnesota* encountered severe weather and lost a seaman overboard.[3]

Later that year, the *Minnesota* joined the Great White Fleet, so called because the ships were painted white to better deal with the heat of tropical climates. Conceived originally as a response to growing tension in East Asia, especially in Japan, the Great White Fleet was the largest display of naval power ever assembled. In addition to being a popular event abroad, designed to improve U.S. relations with several foreign countries, the fleet's cruise "was a highly successful exercise in public awareness. It greatly expanded popular understanding of American foreign relations and defense considerations, particularly in regard to the Pacific Basin."[4]

After putting into the Brooklyn Navy Yard for preparations for its extended cruise around the world, the *Minnesota* sailed for Hampton Roads, where the Great White Fleet would be reviewed by President Roosevelt before departing. Forced to lay off Cape Henry for a day in thick fog, the *Minnesota* was the last battleship to arrive, reaching Hampton Roads on December 11. The sixteen battleships took up position in two parallel lines, with the *Minnesota* at the head of one line, serving as a squadron flagship; Rear Admiral Charles M. Thomas was aboard as Second Squadron commander and fleet second in command. The fleet Marines, under the command of Major Dion Williams, prepared for a parade at the army's Fort Monroe, where Admiral Evans would review them.[5]

Several days of final preparations followed, including coaling the ships. Several glittering social events were held, such as a grand ball onshore on December 13. On December 16 Roosevelt returned on the *Mayflower* and was greeted by a twenty-one-gun salute. As the *Mayflower* proceeded down the line between the two squadrons, bands played and Marines paraded. Roosevelt held a reception on the *Mayflower* for senior naval officers, after which the admirals and captains returned to their ships, weighed anchor, and set sail for the south, firing a final twenty-one-gun salute to the president. Logan Feland and the others aboard the fleet vessels were embarking on the trip of a lifetime.

The fleet steamed southward in double columns as Admiral Evans conducted fleet exercises. By December 23, 1907, the Great White Fleet had arrived in Port of Spain, Trinidad, where it remained until December 29, when it set out for Rio de Janeiro, Brazil. While in Trinidad, the *Minnesota* hosted a Christmas Day reception for officers from the other ships. The visit to Port of Spain was rather low-key, with the major objective being the recoaling of the ships. The Great White Fleet crossed the equator on January 5 and was met by representatives of King Neptune, as each ship conducted the time-honored tradition of baptizing those seamen and Marines who were crossing the equator for the first time.[6]

On January 12, 1908, the Great White Fleet entered the harbor at Rio de Janeiro, with Sugarloaf Mountain as a backdrop. Bands played, guns fired salutes, excursion boats hovered in the harbor, and thousands of people lined the shores to watch the fleet come to anchor. Several days of activities followed, including a reception given by Brazilian president Alfonso Penna. In return, the *Minnesota* hosted a grand reception for the Brazilians.

Maritime artist and journalist Henry Reuterdahl had been chosen by President Roosevelt to accompany the fleet and document its voyage. He also oversaw the installation of a goldfish pond and a fountain on the *Minnesota*. His excellent decorative skills helped atone for a highly critical essay he had published in the January 1908 issue of *McClure's* magazine, calling into question the efficacy and safety of battleship gun turrets. Reuterdahl's article was part of a long-standing debate over battleship design deficiencies, such as the placement of armor belts near the waterline. Despite his controversial article, Reuterdahl was apparently cordially welcomed aboard the *Minnesota*, especially by Admiral Thomas, who agreed with some of his critiques.[7]

On January 22 the Great White Fleet departed Rio de Janeiro, bound for Buenos Aires, Argentina. The Argentinean capital had originally been left off the itinerary, but the Argentineans would have felt slighted if the fleet had visited archrival Brazil's capital and not theirs. Because the Buenos Aires harbor was too shallow for battleships, the United States sent a smaller flotilla of torpedo-boat destroyers into the port, while the battleships exchanged salutes farther out to sea with Argentinean armored cruisers. The Great White Fleet then proceeded southward to its next coaling station in Punta Arenas, Chile, on the north shore of the Strait of Magellan.[8]

By the time the fleet reached Punta Arenas, Admiral Evans had become increasingly ill, so Admiral Thomas unofficially took command of the fleet. The *Minnesota* hosted a dinner for the Chilean dignitaries, and Feland's Marines turned out to receive the guests. After recoaling, the fleet left Punta Arenas six days later, bound for a pass-by of Valparaiso. Because the city lacked a serviceable port, and because of the fleet's tight schedule, it was decided to only promenade the fleet past the harbor at Valparaiso. "The fleet's maneuver in Valparaiso Harbor was a masterpiece of symmetry and timing. When the *Minnesota*, in the middle of the column, came abreast of the Point Angeles fort at the harbor's southern entrance, the ships fired a simultaneous twenty-one-gun salute to Chile."[9]

The Great White Fleet then steamed onward to Peru, where more lavish entertainment, including a bullfight, awaited. After ten days, the fleet moved northward up the coast of Latin and Central America, bound for the next major destination: Magdalena Bay, Mexico. During this time, excitement built on the *Minnesota* and the other ships as the men prepared for the annual target practice competition. Captain Feland served as a division commander in charge of firing the ship's three-pounder guns. According to a letter from the navy placed in Feland's service record, during the competition, Feland's division attained "high average scores of, respectively, 23.44 shots and 13.03 hits per gun per minute, and 29.17 shots and 14.59 hits per gun per minute; the latter being the highest division score of this type of gun in the Navy. Also, the score of gun number 3 (day firing) and gun number 2 (night firing) indicate such a degree of excellence that the right to wear the Navy 'E' has been awarded their crews." The letter went on to commend "the zeal and ability displayed in your [Feland's] duties as a division officer."[10]

From Mexico, the Great White Fleet continued up the West Coast to San Diego, Los Angeles, Santa Barbara, and then San Francisco, participating in various festivities along the way. On May 17 Secretary of the Navy Victor Metcalf reviewed the fleet in San Francisco Harbor. The *San Francisco Call* reported that officers' wives, sisters, and "feminine relatives" were invited to the festivities, listing Mrs. Logan Feland as one of the invitees. The *Minnesota* then sailed to Washington, visiting Bellingham, Seattle, and Bremerton before returning to San Francisco at the end of May.[11]

Captain Feland's exciting cruise was disrupted when he received word that he would not be accompanying the Great White Fleet on the rest of its trip around the world. Instead, he was ordered back to Headquarters Marine Corps for further assignment. Katherine Feland joined her husband in Portland, Oregon, and they crossed the continent together. Feland was then ordered to report to Norfolk to take command of the Marine Guard on the newly commissioned USS *Montana*. A *Tennessee*-class cruiser, the *Montana* had been launched on December 16, 1906, and was commissioned on July 21, 1908, the day Feland joined the ship. While he was aboard the *Montana*, Katherine Feland traveled to Paris to study music, coming home at the end of November when Captain Feland returned to Annapolis and taught briefly at the School of Application. He was then posted to New York City, where he served at the Marine Barracks and then as a recruiting officer. Thus, for Feland, 1908 was filled with varied but typical duty for a Marine Corps officer.[12]

Feland's next experience proved atypical: testifying before a U.S. House of Representatives subcommittee on naval affairs in January 1909. With the advent of the modern navy, several naval officers had questioned the need for Marine detachments aboard ships. In 1908 President Theodore Roosevelt signed Executive Order 969, removing Marines from ships. In response, Thomas Butler of Pennsylvania led the congressional counterattack during discussions of the 1909 naval bill. (Butler had a special interest in the Marines: his son was Smedley Darlington Butler.) Butler's subcommittee called several U.S. Navy and Marine Corps officers to testify; the Marine Corps representatives included Commandant George Elliott, adjutant and inspector Colonel Charles Lauchheimer, Colonel L. W. T. Waller, Major Wendell Neville, and only two captains: Robert "Hal" Dunlap and Logan Feland.

Responding to Congressman Butler's queries, Feland noted that he had served on ships for a total of three and a half years, having just come off the *Montana*. He also testified about his experiences on the *Minnesota*. Feland asserted that removing Marines from ships might have a "harmful" effect on the Corps's efficiency and morale, damaging its military spirit. He had not experienced friction between sailors and Marines, nor between officers of the two services. On the contrary, he noted that when his detachment marched off the *Montana*, the ship's sailors heartily cheered the Marines. Captain Feland observed that eliminating ship duty would deprive Marines of "important duties and opportunities."[13] Fearing

Robert H. Dunlap. Dunlap and Feland served together for more than thirty years.

the Corps's eventual elimination, the other Marine Corps representatives pointed out that it would be more costly to replace Marines with sailors. After hearing the testimony, the House Naval Affairs Committee challenged the president's executive order by passing a resolution that became a rider to the Naval Appropriations Act. The rider stipulated that there would be no fiscal authorization for the Marine Corps unless Marines were returned to battleships and cruisers "at a strength no less than 8 percent of the ship's complement."[14]

Roosevelt backed down and signed the Naval Appropriations Act, and Marines had returned to navy ships by June 1909. The Marine Corps had won a great political victory. In the words of historian Allan Millett, it "marked a political milestone in the Marine Corps's history, for the Corps had by now so developed its own popular constituency in the public and the federal government that it could survive an assault on its least defensible function."[15]

Although he had testified in their defense, Logan Feland would not command any more shipboard Marine detachments. Instead, as the Marine Corps sought to redefine itself for warfare in the early twentieth century, he would become part of another initiative: the Advanced Base School.

In July 1910 Logan and Katherine Feland moved to New London, Connecticut, where the captain would be instrumental in the development of a project long in the works: the creation of an Advanced Base School. Following the Spanish-American War, the U.S. Navy had created the General Board to assist in the formation of policy and strategy. Under the leadership of Manila Bay hero Admiral George Dewey, the General Board had assigned a new task to the Marine Corps: establishing advanced bases around the world to protect the navy's resupply positions. As the navy (with President Roosevelt's strong support) increased its battle fleet, the board determined that overseas bases were necessary to protect the nation's new territories as well as the mainland United States. Plans were made to counter potential attacks by rivals such as Japan, Germany, and even Great Britain. New territories in the Philippines, Guam, and Hawaii meant that the navy could no longer focus primarily on the Atlantic. This became especially clear when the Russo-Japanese War in 1904–1905 positioned Japan as a major force in the Pacific.[16]

The Marine Corps had performed well in establishing an advanced base at Guantanamo during the Spanish-American War. However, successive Marine Corps Commandants had focused on placing Marines aboard ships rather than embracing the new advanced base mission. Several Marine Corps officers studied the issue. Major Dion Williams developed the idea that an advanced base force should consist of a fixed defense component focused on the placement of artillery and harbor mines, as well as a mobile defense component of infantry to help establish and defend the advanced base. In 1909 Major John Russell wrote a paper outlining the principles and specific composition of the advanced base force, including water mines, artillery, and land forces.[17]

Finally, in March 1910, navy officials ordered the Marine Corps to take responsibility for advanced base equipment stored at the Philadelphia Naval Shipyard and to establish a force to use that equipment. After dithering over where to house the Advanced Base School, the Corps established the school at New London, Connecticut.[18]

In New London, the Felands settled into a pleasant life. Katherine Feland continued to sing at various venues, and the couple entertained local citizens as well as fellow Marine Corps officers, including old acquaintance Louis McCarty Little, who was also stationed at New London. Major Melville Shaw commanded the Advanced Base School, and Feland served as an instructor, leading to his emergence as an expert on the subject.[19]

Creation of the Advanced Base School proved to be a timely development, in light of World War I and the technological changes occurring in the world. In the words of eminent Marine Corps historian Clyde Metcalf, "Several Marine officers, particularly Captains Earl H. Ellis and Logan Feland, made extensive studies of the problems connected with advanced bases and their ideas together with the teachings of the Naval War College led to the forming of an advance base organization and the Advanced Base School which worked in conjunction with each other. It was during the period of the existence of these two units that the Marine Corps made its greatest pre-war advance in technical knowledge of weapons other than those of regular infantry."[20] In sum, Logan Feland was instrumental in the development of a concept that would have ramifications throughout the twentieth century and into the twenty-first. The Advanced Base School would lead to the Advanced Base Force, which in the 1920s would morph into the East Coast Expeditionary Force, which would lead to the Fleet Marine Force, created on December 7, 1933. As a result of this progression, the Corps became the nation's amphibious force, a role it performed well in the Pacific during World War II. The Corps retains this mission in the twenty-first century.[21]

Captain Feland's assignment at the Advanced Base School was interrupted by another expedition to Cuba. Diplomatic tensions increased after a revolution broke out in Mexico in 1910; in response, the Marine Corps mounted another mission to Guantanamo, where Colonel Waller headed a provisional brigade of three regiments. Joining Colonel George Barnett's First Regiment, Feland sailed on the USS *Prairie* on March 8, 1911, and arrived shortly thereafter at Camp Meyer, located at Deer Point on Guantanamo Bay. Feland served as regimental adjutant and, as such, was at the center of all administrative duties, ranging from establishing procedures for regimental artillery fire control to carrying out maneuvers. This position called for painstaking attention to detail and a wide knowledge of Marine Corps field operations. Feland had previously served in adjutant positions, dating back to the Philippines. This time, he would do so under the eye of Colonel Barnett, who would become increasingly important to Feland's career, especially after Barnett became Commandant in 1914. Barnett consistently rated Feland as "excellent," giving him the highest grade of 4.0 in areas such as aptitude, attention to duty, manner and bearing, efficiency, general conduct, and health.[22]

Feland's service as the First Regiment's adjutant was interrupted when he received orders to proceed to Camp Elliott in the Panama Canal Zone to serve as judge advocate for the general court-martial of Captain Robert Gilson. Gilson had joined the Marine Corps during the Spanish-American War and served faithfully in the Philippines and in China during the Boxer Rebellion. He left the Corps in 1903 and then rejoined in 1908, serving under Major Smedley Darlington Butler in Nicaragua and Panama. Butler, however, had recently charged Gilson with "conduct unbecoming of an officer, scandalous conduct tending to the destruction of good morals, culpable negligence and inefficiency in the performance of duty and falsehood." Specifically, Gilson was accused of writing checks with insufficient funds to pay his post exchange accounts, embezzling money from Company C's fund to pay his debts, and then lying to Major Butler about his actions. Gilson pleaded not guilty to all charges.[23]

The Marine Corps sent assistant adjutant and inspector Henry Haines to head the court-martial team, which included Majors George Thorpe and Melville Shaw, Captains George van Orden and James Bootes, and two naval officers. The Marine Corps officers all knew one another—perhaps too well. Gilson's defense counsel, Captain Philip Brown, challenged Shaw's presence, and the major was removed "because of prejudice expressed by Major Shaw against the accused."[24]

As the court-martial's judge advocate, Captain Feland served as prosecutor of the case. He began by calling Major Butler to the stand for a lengthy recollection of events. On cross-examination, Gilson's counsel focused on the major's alleged "animus" against the accused, and Butler admitted that Gilson had "severely vexed" him. Feland also called several Marine Corps and bank witnesses to testify about Gilson's handling of his accounts. The defense called witnesses to support the claim of Butler's ill will against Gilson, including Captain "Johnny the Hard" Hughes, an officer with a tough reputation. Gilson also testified in his own defense. The court-martial found Gilson guilty of two of the charges, and it reduced the third to "conduct to the prejudice of good order and discipline." The court recommended that Captain Gilson be discharged from the Marine Corps, a verdict upheld by the navy judge advocate general, the acting secretary of the navy, and the president.[25]

Feland proved to be fair and efficient in carrying out the important, if somewhat distasteful, task of prosecuting a fellow Marine Corps officer. After the court-martial, Feland wrote to his friend Major Butler, assuring "my dear Smedley" that he need not worry about his reputation. Feland wrote that although he had not been able to talk to Smedley's father, he had asked Cyrus Radford to inform the congressman that everything was all right.[26]

Captain Feland returned to Guantanamo Bay in mid-June 1911, just in time to join his regiment for the trip back to Philadelphia. Tensions with Mexico had cooled, and the Marines returned to their former posts. Feland resumed his position as an instructor at the Advanced Base School in New London. As the advanced base concept matured, the Marine Corps gathered more men and material in Philadelphia to form the fixed and mobile regiments that were central to its implementation. When the Corps consolidated its resources, Katherine and Logan Feland moved with the Advanced Base School from New London to Philadelphia in July 1911.[27] In Philadelphia the Felands would become a bit more rooted, spending half a dozen years stationed there, although Captain Feland would be sent on temporary expeditions elsewhere, as was the normal Marine Corps practice for field officers.

The mission of the Advanced Base School was to "train Marine officers and men in the handling, installation, and use of advance base material; to investigate what types of guns, gun platforms, mines, torpedo defenses, and other equipment might be best suited for advance base work; to study such military and naval subjects as pertained to the selection, occupation, attack, and defense of advance bases, or to expeditionary service in general." By 1912, the school had trained about 16 percent of the Marine Corps.[28]

The movement to develop the advanced base concept was interrupted in May 1912 when Feland and other members of the Advanced Base School boarded the USS *Prairie* and headed to Cuba again.[29] Although the U.S. Army of Cuban Pacification had left the island in 1909 when the situation stabilized, U.S. economic interests in Cuba remained significant, "by far the most important of the Caribbean states from the standpoint of foreign trade and investment."[30] Thus, when black Cubans revolted against the government in May 1912 to protest their poor treatment, the U.S. State Department called for Marines to protect the extensive U.S. economic interests there. The *Prairie* reached Guantanamo Bay early on the morning on May 28, 1912.

The First Provisional Regiment was led by Colonel Lincoln Karmany, "who had a reputation among his fellow officers as a tough campaigner and two-fisted drinker"; he had allegedly quipped: "There may be a few good men who don't drink, but they've got to prove it."[31] The Second Provisional Regiment was led by Colonel James E. Mahoney. Because Karmany was the senior colonel, he assumed command of the newly constituted First Provisional Marine Brigade on June 7, and Colonel George Barnett took over command of the First Provisional Regiment, where Feland served as Company B commander in the First Battalion headed by Major Henry Davis. Second Lieutenants Alfred Robbins and John Gray were Feland's junior officers.

After arriving ashore, Captain Feland and his men proceeded by railroad to Soledad, about nineteen miles northwest of Guantanamo. Their primary task was to protect the extensive property of the Guantanamo Sugar Company. Feland dispatched Lieutenant Gray and twenty-four men to San Jose, in the northwest corner of the company's property. While the Marines protected property in various locations scattered throughout Oriente Province, the Cuban army remained free to concentrate on ruthlessly putting down the black rebellion.[32]

Although the area around Soledad remained reasonably peaceful, one night Lieutenant Gray heard sustained rifle fire coming from about a mile away. He telephoned Captain Feland to ask if he should go out and investigate, but "Captain Feland in no uncertain terms put his veto on this procedure." The next day, Gray took some men to inspect the scene of the fight, where they encountered "some evil looking characters" and "a surly looking crew." Gray later recalled that he was "not sorry that Captain Feland had not approved of my request of the previous night."[33]

The Marine Corps did not remain long in Cuba. Most of the men had been withdrawn by mid-July. Feland did not return with his company to Philadelphia; instead, he was again posted to Camp Elliott in Panama, this time to serve on a court of inquiry. He sailed back to New York at the end of July and returned to Philadelphia on August 8. He and his wife had little time together, however, as Captain Feland was dispatched to the Caribbean again in September 1912.

On the island of Hispaniola, the boundary between Haiti and Santo Domingo was in dispute, and an uprising in Santo Domingo threatened the peace. Seeking to assist, the United States sent two commissioners plus nearly 800 Marines in the Second Provisional Regiment under the command of Colonel Franklin J. Moses. Feland served as regimental adjutant as the troopship *Prairie* carried the Marines to their destination. After arriving in Santo Domingo, however, the Marines remained on board the *Prairie* while the commissioners helped sort out several matters, including who would take over the Santo Domingo government. The fighting ceased, a new president was installed, and the Marines departed; Feland arrived back in Philadelphia on December 7.[34]

Two months later, Feland was once more headed to the Caribbean. Because of the continued fighting in Mexico, President William Howard Taft (who had only two weeks remaining in office) was concerned about the threat to U.S. lives and interests, so he sent Marines into the region to be ready for deployment, if necessary. Having overthrown longtime Mexican dictator Porfirio Díaz in 1911, Francisco Madero was facing his own struggles with conservatives, on the one hand, and with more radical revolutionary elements, on the other. On February 9, 1913, fighting broke out in Mexico City, pitting troops loyal to Madero against rebel army troops under Generals Bernardo Reyes and Félix Díaz. Madero's top general, Victoriano Huerta, joined the rebels. The ensuing *La Decena Trágica*

(Ten Tragic Days) resulted in a successful coup d'état by Huerta and Díaz and the death of Madero. On February 19 Huerta became Mexico's president, but opposition quickly arose. Several factions objected to the coup and began "what was to become a Constitutionalist revolution, the year-and-a-half campaign to rid Mexico of Huerta."[35]

Given the shaky situation in Mexico, Marines boarded the U.S. Army transport *Meade* on February 20, bound for Guantanamo Bay. Captain Feland served as adjutant of the First Regiment of the Second Provisional Brigade, which was again commanded by Colonel Karmany. Colonel George Barnett was commander of the First Regiment, and Lieutenant Colonel John Lejeune was his second in command; these two men (both future Commandants) would become increasingly crucial to Feland's career over the next few years. Despite the instability and unrest in Mexico, the Marines were never sent into action. The First Regiment boarded the *Prairie* on April 28 and sailed back to the United States, arriving in Philadelphia on May 2.[36]

During their time in Guantanamo, the Marines took action to solidify the future of the Corps. Back in 1911, officers of the First Provisional Brigade had met during their brief stay in Cuba to consider forming an association to promote the cause of the Marine Corps. That group had included many of the current and future stars of the Corps—L. W. T. Waller, George Barnett, Franklin Moses, John Lejeune, Louis McCarty Little, Harry Lay, Hiram Bearss, and Logan Feland—and many of the same officers found themselves back in Guantanamo in April 1913. Under Colonel Karmany's direction, they met once again to discuss formalizing the support group. On April 25 they formed the Marine Corps Association, with Lieutenant Colonel Lejeune, Captain Harold Snyder, and Captain Davis Wills acting as its Executive Committee. The association was formed "for the purpose of recording and publishing the history of the Marine Corps, publishing a periodical journal for the dissemination of information concerning the aims, purposes and deeds of the Corps, and the interchange of ideas for the betterment and improvement of its officers and men."[37]

In 1915 the Marine Corps Association would create a Board of Control consisting of Major General Barnett, Colonel George Richards, Lieutenant Colonel Lejeune, and retired Captain Frank Evans, who served as secretary and treasurer. The association's constitution set forth its task: "to disseminate knowledge of the military art and science among its members; to provide for the improvement of their professional attainments; to foster the spirit and preserve the traditions of the United States Marine Corps; and to increase the efficiency of its members." The association collected dues with an eye toward producing a professional journal, the *Marine Corps Gazette*, and Feland supported the publication in a surprising way. On the inside back cover of the first issue of the *Gazette*, which appeared in March 1916, Captain Logan Feland and Lieutenant Samuel Bogan advertised their patented "Rifleman's Friend," a paraffinned or celluloid card containing tables designed to take into account windage when firing a rifle. The paraffinned card cost twenty-five cents, and the celluloid one thirty cents.[38]

Once again, Feland had used his technical acumen to address a professional issue: better marksmanship. By the early 1900s, the Marine Corps had begun to place a great deal of emphasis on marksmanship. In 1899 Commandant Heywood had appointed Major Charles Lauchheimer as inspector of target practice, and it was Lauchheimer who had inspected the praiseworthy rifle range constructed by Feland at Annapolis. Lauchheimer supported the establishment of a Marine Corps marksmanship team, and rifle skills were emphasized after Marines were armed with the new M1903 Springfield rifle starting in 1906. Marines subsequently received extra pay if they qualified as marksmen, sharpshooters, or expert riflemen. Their impressive marksmanship would stun the Germans in World War I.[39]

Logan Feland's service in the years 1907 to 1913 demonstrated that Marine Corps personnel were stretched thin: it was difficult to make progress with the Advanced Base School while repeatedly responding to situations in the Caribbean. Captain Feland established himself as a capable and increasingly important leader in the Corps. His appearance before the Butler subcommittee in 1909, his appointment as one of the first instructors at the Advanced Base School, and his service as adjutant in various expeditionary regiments all demonstrated his increasing significance and value to the Corps. His old commander, Colonel Waller, certainly believed that Feland was a top-notch Marine Corps officer. When Waller was ordered to Mare Island, California, in 1911, he lamented that if he had Smedley Butler, "Cyrus Radford, Feland and some other of my old friends [here] we could make things as they should be."[40] After 1913, Captain Feland would become even more significant in the Marine Corps.

5

Prewar Postings, 1913–1917

After returning to Philadelphia at the beginning of May 1913, Captain Logan Feland could finally turn his attention to the Advanced Base School and the creation of an Advanced Base Force. Captain William Fullam, the navy's aid for inspections, had criticized the Marine Corps for its failure to create a viable force. Specifically, Fullam "charged that the Marine Corps had shirked its 'true field' of expeditionary duty and advanced base force training for thirteen years and had demonstrated its lack of interest by 'its failure or inability' to form permanent battalions and to surrender its anachronistic ships guard and Navy yard security functions."[1] Other naval officers supported Fullam's critique in *Proceedings of the U.S. Naval Institute.*

As a result, the U.S. Navy's General Board decreed that the Marine Corps's Advanced Base Force would participate in the 1913–1914 Atlantic Fleet winter exercises in three ways: conduct a landing, set up fortifications, and defend those fortifications. Accordingly, Commandant Biddle focused on solidifying the Advanced Base Brigade in Philadelphia. The force would consist of the First Regiment, focusing on fixed defenses, and the Second Regiment, serving as mobile defense. Feland would command Company C, the submarine mine company, in the First (Fixed) Regiment.[2] The other companies in the First Regiment included artillery, engineer, signal, and searchlight groups. Their task would be to go ashore, set up advanced base fortifications, and mine the harbor to protect the U.S. fleet. The Second (Mobile) Regiment would consist mainly of infantry supported by light artillery and machine guns designed to repulse enemy landings. Each regiment would number about 800 men, which was fewer than optimal but realistic, given the Marine Corps's continuing expeditionary and fleet duties. The brigade needed much more material, which finally started arriving in the summer of 1913, including several types of landing craft. A former ocean liner, the *Hancock*, was refitted to carry the First Regiment.[3]

As the brigade came together, training intensified. Put in command of an artillery company of three-inch guns, Feland's friend Frederick "Fritz" Wise later recalled that "the easy days in Philadelphia were over." The companies drilled and practiced, and Wise noted that his company had to build a "portable railroad," dig pits, build gun platforms, and mount the guns.[4]

As Feland prepared his company, he had to wrestle with issues such as which electrical mines to use, how to transport them, how to rig them to fire properly, and how to lay the mines in the harbor. The mining company had a very important role in the Advanced Base Force. Whereas the navy laid contact mines, the Marines used controlled mines that needed an electrical connection to detonate. The two types of mines worked together: navigation channels could be established using contact mines, and then controlled mines could be used within the channels to determine which ships could pass through it. Captain Feland focused on experimenting with the electrical firing systems of the mines. Although he had been trained at MIT as a civil engineer and an architect, his penchant for technical work made him well suited to the complex electrical engineering required to control the mines.[5]

Finally, in December 1913, the Marine Corps's Advanced Base Brigade boarded ships to begin the winter exercise. The First (Fixed) Regiment's task was to land and establish fortifications on the small island of Culebra, off the Puerto Rican coast, and set up mines in the harbor. Colonel George Barnett commanded the brigade, and Colonel Charles "Squeegee" Long headed the First Regiment, which boarded the *Hancock* in Philadelphia. The Second (Mobile) Regiment, headed by Lieutenant Colonel John Lejeune, assembled at Pensacola, Florida, and embarked on the *Prairie*.

By mid-January, both regiments had landed at Culebra and set up their defenses. Feland's company laid mines to protect Great Harbor. The Atlantic Fleet arrived and tried to enter the harbor; then it landed its shipboard Marines. Observing the exercise, chief naval umpire Captain William Sims pronounced that the defense had won. After the exercise, the Fixed Regiment conducted further artillery tests and attempted to detonate the mines. Unfortunately, Feland's Company C could detonate only one mine.[6]

In a lengthy report, Feland laid out many of the problems encountered during the exercise and made recommendations for solving them. He performed extensive calculations to determine how much time was needed to handle the many supplies required to conduct mining operations. He noted that the absence of appropriate boats had slowed down the laying of the mines. More searchlights were needed to conduct night operations, and many technical details remained to be worked out if the mines were to be exploded correctly. Feland praised the work of his subordinates, crediting the "conscientious and tireless effort given to this most difficult, and in many cases dangerous, work by First Lieutenants Samuel W. Bogan and Howard C. Judson and by the enlisted men as a whole." Despite the problems elucidated in Feland's analysis, regimental commander Long's report to brigade commander Barnett acknowledged that the mining company had done well: "The mine company report indicates clearly the difficulties encountered and the work performed. The mining company, under Captain Logan Feland, performed most creditable work, not only in assembling the mines, but in the establishment of observation stations, mine casements and searchlight, and in operating same."[7]

Having completed a reasonably successful exercise, the Marines departed Culebra on the *Hancock* and the *Prairie* and returned to Pensacola on February 15, 1914.

Meanwhile, a major change was taking place in the Marine Corps: appointment of a new Commandant. Major General William Biddle, scion of a famous Philadelphia family, was nearing mandatory retirement. Biddle had become Marine Corps Commandant in 1911 after a political struggle over the position. Many officers, including Smedley Butler and Fritz Wise, had favored the candidacy of veteran campaigner L. W. T. Waller, which foundered due to Waller's involvement in the Samar incident and his subsequent court-martial. Another candidate, George Barnett, had enjoyed the support of his former Naval Academy roommate, Representative John Weeks of Massachusetts. Powerful Pennsylvania senator Bois Penrose had championed Biddle for the Commandant's slot, and because President Taft needed Penrose's support for some upcoming legislation, Biddle was awarded the job.

Despite some criticism of his seemingly lethargic demeanor, Biddle proved to be a valuable Commandant who championed the advanced base concept. Noted Marine Corps historian Allan Millett credits Biddle with "at least three important reforms that strengthened the Corps's ability to respond to the advanced base mission": "creation of an assistant to the commandant with important responsibilities for military training and preparedness, the creation of permanent expeditionary companies at each Marine barracks, and the institution of mandatory three months' recruit training."[8] Another noted historian, Brian McAllister Linn, describes Biddle as a "transitional commandant who was well suited to guide a Corps itself in transition"; he states that "Biddle's steadfast defense of the Marine Corps's interests and his refusal to stake it all on a new mission until his superiors made an equally firm commitment should not be slighted, for they provided a solid foundation for his successors to build on."[9]

When Biddle announced his retirement in 1913, jockeying for the Commandant's position began anew. Several Marine Corps officers came up for consideration, including L. W. T. Waller, Lincoln Karmany, George Barnett, and John Lejeune. John Weeks, now a U.S. senator, supported Barnett again. Waller had the full support of the Virginia congressional delegation, but his reputation (perhaps unjust) as the "Butcher of Samar" persisted. Karmany (Biddle's favorite) had recently divorced. Lejeune was still a lieutenant colonel and thus a relatively young candidate. In the end, Secretary of the Navy Josephus Daniels chose George Barnett as Commandant.[10]

Barnett had been commissioned into the Marine Corps in 1883 and had performed a variety of shipboard and expeditionary duties, including commanding the maneuvers at Culebra in January 1914, just before becoming Commandant. In 1908 he had married the formidable Lelia Montague Gordon, a wealthy, widowed Washington, D.C., socialite. First in Beijing and then in Philadelphia and Washington, the Barnetts had become prominent on the social scene, and Logan and Katherine Feland would increasingly be included in their social circle. In contrast, Josephus Daniels did not enjoy high society, and eventually the two men's different styles would clash.[11]

Barnett returned to Washington, D.C., to take up his new duties

Major General George Barnett. Barnett was Commandant of the Marine Corps during World War I and strongly supported Feland during his career.

as Commandant on February 24, 1914, turning over command of the Advanced Base Brigade to Lieutenant Colonel Lejeune. Because the Mexican situation had heated up again, the First Advanced Brigade lingered in the Caribbean rather than returning to Philadelphia. The Mobile Regiment boarded the *Prairie* and sailed for the Mexican coast, but Captain Feland and the Fixed Regiment got a respite, visiting New Orleans for a month, in time for Mardi Gras. Feland and his friend Captain "Hiking Hiram" Bearss served on a general court-martial board at the end of February, after which they requested ten days' leave to return to Philadelphia, but the request was denied.[12] The Mexican situation was becoming critical, and the Marine Corps needed its key officers to be ready for action.

Meanwhile, President Woodrow Wilson continued to pressure the Mexican government of Victoriano Huerta. The United States maintained troops along the Texas-Mexico border and had Marines stationed in the Caribbean, waiting to intervene in Mexico if the opportunity presented itself. Hostilities almost occurred over a minor incident at the eastern port of Tampico, when U.S. sailors were detained there. Rear Admiral Henry T. Mayo demanded an apology and a gunfire salute to the U.S. flag but got neither. Shortly thereafter, it was reported that the German steamer *Ypiranga* would soon arrive at Vera Cruz, bearing arms for Huerta's forces. Wilson used this as an excuse to order Marines from Lejeune's force and fleet Marines to converge on Vera Cruz for a possible landing. In addition, the *Hancock*—with Feland aboard—was dispatched from New Orleans to join the U.S. attacking force.[13]

On the morning of April 21, 1914, U.S. Marines under the overall command of Lieutenant Colonel Wendell Neville landed at Vera Cruz and attempted to seize the customhouse. Mexican soldiers resisted, and a battle broke out. The *Hancock* arrived on April 22, and the men of Colonel Long's First Regiment went ashore and took up positions in the town. Urban fighting ensued, as Mexican soldiers and naval cadets put up a brief resistance. The Marines cleared the streets block by block, building by building.

As part of Major Robert "Hal" Dunlap's Second Battalion, Captain Feland's Second Company landed at about 12:15 p.m. and marched into town to "search houses for arms and ammunition, arrest all persons having arms in their possession and to shoot all snipers." When the Marines landed, "the crew of an English Warship gave them three cheers. Captain

Logan Feland ordered his Company—'With ball cartridges—LOAD—A state of war exists—use your own discretion—Squads right, march!'"[14] As darkness fell, Dunlap took Feland's and Captain Hiram Bearss's companies outside the city, where they "joined Major Butler's Battalion in building a trench against a possible counterattack from the enemy outside." At the end of the day, Feland's company was posted on picket duty on the outskirts of Vera Cruz. The next day, his company continued to search for arms in the city. Most of the resistance ceased after the Marines' second day ashore.[15] Although the fighting did not last long, the Marine Corps had proved that it could deploy rapidly and effectively.

On May 5 Colonel Waller arrived to take over command of the Marines in Vera Cruz, reporting to U.S. Army brigadier general Frederick Funston, who had briefly commanded in Cuba in 1906. When the U.S. Army troops arrived on April 29, the fleet Marines returned to their vessels, but a Marine contingent would remain in Vera Cruz until mid-December 1914.

Feland departed for the United States on November 3 aboard the *Buford* and arrived home ten days later for what he expected to be a month-and-a-half leave of absence. His leave was cut short, however. After a quick trip to Kentucky to visit his sister Mary in Owensboro and his mother in Hopkinsville, Captain Feland returned to Philadelphia on December 5, 1914, and reported for duty with the Second Company, Advanced Base Force.[16]

Feland once again took up the problem of mine warfare. He continued to work on improving the control system for firing electrical mines and applied for a patent for such a system on March 23, 1915; the patent was granted on October 14, 1919.[17] Feland and his company also practiced on maneuvers. In one exercise in the waters off the Philadelphia Naval Shipyard, in two hours Feland's company assembled and sowed twenty mines and connected wires to the firing board. Feland's technical interactions extended beyond the Marine Corps. He consulted with navy officials, especially at the Torpedo Station in Newport, Rhode Island, and delivered a lecture on mines to the army's Coast Artillery School at Fort Monroe, Virginia. During this period, Captain Feland also performed other typical duties, such as serving as a board member of a general court-martial and on an examining board for promotions.[18]

When Feland had time off, he and Katherine began to spend more and more time in the Pocono Mountains, about 150 miles north of Philadelphia. Pike County, Pennsylvania, was relatively unspoiled wilderness and sparsely populated, with slightly more than 8,000 residents counted in the 1910 census. Although he was comfortable in society, Feland still loved the outdoors and enjoyed hunting and fishing. Pike County was a good antidote to life in Philadelphia and the demands of the Marine Corps. Feland would later build a cabin there in anticipation of his retirement.[19]

The Felands became more prominent in Philadelphia society primarily because of Katherine's musical appearances. She sang at a variety of venues, and her picture appeared in the *Philadelphia Inquirer*. She sang with the Strawbridge and Clothier Chorus, a well-known, well-regarded group of more than 200 singers that had been sponsored by the Philadelphia department store since the early 1880s. Soon after Logan Feland returned from Vera Cruz, Katherine sang in the annual A. J. Drexel Biddle concert for the benefit of religious work. A few weeks later, in early January 1915, she sang at a Drexel Institute concert.[20] The connection with Philadelphia millionaire A. J. Drexel Biddle would prove to be an important one for the Felands.

After the outbreak of war in Europe in August 1914, national debate about U.S. participation remained contentious. Some leaders believed the United States should remain neutral, relying on its small professional army for protection if attacked. Others, such as former president Theodore Roosevelt, thought U.S. participation in the war was desirable and inevitable and sought to increase U.S. preparedness. They encouraged the creation of a large citizen army to supplement the professionals.[21]

Major General Leonard Wood encouraged preparedness. His was a highly qualified perspective because of his position as a physician, Medal of Honor recipient, Rough Rider, former military governor of Cuba and the Philippines, and U.S. Army chief of staff. At his urging, military training camps for college students began in 1913 at Gettysburg, Pennsylvania, and Monterey, California. After August 1914, and especially after the sinking of the *Lusitania* in May 1915, the impetus grew for the creation of other training camps to prepare business and professional men for military service. The most famous camp was established at Plattsburgh, New York, 150 miles north of Albany, and gave its name to the overall movement.[22] The camp drew some of the educated elite of the Eastern Seaboard, including lawyers, bankers, politicians, professors, and even the mayor of New York City, John Purroy Mitchel. Other camps near Chicago and San Francisco attracted similar trainees. Although General Wood saw these men as potential U.S. Army soldiers, in Philadelphia, the training camp movement eventually took on a decidedly Marine Corps flavor.

Anthony J. "Tony" Drexel Biddle, son of a banker and scion of one of Philadelphia's oldest families, was rich, well known, and eccentric. As a somewhat puny youngster, he took up sports and Christianity, combining the two into a movement called "muscular Christianity," which, at its peak, had nearly 300,000 adherents who came primarily from his Bible classes. Biddle was, among other things, a reporter, author, publisher, boxer, and martial arts specialist. He was also a strong proponent of military preparedness.[23]

After war broke out in Europe in 1914, Biddle became alarmed at Germany's actions and encouraged the United States to increase its readiness by training more men to fight. Consequently, in October 1915 the Drexel Biddle Military Instruction Camp was created when fifty business and professional men, including Tony Biddle himself, started to train at the Biddle estate in the Philadelphia suburb of Lansdowne. Under the command of Colonel J. Campbell Gilmore, U.S. Army, the training was rudimentary at first, focusing on military etiquette such as folding a flag, but it progressed to include signal work. The camp attracted a great deal of attention when it was visited by Philadelphia notables, including Logan and Katherine Feland. Captain Feland continued his interest in the Drexel Biddle training camp, which in November 1915 welcomed another group of seventy-five volunteers. This camp featured advanced training such as "a stiff bayonet drill, extended order drills, skirmish and firing line practice." The camp added a hospital corps and a field ambulance, as well as an "electric signaling car," on which a searchlight was mounted. The new camp members also watched a group of Pennsylvania National Guard engineers construct a pontoon bridge. At the camp's religious ceremony, Katherine Feland served as vocalist.

Toward the end of the camp, Tony Biddle hosted a dinner for the Marine Corps Commandant, Major General George Barnett, and his wife, Lelia. The Felands attended, as did Captain James Carson Breckinridge, Barnett's aide-de-camp.[24] The dinner played a part in Commandant Barnett's approval of the Marine Corps's participation in Biddle's Philadelphia military training camp, in which Feland would have a major role.

During the winter of 1915–1916 the preparedness movement gained steam, despite some strong national opposition. In February 1916 Captain Feland attended a dinner in Philadelphia where 300 people gathered to hear a speech by Hudson Maxim, the inventor of smokeless gunpowder (his brother Hiram had invented the Maxim machine gun). Maxim vehemently castigated the "Lilliputians of pacifism" and called for universal military service.[25] Given his interest in hunting, his military background, and his fascination with technology, Feland must have been captivated by Maxim's speech.

In April 1916 Biddle presided over a dinner hosted by the Philadelphia Preparedness Campaign Committee, which was trying to raise half a million dollars to finance a citizens' army of 48,000 men. Having been relieved as U.S. Army chief of staff but still a strong proponent of military training camps, Major General Leonard Wood spoke to the gathering, as did Commandant Barnett. Though recognizing that "peaceful arbitration of conflicts should be strived for," Wood believed that "it is the strong, well-prepared nation which determines whether arbitration is to be employed or force resorted to, not the weak and unprepared nation." Barnett touted the Marine Corps, which "represented preparedness in the highest sense of the word," and spoke of Marine Corps exploits. He pledged support for the citizens' army and called on Congress to do the same. Katherine Feland sang "The Star-Spangled Banner." All told, more than $13,000 was raised in this first of a series of planned fund-raisers.[26]

The preparedness movement continued to gather steam not only in Philadelphia but also in other cities. A national debate ensued over what became the National Defense Act of 1916. The act contained provisions for the funding of military training camps that had been privately funded in the past. In 1916 more than 16,000 men attended regular army instruction camps, four times the previous year's total. Separate from but parallel to the army, the Marine Corps became more involved with the military training movement.[27]

Biddle's discussion with army officials about creating a military training camp in Philadelphia did not lead to their support, so he turned to Barnett. Given the long-standing ties between Philadelphia and the Marine Corps—dating back to Tun Tavern, the so-called birthplace of the Corps—Barnett proved more amenable to the idea of a Philadelphia training camp. The camp concept dovetailed with Barnett's desire to increase the size of his organization. The Naval Appropriations Act of 1916 eventually authorized an increase in the Marine Corps from just over 10,000 officers and enlisted men to more than 15,000, with a possible increase in a national emergency to more than 18,000 Marines. It also created a Marine Corps Reserve.[28]

With $31,000 appropriated to set up training camps, Commandant Barnett approved the Marine Corps's participation in the program and named Captain Feland, head of the Philadelphia Marine Barracks, to lead the new training camp. For this venture, Feland had several capable assistants, including Captain Frank Halford, Lieutenant Ralph Stover Keyser, Captain Andrew Drum as camp quartermaster, and Tony Biddle as camp adjutant.[29]

First, Feland sent a detachment to the estate of Mrs. George Childs Drexel in Lansdowne to create the new military camp. The Marines laid out streets, installed water mains and electric lights, put up tents, established a telephone system, and set up six field kitchens. The Philadelphia Military Training Camp officially opened on July 21, 1916. On Sunday, July 23, in front of thousands of spectators, Marine Corps Commandant Barnett and his aide, Captain Earl Ellis, made a formal inspection of the camp. Katherine Feland presented the camp with a "beautifully embroidered silk flag," and Lieutenant Keyser led a well-received machine gun demonstration.[30]

The camp's initial 200 recruits soon swelled to 500 men willing to undergo three full weeks of military training to receive a commission in the Marine Corps Reserve. The recruits could either spend three weeks in a row at the camp or two weeks and subsequent weekends, to accommodate the businessmen who signed up. The recruits were issued Marine Corps gear, including uniforms, rifles, and tents. Between reveille at 0530 and taps at 2100, a full day of training was carried out. The training regimen included marching and drilling, maneuvers, signals work, small-arms practice, machine gun drills, first-aid instruction, lectures on hygiene, and even artillery practice with three-inch field pieces, standard Marine Corps weapons.[31]

Each weekend, spectators gathered to review the troops. On one Sunday, notable Philadelphians and others from Washington, Baltimore, and New York City watched the recruits conduct drills and carry out a sham battle in which Captain Drum headed the offense while Lieutenant Keyser led the defense.

On August 28, 1916, the Philadelphia Military Training Camp had its final review. The event generated great interest and publicity. General and Mrs. Barnett attended, as did Katherine Feland and Cordelia Biddle. A *Philadelphia Inquirer* photograph portrayed the three women together. A smaller photo showed Barnett striding resolutely alongside Captain Feland, with Ellis following. Feland addressed the assembled men, calling for volunteers to form the first Marine Corps Reserve unit. Seventy-four percent of them volunteered. Barnett praised these men, who would "form a nucleus of a force upon which the United States will at some time depend to form its first line of defense."[32]

The Philadelphia Military Training Camp proved to be a great success. Writing in *Marines Magazine,* Corporal James Wisner related his visit to the Lansdowne camp and noted, "It was an agreeable surprise to see the results obtained during the short period the camp has been in existence." Wisner concluded that "the Lansdowne camp is a splendid advertisement for the Marine Corps and will undoubtedly stimulate recruiting in a large degree, particularly at this time when a material increase in personnel is expected."[33]

Captain Feland and Lieutenant Keyser would fight together at Belleau Wood in World War I and eventually retire as major generals. Tony Biddle would join the new Marine Corps Reserve and become a renowned instructor in the art of hand-to-hand combat in both world wars, specializing in boxing, jujitsu, and bayonet training. He would write a manual on individual combat, *Do or Die*, that was used by the Corps, and he would be cited by the secretary of the navy for his service. Biddle eventually retired as a Marine Corps Reserve colonel and died in 1948.[34]

Just prior to the Philadelphia Military Training Camp, Captain Logan Feland had appeared on July 13 and 14 before a Marine Corps examining board, as he was being considered for promotion to major. Colonel Charles Doyen headed the board, which also included Major George Thorpe and Major John H. Russell. Feland performed well on the two-day examination, scoring a 3.58 (out of 4) average. On September 14, 1916, he was promoted to major, subject to confirmation, with the promotion retroactive to August 29.[35]

Socially, the Felands continued to solidify ties with the Barnetts. Katherine Feland hosted a tea for Lelia Barnett in November 1916 at the Feland residence at the Philadelphia Naval Shipyard. In turn, the Barnetts invited the Felands to a dinner party in Washington in January 1917. Prominent political, social, and military dignitaries attended, along with their wives. These included Secretary of State Robert Lansing, Supreme Court Justice Mahlon Pitney, USMC Quartermaster Brigadier General Charles McCawley, USMC Adjutant and Inspector General Charles Lauchheimer, Colonel Charles Doyen, Solicitor General John W. Davis, and Naval Academy Superintendent Edward W. Eberle. Katherine Feland sang after dinner. The Felands and the Eberles stayed at the Commandant's house at "Eighth and Eye."[36]

McCawley and Lauchheimer were key Marine Corps staff officers (often disliked by line officers, who served on expeditionary forces and on ships), and both had been promoted to brigadier general in August 1916, when legislation expanded the Corps. Lauchheimer had been a classmate of Barnett's at the Naval Academy, and McCawley was the son of a former Commandant; both had strong political connections. Lauchheimer had had a contentious relationship with the previous Commandant (William Biddle), resulting in a board of inquiry and Lauchheimer's temporary exile to the Philippines. Doyen, another of Barnett's Naval Academy classmates, had commanded expeditionary forces in the Philippines and the Caribbean, and he had been Feland's commander when the latter taught at the School of Application at Annapolis.

Feland was thus associating with key Marine Corps officers as he and his wife climbed the social and professional ranks. Their climb did not pass without comment. Back in 1915, L. W. T. Waller had noted to John Lejeune, "I do not write to Feland because for some reason he has taken a queer dislike to me and we who were friends see nothing of each other. He and his wife have never called on us although I have seen them in the yard calling on all the others. I am rather glad she has not called as it has saved us a lot of trouble."[37]

In late January 1917 Major Logan Feland was transferred to the Headquarters Detachment of the Fixed Defense Force of the Advanced

Base Force, where he carried out various duties. In 1915 two German cruisers, the *Kronprinz Wilhelm* and the *Prinz Eitel Friedrich*, had been interned, and in October 1916 the men and ships had been sent to the Philadelphia Naval Shipyard. The men remained there until March 26, 1917, when Marines commanded by Major Feland supervised their shipment by train to internment camps at Forts Oglethorpe and McPherson in Georgia. Feland also continued to do administrative and technical work. For example, in March 1917 he was charged with inspecting two armored cars under development for use by the Marine Corps.[38]

Feland spent most of the years immediately preceding U.S. entry into World War I Stateside, with the exception of brief exercises in Cuba and several months in Mexico. He helped the Marine Corps prepare for the war in three ways: First, he was a technical expert, leading the development of electrically controlled mines, which were at the heart of advanced base defense. Second, he led the men in his company, which played an important role in the Advanced Base Force. Finally, he led his fellow citizens at the Philadelphia Military Training Camp. As World War I approached, the Marine Corps increasingly prepared for its greatest challenge.

Commandant George Barnett had anticipated the need for a larger Marine Corps. In May 1913 he had issued orders to the adjutant and inspector, the quartermaster, and the paymaster to submit quarterly reports on "preparedness for war." Within a week of the outbreak of fighting in August 1914, General Barnett had sent the assistant quartermaster, Major Henry Roosevelt, to England and France to observe conditions there and report back. Roosevelt reported on subjects ranging from clothing to aviation to the morale of the French soldiers and citizenry. A year later, Barnett's assistant, John Lejeune, prepared a memorandum for Secretary of the Navy Josephus Daniels covering a variety of topics, such as field artillery and machine guns, entrenchment, aviation, and preparedness.[39] Barnett lobbied strongly and effectively for more men and officers, citing the possibility of U.S. participation in the European war, along with the Marine Corps's continuing commitments in such places as Haiti and Santo Domingo. In August 1916 the Naval Appropriations Act not only authorized the creation of eight new generalships but also added 5,000 men to the Corps.

On April 6, 1917, Congress declared war on Germany. The next day, Logan Feland was ordered to join Brigadier General Waller and Colonel

Charles Long in witnessing eight-inch howitzer tests at Bethlehem, Pennsylvania.[40] The howitzers would soon be needed.

Commandant Barnett then lobbied for even more men and argued that a Marine Corps Brigade should be formed to accompany General John J. Pershing, the newly designated commander of the American Expeditionary Force (AEF), to France. Barnett prodded Secretary Daniels and Chief of Naval Operations William Benson, who in turn convinced Secretary of War Newton Baker to send a Marine Brigade to France. Once again, the Marine Corps would be among the "First to Fight."[41] And first among the Marines would be Logan Feland. On May 22 he received confidential orders that he would be going to France with Pershing. Also chosen to accompany Pershing and the first small AEF contingent was Feland's friend Lieutenant Colonel Robert "Hal" Dunlap.[42]

The day before receiving these orders, Feland had appeared before a Marine Corps examining board headed by Colonel Long. He was given a "duties of higher command" problem to consider overnight and then report back the next day with his answer. He received a mark of 3.47 on the problem, which, when combined with a 3.87 for "general efficiency," resulted in the recommendation that Feland be promoted to lieutenant colonel. His promotion was eventually approved by the Senate in October 1917, retroactive to March 26, 1917.[43]

After languishing as a captain for more than a dozen years (standard practice in the Corps), Feland had advanced two ranks in the short span of nine months. It was the beginning of a meteoric rise. Feland had little time, however, to consider his promotion or other matters: he had to report to Governor's Island, New York, on May 28, 1917, to embark with General Pershing's advance party on the SS *Baltic*, bound for Europe.

6

World War I through Belleau Wood

On the gray, rainy morning of May 28, 1917, nearly 200 men gathered in presumed secrecy at Governor's Island, New York, to board a White Star Line passenger vessel, the SS *Baltic*. This group constituted the advance team that would accompany General John "Black Jack" Pershing to initiate the United States' military effort in France. Dressed in civilian clothes, the men were supposed to meet furtively, but the secret was not perfectly kept: General Pershing's aide had marked his luggage "General Pershing, Paris, France," and it sat on the pier awaiting shipment, for any German spy to see.

This small contingent included a number of men who would achieve prominence in World Wars I and II. One was James Harbord, a longtime cavalry officer who had served twelve years in the Philippines, where Pershing had become acquainted with his skills. Harbord became Pershing's first chief of staff and would play a large role in Logan Feland's rise in the ranks during the war; their friendship would continue until Feland's death.

Other members of the group included future generals Hugh Drum, Fox Conner, and John Hines and future quartermaster general A. W. Brewster. Future tank commander and World War II general George S. Patton Jr. sailed on the *Baltic*, as did future air ace Eddie Rickenbacker (at that time, a sergeant performing duty as a chauffeur). The group also numbered two of the Marine Corps's best and brightest officers: Logan Feland and Robert Dunlap.[1]

The men were ferried downriver to the *Baltic*, which left in the late afternoon. James Harbord noted in his book written after the war: "There was no inspiring view of the New York skyline, no-Napoleon-on-the-Bellerophon-gazing-at-the-fast-fading-shores-of-France for us, for it was cold and raw, and a fog like a pall settled over the green shores of Long Island."[2] When the *Baltic* reached open waters, it turned north toward Newfoundland, on the way to its final destination of Liverpool, England. Already, Pershing's staff started to gel, and their training began. Officers studied French for two hours each day. Feland's service record indicated that he could already speak French, which he most likely picked up at the Ferrell School in Hopkinsville. In addition to French lessons, Pershing's contingent worked on staff planning.[3]

As the *Baltic* turned eastward and headed across the North Atlantic, concern grew over potential German U-boat attacks. When the *Baltic* approached the British Isles, however, U.S. destroyers arrived to accompany the ship to Liverpool. In the meantime, Pershing's men continued their preparations, including typhoid shots, lectures by the British officers on board, and a warning about venereal disease. One evening the men were entertained with a benefit concert for war orphans. Finally, on the evening of June 7, they sighted land. On June 8 the *Baltic* docked in Liverpool, where Pershing's contingent received a hearty welcome by the lord mayor of Liverpool as a band played "The Star-Spangled Banner" and "God Save the King." Then Pershing's party boarded trains for London, where they met a host of British and American authorities, including U.S. ambassador Walter Hines Page and the British secretary of state for war, Lord Derby.

Lieutenant Colonel Feland and the other officers enjoyed what would undoubtedly be their best beds of the war at the Savoy Hotel. The enlisted men were given historical, if not plush, accommodations at the Tower of London barracks. There followed a round of social events and conversations with British military colleagues before the Americans left for Paris on June 13, 1917. They crossed the English Channel by boat to Boulogne, where they were given a grand reception. They continued to Paris by train and arrived at the Gare du Nord, where Marshal Joffre, General Foch, and other French dignitaries, along with a huge crowd, greeted them as a band played "The Star-Spangled Banner" and "La Marseillaise."[4]

Feland quickly got to work, serving on a board created to compile port regulations for the disembarkation of troops. The United States was about to send thousands of men and tons of material to France, and some sem-

Charles Doyen. Doyen was the first commander of the Fifth Regiment and then the Fourth Marine Brigade during World War I.

blance of order needed to be established at the receiving ports. From June 24 to July 2, Feland served as assistant landing officer at Saint-Nazaire, France, on the Bay of Biscay. On June 27 he greeted the men of the Fifth Regiment, under the command of Colonel Charles Doyen. Feland had previously been designated the regiment's second in command.

Within days after the United States declared war on Germany, Commandant Barnett had pushed for an expanded Marine Corps. A threefold increase in numbers was approved on May 22, 1917. Recruits poured into Marine Corps staging grounds at Parris Island, South Carolina, Philadelphia, and a newly leased base at Quantico, Virginia. Several of these new recruits would be assigned to a strengthened Fifth Regiment of Marines slated for shipment to France to serve under the War Department, not the Navy Department. Comprising three battalions of three companies each—a headquarters company, a supply company, and a machine gun company—the Fifth Regiment would be commanded by Colonel Charles Doyen. An 1881 graduate of the U.S. Naval Academy, Doyen had joined the Marine Corps two years later and subsequently spent much of his time in typical officer postings, such as on ship detachments and with expeditionary forces in the Philippines, Cuba, and Santo Domingo. Several veteran Corps campaigners joined Doyen as leaders in the Fifth Regiment, including Julius Turrill, Andrew Drum, George Shuler, Fritz Wise, Holland Smith, and Benjamin Berry.[5]

In early June 1918 the regiment sailed to France aboard three transports: the *Henderson*, the *Hancock*, and the *DeKalb*. Despite a few submarine scares, the three transports arrived safely at Saint-Nazaire, where the regiment's second in command, Lieutenant Colonel Logan Feland, awaited their arrival.[6] The Fifth Regiment, which was initially assigned to the U.S. First Division, set up camp and performed provost and guard duty. On July 16 the regiment climbed aboard the infamous "forty men and eight horses" boxcars of the French railroad system for the trip to Gondrecourt, in the northeastern province of Lorraine.[7]

In Gondrecourt, Feland and the Fifth Regiment trained under the tutelage of the French *Chasseurs Alpins* (Blue Devils), an elite mountain troop. Training focused on "various phases of attack and trench work," including the construction of first-line trenches, assembly and disassembly of machine guns, machine gun drills, automatic rifle instruction, pistol and rifle target practice, grenade instruction, signal drill, bayonet exercises, night attacks, combat formations, and other fighting techniques. General Pershing inspected the Marines on August 1, and on August 6 Doyen and Feland joined General D'Arman de Pouydraguin, commanding general of the Forty-Seventh Division of the *Chasseurs Alpins*, to review the Second Battalion as it carried out drills in trench building, grenade throwing, and attack formation. On August 17 Pouydraguin returned for another inspection, accompanied by General Pershing and French general Philippe Petain, commander of French forces. The generals appeared quite satisfied with the inspection.[8]

To understand trench warfare better, officers of the Fifth Regiment were sent to various parts of the Western Front to observe French fighting units. From August 21 to 23, Feland spent time with the Fifty-Fifth Regiment of French infantry as it successfully attacked at Côte de Poivre, north of Verdun, which had seen intensive fighting for nine months in 1916.[9] Then, at the end of October 1917, Feland received a new assignment: chief of staff of the newly formed Second Division.

As the United States geared up for war, more divisions were needed, and Commandant Barnett seized the opportunity to create a second Marine regiment for service in France to constitute a two-regiment Marine Brigade.[10] Thus, the Sixth Regiment was activated on July 16, 1917, under the command of Colonel Albertus Catlin, with Lieutenant Colonel Harry Lee as second in command. Made up primarily of newcomers to the Corps, the Sixth Regiment went through intensive training at the new Marine Corps base at Quantico, Virginia, before shipping out piecemeal to France starting in September 1917. Meanwhile, on September 24 the Fifth Regiment boarded two trains bound for the towns of Breuvannes and Damblain; the latter would be the site of regimental headquarters. Lieutenant Colonel Feland remained in command of the Marines at Breuvannes, while Major Fritz Wise commanded at Damblain. Eventually, the Sixth Regiment would join the Fifth Regiment to form the Fourth Marine Brigade, which was officially organized on October 24, with Doyen in command as a newly appointed brigadier general.

To form the new Second Division, the Fourth Marine Brigade would be coupled with the U.S. Army Third Brigade, consisting of two regular army regiments, the Ninth and the Twenty-Third. As the Second Division came into being, it was assigned a training sector at Bourmont, about fifty miles south of Gondrecourt. Doyen proceeded to Bourmont to

Wendell "Buck" Neville (seated, left), Logan Feland (seated, right), and Fifth Regiment officers (standing behind them). Neville led the Fifth Regiment during the iconic Battle of Belleau Wood, while Feland served as second in command. (Marine Corps Archives)

establish Second Division headquarters, which he would command temporarily until Major General Omar Bundy became available to take over on November 7. Accompanying Doyen was Feland as chief of staff and Harry Lay as adjutant. After Bundy took command, Feland stayed on as chief of staff for a short time. On January 1, 1918, Colonel Wendell "Buck" Neville assumed command of the Fifth Regiment, and on January 27 Feland returned to the Fifth Regiment as its second in command.[11]

With the Fifth Regiment now under the solid command of Neville and Feland, training intensified. The creation of the Sixth Machine Gun Battalion under Major Edward Cole meant that the Fourth Brigade had to coordinate action with its machine gunners. In addition, artillery demonstrations gave the Marines an idea of how they would be supported by guns of various sizes. They practiced for gas attacks, bayonet

American Expeditionary Force commander John "Black Jack" Pershing (center left), Wendell "Buck" Neville (behind him), Logan Feland (center back), and Fritz Wise (foreground) confer.

combat, and signaling; they held small group maneuvers as well as larger brigade maneuvers. On February 10, 1918, General Pershing visited Doyen's Fourth Marine Brigade and seemed quite pleased with its training progress.

In mid-March the Fourth Brigade moved to the battlefront, positioning itself in the Toulon sector between Verdun and Saint-Mihiel. Although the area was fairly quiet, the Marine regiments rotated into the front lines one battalion at a time, with the other two battalions in reserve. The men on the front lines sent out patrols and raiding parties, manned machine gun posts, and set up telephone lines and first-aid stations. It was not until April 1, 1918, that the first Marine was killed: Private Emil Henry Gerhke died instantly when hit by a German artillery shell fragment.[12] Many more Marines would die in just a few months.

Up to that time, fighting had been sporadic in the Toulon sector. On April 13 the Sixth Regiment suffered its first serious losses when it was struck by a gas attack. On April 17 the Fifth Regiment carried out a successful raid, resulting in two men receiving the French Croix de Guerre. The regiment successfully repulsed a German raiding party on April 21.

On April 29, AEF commander General Pershing informed Brigadier General Doyen that he had failed his mandatory physical examination; consequently, Doyen would be sent back to the United States. In Doyen's place, Pershing named James Harbord, a U.S. Army general and his chief

James Harbord. Harbord, a U.S. Army general, commanded the Fourth Marine Brigade during the Battle of Belleau Wood and subsequently the U.S. Second Division. He relied extensively on Feland during Belleau Wood, and the two remained friends after the war.

of staff, to lead the Fourth Marine Brigade.[13] This move would test Harbord, as it was his first true wartime command. It would also prove significant for Feland, who would soon demonstrate his worth to his new brigade commander.

Feland and the rest of the Fifth Regiment remained in the Verdun sector until mid-May, when they were sent back to a rest and training area. Then the Fourth Brigade moved just northwest of Paris to begin open warfare training. Pershing was insistent that U.S. troops would not get bogged down in trench fighting.

In the meantime, German general Erich von Ludendorff had launched his second major spring offensive, designed to drive a wedge between the British and French armies. On May 27 he followed with yet another major offensive directed at the French troops, who were weary from nearly three years of fighting. The attack proved successful, as the Germans rolled up mile after mile, advancing toward Paris. Fortunately, the new U.S. troops arrived in a timely fashion, helping to blunt the German offensive and shore up the Allied war effort.[14]

After celebrating Memorial Day on May 30, the Fourth Brigade received orders to proceed to the front northwest of Chateau-Thierry. Immediately the Marines were thrust into the breach in an attempt to stop the German advance. Streams of French troops were heading away from the battlefield, and when a French officer advised him to fall back, Captain Lloyd Williams supposedly replied, "Retreat, Hell, we have just come—let the Boche retreat." Years later, Fritz Wise would claim that he had uttered those famous words, shortened to "Retreat, Hell, we just got here." After the war his friend Logan Feland would write an article for the *Marine Corps Gazette*, humorously noting that although Williams had likely used the same language, "Colonel Wise had been in the Marine Corps twenty years longer and naturally knew more about 'cussing' than Captain Williams."[15] No matter who said it, the Marines were there to stay.

By June 2, 1918, the Fourth Brigade was in place just west of Belleau Wood, an old hunting preserve that was a morass of trees, ravines, and huge boulders. For the first few days the Marines played a defensive role, repelling several German attacks with devastatingly accurate rifle fire from a long distance. The strong resistance surprised the Germans, who would allegedly start to call their new opponents "Devil Dogs."[16]

The Germans knew the Americans would be coming to the front, but according to retired Lieutenant Colonel Ernst Otto, writing ten years later, the overarching question was: "How will the American troops behave in a pitched battle?"[17] The answer was, with a strong will, courage, and bravery. Feland would be one of the strongest, once he found himself in the thick of the fighting.

As second in command of the Fifth Regiment, Feland had no direct supervisory duties, so he was free to move between regimental headquarters, where Colonel Neville had to remain, and the battlefront. On June 3 Neville sent Feland out to reconnoiter the situation and report on the disposition of Wise's battalion.[18] During the Battle of Belleau Wood, both Colonel Neville and General Harbord depended on Feland to carry out various duties. Harbord would increasingly manage the situation himself, often bypassing his regimental commanders Neville and Catlin.

After successfully stopping the Germans' advance, the Marine Corps turned to the assault on Belleau Wood itself, which would become an iconic event for the Marine Corps. In the words of two prominent Marine Corps historians, "The three-week struggle for Belleau Wood ranks as one of the greatest battles of the twentieth century of the U.S. Marines, a touchstone that compares with Iwo Jima in 1945 and the Chosin Reservoir in 1950."[19]

On the evening of June 5, Lieutenant Colonel Feland appeared at Major Julius Turrill's battalion headquarters to instruct two of Turrill's company commanders, Captain George Hamilton and First Lieutenant Orlando Crowther, where to attack the next day. Turrill's troops would advance on Hill 142 to the northwest of Belleau Wood in the first phase of the day's attack plan. The second phase called for other Marines to advance on Belleau Wood and the town of Bouresches, near the southeast corner of the wood.[20]

As dawn approached on June 6, Turrill's Marines moved out at 3:45 a.m. toward Hill 142. Despite furious fighting and heavy casualties, the attack moved forward quickly. In particular, Captain Hamilton and Gunnery Sergeant Charles Hoffman distinguished themselves: Hoffman received the highest military award, the Medal of Honor, for killing or dispersing twelve Germans armed with five light machine guns, and Hamilton received the second highest award, the Navy Cross, for his actions and leadership that day. By 6:30 a.m., Feland reported to Neville that Turrill's men had proceeded north of Hill 142, far outdistancing French troops on the left flank. Feland requested that an additional reserve company be moved into the gap between the two Allied forces, and he reported that everything was "going well."[21]

In his characteristic way, Feland was being optimistic when he said things were going well. The Germans counterattacked Turrill's men throughout the day, and the battalion suffered horrendous losses. Nevertheless, with the help of an engineering company sent by General Harbord, the Marines consolidated their gains on Hill 142 and held the line. Feland's upbeat report reflected a common dilemma faced by military men in the heat of battle. Although it is important to be positive and confident, especially in difficult circumstances, there is a fine balance. Being too optimistic can blind commanders to the realities of the situation, whereas being pessimistic can have a deleterious effect on morale, making a bad situation worse. At the time of Feland's report, the attack on Hill 142, though bloody, had proceeded better than envisioned. The Marines had performed well in their first real test in World War I.

Late in the afternoon, the Fifth Regiment implemented the second phase of the battle plan and moved out toward Belleau Wood. Having heard from the French that the wood remained lightly defended by the Germans, General Harbord had not ordered a heavy artillery barrage prior to the attack. As the assault moved forward, the "fog of war" descended. Confusion reigned when some units did not shove off on time and others lost contact with units that were supposedly on their flanks. As the Marines approached Belleau Wood, they discovered that it was much more heavily defended than anticipated. During the fierce fighting the Sixth Regiment's commander, Colonel Catlin, suffered a severe wound to the right shoulder, and Lieutenant Colonel Harry Lee, the regiment's second in command, took his place at the front. Battalion officers such as Burton Sibley and Benjamin Berry led the attack, making some headway into Belleau Wood and then trying to consolidate the ground won. Reports of successes turned out to be overly optimistic.[22]

At this juncture, Lieutenant Colonel Feland was supposed to initiate an attack into the northern section of Belleau Wood from Hill 142. He recognized the perilous state of Turrill's battalion but prepared for battle anyway. At 6:45 p.m. Feland requested additional ammunition from General Harbord and reported that everything was set for the attack. He then found out that the French were not in position on the left flank, leaving the Marines in a bind. He sought to postpone the attack until after an artillery barrage on the wood, which Harbord approved. Later, after learning that Feland still had not attacked, Harbord told the Kentuckian to consolidate his position and await the arrival of Wise's battalion in the morning. Regarding Feland's hesitation, historian and retired Marine Corps officer Ron Brown notes: "Lieutenant Colonel Feland wisely held the battalions in place when the French failed to advance rather than needlessly expose his men to devastating flanking fire. When his decision was later questioned, Feland replied that such an attack would have gained nothing but the senseless slaughter of the attackers. He correctly deduced that there was too much open ground and too few men to carry the position without French support."[23] Feland's decision saved the lives of many men. On that day, June 6, the U.S. Marine Corps suffered more casualties than in all its previous history: 31 officers (6 killed) and 1,056 men (222 killed).[24] If Feland had led his men forward, the numbers would have been worse.

Feland's actions on June 6 would be mentioned on July 8, 1918, in General Order 40 of the Second Division: "During gas alarm on the morning of June 6, while on duty at Regimental P.C. [Post of Command], [Feland] was notified that the 8th Machine Gun Company, with the 17th Infantry Company following, could not find the route to go into action. Finding the 8th Machine Gun Company with the Infantry Company, Lieutenant Colonel Feland led them through Champillon, found the 17th Company, took them according to plan of Battalion Commander. He then went to the P.C. of the Battalion Commander, volunteered to perform any duty that would help, which assistance was of great value, displaying a high type of courage."[25]

In preparation for attacking the northern part of Belleau Wood the next day, June 7, General Harbord ordered Wise to move out at 2:00 a.m. to hook up with Feland and bridge the gap between Turrill's and Berry's battalions. Wise later recalled, "That was the damnedest order I ever got in my life—or anyone else ever got." He noted, "It was dark as pitch. Finding Feland would be a miracle." In fact, his runners did have trouble finding Feland, and at 5:00 a.m. the two Marines had not yet made contact. Finally, at 5:45 a.m., Colonel Neville reported to General Harbord that his two officers had established communication.[26] Soon after arriving in the gap between Turrill's and Berry's positions, Wise's battalion encountered strong fire from the Germans, and for most of the day the Marines consolidated their positions and tended to their wounded.

General Harbord ordered another attack on Belleau Wood on June 8, this time led by Sibley's battalion. By nightfall, the Marines had captured only a small portion of the southern part of Belleau Wood and had a tentative hold on the village of Bouresches, taken under the leadership of Thomas Holcomb. Disorder reigned. General Harbord finally ordered a massive bombardment of Belleau Wood on June 9 to support the ground troops.

Next up to lead the attack was "Johnny the Hard" Hughes. His battalion attempted to take over the southern portion of the wood on June 10. Although Hughes's men regained most of the ground vacated by Sibley's troops, the misinformed General Harbord believed the Marines were in control of a much larger portion of the wood. He therefore decided to send Wise's battalion toward the northern part of the wood on June 11 in an effort to capture Belleau Wood and achieve a solid victory.[27] Consequently, at 4:30 a.m. on June 11, Wise's troops attacked, although farther south than planned. Confusion reigned again. Overly optimistic reports followed, indicating that the wood had finally been captured. It had not; the northern portion had not even been entered.[28]

Even as the Battle of Belleau Wood was being fought, Feland received a commendation. On June 10, 1918, the French army awarded him a Croix de Guerre with a bronze star for his actions on the battlefield.[29] During the first week of the war, Feland had been tireless as he moved about the battlefield offering his help. A regimental history written soon after the war noted, "Almost every day he [Feland] might be seen along the lines, encouraging the officers and men and improving the situation by wise suggestions. On several occasions, he relieved tired Battalion commanders in order that they might be able to move to the rear for a time and gain much needed rest and food."[30]

At midmorning on June 12, Lieutenant Colonel Wise met with General Harbord, Colonel Neville, and Lieutenant Colonel Feland to discuss the situation. The officers were convinced that the battle for Belleau Wood was nearly over, but the fighting continued. Despite overwhelming casualties, Wise's Marines pushed northward, deeper into Belleau Wood, following another artillery barrage. Well dug in, the Germans resisted with machine gun fire. Hand-to-hand combat ensued as the Marines tried to clear out the wood in small-unit fighting. As evening fell, the Marines consolidated their gains and formed a thinly held line of defense. From a dying German prisoner captured by one of his units, Wise heard news of an impending German counterattack. Subsequently, at Fifth Regiment headquarters, Feland ordered an artillery bombardment of the area surrounding Belleau Wood. The bombardment did not stop the Germans completely, however. They attacked from the north toward Bouresches, a small village in the southeast corner of the wood. Major Maurice Shearer's Third Battalion, Fifth Regiment, successfully defended the town.[31]

By this time, the Marines were exhausted after nearly two weeks of fierce fighting. Various units started rotating to the rear for recuperation as U.S. Army units from the Third Brigade, Second Division, moved in to relieve the beleaguered leathernecks. Not all the Marines, however, could look forward to a respite.

On the morning of June 14 Harbord appeared at the Fifth Regiment's command post to talk to Neville and Feland. As Feland later wrote: "He [Harbord] went over the situation, that Holcomb had not been able to relieve Wise due to losses from gas and said the situation was not satisfactory. He told me to go down to the woods and 'get things straightened out.' I asked why [sic] my authority would be and General Harbord said 'To command everything in the woods.'"[32] Feland had at his command a group comprising elements of both the Fifth and Sixth Regiments, including a battalion commanded by Holcomb. Feland recollected that he started for the front lines "to correct what I believed [was] the most dangerous element of the situation." The line held by Wise and Holcomb was tenuous and had not been extended as reported, and the gap between Turrill's and Wise's battalions "would enable a determined thrust by the enemy to be easily successful."[33] In Feland's view, there were still plenty of Germans in the wood, and as some Marines were withdrawing and others were moving forward with army units, the Germans proved that they were still formidable opponents: they shelled the Americans with gas, causing many casualties and great confusion.[34]

Feland went forward to find his friend Fritz Wise. As Wise later related, the Kentuckian told him that "General Harbord is sore as hell because you didn't clean out the wood." Wise pointed out his great losses, with half the battalion as casualties. Feland then went forward to reconnoiter the lines of defense for himself, taking along Captain Rosewell Winans from Turrill's battalion. Based on an earlier reconnaissance, Winans believed that if properly supported, he could advance through the wood. Feland developed a plan of attack and apprised Colonel Neville, but the Fifth Regiment's commanding officer was not convinced of its feasibility, having heard contradictory information. Chagrined, Feland offered to be relieved of his command, but Neville quieted down and agreed to the attack plan, as did Harbord.[35]

Later in the afternoon on June 14, Feland sent a message to Neville in which he stated that "many men are getting to the rear on various excuses and never returning to the line." Feland took a dim view of this "considerable loss of strength" and thought the military police "should be instructed to prevent it." He also acknowledged, however, that "unless an immediate relief for this Brigade is found we are in the gravest danger of losing all we have gained. Under the strain the morale may snap at any time."[36] Feland's message revealed that he was a commander who would brook no shirking, but he recognized the tremendous burden the Marines had borne over the last couple of weeks. Feland continued to be assertive and hoped that the Germans would quit, telling Turrill to "remind Winans to call on the Boches to surrender when he begins work in the morning."[37]

Winans's attack on the morning of June 15 proved successful. The Marines gained more ground in the wood, leaving only a small portion in the northwest corner under German control. Despite this apparent success, the battle lines remained unclear; Feland asked Neville if "aviation" could ascertain where Winans's Marines were located. The Kentuckian spent the rest of the day trying to consolidate gains and figuring out the next course of action. Wise's intelligence officer, Captain William Mathews, would later note that Feland had "exposed himself time after time to heavy fire" and "was on the go day and night."[38]

Feland remained in command of the troops in Belleau Wood until noon on June 16, when he turned over command to newly arrived troops from the U.S. Army's Seventh Infantry; he then returned to Fifth Regiment headquarters. Later that afternoon, Feland told Harbord that only a small force of Germans remained in Belleau Wood. Unfortunately, in the words of historian Robert Asprey: "Logan Feland's appreciation of the enemy situation, which Harbord approved, was over-optimistic. The remaining German defenses in Belleau Wood were not as weak as he believed."[39] The Germans were more numerous and held more ground than Feland thought, and they could be reinforced from the north. Fortunately for the Americans, the Germans had also suffered massive casualties in the fighting and were weak.

Even though the Seventh Infantry had replaced the Fourth Marine Brigade, Harbord left Feland in command of Belleau Wood itself, while Neville commanded the overall sector. Harbord himself, however, continued to issue orders to unit commanders, as he had done throughout the battle. The army troops would try to envelop the remaining German troops in the wood, per Feland's plan. Unfortunately, the ill-prepared and unseasoned army troops failed to rid Belleau Wood of the remaining Germans. The fighting was so fierce that the Americans' hold on the wood was in doubt. Feland would later note that were it not for the consolidated line established by the Marines on June 16, "the 7th Infantry Battalion [sic] would have lost the Wood during the first or second attack made by it. The Marines might have lost it at any time before this line was formed if the enemy had attacked with determination in this gap."[40]

Major Shearer's Third Battalion, Fifth Regiment, returned to the wood, and Harbord ordered the Marines to advance in sharpshooting pairs. Feland did another reconnaissance and determined that the Germans still held a large part of the northern section of the wood, but Harbord ordered the attack to proceed as planned on June 23. After faltering initially, Shearer's men pushed on. By the morning of June 26, Shearer would report in soon-to-be-famous words: "Belleau Wood now U.S. Marine Corps entirely."[41]

Chicago Tribune correspondent Floyd Gibbons had written an article about the attack on Belleau Wood, noting the specific contributions made by the Marines. Because Gibbons had been presumed mortally wounded, a censor, who was a friend of his, allowed Gibbons's article to be published. The resulting publicity helped make the Battle of Belleau Wood a Marine Corps legend, but it also aroused the jealousy of army officials, who would suggest after the war that Belleau Wood had been a minor affair.[42]

The Battle of Belleau Wood certainly was not a minor affair for the Marine Corps in terms of casualties. The Fourth Brigade suffered a nearly

55 percent casualty rate, or about 4,000 men. The original companies were decimated, but new replacements came in and served well. In recognition of this heroic effort, the French army issued an order renaming Belleau Wood the *Bois de la Brigade de Marine.*[43]

For Logan Feland, the Battle of Belleau Wood established his solid reputation as a leader who was not afraid to go toward the action. Snippets of reports revealed a reasonably cool Feland taking command whenever and wherever necessary during the battle. Several years later, one of Wise's officers, Captain Joseph Murray, remembered an incident: "I was awakened some time in the early morning by a familiar voice and saw Colonel Logan Feland sitting on the edge of a foxhole talking through the field phone." After identifying himself by his call sign—Slap Six—Feland went on to identify himself further, according to Murray:

> "Oh, Hell, this is Feland and I'm here at Wise's. This battalion is not going to attack at 'H' hour. . . . Yes, I can see how it is. What? . . . You'll have to take my word for it, Sir. . . . What's that? I'll take a Court if you want, but they are not going to attack at—er—H hour." And he hung up. All said quiet calmly too. In fact, that was the nearest to being excited that I ever saw Colonel Feland under fire and Charley Dunbeck told me that during the last trying days of the War, which I missed, Colonel Feland, then commanding the Fifth Regiment was the only officer above the rank of Major, excepting Lieutenant-Colonel Turrill, that he ever used to see up in the *real* front line.[44]

Years later, James Harbord wrote to the secretary of war and noted that, during Belleau Wood,

> There were probably few days in which I did not have occasion to see this officer [Feland] and to make use of his service. The importance of the service he rendered to his country, to the Army, and to his own Corps by his conduct during that forty days can hardly be overstated. As Lieutenant Colonel of the Fifth Marines he inspired and supported his Commanding Officer in a most efficient manner. Not having a regular command he was free for special details by his Colonel and by myself. Time and again

Logan Feland wearing his new Distinguished Service Cross.

when conditions were in doubt on some part of the fighting line, or when a commander was needed for combined battalions or to straighten out a difficult situation by the presence of a field officer in whom I had entire confidence, Colonel Feland was used and he never failed to justify the confidence held in him.[45]

On July 9 Feland and the rest of the Fourth Brigade rotated to the rear to a reserve line west of Belleau Wood. For his actions at Belleau Wood, Lieutenant Colonel Logan Feland received the Distinguished Service Cross, the second-highest award for military valor, after the Medal of Honor, and the highest award received by Marine Corps ground officers during World War I. The citation accompanying Feland's award read:

> The President of the United States of America, authorized by Act of Congress, July 9, 1918, takes pleasure in presenting the Distinguished Service Cross to Colonel Logan Feland (MCSN: 0-284), United States Marine Corps, for extraordinary heroism while serving with the Fifth Regiment (Marines), 2d Division, A.E.F., in action during the operations at Bois-de-Belleau, June 6–14, 1918. Colonel Feland distinguished himself by his energy, courage, and disregard for personal safety in voluntarily leading troops into action through heavy artillery and machine-gun fire. His efforts contributed largely to our successes at this point.[46]

Feland would be the highest-ranking Marine Corps officer to win the Distinguished Service Cross during the war.

The Battle of Belleau Wood made Feland a war hero, solidifying his reputation as a top Marine. Because of his valuable service at Belleau Wood, Feland would also gain the long-lasting friendship and patronage of James Harbord. In his reminiscences after the war, Harbord credited Feland with being "of more mature judgment than many of his contemporaries. His common sense was very evident, his courage beyond reproach, and he was a reliance every time I had to send someone to straighten out a difficult situation."[47]

The stage was set for Feland's new leadership challenge: commander of the Fifth Regiment.

7

From Soissons to the
Return Home

During the first week of July 1918, the Fourth Marine Brigade finally got a major respite from fighting. Pulled back into reserve, the Marines regrouped, taking in new replacements and preparing for future combat. General Pershing made significant command changes. Second Division commander Omar Bundy moved up the ladder to head an army corps. Brigadier General James Harbord became Second Division commander and received a promotion to major general. Wendell "Buck" Neville was promoted to brigadier general and replaced Harbord as head of the Fourth Marine Brigade, and Lieutenant Colonel Logan Feland took command of the Fifth Regiment. Given his new responsibilities, in August, Feland would get official notification of his promotion to colonel, retroactive to July 1, 1918.

Feland inherited a regiment that had been decimated by the Battle of Belleau Wood. In nearly five weeks, it had lost about 500 men, with another 44 officers and more than 1,500 men wounded. Despite these losses, the regiment still included some outstanding veterans of the fierce battle against the Germans. Major Julius Turrill, who had received the Distinguished Service Cross (DSC) for his role at Belleau Wood, still commanded the First Battalion. The Second Battalion would be commanded by Major Ralph Stover Keyser, who had worked for Feland in 1916, during the Philadelphia Military Training Camp, before becoming an aide to Commandant Barnett. Toward the end of the Belleau Wood struggle, Harbord had relieved Fritz Wise of command of the Third Battalion, due to exhaustion. After recovering, Wise was eventually promoted and sent to command a U.S. Army regiment. Major Ralph Shearer, also a

DSC recipient for his part at Belleau Wood (his men had gained control of the last part of the wood), took over command of the Third Battalion. Other Marine Corps notables who served in the Fifth Regiment included writer and illustrator Lieutenant John Thomason, the future "Kipling of the Corps," known for his stories about the Marines.[1]

With Feland's new assignment came great responsibility. He would have little time to restore and reorganize his unit. On July 15 the Germans began their fifth and last offensive of the year, striking on a broad front in the Champagne and Marne regions. On leave in Paris, Major General Harbord drove back to Second Division headquarters to prepare for a major Allied counteroffensive after the German attack bogged down. The Second Division would be thrown into the battle south of the town of Soissons, north of Belleau Wood.

On July 16 Feland received orders to move his regiment hastily to the forest at Villers-Coterets, near Soissons. The Forêt de Retz would be the staging ground for an attack eastward through the wheat fields toward the Beaurepaire Farm. Feland's Fifth Regiment would lead the Marine Corps attack, with the Sixth Regiment held in reserve. Because Colonel Albertus Catlin had been severely wounded at Belleau Wood, the Sixth Regiment was now commanded by Colonel Harry "Light Horse Harry" Lee, Catlin's second in command. In a new twist, French tanks would support the ground troops during the attack.[2]

After riding in cramped French camions for up to thirty hours, the Fifth Regiment slogged in extreme darkness and through rain and mud in an exhausting twelve-mile march to take up their attack positions in the Forêt de Retz. *New York World* newspaperman Joseph A. Brady, serving as a Marine lieutenant, described the move, which left the men starving and thirsty. Then "night came, and with it rain and lightning, and thunder, and action." According to Brady, at about five miles into the march, Colonel Feland gathered his officers in a small clearing and "told us briefly that we were going to attack and attack big—along a thirty mile front." Then Feland asked Brady to accompany him to the front of the regiment to find the French guides who were supposed to direct them to their jumping-off place. The two went off into the rainy darkness, stopping every so often to inquire about the guides. After a six-hour march, the regiment halted—hungry, tired, confused, and with little ammunition.[3]

The ensuing attack on July 18 had been hastily planned. Attack orders were sketchy, and maps were almost nonexistent. Feland's regiment would attack on a rather wide front, requiring the battalions to go forward two abreast and then wheel southward in a complicated maneuver. Rather than having the mobility to go out and scout the battlefield before making decisions, as he had done at Belleau Wood, Feland would be tied to the regimental command post and would have to rely primarily on runners for communications with his battalion commanders. In a comprehensive examination of the battle, historians Douglas Johnson and Rolfe Hillman assert: "Of the twelve regimental commanders in XX Corps, none faced a more daunting situation than did Lt. Col. Logan Feland into bringing his 5th Marine Regiment onto the battlefield and directly into action."[4] In short, Feland's first regimental command in battle would be an enormous challenge right from the beginning.

The attack on July 18 was also hastily executed. Feland set up headquarters at a crossroads and established a telephone line back to Brigadier General Neville's brigade headquarters. Major George Shuler served as Feland's adjutant, and he also had two runners. The attack kicked off with Turrill's and Keyser's battalions moving toward their objectives through a small portion of the Forêt de Retz and beyond. According to Johnson and Hillman, "That would virtually end Feland's command impact on the 5th Marines for that day. His regiment was about to detonate, with control fragmenting to battalions, companies, and errant detachments."[5] For Feland, the Battle of Soissons would underscore the haphazard nature of warfare. Forced to rely on spotty communications and remain far from the front lines, he found himself in a situation similar to that of General Harbord during Belleau Wood. Unlike Harbord, he had no one to spare who could act as his eyes and ears. Fortunately, his unit commanders would do a tremendous job that day.

The Fifth Regiment engaged in some sharp fighting during the day, but the Marines moved ahead steadily. In one incident, Acting Gunnery Sergeant Louis Cukela attacked and cleared three German machine gun emplacements, a feat that earned him the Medal of Honor. In another action, Sergeant Matej Kocak took out a German machine gun emplacement and rallied French Senegalese troops to carry out a bayonet attack, also earning a Medal of Honor. The future "Kipling of the Corps," Lieutenant Thomason, was wounded while eliminating a German machine gun post and earned a Navy Cross.[6]

The Fifth Regiment bore the bulk of the fighting on July 18 under extremely difficult conditions, but with good results. At one point, Major Keyser reported to Feland that his battalion was "utterly exhausted, having had no hot food or drink for 60 hours."[7] Casualties remained lighter than at Belleau Wood, although several company commanders were killed or wounded. The regiment gained nearly four miles of ground, a magnificent advance in World War I's trench warfare–dominated stalemate. Thomason would later write: "That always remains . . . the marvel of the Soissons fight—how those men, two days without food, three nights without sleep, after a day and a night of forced marching, flung off their weariness like a discarded piece of equipment, and at the shouting of the shells sprang fresh and eager against the German line."[8]

By nightfall on July 18, Feland had moved his command post forward to Vauxcastille, and the next morning he moved it to a large tunnel in Vierzy. Feland's Fifth Regiment spent most of July 19 on the defensive, trying to dodge German artillery and airplanes. Turrill's First Battalion joined Feland and his headquarters unit in the Vierzy tunnel to avoid the intense German bombardment. While this was happening, Lee's Sixth Regiment endured the heaviest fighting on the second day of the attack, with nearly half its men killed or wounded. Nevertheless, at the end of the two-day Battle of Soissons, the Fourth Marine Brigade had collectively advanced more than six miles into the heart of the German lines, capturing 3,000 German prisoners and quantities of artillery, machine guns, and other supplies. This was clearly a breakthrough achievement. Feland's Marines led Pershing's war of maneuver, which would replace the stalemated trench warfare of the previous four years.

In their analysis of the battle, Johnson and Hillman note that Soissons "reflected an army in transition. The 'laws of trench warfare' demanded that senior commanders remain in their headquarters, tethered to the end of a telephone wire." In the more open warfare characterized by the Battle of Soissons, the Second Division and Feland's Fifth Regiment soon learned to act more independently and effectively. Warfare was changing, and Feland and his men adapted quickly. Despite the lack of preparation—specifically, reconnaissance—the Battle of Soissons once again proved that U.S. ground troops could perform admirably in the face of German opposition. It was apparent, however, that the German army was much weakened. Some historians believe that Soissons was the beginning of the end for the Germans.[9]

Feland understood and appreciated what his Marines were achieving and the circumstances under which they worked. In his after-action report, reflecting his characteristically upbeat manner, Feland lauded the "zeal and perseverance of officers and men in overcoming the many difficulties of the march of approach on the night of July 17–18 and the fact that they did by almost superhuman efforts overcome all these difficulties and obstacles and were ready to follow the barrage at the hour appointed." Although Feland could be critical of those who shirked their duty, he never failed to recognize and praise his men and to make sure the higher-ups were aware of the conditions under which they fought. Feland noted the regiment's steady progress, which occurred with "as little confusion as could be expected, considering the coming into our sector of attack elements of other brigades and divisions." He reported that "a full share of captured enemy, guns and machine guns" had fallen to his regiment. He also acknowledged that the forwarded reports of his battalion commanders better described the battle, "since the battalion commanders were nearer the front and always had a better idea of the situation than I could have at the P.C. [Post of Command] assigned me."[10] Feland clearly had difficulty with the notion of command from behind.

Feland had served on two battlefields—Belleau Wood and Soissons—where the style of war was shifting. There were no trenches; instead, there were forests, which were difficult to reconnoiter, as well as open ground. He realized that officers in the field had to be given greater autonomy in decision-making, which led to a dilemma still facing military commanders today: how to give subordinate officers on the front lines the autonomy they need to make quick, necessary decisions while maintaining control of the overall battle to ensure that objectives are met.

For Logan Feland personally, the accolades continued to accrue after Soissons. He was awarded another Croix de Guerre and was made a member of the French Legion of Honor. He was also cited in Second Division orders for gallantry. After the war, he was notified that he had received both the Army and Navy Distinguished Service Medals for his leadership at Soissons.[11]

Shortly after the battle, General Harbord recommended that Feland be promoted to brigadier general, along with Wendell Neville and Albertus Catlin, both of whom were above Feland in rank and seniority and had earned Medals of Honor at Vera Cruz. Noting Feland's work at Belleau Wood and Soissons, Harbord asserted that the Kentuckian's "steady coolness and the confidence that he inspires in officers and men place him, notwithstanding his junior rank, on a level with the other two officers for preferment."[12] Feland proved to be ambitious and wrote to Secretary of the Navy Josephus Daniels, through Commandant Barnett, citing several factors that warranted his promotion: his "long and admirable service in the Marine Corps," including the fact that he was the longest-serving Marine in France and had taken part in all the Corps's fighting; his receipt of the DSC and Croix de Guerre; and General Harbord's recommendation. Feland's request was also endorsed by his immediate commander, Buck Neville.[13]

Despite his family's long connections to the Republican Party, Feland's promotion was supported by some key Democrats. In August, Owensboro newspaper editor and publisher Urey Woodson, a member of the Democratic National Committee, wrote to Secretary Daniels in support of Feland. Woodson cited many of the same arguments Feland had noted in his own letter to Daniels. Ollie James, Democratic senator from Kentucky and chairman of the Democratic National Conventions of 1912 and 1916, also wrote to Daniels on Feland's behalf.[14] The promotion, however, would have to wait: there was more intense fighting to come.

The Second Division and its Fourth Marine Brigade had fought well at Soissons under General Harbord's command. General Pershing, however, had grave concerns about the increasing amount of men and supplies arriving in France as the United States ramped up its war effort. Consequently, Pershing tapped Harbord to be commander of the Services of Supply, headquartered at Tours. Harbord would spend the rest of the war indefatigably coordinating the massive amounts of material needed to prosecute the war successfully. Command of the Second Division passed to Brigadier General John Lejeune, who had arrived in France with Earl "Pete" Ellis in early June 1918. Lejeune had kicked around in various short-term postings, including three days as commander of the Fourth Brigade, before settling in as Second Division commander on July 29, 1918, and becoming a major general a week later. Lejeune's appointment marked the first time a Marine would command a U.S. Army unit

Major General John Lejeune. Lejeune is wearing the Second Division Indian-head patch on his left shoulder.

at such a high level. Neville remained in command of the Fourth Brigade, and Ellis served as his adjutant, with Feland and Lee still commanding the Fifth and Sixth Regiments, respectively. This upper command structure would remain in place until the end of the war.

On July 31 Colonel Logan Feland moved his Fifth Regiment to the

Marbache sector, near Nancy in eastern France. The sector was relatively quiet, and no one could deny that the regiment needed some time to regroup. Assistant Secretary of the Navy Franklin D. Roosevelt visited and reviewed the Marines. Feland set about reorganizing his staff; Julius Turrill became the regiment's second in command. A native of Vermont, Turrill had joined the Marine Corps in October 1899 and had served in the Philippines, Cuba, and Guam; he was a distinguished graduate of the U.S. Army's School of the Line at Fort Leavenworth, Kansas. Like Feland, Turrill had received a DSC for his bravery at Belleau Wood.[15] After two weeks of well-deserved rest, the Fifth Regiment moved again, southeast of Toul. Under the direction of Lieutenant Colonel Turrill, the regiment underwent additional training. New replacements joined the veterans to hone their skills on the firing range, practice grenade throwing, and prepare for the next battle.[16]

On September 2, 1918, the Fifth Regiment moved again, taking up positions near Saint-Mihiel. By September 10, Colonel Feland had established his headquarters at Manonville. The next task was a major offensive to reduce a German salient in the Allied lines near Saint-Mihiel. This time, the Fourth Marine Brigade would follow the Third U.S. Army Brigade into battle. The attack was launched on September 12, 1918, and the Third Brigade relinquished the lead to the Fourth Marine Brigade on September 13. The Second Division met its objectives quickly, and by September 16, the Fourth Brigade had been relieved by other U.S. Army troops. The Battle of Saint-Mihiel resulted in relatively few casualties for the Fourth Brigade: the Fifth Regiment suffered 27 dead and 143 wounded.[17] The next battle would be harder on Feland's regiment.

Having stopped the German offensives, the Allied armies geared up to carry out a major offensive of their own. The British would push forward toward Cambrai, the French toward the Aisne, and the Americans toward the Meuse-Argonne sector.[18] Major General Lejeune convinced the French that his Second Division could take a low but well-fortified ridgeline at Blanc Mont (not to be confused with the much larger Mont Blanc in the Alps).[19] The Fourth Brigade relieved French troops north of Somme-Py, three miles from Blanc Mont, by October 2, 1918.

Initially, Brigadier General Neville planned to array his two regiments side by side across the attack front, with the regimental battalions stacked in columns and supported by machine gun companies. French divisions would flank the Fourth Brigade, and French tanks would support the attack, which would take place as a rolling artillery barrage crept toward the German lines. Initial jumping-off positions put the Fourth Brigade in a jangle of occupied German trenches. This time, the Sixth Regiment would lead the attack, with the Fifth Regiment to follow. Feland's Fifth Regiment now had new battalion commanders: Major George Hamilton commanded the First Battalion, Major Robert Messersmith the Second Battalion, and Major Henry Larsen the Third Battalion. Lieutenant Colonel Turrill remained Feland's second in command.

At 0530 on October 2, the attack began. Heavy machine gun fire impeded the Marines, and German positions on the left flank, the Essen Hook, needed to be cleaned out, which was accomplished by midafternoon. By then, the Sixth Regiment held the lower slopes of Blanc Mont but required assistance. Colonel Feland was ordered to move his regiment forward to shore up the attack. A large gap had appeared on the left, where the French troops had faltered while the Americans advanced. Feland sent units to close the gap, but this forced him to postpone his major attack on the Saint-Etienne Heights. The attack recommenced the next morning, in what would become a momentous day in the history of the Fifth Regiment.[20]

Driving forward on October 5, the Fifth Regiment soon became enveloped in a narrow wedge between the German lines. Casualties mounted precipitously as Feland's regiment tried to hold on and consolidate its gains, despite withering fire from machine guns and artillery. Feland's Marines repulsed a German counterattack, but at great loss, including two Medal of Honor recipients: First Lieutenant Henry Hulbert and Sergeant Matej Kocak, who had just received his medal after Soissons. Once again the fog of war descended, and the company commanders bore the brunt of decision-making during the battle. In the words of Marine Corps historians: "Even the battalion commanders, the only senior officers engaged in the actual fighting, lost contact with some of their companies for hours at a time. Col. Logan Feland, struggling to make sense of the dire, fragmented reports drifting in from his besieged regiment, could do little to ease the crisis. Neither Neville nor Lejeune were near enough to the fighting to discern the critical turn of events."[21]

Commanding the First Battalion, the stalwart Hamilton summarized the dire situation in a message to Feland early on the morning of Octo-

George Hamilton. One of Feland's most trusted and valuable World War I battalion commanders, Hamilton led the Marines across the Meuse River on the last night of the war. He later became an aviator and died in a plane crash during Marine Corps maneuvers. (Courtesy of *Leatherneck* magazine)

ber 5: "This battalion will go, or attempt to go, where you order it. You should understand though that your regiment is now much depleted, very disorganized, and not in condition to advance as a front line regiment even though the enemy forces in front are found to be small. It is hard to say 'can't,' but the Division Commander should thoroughly understand the situation and realize this regiment *can't* advance as an attacking force. Such advance would sacrifice the regiment."[22]

After Hamilton's report, Feland called Ellis at Fourth Brigade headquarters to report that although the regiment had "got along all right last night," he could not ascertain the strength of his companies; reports indicated, however, that they were "very badly depleted and disorganized." Shortly thereafter, Second Division commander Lejeune, in a message to Feland, acknowledged: "Fine work out there. That was hard work." He then informed Feland that Neville would send in the Sixth Regiment to relieve the Fifth.[23]

Feland's Marines had captured Blanc Mont, but at a devastating price. During the battle, the Fifth Regiment suffered a nearly 60 percent casualty rate of killed or wounded. Feland's Marines held the line for four days before being relieved and sent south to recuperate. The Germans continued to retreat, as the Allies prepared for another attack.[24]

In the aftermath of Blanc Mont, Feland had to deal with an extremely difficult personnel issue. At one point, he had written to his battalion commanders: "It is the earnest desire of the Brigade and Division Commanders as well as my own to rid the regiment and in some cases to rid the Marine Corps of such officers as have shown by their conduct and lack of efficiency that they are not fit to hold commissions." Feland listed three classifications of such officers. The first were those men displaying cowardice or "culpable inefficiency which endangered some unit." Feland asserted that these men should be court-martialed. The second category included "officers who have shown by their lack of efficiency, zeal and by their general conduct to have demonstrated clearly that they are unfit to hold commissions in any grade." Feland believed these officers should be discharged for the good of the regiment and the Corps. The third category consisted of officers who were unfit to lead at their current grade but might render good service in a lesser grade.[25]

After Blanc Mont, Major George Hamilton reported that during the battle he had seen several men, led by officers, running to the rear. One of these officers, Major Robert Messersmith, offered an explanation, claiming "that he had lost all his officers," but, Hamilton noted, Messersmith "didn't show any initiative or leadership." Hamilton also reported that he and Captain James Nelms had been forced to draw their pistols to stop the "rout."[26] Faced with Hamilton's report, Feland felt obligated to initiate an inquiry. He tasked his second in command, Lieutenant Colonel Turrill, to investigate.

Pennsylvanian Robert Messersmith had joined the Marine Corps in 1909 and had participated in expeditions to Cuba with Feland. Within seven years, he had achieved the rank of captain. Commanding a Sixth Regiment company during the Battle of Belleau Wood, he had been gassed and evacuated. He later rejoined his unit and suffered a head wound at Soissons. After recuperating, he had been transferred to the Fifth Regiment in August and promoted to major on a temporary basis. At Blanc Mont he had commanded the Second Battalion. In sum, Messersmith was a battle-seasoned veteran.[27]

Turrill's report outlined the circumstances leading up to Messersmith's actions. His battalion had been in support of the leading Third Battalion, which encountered heavy fire and, because it had no cover, started to fall back. Instead of holding his line, Messersmith and his battalion also fell back, until running into Major Hamilton and Captain Nelms of the First Battalion (the second reserve). Turrill concluded that "Major Messersmith was not awake to the true tactical situation and did not initiate any steps to avert the danger of a panic. Thereby he displayed *lack* of *leadership*. As Battalion Commander, he was responsible that his line did not give way at this time." Noting that the "cuffs of his blouse and field glass case were penetrated by bullets," Turrill acknowledged that "Major Messersmith had displayed no lack of courage."[28]

After considering Turrill's report, Feland recommended that Messersmith "be assigned some duty, outside this division, if in command of troops, or not in command of troops if within this division." Messersmith ended up being reassigned to Feland's Fifth Regiment headquarters to serve as liaison to Neville's Fourth Brigade headquarters, a position he held until January 1919.[29] Faced with a difficult decision, Feland displayed empathy and understanding toward his battle-scarred subordinate. Instead of court-martialing Messersmith or seeking his dismissal, Feland used Turrill's report to determine that Messersmith was one of those officers who might benefit from a change of duty. He never recommended that Messersmith be reduced in rank. Messersmith remained in the Marine Corps after the war and later served under Feland in Nicaragua in 1928.

After the Battle of Blanc Mont, both Feland and his regiment continued to receive honors. Having been cited for the third time by the French, the Fifth Regiment's Marines were entitled to wear a red and green *fourragère* (a braided cord) on their left shoulders. On October 16, 1918, Second Division commander Lejeune wrote to General Pershing and recommended that Feland be promoted to brigadier general.[30]

Even before the Allied success at Blanc Mont and other areas of engagement, German general Erich von Ludendorff had warned his government of the possible collapse of the German front. Conditions in Germany itself also continued to deteriorate, as the Allied blockade took a toll on the civilian population. Consequently, in the first week of October, the German government had approached President Woodrow Wilson to negotiate an armistice.[31]

Even as armistice negotiations began, the Allies continued their "Grand Offensive." The Battle of Blanc Mont and the Meuse-Argonne campaign were part of the larger Allied breakthrough effort. At the end

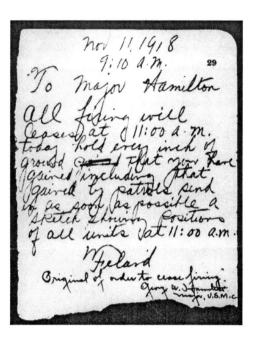

Feland's "Hold every inch of ground" note. Feland sent this message to George Hamilton after the announcement of an armistice on November 11, 1918.

of October 1918 the entire Second Division moved to Charpentry, on the eastern edge of the Argonne forest. The next major attack kicked off on November 1. The Marines followed a rolling artillery barrage, with each battalion leapfrogging to the front to lead the attack at various points during the day. Despite suffering heavy casualties, the Marines pushed forward, capturing many prisoners and artillery. Having lost their allies, and facing a naval mutiny at home, Germany military leaders withdrew their troops to the east bank of the Meuse River. It became apparent that the Germans were on their last legs.[32]

As the war was winding down, the Fourth Brigade prepared to cross the Meuse River. On the night of November 10–11, 1918—the last night of the war—elements of Feland's Fifth Regiment, with Major George Hamilton in command, made it across the Meuse and set up positions on the east bank. Feland received word of the armistice on the morning of November 11 and sent a note to Major Hamilton at 9:10 a.m., notifying him of the 11:00 a.m. cease-fire and enjoining him to "hold every inch of ground that you have gained including that gained by patrols" and to "send in as soon as possible a sketch showing positions of all units at 11:00 a.m."[33]

Feland's note arrived late, but the Marines suffered no casualties after the cease-fire officially commenced. Some of Hamilton's units continued to seek out the enemy, unaware of the armistice. For instance, troops under Captain Samuel Cumming engaged with the enemy until 2:15 p.m. After being informed by the Germans that an armistice had been signed, Captain Cumming finally received confirmation from regimental headquarters that the war had indeed ended.[34]

Colonel Logan Feland, the longest-serving Marine in France during World War I, had led his Fifth Regiment in some fierce fighting. He had proved himself brave and intelligent and a good commander. In an assessment of Feland many years later, William Mathews, Wise's intelligence officer and future *Arizona Daily Star* newspaper editor, asserted that at the time of Belleau Wood, Feland was already "the brains of the 5th Regiment. He was second in command. It was Feland who was out visiting all of the units in the front line. A superior, Colonel Neville, never, to my knowledge, approached our front line unit. Feland was the ablest of all of the higher ranking officers that I knew. He was soft spoken, but firm, just and highly intelligent. In appearance he was at least 6 feet tall, but was comparatively slender. He had a studious, weather beaten face."[35]

Before Feland and the Fifth Regiment could go home, however, there was more work to do. The Second Division had been chosen to serve in the occupation of Germany until a peace treaty could be signed. The American Third Army had been created to occupy parts of Germany on the west bank of the Rhine, with the Second Division included as a veteran unit. So, on the cold, rainy morning of November 17, 1918, Colonel Feland led his Fifth Regiment on the march to the Rhineland. The column of Marines moved cautiously but steadily, keeping in mind that although an armistice had been signed, there was no peace treaty in place. As the Marines marched on, the German army pulled back and then dissipated. In miserable weather, Feland's regiment marched through France, Belgium, and Luxembourg, welcomed by the inhabitants who had been liberated from German control.

The Fifth Regiment crossed into Germany on December 1 and continued marching until it reached the Rhineland sector around Koblenz, where the Second Division would be in control, on December 16. Colonel Feland established his regimental headquarters in the Schloss Monrepos in Neuwied, controlling the valley of the Wied River north of Koblenz.[36]

The Schloss was the home of Prince William Frederick of Wied and was still inhabited by his wife and sister. The family entertained Feland and his old friend Fritz Wise, serving tea when the latter stopped by for a visit after Christmas.[37] Once the Marines had settled in the various small towns around the Schloss, they were kept busy by a host of activities designed to keep them out of trouble. The men patrolled, drilled, attended classes, participated in sports, and marched in numerous reviews.

For Logan Feland, this seemingly idyllic postwar command would not last long. On March 12 he got the good news that he would be receiving his first star, having been promoted, at least temporarily, to brigadier general. Also receiving temporary promotions to brigadier were Feland's colleague and developing rival Smedley Darlington Butler and Harry Lee, commander of the Sixth Regiment. Whereas Lee, like Feland, had commanded Marines in the heat of battle, Butler had been relegated to the rear, serving first in Haiti and then in the coastal city of Brest, France. In France he did an excellent job cleaning up Camp Pontanezen, located at a major port of disembarkation for troops arriving from the United States. Despite his efforts to get to the front, where he hoped to serve with his good friend John Lejeune, Butler languished in the rear and blamed Commandant George Barnett for keeping him out of the action.[38]

Feland's promotion was retroactive to March 9, 1919, placing him at number nine on the lineal list of Marines. At the top stood Major General Barnett, the Commandant, followed by John Lejeune and the aging L. W. T. Waller. Veterans Joseph Pendleton, Eli Kelly Cole, Charles Long, and Wendell Neville followed, just in front of Butler and then Feland. In achieving his star, Feland leapfrogged over many other capable officers, such as Robert "Hal" Dunlap, James Carson Breckinridge, Ben Fuller, and John Russell, as well as venerable veterans such as Lincoln Karmany. The promotion was reported in newspapers across the country, including in Feland's hometown of Hopkinsville.[39]

Accolades continued to accrue as Feland became one of the most highly decorated Marines of World War I. No Marine Corps ground officer received the highest award, the Medal of Honor, during the war, but as noted earlier, Feland received the second-highest award, the Distinguished Service Cross, for his heroic actions at Belleau Wood. For his other wartime contributions, Feland received both the Army and Navy Distinguished Service Medals and the French Croix de Guerre with

Logan Feland and Harold Snyder. During the occupation of the Rhineland after the war, Snyder took over command of the Fifth Regiment when Feland was promoted to brigadier general. (Courtesy of *Leatherneck* magazine)

Bronze Star, Gold Star, and four Palms; he was also made an officer of the French Legion of Honor.[40]

On March 21, 1919, at a review in Hausen, Germany, newly appointed Brigadier General Logan Feland passed command of the Fifth Regiment to Colonel Harold Snyder. He then traveled to Paris, where he would meet Secretary of the Navy Josephus Daniels and accompany him on a European tour.[41]

After arriving in Brest on March 23 and being entertained at Camp Pontanezen by Butler, Daniels arrived in Paris on March 25. Three days later, Daniels visited the World War I battlegrounds at Chateau-Thierry, Belleau Wood, Soissons, and Rheims, accompanied by Feland and Major Charles Busbee, an old friend and prominent Raleigh, North Carolina, attorney. The Daniels party then traveled to Italy before heading to Germany to see the occupation troops. In mid-April the group visited the Second Division in the Rhineland, where Generals Lejeune and Neville, along with Colonel Snyder, hosted a number of dinners and receptions. Feland and his aide, Lieutenant Henry Glendenning, attended these festivities, along with several rear admirals and the secretary's wife and son, Marine Corps lieutenant Josephus Daniels Jr. Secretary Daniels reviewed the Second Division on the plains of Vallendar on Good Friday, pinning Distinguished Service Crosses and Croix de Guerres on several Marines.[42]

On Easter Sunday, April 20, 1919, Secretary and Mrs. Daniels and his official party attended a luncheon with the Eighteenth Company, Second Battalion, Fifth Regiment, which was commanded by Captain John R. "Rollie" Foster of Flemingsburg, Kentucky. A host of Marines accompanied Secretary Daniels, including Generals Lejeune, Feland, and Lee; Colonel Snyder; and Captains Charley Dunbeck and Gilder Jackson, who had served under Feland during the war. The luncheon was an informal affair, with a menu featuring "Soup a la Shrapnel," "Boef au petite Whizz Bang," "Box Barrage Dressing," "Shell Shocked Peaches," and other cleverly named dishes.[43]

Feland accompanied the Daniels party until he received orders, dated April 14, 1919, to proceed to the United States and report to Headquarters Marine Corps. He was leaving the World War I European theater after nearly two years. As Secretary Daniels and the rest of his party visited Belgium and then sailed to England, Feland made his way to the French port of Brest, where he boarded the SS *Von Steuben* on May 5, bound for the United States.

8

The Dominican Republic, 1920

On May 13, 1919, the SS *Von Steuben* arrived in Hoboken, New Jersey, with Brigadier General Logan Feland aboard. The rest of the Fourth Brigade would not leave Europe until July, after the peace treaty had been signed at Versailles. Feland spent a few days with his wife in Philadelphia, where she had remained throughout the war. He then reported, as ordered, to Headquarters Marine Corps in Washington, D.C., where he participated in a Belleau Wood remembrance ceremony in early June. Keynote speakers included Secretary of War Newton Baker and Secretary of the Navy Josephus Daniels, along with the Commandant of the Marine Corps, Major General George Barnett. General Feland also made remarks about the battle, and his wife Katherine sang in a music program led by the Marine Band. The Felands thus quickly reintegrated into the Marine Corps and Washington society.[1]

Before taking up his new duties, General Feland was granted a well-deserved leave that was supposed to last until August 1, 1919. Just as they had done before the war, the Felands vacationed at Rockbound Camp in Glen Eyre, a hunting and fishing retreat where the general could pursue his favorite leisure activities. There in rural Pike County, the Felands left the war behind. They would return to this refuge repeatedly during the 1920s, and in 1922 the Felands would pay five dollars to purchase three and a half acres in Rowlands, in the Township of Lackawaxen, in an area known as "Little Norway." Before 1927, when Feland left for Nicaragua, they would have a cabin built on the property, with Feland overseeing the architectural and construction details from his post at Quantico.[2]

During this period the Felands also made a trip back to Ohio and

Kentucky. Katherine Feland appeared in June at a Methodist centenary convention in her hometown of Columbus. As fifty veterans unfurled a huge flag with stars commemorating the Methodists who had served in the war, Katherine sang "The Star-Spangled Banner." General Feland arrived in Owensboro, Kentucky, on June 24 to visit his sister, Mary Gilmour, and her family. He was to be the guest of honor and a key speaker at a Fourth of July picnic hosted by the newly created American Legion group. He also spoke briefly to the local Rotary Club, where he professed to be glad to be home.[3]

Brigadier General Feland's leave was cut short by a week, however, when he was ordered to temporary duty with the Office of the Chief of Naval Operations. Newly formed in 1915, with Admiral William Benson as its head, the office had overseen the large increase in the navy during World War I. The chief of naval operations (CNO) served as the third-ranking person in the Department of the Navy, behind the secretary and assistant secretary. The office was responsible for "operations of the fleet and . . . the preparation and readiness of plans for its use in war." Thus, the CNO was in charge of a variety of units, ranging from the Office of Naval Intelligence to the Bureau of Aeronautics. Benson and Feland were already acquainted. From 1913 to 1915 Benson had been commandant of the Philadelphia Naval Shipyard, where Feland had served as head of the Marine Barracks. Now Benson had a special project for Feland: creating plans for a possible war with Mexico.[4]

Since the beginning of the Mexican Revolution in 1910, the U.S. government had kept a wary eye on Mexico. Part of the reason was a desire to maintain access to the Mexican oil needed by the U.S. fleet. The occupation of Vera Cruz in 1914, in which Feland had taken part, was one manifestation of this concern. After entering World War I, the U.S. government remained anxious that Carranza's government might shut down the oil fields or that Germany might sabotage them. During the war, the Marine Corps had kept first a regiment and then a brigade at Galveston, Texas, in the event intervention should be necessary again. After the war, with the continuing transition from a coal- to an oil-driven fleet, the Department of the Navy retained an interest in the Mexican oil fields, particularly those near Tampico.[5]

Consequently, Logan Feland was commissioned to study the situation, and he produced a report titled "Occupation of Oil Fields, Tampico and Tuxpam." He defined the mission as follows: "To seize and hold the ports of Tampico, Port Lobos and Tuxpam and the Western and Southern oil fields. This involves the protection of life and property and the maintenance of order within the area." Borrowing from previous material prepared by the Military Intelligence Division of the U.S. Army general staff, Feland laid out the various transportation approaches to the region by road, ship, and railroad. In estimating opposition forces, he cited numbers obtained in 1918 but cautioned that because of the fluid situation in Mexico, "it would be well now to anticipate that these forces might be fifty percent larger at any time." He believed that the forces of Tampico rebel leader Manuel Pelaez would be neutral at first but would become hostile "when deprived of the revenue now levied on the oil companies." Nevertheless, this hostility would probably not occur until after the two weeks the occupying U.S. force would need to complete its mission. Feland estimated that five regiments of infantry and support units would be necessary to secure the area. He recommended that naval forces include at least three battleships, a cruiser, more than a dozen destroyers, and several support ships, including an aviation ship. Feland noted that aviation would be helpful in reconnaissance. He advised that the troops be landed in two or three places and that their expansion outward should be by the "*best* and *most* practicable routes of approach. The various railroads and waterways should be used to the limit of their capacities."[6]

Even as Feland was working on his report, Commandant Barnett sought other views on the seizure of the Mexican oil fields, most notably from Earl "Pete" Ellis. Ellis had served as General Lejeune's adjutant and operations planner at the Second Division and as Colonel Harold Snyder's second in command of the Fifth Regiment after Feland left in March 1919. Ellis arrived home with the Fifth Regiment in August 1919 and took leave in his hometown in Texas. From there he traveled to Tampico in September and remained in the area for a month, producing a plan for the invasion of the Tampico oil fields based on his observations. This was followed in September 1920 by another report prepared by Marine Corps staff at Quantico under the command of Smedley Darlington Butler.[7] Despite the planning by Feland and his colleagues, the Marine Corps never invaded Mexico after the occupation of Vera Cruz in 1914.

On August 8, 1919, Brigadier General Feland joined the other members of the Fourth Brigade and their army colleagues in the Second Divi-

Logan Feland and others awaiting the Second Division parade in New York City in August 1919.

sion for a parade in New York City. Major General John Lejeune led the parade on horseback as the division marched up Fifth Avenue to the cheers of hundreds of thousands of spectators and passed a reviewing stand containing, among others, Assistant Secretary of the Navy Franklin Roosevelt and Commandant George Barnett. After this event, Feland and the rest of the Fourth Brigade proceeded to Washington, D.C., for another parade on August 12. This time, only the Marines marched up Pennsylvania Avenue. The Marine Band played as Wendell Neville led the Fourth Brigade past the reviewing stand in front of the White House, where President and Mrs. Wilson watched the parade, joined by Roosevelt, Barnett, Lejeune, Congressman Thomas Butler, and others. After the parade, Logan and Katherine Feland joined other Marine notables such as Barnett, Lejeune, Neville, Snyder, Catlin, Lee, Dunlap, Shearer, Keyser, and Holcomb at a dinner sponsored by Roosevelt.[8]

This was the Fourth Brigade's swan song. The Marine Corps quickly began to contract as thousands of brigade members were demobilized. The Marine Corps declined from a high of nearly 75,000 men and women at the height of the war to an immediate postwar contingent numbering about 17,400.[9] During this retraction, several Marine Corps officers, including some temporary generals such as Ben Fuller, Cyrus Radford, and John Twiggs Myers, were reduced in rank to their prewar status. Speculation grew as to where the remaining Marine Corps generals would be located. Because of competing interests and jockeying for position, tensions increased at Headquarters Marine Corps. At the end of August the *Washington Post* reported that John Lejeune would command the relatively new Marine base at Quantico, but positions had not yet been determined for Eli Cole, Wendell Neville, Smedley Darlington Butler, and Logan Feland. A month later the *Post* confirmed Lejeune's appointment as commander of the Marine Barracks at Quantico and reported that Butler would command a brigade at Quantico and Feland would command Marines in Santo Domingo, Dominican Republic. The *Post* noted, however, that Secretary of the Navy Daniels had delayed those orders, perhaps having something else in mind for Butler and Feland.[10]

Daniels did not change the assignments, however, and on October 23, 1919, Brigadier General Logan Feland received official orders to proceed to New York City en route to his posting as commander of the Second Provisional Brigade, Dominican Republic. After picking up his first passport (he had not needed one for expeditionary duty), Logan and Katherine sailed on the SS *Algonquin* to Santo Domingo at the beginning of November. They would spend six happy months together until Katherine's return to the States in June 1920, ahead of Feland's reassignment.[11]

Feland was entering a situation with a long and contentious history. Comprising Haiti and the Dominican Republic, the Caribbean island of Hispaniola had been the scene of encroaching U.S. influence before World War I because of its strategic and economic value. Strategic issues included protection of the new Panama Canal; economic interests were increasingly tied to the growing Dominican sugar industry. In 1915 Marines landed in Haiti to help stabilize the country. In April 1916, on the other half of the island, the Dominican minister of war, General Desiderio Arias, led a revolt against the government of President Juan Isidro Jimenez. Consequently, on May 5, 1916, Marines under the command of Fritz Wise landed in Santo Domingo to protect the U.S. legation and consulate and to aid President Jimenez. After Jimenez resigned, Wise helped broker a truce between the fighting factions. More and more

Marines moved into Santo Domingo and eventually spread throughout the country as the Dominican civil government collapsed.

Arriving a week after Wise's Marines first landed, Rear Admiral William Caperton, commander of the Atlantic Fleet Cruiser Squadron, oversaw the gradual occupation of the Dominican Republic. By the end of June 1916, many more Marines under Colonel Joseph "Uncle Joe" Pendleton had arrived and set about restoring order as armed bands continued to roam the countryside. Several skirmishes with these rebels, or "bandits," ensued. Given the continued conflict and disarray in the country, on November 29, 1916, Caperton's successor, Captain Harry Knapp, proclaimed a U.S. military government in the Dominican Republic, with an eye toward restoring peace and prosperity.[12]

Under the military government, U.S. Navy and Marine Corps officials took control of key components of the Dominican government, such as the Ministries of the Interior and Police, War, and Navy. The military government also established provost courts, initiated censorship of the press, created a secret service, and disarmed a large part of the population. The U.S. military government abolished the Dominican army and established a new, presumably depoliticized, national police force: the *Guardia Nacional Dominicana*. The Marines trained the *Guardia* in military fashion. Its duties included enforcing civil laws, acting as judicial police, guarding the coastline and frontier with Haiti, patrolling the few available highways, and assisting the Marines in combating insurgents. Because of a perceived notion that the Dominicans could not lead the *Guardia* themselves, Marine Corps junior officers, noncommissioned officers, and even privates served as *Guardia* officers.[13]

Knapp's new military government attempted to implement reform in key areas, including the improvement of road networks, public works projects, educational reform, and public health and sanitation projects. Despite these efforts at modernization, the Dominicans resented and resisted the changes imposed on them. They were slow to join the *Guardia*, believing it to be a repressive tool of their occupiers. They greatly resented the Marine-administered provost courts, which had jurisdiction over civil as well as military matters. The Dominicans also charged the Marines with cruelty and atrocities.[14]

In August 1918 Brigadier General Ben Fuller succeeded Pendleton in leading the Marines, and in February 1919 Rear Admiral Thomas

Snowden arrived to serve as military governor of Santo Domingo. Snowden, a Naval Academy graduate who had served as a battleship squadron commander in the Atlantic Fleet during World War I, did not get along with the Dominicans as well as his predecessor had. The country had been previously divided into two major districts: the north, with its base in Santiago, and the south, around the capital of Santo Domingo. Because most of the resistance fighting occurred in the east, Snowden created a third district—centered around San Pedro de Macoris—which was staffed by the newly arrived Fifteenth Marine Regiment under the command of Colonel James Carson Breckinridge.[15]

The Marines had difficulty dealing with the ongoing Dominican resistance. Historian Bruce Calder has noted several factors that hampered the Marines in what became a classic guerrilla war. Although the Marines had superior organization, weaponry, and training, the Americans had lost their focus on fighting guerrilla wars. Their problems included an inability to distinguish between legitimate rebels and mere outlaws (the Marines lumped everyone together as "bandits"), futile pursuits, susceptibility to ambush, and lack of permanent control. The Marines were strangers in the land, whereas the Dominican guerrillas blended in. The guerillas had mobility, knowledge of the terrain, and a good intelligence network. Admiral Snowden continued to downplay the seriousness of the resistance as the Marines adopted a policy of containment throughout the country.[16]

Such was the situation in the Dominican Republic when Feland arrived (replacing Fuller) and reported to Snowden. Feland took command at Second Provisional Brigade headquarters in Santo Domingo. Colonel Dion Williams commanded the Marines in the Northern District, Colonel Carl Gamborg-Andreson in the Southern District, and Breckinridge in the Eastern District. All three men were seasoned Marines, having served since the beginning of the century.[17]

The Marines in the Dominican Republic carried out combined civil-military duties. In the early days of the military occupation government, Pendleton had served as minister of war, navy, interior, and police, while Colonel Rufus Lane had served as minister of foreign relations, justice, and public instruction. The district commanders continued to have wide-ranging authority. In a letter to his mother in March 1919, shortly after arriving, Colonel Breckinridge noted, "I am the Military Commander of the Districts of Saibo and Macoris which include the Eastern end of the island, the only place where there is trouble; it is all in my back yard. The powers vested in the Military Commander are rather appalling, really there is no limit except death itself."[18]

As commanding general, Feland would also face a host of issues, many of which were not military. Although he had gained some experience dealing with civil and military issues in Cuba, serving in the Dominican Republic would increase his understanding of these sometimes complementary, sometimes conflicting roles. This dynamic tension would foretell similar Marine Corps experiences in Iraq and Afghanistan in the twenty-first century.[19]

Fortunately for Feland, the Northern and Southern Districts were relatively calm by the time he arrived in the Dominican Republic in December 1919. Colonel Breckinridge and his men had borne the brunt of fighting the disaffected Dominicans. Breckinridge moved through his district on horseback, in one case covering nearly 800 miles in muddy, mountainous terrain that lacked proper trails, as he visited his men and the local inhabitants. He reported several incidents of Marine contact with bandits, but by April 1920, Breckinridge could write home, "My work is almost over, and I have begun to close it up. Soon there will be little or nothing for me to do. My bandits are all working or dead, and I will be looking for a new job, but I would not have missed winding this up for anything."[20]

Soon after his arrival, Feland reported to Commandant Barnett about a single ten-minute skirmish between bandits and the *Guardia* but noted, "With the exception of the foregoing [skirmish], conditions throughout the Republic have been quiet."[21] Despite this early assessment, real and potential problems existed, and Feland requested more Marines. Believing that the 2,000 men designated for Santo Domingo constituted a bare minimum, which the Corps was having difficulty maintaining because of postwar reductions, Feland urged Barnett to increase the force to 2,500 men—a request supported by Snowden in correspondence to the CNO, Admiral Robert E. Coontz. When reinforcements proved slow in coming, Feland and Snowden continued to press for more men. They feared that if labor unrest provoked by rebellious politicians resulted in a revolt against the government, the existing Marines would not be able to contain it. Noting that organized resistance had disappeared in the countryside, largely because of the efforts of Breckinridge and his men, the two commanders still believed that an additional 500 men were needed to ensure stability. Feland and Snowden's concerns continued as the Marine Corps responded slowly to their requests for more men.[22]

The Marine Corps was still in flux, still downsizing from World War I. Commandant Barnett continued to argue for an expanded Marine Corps, and he would eventually be authorized a total of 20,000 men. This would take time as the Corps sorted out who would remain and who would be allowed to rejoin after demobilization. One of Feland's best World War I commanders, George Hamilton, struggled with the issue of whether he should stay in the Corps, leaving briefly before being accepted back. In addition, "the Corps had lost a great number of prewar non-commissioned officers, on whom it had previously depended for much of its cohesion."[23]

In an effort to better communicate with and guide his Marines, Feland published a twenty-three-page brigade order in early January 1920. It covered a variety of topics, such as who had the right to carry arms, rules and regulations for the provost courts, how to handle the remains of deceased Marines, rules for dealing with the *Guardia*, how to maintain morale, proper record keeping, and other administrative matters. Always a believer in the value of training, Feland set up training centers in Santiago to cover the Northern District and in Santo Domingo to cover the Southern and Eastern Districts. He also instituted a seven-week training regimen for companies, after which they would be sent to different areas. This instruction was designed to "train troops for service in 'small wars.'" Feland invited Commandant Barnett to visit the Dominican Republic to see these new training centers.[24]

Snowden and Feland were right about the need for more troops: resistance in the Dominican Republic increased in 1920. In February a new nationalist organization, the *Union Nacional Dominicana*, mobilized the elites and the middle class. After Snowden relaxed the censorship rules in March, newspapers in Santiago and Santo Domingo called for an immediate end to the U.S. occupation and threatened violence. Snowden feared that agitation was growing, particularly in light of the *Semana Patriotica*, a so-called Patriotic Week held from June 12 to 19. Pete Ellis, Feland's intelligence officer, reported on the *Semana Patriotica* and concluded that one of the leaders was hoping to foment armed revolution in the autumn but added, "not that he believes it would possibly succeed"; however, "it would afford a good literary and diplomatic weapon by attracting United States and foreign attention."[25]

The Dominicans remained hostile to reforms, and Snowden feared attacks on Marine Corps officers by a society of assassins. Snowden's own life had been threatened. He wanted an immediate surge to 2,500 men, and 2,950 Marines in Santo Domingo by October 1, 1920. CNO Coontz agreed to the 2,500 men but balked at the 2,950.[26]

While Snowden was in Haiti in July 1920, Feland became acting military governor of Santo Domingo. As such, he dealt with a variety of issues and crises, such as a dispute over management of the municipal lottery, construction of a new barracks for the *Guardia*, civil service appointments, and the "sending of any injurious, scurrilous or defamatory anonymous letters." Seeking to clarify the military government's position, Feland promulgated twelve executive orders covering these issues before Snowden resumed command on August 19, 1920.[27]

By midsummer 1920, Feland reported that conditions in the Dominican Republic were "outwardly quiet except for the operations of certain professional agitators and occasional unimportant bandit raids. There is, however, an undercurrent of hostility among the people, especially in and around the towns. The country people are generally friendly. The friendly inclined, of whatever class, are afraid to express their friendship openly." He noted that all the districts were patrolled when men were available, but some ungarrisoned areas needed a temporary or permanent presence "to insure quiet and protect the people against bandit raids." Regarding Marine Corps morale, Feland reported that the brigade's health was "excellent," but he expected a slight increase in sickness during the rainy season. Venereal disease rates were below normal. He believed the "spirit" of his men was "excellent in the field, very good in the small towns, and good in large towns." In the field there was "plenty of out-door exercise, little liquor and few prostitutes." This was not the case in large towns, so Feland wanted more money to keep the men busy in "more systematic military work, athletic sports, and amusement." Amusements included movies, which were divided evenly among the three districts for the enjoyment of the troops. Athletics included a brigade field meet in Santiago on September 4–6.[28]

Feland's fiscal-year-end report to the Commandant after June 30 reiterated his assertion that "all organized military resistance to the Military government has disappeared. Bandit activity for the year has been considerably reduced over former years and is confined almost entirely to the Eastern District." He noted that although "the attitude of the native population is outwardly friendly . . . there is a strong undercurrent of unrest which is kept alive by the anti-american [*sic*] propaganda of professional politicians."[29]

In a private letter written at the end of July to Secretary of the Navy Daniels, Feland also blamed "professional politicians and grafters who flourished here in the old days" for some of the recent agitation. He believed that people residing in the countryside, particularly small farmers, appreciated the U.S. presence and peacekeeping efforts, as did about half the people in the cities. The other half resented the Americans "due to the antipathy between the Latin and the Anglo-Saxons. Also, in the cities they come in contact more with us and so feel more the humiliation of being governed by those of alien race and customs." Following Patriotic Week, in which newspapers' vitriol toward the Americans increased, Feland called in some of the journalists and warned them that such agitation would not be tolerated. Some complied; others he had arrested, and they were awaiting trial.[30]

While Feland was dealing with the tinderbox situation on the island, events in Washington had come to a head in the case of Commandant George Barnett. Barnett had gradually fallen out of favor with Secretary of the Navy Daniels and had earned the enmity of two powerful figures: Brigadier General Smedley Darlington Butler and his father, Congressman Thomas Butler. Stationed in Haiti when World War I broke out, the younger Butler had clamored to lead combat troops in France. Instead, he became head of the disembarkation base at Camp Pontanezen, near Brest. Although he did an excellent job there, Butler was unhappy with this admittedly rear-echelon job. As part of a growing feud with Barnett, Congressman Butler successfully blocked legislation that would have promoted Barnett to lieutenant general. He also insulted the Commandant and his wife when he saw them sitting in the congressional gallery, pointedly noting, "The place for fighting men is at the front, not here in the gallery."[31]

Subsequently, Daniels notified the Commandant that he would not be serving his full four-year term, forcing Barnett out in June 1920. In Barnett's place, Daniels appointed the man he had long wanted as Commandant: John Archer Lejeune, former commander of the Second Division. Barnett did not go easily, however; he refused to retire. At the suggestion of Lejeune, Daniels created a new position—head of the Department of the Pacific—and exiled Barnett to San Francisco. Lejeune also successfully lobbied Daniels to create a new major general's slot so that Barnett would not be demoted.[32]

Midway through his service in Santo Domingo, Feland learned that his old mentor, Barnett, had been ousted. Lejeune's ascendancy to the Commandant's position resulted in a new opportunity for Feland. Seeking to modernize and reform the Marine Corps, Lejeune decided to reorganize Headquarters Marine Corps and create a new division that would control operations, training, military education, intelligence, and aviation. He appointed Feland's World War I commander, Wendell "Buck" Neville, as Assistant to the Commandant, replacing Charles Long. To lead the new Division of Operations and Training, Commandant Lejeune picked a man considered by many to be one of the brightest Marines: Brigadier General Logan Feland.[33]

While in Santo Domingo, Feland remained attuned to the Corps's overall strategic needs. His active, logical mind recognized potential needs and evolving roles. In one case, Feland and Ellis developed contingency plans to use the Second Brigade in operations outside the Dominican Republic. For example, what if the Second Brigade were called on to help with a problem in Panama? Feland and Ellis developed scenarios, anticipating needs.

In addition, Feland recognized and supported Lejeune's ideas for reform. In a letter to the Advanced Base Force mining company officer, Julian Smith, Feland noted that he agreed with Lejeune that "all mine work should be turned over to the Navy." He stated that if the Corps would "take over the guns, communications and searchlights for an advanced base outfit and really get to work on it, we [the Corps] will have bitten off quite a mouthful."[34] Feland had the maturity and perspective to recognize where the mining of harbors should fit organizationally. He did not blindly champion its position in the Corps simply because he had worked with mines in the past. His ability to understand the "big picture" was the hallmark of a leader. Feland clearly saw what the Marine Corps could and should, do, and he understood the manpower needed to do it.

Feland received orders in September 1920 to return to Washington as soon as his replacement, Brigadier General Charles Long, arrived in Santo Domingo. Meanwhile, he continued to travel around the Dominican Republic and inspect his Marines. On one trip, he crossed the island on horseback with an escort provided by the Forty-Fourth Company, Mounted, heading to the Northern District commanded by Dion Williams. After inspecting a few outlying posts, Feland proceeded to the Northern District headquarters in Santiago, where he observed the Labor Day field meet of the Marine Brigade.[35]

On a trip to the Eastern District, commanded by Breckinridge, General Feland arrived at Seibo. The next day the battalion commander, a Major Reno, insisted on leading Feland's party for the rest of its journey. Unfortunately, the major got lost. Chafing in the saddle after a long, seemingly fruitless ride around the countryside, Feland finally had enough and insisted that Sergeant Bill Hensley take the lead. After arriving successfully at his final destination, Feland shook hands with the sergeant and thanked him, but he ignored the major. The general expected more from his officers; he did not brook nonsense or incompetence.[36]

In the first week of October, Feland flew by Marine Corps airplane to San Pedro de Macoris to inspect the Eastern District again. After the inspection, Feland's plane managed to get off the ground in a severe crosswind, but the accompanying plane wrecked during takeoff.[37] The incident underscored the dangers of flying, although Feland remained intrigued by the growing importance of military aviation and would continue to fly in his future command in Nicaragua.

Before leaving Santo Domingo, Feland recommended to Snowden that Breckinridge be appointed head of the *Guardia Nacional Dominicana*, a post held by a Marine Corps officer since its inception in 1917.[38] Breckinridge became *Guardia* commander on October 5, 1920, succeeding Colonel George Reid.

Feland also reported once more on the state of Marine Corps activities in the country. With his characteristic optimism, he asserted that the situation was "outwardly quiet except for occasional bandit raids." He acknowledged, however, that "the bands are increasing in number." This resulted in "extensive patrolling during the month designed to counteract the increase in brigandage and spread of revolutionary propaganda," which had "an excellent effect." He concluded again that brigade spirit was "excellent in the field—very good in small towns and good in large towns."[39] The situation remained tenuous, but the Marines seemed content.

In retrospect, historians viewed the situation in the Dominican Republic differently. The buildup of the *Guardia* had increased, but the population regarded the new force with disdain, as a tool of the occupiers. Agitation grew throughout 1920, and resistance to the U.S. occupation became stronger both within the country and internationally, including in the United States. Magazines such as the *Nation*, labor groups such as the American Federation of Labor, and congressional leaders continued to question the U.S. occupation of Santo Domingo. Presidential election politics also played a part in raising the issue of the U.S. role there. Bad publicity regarding Marine atrocities, primarily in Haiti, prompted a visit to the island by Commandant Lejeune and his protégé Smedley Butler, but they spent only a couple of days in Santo Domingo.[40]

Facing opposition in both the Dominican Republic and the United States, the U.S. government devised the Wilson Plan. Snowden publicly announced the plan on December 23, 1920, which called for the gradual withdrawal of U.S. control over the Dominican Republic. Consequently, the last Marines would leave the Dominican Republic on September 18, 1924.[41]

As Feland's tenure in Santo Domingo was ending, Snowden recommended that he be considered for the major general's slot that had opened up with the announced retirement of L. W. T. Waller. Like Harbord in World War I, Feland's in-country commander was impressed with the Kentuckian's work. Snowden commended Feland's dedication and cooperation. The admiral had looked to Feland for "advice and judgment in many important and difficult questions" and had "found his judgment excellent, clear and decisive." Feland had "shown great zeal, energy, and ability" in improving the brigade's organization, training, and efficiency. Noting that Feland was fifty-one years old, Snowden commended the general's activity and physical strength, evidenced by his use of horses and planes to travel the Republic to visit his Marines.[42]

Brigadier General Logan Feland left Santo Domingo on the USS *Gulf-port* and arrived in Charleston, South Carolina, on November 3, 1920. He proceeded to Headquarters Marine Corps to take up his new duties. On December 1 Feland became the director of the Division of Operations and Training (DOT), reporting directly to Commandant Lejeune. He would remain in that position until July 1923, when he would replace Neville as Assistant to the Commandant.

As director of operations and training, Feland oversaw key aspects of the Corps: operations, which included war planning, mobilization, and advanced base and expeditionary forces; training; military education, including Marine Corps schools; military material, including inventions; military intelligence; and aviation. In one of his few published writings, Feland explained that the DOT served as a quasi-staff to the Commandant, providing advice after extensive study of the relevant issues regarding purely military matters. Feland was careful to point out that decision-making rested with the Commandant, but in order to make those decisions, the Commandant needed correct, up-to-date information, which the DOT could provide.[43]

His appointment as director of operations and training underscored Feland's value to the Corps. As DOT director, he would perform a wide variety of duties and responsibilities as Commandant Lejeune tried to modernize the Corps's administrative structure and solidify its status, which was always under scrutiny by the navy and Congress. Feland would help oversee the Corps's development in the early 1920s, first as DOT director and then as Assistant to the Commandant. While Lejeune's good friend Smedley Butler would command the newly created East Coast Expeditionary Force (successor to the Advanced Base Force) at Quantico, Logan Feland would be at the heart of operations at Headquarters Marine Corps.

9

Headquarters Marine Corps

Commandant John Lejeune "envisioned the Division of Operations and Training as the springboard for Marine Corps doctrine and planning."[1] As the first director of DOT, Brigadier General Logan Feland would be involved in many issues and responsible for many decisions that would impact the Marine Corps administratively.

Upon his return to Washington from Santo Domingo, Feland began to attend Lejeune's weekly management meetings, initiated in the summer of 1920, to discuss relevant Corps issues. Attendees included Wendell Neville, Assistant to the Commandant; Smedley Darlington Butler, commander of the East Coast Expeditionary Force at Quantico; Harold Snyder, who had been Feland's second in command in the Fifth Regiment; and occasionally, Feland's old friend Robert Dunlap, who had commanded a U.S. Army artillery regiment during the war. These battle veterans were joined by staff officers such as adjutant and inspector Henry Haines, quartermaster Charles McCawley, and paymaster George Richards.[2]

Although Feland seldom spoke up at these meetings, he did comment on the importance of advanced bases in the Corps's future. At the conference held on December 14, 1920, Feland stated that he "believed it to be a matter of vital importance to the Marine Corps to build up that part of each expeditionary force which is to handle advanced base material." He noted that plans were in progress for joint maneuvers in which the army, navy, and Marines would participate. He anticipated that these maneuvers would involve the navy "seizing a point," the Marines taking it over and "putting it in a temporary state of defense as an advanced base," and

Commandant Lejeune and his Headquarters generals. Logan Feland stands on the right, and Wendell Neville is second from left, next to Lejeune in the center.

then, after the fleet "carried out a problem of securing a line of communication," the army relieving the Marines. Feland believed the Marines would have "a difficult job, requiring a great deal of preparation so far as handling advanced base material is concerned," and he recommended that they start planning right away, as the army and navy were already at work. Commandant Lejeune agreed, noting that he had ordered General Butler to fill vacant positions as soon as possible. Feland's comments at this meeting reflect his far-ranging appreciation of the challenges facing the Marine Corps as it transitioned from a strictly defensive advanced base force to a more mobile expeditionary force designed to participate in joint maneuvers.[3]

In addition, Feland sometimes expressed an opinion about seemingly incidental matters, such as proposing that Marines always wear their uniforms in public. Reflecting his strong technological background, he believed that gunnery sergeants should possess highly technical skills. He appreciated Marine Corps traditions but also recognized the need for change.

The Kentuckian also recognized the changing world situation, especially in East Asia. Prior to World War I, Japan had solidified itself as the major power in East Asia after the defeat of China in the Sino-Japanese War of 1895 and the defeat of Russia in the Russo-Japanese War, settled by the Treaty of Portsmouth in 1905. As a result of post–World War I peace treaties, Japan had acquired some former German colonies in the Pacific, as mandated by the League of Nations. Given these developments, Feland's Division of Operations and Training needed to create extensive plans to deal with any threat from Japan, including war. To undertake this task, the Corps tabbed Feland's close colleague, the brilliant but flawed Earl "Pete" Ellis.

Feland had always strongly supported Ellis. When Commandant Barnett offered Ellis's services as intelligence officer in 1920, Feland had jumped at the opportunity. Ellis had also served well as brigade operations and training officer and as acting chief of staff. Before leaving Santo Domingo, Feland had written to Lejeune, praising Ellis's efficiency in creating effective intelligence reports. Feland underscored Ellis's "untiring energy, thorough knowledge of the ends to be attained and the means of doing so, and devotion to the work in hand."[4]

Shortly after Feland took command of the Division of Operations and Training, Ellis returned from Santo Domingo and became head of the DOT's Intelligence Section. In that capacity, he studied U.S. interests in the Pacific and produced a treatise titled "Advanced Base Operations in Micronesia," foreshadowing Corps landings throughout the Pacific during World War II. Specifically, Ellis's study focused on the need for amphibious assaults in the region in the event of war with Japan.[5]

While he was still in Santo Domingo, Ellis had written a confidential memo to Commandant Lejeune requesting permission to make "necessary reconnaissances" in South America and the Pacific to gather information. Ellis noted that, if necessary, he was willing to take personal actions, such as submitting an undated resignation or traveling as a civilian, to "ensure the United States would not be embarrassed through my operations." Ellis hoped to depart by December 1, 1920. Approving and forwarding Ellis's request, Brigadier General Feland added, "In studying the problem of Santo Domingo I have necessarily been [led] to a consideration of our relations with all Latin American countries. It appears probable that the peace of the United States will be seriously disturbed by some

Earl "Pete" Ellis. Feland supervised the brilliant but self-destructive Ellis, who developed a plan for Marine Corps amphibious assaults in the Pacific and would die while on a spying trip to Micronesia in 1923.

Latin American combination fostered by the intrigues of Oriental Countries whose policies are inimical to those of the United States. I believe it desirable that the Marine Corps (and the Navy) secure all necessary information as to possible theatres of operations in South America and the Pacific Ocean as soon as practicable."[6]

Ellis would not go to the Pacific, however, until 1921. In the meantime, his health deteriorated. A heavy drinker, Ellis was admitted to the naval hospital in Washington just before Christmas 1920 and diagnosed with "psychasthenia," a psychological disorder. In Ellis's case, this manifested as headaches, insomnia, tremors of the fingers, appetite loss, depression, and "difficulties in thinking." In mid-January 1921 he was released from the hospital and given ninety days' leave. He seemed to function well enough when he resumed his duties in mid-April, producing his treatise on Micronesia. And once again, he requested permission to visit the Pacific Islands.[7]

Ellis left on his long-awaited trip to the Pacific in May 1921 and remained in the area until his death, under somewhat mysterious circumstances, in May 1923 on the island of Palau. In June 1922 Ellis cabled General Feland, requesting an extension of his leave as he recuperated from an illness at Cavite Naval Station in the Philippines. Ellis noted that he possessed the necessary funds to stay. Feland apparently granted his permission and then lost contact with Ellis. He did, however, keep in touch with Earl Ellis's brother, John. In January 1923 John Ellis contacted Feland because payments into his brother's bank account had stopped. Feland told John that if Earl approached him for funds, the general would take care of it, but Feland thought it unlikely that Earl would contact either one of them.[8]

Ellis's whereabouts in the Pacific remained largely a mystery as he undertook his secret mission. It is known that, after stops in New Zealand, Australia, and the Philippines, Ellis went to Yokohama, Japan, where he was treated for alcoholism in a U.S. naval hospital. From Yokohama, Ellis set off for the Japanese-controlled islands in the Pacific, first heading south to Saipan and then to Palau in the Caroline Islands. He traveled east into the Marshall Islands before heading back to Palau. Ellis, who was being watched by Japanese authorities, continued his downward alcoholic spiral.[9]

In May 1923 Feland apparently became concerned and asked John Ellis to contact him "at once" if he heard from his brother. He also suggested that John contact Earl's bank in Newport, Rhode Island, and inquire when his last check had been written, hoping to find a clue as to his whereabouts.[10] Soon thereafter, they learned that Earl Ellis had died in Palau on May 12, 1923, after drinking two bottles of liquor.

In response to an inquiry from Earl's older brother, Ralph (managing editor of the *Kansas City Journal-Post*), Feland offered to help the family sort out Earl's personal affairs and accounts with the Marine Corps. Feland closed his letter with a personal note, telling Ralph Ellis how much he "deeply and sincerely regretted Earl's death." He cited Ellis's contribution to the Marine Brigade during the war and recalled serving with him in Santo Domingo, where Ellis had "continued to give all his energy and devotion to the service, working harder than he should, in spite of my urging him to ease up." Feland noted that he had approved the Pacific trip because Ellis had "felt so sure that this would enable him to recover his health. When it was arranged, he was happier than I have ever seen him."[11]

Feland continued to correspond with the Ellis brothers through June, noting that it was difficult to get Earl's stored goods released from Palau without a will, an executor, and legal proof of his death. In a letter to Ralph Ellis, Feland wrote: "In your last letter you spoke of having some notes, pictures, etc., which Earl collected on his Pacific travels. If this includes any material collected on this last trip, I would suggest that you take very particular care of such material. In case any such is found, I think it would be well for you to send it to me here at Headquarters. If you feel inclined to do so, you might send me all such material, notes, pictures, maps, etc., and if you desire, I will return that which is not necessary to be kept here."[12] Obviously, Feland hoped to obtain the results of Ellis's spying trip. Feland eventually arranged for Earl's trunks and boxes to be returned to his family. Ralph Ellis subsequently wrote to the Commandant, expressing his thanks, and in another letter he characterized Lejeune and Feland as "two of Earl's closest friends."[13]

Ellis's death was one of the more puzzling events that occurred during Feland's command of the DOT. Rumors swirled: had the Marine Corps spy been killed by the Japanese? Whatever the case, Ellis's seminal work on advanced bases in Micronesia foretold of a future war the Marine Corps would undertake against Japan.[14]

His advocacy for and monitoring of Ellis's intelligence-gathering trip to Micronesia demonstrated Feland's ability to adapt to changing conditions. He did not simply look to the past and focus solely on the "small," or "bush," wars reflected in expeditions to Central America and the Caribbean; nor did he simply look back to the grand battles fought in

World War I. Feland looked forward. He knew that the Marine Corps's role would be changing, given the new conditions in East Asia and the Pacific. These conditions would impact planning and training and especially the evolution of the Marine Corps's Expeditionary Forces. In sum, Feland had a global view of events and was continually evaluating how his Marine Corps might be affected.

Brigadier General Feland also foresaw the increasing use of new technology, such as the airplane. As director of operations and training, Feland officially supervised the development of Marine Corps aviation in the early 1920s. His interest in this new weapon of war may have dated back to the Culebra maneuvers of 1914, when airplanes had been used for scouting. It is unclear whether Feland himself went up for an observational flight during the Culebra maneuvers, but he was probably aware of a previous flight by the first Marine Corps aviator, Alfred Austell Cunningham, at Guantanamo in 1913. Cunningham had reported spotting a naval minefield from the air, and as commander of the Advanced Base Force mining company, Feland would have been interested in this new development.[15] As the temporary chief of staff of the Second Division, Feland had lunch with Cunningham in December 1917. Historians can only surmise what their conversation covered. Certainly, by 1920, Feland had become very aware of the benefits of Marine Corps aviation. While commanding in Santo Domingo, Feland had flown to various parts of the island to review his Marines.[16]

In 1920 Lieutenant Colonel Thomas Turner replaced Cunningham as director of Marine Corps aviation. The following year Turner demonstrated "the practicality of long-distance aircraft deployments" when he "led a flight of two DH-4s from Washington, D.C., to Santo Domingo, establishing a record for the longest unguarded flight over land and water made up to that time by American Navy or Marine Personnel." For this feat, Turner received the Distinguished Flying Cross. Feland and Turner knew each other well and were duck-hunting friends, as evidenced by a *New York Times* photograph of the two men sitting in a Quantico duck blind.[17]

In July 1923 Lieutenant Colonel Frank Evans wrote to Feland from Haiti, suggesting that the Marines attempt a record long-distance flight from Hispaniola to St. Louis, Missouri, where the National Aero Congress and International Air Races were scheduled to take place in October.

Evans credited the idea to two Marine pilots, Ford O. Rogers and Horace D. Palmer.[18] Feland and Turner obviously approved of the proposal, and Palmer and Rogers made the record-breaking flight from Haiti, arriving in St. Louis on September 28. Along the way, they landed at Bolling Field in Washington, D.C., where they were greeted by Feland, Turner, and Rear Admiral William A. Moffett, chief of the navy's Bureau of Aeronautics.[19] Feland, Turner, Moffett, and Secretary of the Navy Edwin Denby (a former Marine) gathered a few days later at the Aero Congress in St. Louis, where they watched as naval aviators, including Marine Corps lieutenant Lawson Sanderson, swept the Pulitzer Trophy competition at the International Air Races. Afterward, Palmer and Rogers proceeded to San Francisco before turning around and flying back across the country and eventually back to Santo Domingo. In sum, "The trip of 10,953 miles in 127 hours of actual flying time was recorded as the second-longest trip in the history of aviation. In 1919, the winner had been a twin-engine World War I Vickers 'Vimy' bomber, which made the 11,063-mile trip from London to Darwin, Australia, in 29 days. In this case, it was not all bad for the Marines to place second."[20]

Feland's interest in aviation would continue after he left Headquarters Marine Corps. In 1926, while serving as commander of the East Coast Expeditionary Force at Quantico, he would sign up for an aviation observer's course, which he believed would be of great value to any brigade commander. He attended the course only briefly, however. He was deemed physically unfit because of tachycardia (high heart rate) and problems with his depth perception.[21] In sum, Feland recognized and understood the importance of aviation early on, and he did what he could to promote it and utilize it. The technical aspects must have appealed to him, but he also appreciated the practicalities. His knowledge of and interest in aviation would come in handy when he commanded Marines in Nicaragua later in the decade.

As part of his duties as director of operations and training, Feland appeared at public events. One such occasion brought him back to Kentucky, where he attended the Armistice Day celebration and parade in Louisville in November 1922. The day before the November 11 parade, he spoke at the Girls' High School, the Louisville Board of Trade luncheon, and the annual Kiwanis Club dinner. During his Board of Trade speech at Louisville's famed Seelbach Hotel, Feland addressed a favorite theme: the Marine Corps's role as part of the U.S. Navy. He underscored Commandant Lejeune's policy of solidifying ties between the two groups, and he appealed to the audience to support the U.S. Navy as a "business proposition," citing Britain's place in world commerce "as an example of what an adequate navy will accomplish." Continuing with the business analogy, Feland equated the navy with insurance: "insurance of protection for the enterprises necessary to the development of new foreign markets for American goods." Feland then cited a historical example his fellow Kentuckians could relate to: more than 500 Kentucky riflemen had served as Marines in the Battle of Lake Champlain. He also mentioned two famous Kentuckians who had served as navy admirals: Rear Admiral John Crittenden Watson, a Civil War and Spanish-American War veteran who was still alive, and Rear Admiral Hugh Rodman, who had commanded a battleship fleet in the Atlantic during World War I and had recently served as commander in chief of the Pacific Fleet.[22]

Feland's host during his visit was Ellerbe Carter, a Kentucky National Guard officer who had served with the U.S. Army in France during World War I and had founded a brokerage firm in Louisville. Feland was the main guest of honor at the city's Armistice Day parade. The next day, the *Louisville Courier-Journal* published a front-page picture of Feland standing front and center on the reviewing stand, smiling broadly, and towering over Kentucky governor Edwin Morrow, Louisville mayor Huston Quin, and Carter. That evening, Feland attended a ceremony at Warren Memorial Presbyterian Church, where he presented flags representing the Allied nations that had fought in World War I.[23]

Feland's Kentucky connections extended beyond the commonwealth. As a member of the Kentucky Society of Washington, D.C., he kept up social contacts with the Kentucky congressional delegation, such as senators Richard Ernst and A. O. Stanley (his fellow initiate into Sigma Alpha Epsilon fraternity at Kentucky Southern College). He interacted as well with other prominent Kentuckians, including Supreme Court justices Louis Brandeis and James Clark McReynolds and Admiral Rodman, who had served as commander of the Pacific Fleet before another Feland acquaintance, Admiral Edward Eberle (Feland had known Eberle since they were stationed together at Annapolis, early in his career).[24]

After the war and during the 1920s, Logan and Katherine Feland

Commandant John Lejeune presenting medals. Feland (third from left) looks on proudly as Lejeune bestows medals on his fellow Fourth Brigade officers for their actions in World War I.

appeared often on the society page of the *Washington Post*. Katherine Feland had remained in Philadelphia and continued her musical career while her husband was overseas, and after they moved to Washington, D.C., she continued to sing at various events. Shortly after his return from France, on June 3, 1919, the Felands attended a Belleau Wood remembrance at the Marine Barracks, accompanied by Secretary of War Newton Baker, Secretary of the Navy Josephus Daniels, and Major General and Mrs. George Barnett. Brigadier General Feland paid tribute to those Marines who had served at Belleau Wood, and Katherine Feland provided musical entertainment, along with the Marine Corps Band.[25]

Katherine Feland gave many concerts and recitals, and after one such event, the *Washington Post* gushed: "In addition to being a singer of unusual attainments, Mrs. Feland is a woman of distinguished beauty and a charming stage presence." On another occasion, the *Post* published a full-length picture of Mrs. Feland, accompanying an article titled "Fashions of Capital Women."[26]

Katherine Feland also became involved in charitable activities while living in Washington. For example, she joined an effort to raise $200,000 for the Florence Crittenton Home for Girls and sang at Marine Corps activities to raise money for a Belleau Wood memorial.[27]

Katherine Feland proved to be a formidable woman. On one occasion, she and the general were attending a Lafayette Day dinner at the Chevy Chase Club and were seated at the head table with General Pershing, labor leader Samuel Gompers, and painter and author Marietta Minnigerode Andrews. Gompers gave a speech in which he claimed that "labor had done its share toward the winning of the war." Pershing disagreed and, in fact, "denied that organized labor had been loyal to the country in its hour of need and claimed for the soldiery the honor of having won the war in spite of all the handicaps imposed upon the country by enemies within itself." Gompers's and Pershing's competing comments caused tension in the room, and when Andrews stood up to "read a little ode," this did nothing to lighten the mood. Then Katherine Feland acted. Andrews later described the scene:

> Inconsequential as my own contribution, it remained for Mrs. Feland, wife of General Logan Feland of the Marine Corps to relieve the tensity [sic] of the situation. Immediately after me, she rose, stately, Juno-esque, exquisitely gowned; stood calmly surveying the company (and being surveyed!) then in a powerful, well-schooled voice, without accompaniment, sang the National Anthem. All were instantly on their feet—soon hundreds of voices took up the strain. A common sympathy spread throughout the company; the reaction had come. Happy faces, cordial greetings, polite congratulations, general good-humor, marked the occasion. The dancing set betook themselves to the ballroom.[28]

Brigadier General Feland participated in numerous other social events, usually related to his membership in various military-related organizations. Before the war, Feland had become member number 1,549 of the Military Order of the Carabao, an organization with a history dating back to 1900. When members of the international military force that had served in China during the Boxer Rebellion formed the Order of the Dragon, those men who had remained in the Philippines during the "Punitive Expedition" created their own society in November 1900 in parody of the Dragons, choosing as their symbol the lowly carabao, or water buffalo. The Philippine veterans organized into local clubs called "corrals," which held annual events called "wallows," where liquor, satirical skits, and convivial good times reigned. The infamous 1913 wallow in Washington, D.C., had been attended by Secretary of the Navy Josephus Daniels, a well-known teetotaler. The secretary apparently reported to President Wilson that the entertainment got out of hand when the Carabaos sang "Damn, Damn, Damn the Insurrectos." Offended by this slight to Filipinos, for whom the new Democratic administration desired independence, Wilson rejected his honorary membership in the Order of the Carabao and had his secretaries of war and navy issue reprimands to several military men.

In 1920 Feland's former Fifth Regiment commander, Major General Wendell "Buck" Neville (member number 690), was elected head of the order, a position known as the Paramount Carabao. Admiral Edward Eberle would also serve as Paramount Carabao in 1924–1925. Other famous Carabaos of the period included Feland's Fourth Brigade commander James Harbord (member number 1,821), General John Pershing (144), and famed army aviator Billy Mitchell (1,300), as well as Feland's Marine Corps colleagues James Carson Breckinridge (1,381), "Hiking Hiram" Bearss (450), and Fritz Wise (1,379).[29]

Brigadier General Feland also participated in several other organizations, including the Second Division Association, the Military Order of the World War, and the Baltic Society. The Second Division Association had been founded after World War I and held annual reunions around the country. In its early years, Commandant Lejeune played a prominent role in the national association. Feland served as president of the association's District of Columbia branch in 1923 and would eventually serve as president of the national association in 1935.[30] Founded in 1920 in Detroit, the Military Order of the World War supported a strong U.S. military presence. In the words of its founding commander in chief, Major General George H. Harries, its purpose was the "awakening of congress and the rest of the country against the dangers of pacifism, insufficient defense and radicalism." Feland served on the board of the Washington, D.C., chapter.[31] Initially a 1923 reunion of the officers who had accompanied Pershing on the SS *Baltic*, the Baltic Society eventually expanded to a yearly celebration that included men of all ranks who had sailed to France with Pershing.[32]

It was at Baltic Society and Second Division Association events that Feland became reacquainted with U.S. Army general James Harbord. After being promoted to major general, Harbord headed a commission sent by President Wilson to Turkey and Armenia in 1919. The commission investigated the plight of the Armenians under the old Ottoman Empire and the emerging Turkey of nationalist leader Mustafa Kemal Atatürk, who created the modern Turkish secular state. When Pershing became U.S. Army chief of staff in 1921, Harbord served as his deputy. Harbord retired from the army at the end of 1922 to become president of the Radio Corporation of American (RCA).[33]

In 1922 Feland was a member of a small committee established to raise money to commission a portrait of Harbord. Secretary of the Navy Edwin Denby, a former Marine who had served during World War I, presented the portrait to the Army and Navy Club in Washington in May 1923.[34] Although Harbord did not attend the unveiling of his portrait, he corresponded with Feland, and in June 1923 the two men sat together at a dinner. Afterward, in preparation for a speech, Harbord asked Feland to provide information about the officers and men killed at Belleau Wood. Feland complied. A few months later, the ambitious Feland asked for Harbord's help in obtaining the temporary major general position that was expected to open up. Commandant Lejeune had arrived in France after the Battle of Belleau Wood, and Feland hoped that Harbord could enlighten Lejeune about the Kentuckian's value to the Fifth Regiment and the Fourth Marine Brigade during that campaign.[35]

Although he was retired from the army by 1923, Harbord still exerted a lot of influence in Washington because of his impressive military background, his position as president of a major U.S. corporation, and his participation in Republican politics. In response to Feland's request, Harbord wrote to Commandant Lejeune, noting that the pending retirement of George Barnett in December offered opportunities for others to advance. He recommended that Buck Neville be promoted from temporary to permanent major general and that Feland be given the temporary grade of major general. Harbord cited his acquaintance with Feland since May 28, 1917 (the sailing date of the *Baltic*), and noted his "excellent opportunity to observe his [Feland's] deliberate and studious habits." Reminding Lejeune that he had commanded the Fourth Brigade during Belleau Wood and the Second Division at Soissons, Harbord asserted: "I cannot praise too highly the efficiency of General Feland as shown in those trying days. He was the principal reliance of General Neville in the command of the 5th Marines, and of myself, as Brigade Commander, when an Officer of Field Rank and not in command of a Regiment was needed in any critical place or moment during the strenuous fighting in and around the Bois de Belleau." Observing that Feland's bravery had won him the Distinguished Service Cross, Harbord recalled that Feland had been "'on the job' day and night" and that on many occasions Harbord had sent Feland "to steady, by his example, less competent Commanders. He never failed me in any instance, and I attribute a very substantial portion of the fame so worthily won by the Marine Brigade to the efficiency of Logan Feland." Harbord summarized by saying that he had "studied the list of Line Brigadiers in the Marine Corps" and could "see none whose record or efficiency should warrant promotion ahead of General Feland." Harbord concluded that he was quite sure that Feland's promotion "would meet with the enthusiastic endorsement of every Veteran of the old Marine Brigade of glorious memory."[36]

A few days later Commandant Lejeune replied to Harbord, thanking him for the letter, which would be brought to the attention of the secretary of the navy, and noting that copies would also be put in Neville's and Feland's military records. He added, however, that the secretary of the navy had announced Neville's permanent grade promotion some time ago and that Joseph Pendleton, the senior Marine Corps brigadier general, would receive the temporary major general slot.[37]

Feland thanked Harbord for writing to Lejeune on his behalf. Unfortunately for Feland, he was once again stymied by a Marine Corps system based on seniority, as defined by position on the lineal list. Back in 1916, Feland had submitted a memo to the secretary of the navy asking that he be placed ahead of other officers promoted to major on the same day, given that Feland had more commissioned service. A similar request by Major Arthur Marix had already been denied by the Navy Department, and Commandant George Barnett suggested to the navy's judge advocate general (JAG) that Feland's request also be denied. The issue centered on whether a promotion could be construed as an "appointment," which was the relevant event for determining one's position on the lineal list. The Navy Department concluded that it could not; the issue had been decided years ago, and that decision should not be changed. In sum, Feland's 1916 attempt to move ahead on the lineal list had failed.[38] In 1924 he would try again, this time by attempting to leapfrog over a former friend who had become a serious rival: Brigadier General Smedley Darlington Butler.

Feland had been an usher at Butler's wedding in 1905, he had successfully prosecuted at a contentious court-martial initiated by Butler, and
he had been promoted to permanent brigadier general at the same time
as Butler. But relations between the two men had cooled over the years.
During World War I Butler had resented being left out of the action,
commanding troops at the staging area in Brest. He also derided Marine
Corps officers, primarily staff officers serving at headquarters, who were
deficient in so-called bushwhacking experience on expeditions and had
spent time at the Naval War College or other military schools. Having
joined the Corps at age sixteen, Butler lacked higher education, but he
certainly made up for it in service and bravado. A two-time Medal of
Honor recipient (although he had tried, unsuccessfully, to return the one
awarded after Vera Cruz, believing he had not earned it), Butler was the
publicity hound of the Marine Corps.

In contrast, Feland was highly educated, with a college degree; his time
spent at military schools had been as a teacher, not as a student. He could
not be faulted for his lack of expeditionary duty, and he had certainly proved
his courage under fire during World War I. Unlike the Butlers, Katherine
and Logan Feland played a prominent role in Washington, D.C., society.
They had also been close to the Barnetts. Butler, however, loathed the former Commandant and had conspired to have him removed.

By 1920, the stage had been set for Logan Feland and Smedley Darlington Butler to become strong rivals—a rivalry that played out over the
decade. Feland thought he was better qualified than Butler to be a Marine
Corps major general, and he fervently believed he should be ahead of Butler on the lineal list. Toward this end, in October 1923 he wrote a two-
page, single-spaced letter to Secretary of the Navy Edwin Denby. Feland
argued that because he had been in the U.S. Volunteer Army during the
Spanish-American War, he had been in commissioned service longer than
Butler and should therefore be ahead of him on the lineal list.[39]

In turn, Commandant Lejeune wrote to the secretary outlining the
service of each man, both of whom had been commissioned as brigadier
generals on the same date: March 17, 1921, retroactive to June 4, 1920.
Lejeune's analysis revealed that the combination of volunteer service and
Marine Corps service favored Feland—by three days: Feland had twenty-
one years, ten months, twenty-four days, while Butler had twenty-one years,
ten months, twenty-one days. In December Lejeune wrote to the secretary

again, noting that after a failed attempt to garner Senate approval for the promotions of Butler, Feland, and Harry Lee to brigadier general, their names had been resubmitted to the Senate, and the president had approved the commissions. Lejeune stated, "It was unquestionably the *intent* of the Secretary of the Navy, and of the President, and of the Senate, that Brigadier General Butler should be senior to Brigadier General Feland." In addition, Lejeune believed that, according to the National Defense Act, only service in the Marine Corps counted toward seniority.[40]

In the end, the navy's JAG office interpreted the law to mean that only Marine Corps service could be counted. By this measurement, Butler had twenty-one years, ten months, twenty-one days, while Feland had only twenty years, ten months, twenty-eight days.[41] Butler remained ahead of Feland on the lineal list.

Despite this setback, Feland would try again in 1924, when Pendleton retired. Harbord again interceded on Feland's behalf, this time writing to Secretary of War John Weeks. Harbord underscored Feland's valuable service at Belleau Wood: "Time and again when conditions were in doubt on some part of the fighting line, or when a commander was needed for combined battalions or to straighten out a difficult situation by the presence of a field officer in whom I had entire confidence, Colonel Feland was used and he never failed to justify the confidence held in him." Harbord realized that the secretary of the navy would probably promote the more senior Eli Kelly Cole to the major general's slot, "but however honorable and creditable may be the record of that officer it contains no such chapter as that which General Feland wrote by his splendid service in the Marine Brigade." Harbord could only hope that Weeks would speak to the new secretary of the navy, Curtis Wilbur, on Feland's behalf.[42] Once more, however, Feland was disappointed when Cole was promoted to major general in June 1924.

Feland's efforts to obtain a promotion to major general revealed that he was willing to use the system (as evidenced by his attempt to establish his seniority over Butler), but they also reflected his dissatisfaction with a system based on seniority rather than ability. Commandant Lejeune considered implementing a merit-based system, but that change would not take place until 1934, after both Lejeune and Feland had retired. Feland would have to wait another half a dozen years before becoming a major general.

10

Assistant to the Commandant

As the 1920s progressed, the U.S. Marine Corps under Commandant John Lejeune continued to search for its identity. Greatly reduced after the end of World War I, the Corps had difficulty deciding which direction to take.

The world situation had changed dramatically. In East Asia, Japan emerged from the war with greater interests and responsibilities in the Pacific, as it assumed control of formerly German-held islands. U.S. Navy War Plan Orange recognized the possibility of a Japanese threat, and in early 1920 Chief of Naval Operations Robert Coontz had recommended that the Marine Corps create an expeditionary force on the West Coast to counter possible Japanese incursions in the Pacific. This expeditionary force, along with a similar one set up at Quantico, Virginia, would carry forward the prewar concept of advanced base forces.[1]

An emphasis on what became known as amphibious warfare grew fitfully during the 1920s under Commandant Lejeune. He not only supported the Corps's traditional role on ships and in small war expeditions but also recognized the need to adapt for future amphibious operations. Earl "Pete" Ellis had painted a convincing picture in his Operation Plan 712, "Advanced Base Force Operations in Micronesia," approved in July 1921. It served as Lejeune's justification for ordering that "henceforth the Marine Corps would use it to guide war planning, field exercises, equipment development, and officer education."[2] Those tasks devolved to the Division of Operations and Training (DOT), commanded by Brigadier General Logan Feland.

Soon after returning from Santo Domingo to take up his DOT position, Feland had spoken up about the need for combined maneuvers involving the U.S. Army, the U.S. Navy, and the U.S. Marine Corps. Under his guidance, the DOT oversaw training and war planning, and Feland ordered Julius Turrill, Henry Larsen, and Dion Williams to prepare for combined maneuvers at Culebra. He asked them to prepare memoranda addressing various issues, such as proper training for the evolving expeditionary force, appropriate uniforms, and adequate artillery. These studies intensified after Feland became Assistant to the Commandant in 1923.[3] Hence, Feland advocated early, proper training for the evolving Marine Corps role.

Feland also recognized the continuing need to be part of the navy. After training exercises in the Caribbean in 1924, Feland wrote a brief article for *Leatherneck* magazine, reminding Marines of their historical ties to the navy. Noting that in many places where Marines served the U.S. Navy presence remained slight, Feland chided that sometimes Marines are "prone to forget that our chief duty is one of cooperation and helpfulness to the Fleet." He asserted, "We are part of the Navy and our history could never have been made except as a part of the Navy. Our life in the Navy is permanent; every other episode, no matter how striking, is temporary."[4]

In supporting the traditional Marine Corps ties to the navy, General Feland echoed the position of Commandant Lejeune. Unlike his friend Smedley Butler, who had developed an intense dislike for navy men, especially Annapolis graduates, Lejeune valued his Naval Academy background. He believed the Marine Corps should draw most if not all of its officers from the Naval Academy, as had been the case when he graduated. In the 1920s Lejeune underscored Marines' role in support of naval fleets, especially in operations onshore.[5]

Throughout the 1920s, however, the Marine Corps would be assigned other duties that interfered with progress in strategic directions. One unusual assignment came at the end of 1921. Over the past couple of years there had been several U.S. mail robberies, so Postmaster Will H. Hays asked President Warren Harding to detail Marines to protect the mail trains. On November 7, 1921, Harding forwarded that request to Secretary of the Navy Edwin Denby, who in turn passed it along to Commandant Lejeune. Feland had been on extended leave at his vacation refuge in Pennsylvania since September 16 when, on November 9, he received a

Postmaster General Will Hays and Logan Feland discuss the Marine mail guards, 1921. (Library of Congress)

priority message revoking his leave and ordering him to return to Washington immediately.[6]

It was Feland's task to put the Marine mail guard into effect. Marines were taken from the expeditionary forces at Quantico and San Diego and assigned to various key locations around the country. Feland drew up special orders for the Marines assigned to guard the mail, instructing them to keep a rifle, shotgun, or pistol always in hand and to make the most effective use of these weapons, "shooting or otherwise killing or disabling any person engaged in the theft or robbery" of the mail. Feland followed up with some supplementary orders for guard company commanders, noting that shotguns were to be "carried with filled magazine and empty chamber, in order to avoid accidents," and that "the Marines should be continually reminded that they will use their firearms to wound or kill, *only* when necessary to prevent robbery or theft of the mails. The use of firearms except for this purpose must be avoided." Ever mindful of his troops' well-being and the need to maintain good relationships with the communities where they were stationed, Feland ordered that "commanding officers must take steps to provide a suitable Christmas and New Year for their commands" and suggested "enlisting the good offices of local Welfare organizations."[7]

Marines continued to guard the mail until March 1922. During that time, no robberies took place, and the Marines returned to their normal posts. The new postmaster general, Hubert Work, sent Commandant Lejeune a letter thanking the Corps for its service and extended his "personal thanks and appreciation" to General Feland "for the masterful and efficient means by which these operations have been conducted and brought to such a successful conclusion." In turn, Lejeune sent Feland a copy of Work's letter and added his personal commendation "for the able and efficient manner in which this unusual situation was met."[8]

In 1923 the Marine Corps leadership changed. In July the Assistant to the Commandant, Major General Wendell "Buck" Neville, took over command of the Department of the Pacific in San Francisco (a slot that had been created for former Commandant George Barnett after his ouster in 1920). Consequently, on July 13, 1923, Brigadier General Logan Feland gave up his position as director of the DOT to succeed Neville as Assistant to the Commandant, a post he retained for two years.[9]

The assistant's job was an important one. It had been a stepping-stone for Lejeune on his path to Commandant, as it would be for four future Commandants: Wendell Neville, Ben Fuller, John Russell, and Alexander Vandergrift. As Assistant to the Commandant, Feland was in a position to help develop the Marine Corps and move it forward. Under Lejeune's leadership, the Corps continued to adapt to its postwar status during the 1920s. Lejeune implemented innovations such as the Marine Corps Institute, a correspondence school that offered both military and basic education, as well as the new Marine Corps Schools at Quantico, providing better training for officers. He also supported the organization of the Marine Corps League, which still brings together former and current Marines in support of Corps activities. Lejeune also placed a premium on publicity to bolster the image of the Marine Corps.[10]

The Marine Corps had established a Publicity Bureau back in 1911, and publicity remained a key component of Corps activity. The Marine Corps's image had been aided by its actions during the Spanish-American War, when it claimed to be "The First to Fight," and in World War I, when the Corps ballyhooed its reputation as the "Devil Dogs" of Belleau Wood. At the start of the war, the Corps had utilized the recruiting

Commandant John Lejeune and Assistant to the Commandant Logan Feland.

posters of Howard Chandler Christy and James Montgomery Flagg to attract top-notch talent. One of Flagg's more famous World War I recruiting posters featured future famed aviator Ross Rowell in his field uniform standing steadfast before the American flag, underscored with the slogans "First to Fight" and "Always Faithful" and the exhortation to "Be a U.S. Marine."[11]

In the early 1920s Brigadier General Smedley Butler served as a key figure in Marine Corps publicity. His father, Thomas, remained an influential U.S. congressman and chairman of the House Naval Affairs Committee. Though still disappointed by his failure to gain combat experience in the war, but happy with the demise of Commandant Barnett and the rise of his friend Lejeune, General Butler threw himself into his new duties as commander of the East Coast Expeditionary Force at Quantico and embarked on several ventures that brought publicity to the Corps. For instance, he created a Marine Corps football team that, at its height, played at a new stadium at Quantico and faced the University of Michigan in Ann Arbor. For four years, Butler also oversaw some unique Marine Corps maneuvers carried out on nearby Civil War battlefields.[12]

The first "Civil War" maneuver took place in the fall of 1921 near the Wilderness battleground. The event drew several notable spectators: President and Mrs. Harding, Secretary of the Navy Denby, Assistant Secretary of the Navy Theodore Roosevelt Jr., Congressman Thomas Butler, chief of naval operations Admiral Robert Coontz, and General James Harbord.[13] In 1922 the maneuvers took place at Gettysburg, entailing a long march for the Quantico Marines. En route to the Gettysburg battlefield, they stopped overnight at various camps named after Marine Corps generals, including Camp Feland at the Frederick, Maryland, fairgrounds. The Corps garnered national attention as President Harding watched the Marines reenact Pickett's famous charge. The Gettysburg maneuvers were marred by a tragic accident: the death of George Hamilton, who crashed his plane during the event.[14]

Hamilton had been one of Feland's battalion commanders in the Fifth Regiment, and the two had continued to communicate after the war. While in Santo Domingo, Feland had learned that Hamilton was considering leaving the Corps and had written to his young colleague, emphasizing how important Hamilton's wartime service had been. Feland expressed his hope that Hamilton would get his requested six-month leave of absence and signed off, "sincerely your friend." Along with Lejeune, Neville, Julius Turrill, and Thomas Turner, Feland would serve as an honorary pallbearer at Hamilton's funeral and burial in Arlington Cemetery.[15]

In 1923 the Marine Corps East Coast Expeditionary Force carried out its maneuvers by marching through the Shenandoah Valley to New Market, Virginia. There, it re-created a Civil War battle made famous by the heroic appearance of Virginia Military Institute (VMI) cadets supporting the Confederate cause. Current VMI cadets re-created their role in the battle and then squeaked by to victory over the Marine Corps team in a football game.[16]

Feland recognized the value of the maneuvers for training. When reviewing the plans for the New Market maneuver as director of operations and training, he noted that the same result might be obtained by shorter trips out and back from Quantico. Nevertheless, he approved the maneuver because of the enormous publicity boost it gave the Corps. His detailed review of the New Market plans focused on proper training and the needs of the troops. Feland's main concern was that the Marines serving in navy yards would not be given adequate training in preparation for

the maneuver. He believed they should get the same six weeks of marching with full packs that the Quantico Marines would get before making
the arduous journey to New Market. If that training could not be provided, Feland advised that the navy yard Marines should simply join the
other participants at the maneuver grounds. He advocated that one or the
other option be followed, "with no half-way compromises."[17]

In 1924 the Marine Corps held the last of its Civil War maneuvers
in September, re-creating the Battle of Antietam. At the end of the exercise, the Marines marched through downtown Washington, D.C., where
they were reviewed by President and Mrs. Coolidge and U.S. Navy and
Marine Corps dignitaries.[18] Butler, however, was not the East Coast Expeditionary Force commander at the 1924 maneuvers; instead, the Marines
were led by Brigadier General Dion Williams. Butler had taken a leave
of absence from the Corps, and since the beginning of the year he had
been the director of public safety in Philadelphia. Butler nevertheless
motored down to Frederick, Maryland, to review the expeditionary force
as it marched through town. Although Butler would spend a couple of
years trying to reform the Philadelphia police department, especially its
enforcement of Prohibition laws, he never strayed too far from the Marine
Corps.[19]

While Butler was temporarily away from the Corps, Feland continued
to be involved in the development of amphibious warfare. In the spring
of 1925 the Marine Corps and the U.S. Navy prepared for a joint exercise
designed to test their cooperation and the ability to mesh complementary
skills to achieve higher goals. The exercise, conducted in April, involved
a joint assault on an enemy represented by U.S. Army troops and naval
forces in Oahu, Hawaii. Drawing from the expeditionary forces at San
Diego and Quantico, the Marine Corps provided 120 officers and 1,500
enlisted men to represent a landing force of 42,000 men. Designated the
Blue Marine Expeditionary Force, the attacking group was led by Major
General Buck Neville. Brigadier General Logan Feland led the so-called
First Marine Division, while Brigadier General Dion Williams led the
Second Marine Division. Feland's old commander and SS *Baltic* compan-
ion, Colonel Robert Dunlap, played a major role as the Blue Force's chief
of staff, responsible for much of its planning.[20]

Much to his chagrin, Feland had little to do during the exercise, other
than observe. At one point, a junior officer saw Feland "with his arms full

of maps and what-nots" as the general was going ashore with his skeleton headquarters group. When the officer volunteered to help, "General Feland said, 'No, I want to carry them myself 'cause as far as I can see, that's about the only damn thing I've got to do in this exercise.'"[21] The Kentucky general had a sharp wit, as well as a desire to be part of the action.

The Oahu exercise proved reasonably successful. In the words of historian Leo Daugherty, "In sum, the Oahu Maneuvers of 1925 pointed the services in the right direction despite the bitter interservice relations of the first half of the decade."[22] The exercise showed Marine Corps leaders that there were some serious deficiencies in communications, interservice cooperation, and ship-to-shore transportation. The Marine Corps would not tackle these problems until the following decade, however, because other issues and crises intervened.

Soon after returning from the Oahu exercise, Feland rotated out of his position as Assistant to the Commandant and became commander of the East Coast Expeditionary Force at Quantico, while Dion Williams moved from DOT director to Assistant to the Commandant. The Felands kept an apartment in Washington, where they continued to entertain. For example, they gave a party for Major General Eli Kelly Cole, who was in charge of the Quantico base.[23]

Meanwhile, General Feland's professional interest in aviation continued. In August 1925 he and his hunting buddy, Marine Corps aviator Thomas Turner, attended a test of machine gunnery against air targets at Fort Tilden, New York. The test revealed that the machine guns did little damage to towed targets and helped the two Marines understand the advantages of aerial bombing.[24] In September, Feland, Turner, Williams, and Lejeune attended Marine Corps maneuvers featuring aviation and artillery at the U.S. Army's Fort Meade in Maryland. Once again the Corps received good publicity, and the *New York Times* published a photograph of Feland, Lejeune, and Williams being driven around in a large open convertible while observing the maneuvers. Feland would soon have a better understanding of the efficacy of aerial bombing and would implement it against ground targets.[25]

Over the next couple of years, the Marine Corps got both good and bad publicity. At the end of 1925, Smedley Butler left his civilian appointment in Philadelphia and returned to the Corps. He and his family moved to his next posting in San Diego, California, in January 1926 and, within a few weeks, Butler became involved in a major controversy that generated bad publicity for the Corps.

Back in Philadelphia, Butler had become not only a staunch upholder of Prohibition laws but also a teetotaler. Soon after moving to San Diego, Butler attended a party at the home of Colonel Alexander Williams, and Butler suspected that Williams was intoxicated. Later that day, Williams appeared to be drunk at a party at the local Hotel Coronado. Struggling to reconcile his loyalty to a fellow Marine (whom he had previously commanded in Haiti) with his public utterances against the outlawed demon rum, Butler decided to press charges against Williams for intoxication. A bitter court-martial ensued, and the trial was covered by the national press. Future Commandant Ben Fuller and James Carson Breckinridge were among the court's members, and future Commandant Clifton Cates served as Williams's assistant defense counsel. After contentious testimony about whether Williams was intoxicated or merely sick, the court-martial found him guilty. Williams was reduced by four numbers on the Marine Corps lineal list and transferred to the San Francisco recruiting district.

Ironically, the month after his conviction, the *Marine Corps Gazette* published an article written by Williams in which he concluded, "Everything in San Diego points to its probable development into the largest and most efficient Marine Base in the United States." Williams would not be around to see the base develop: at the end of September 1926 he drove his car off a San Francisco Embarcadero pier and drowned. A naval inquiry deemed his death an accident, and Feland served as an honorary pallbearer at Williams's interment in Arlington National Cemetery.[26]

Marine Corps publicity would take a better turn in late 1926 when Feland and Butler made the news again, this time in conjunction with a new postal crime wave. Postal thefts had been on the rise since 1923, exceeding $20 million in losses in more than eighty episodes in 1926. The final straw was the shooting of a mail truck driver and the theft of $150,000 in Elizabeth, New Jersey, in October 1926. Postmaster General Harry New asked Secretary of the Navy Curtis Wilbur for Marine Corps assistance in protecting the U.S. mail, and Wilbur ordered John Lejeune to provide armed guards for the postal service.[27] This time, 2,500 Marines would be dispersed throughout the country, which was divided into two zones of command under Brigadier Generals Feland and Butler.

Feland commanded the larger zone, the Eastern Mail Guard, comprising states located east of a line running along the borders of Montana, Wyoming, Colorado, and New Mexico. He oversaw detachments in sixteen major cities, including Boston, Atlanta, St. Paul, and Fort Worth. Never content to command from his desk, Feland spent the next couple of months visiting these cities and meeting with local postmasters, city officials, Marine Corps mail guard commanders, and Corps recruiters. In his travels, Feland reconnected with many well-known Marines, including aviator Alfred Austell Cunningham, who commanded the mail guard in New Orleans.

The newspapers had a heyday with the idea of the Marine Corps guarding the mail. Many articles gave details of Feland's distinguished military career, especially his expeditionary duties and his many World War I decorations. Most referred to Feland as a Kentuckian; some referred to him as a "Devil Dog." Called "Shoot-to-Kill" Feland in the *St. Louis Globe-Democrat*, Feland was quoted as saying that the Marines guarding the mail had been ordered to "shoot to keep from getting killed." Feland's photograph—both head-and-shoulder shots and some formally posed pictures—appeared in most of the major newspapers throughout the eastern mail zone. One often-reprinted photograph showed Feland and Postmaster General New in Washington inspecting a Marine Corps sergeant.[28]

This second Marine Corps campaign to guard the mail lasted until mid-February 1927, when, once again, the postal thefts ceased abruptly. The Marine Corps had gained positive publicity, and Feland had become a public figure beyond the Eastern Seaboard. People across the United States had now heard of the Kentucky Marine. They would soon learn more about him when his next assignment—on the distant shores of Nicaragua—made him not only a national but also an international figure.

The United States faced critical situations in China and Nicaragua at the beginning of 1927. Fighting had broken out between different factions in both countries, and the need to protect U.S. interests increased. President Calvin Coolidge decided to send Marines to both countries.

Commandant John Lejeune believed the two expeditions to China and Nicaragua would be beneficial for the Marine Corps, "not only as evidence of its usefulness, but as training for the officers and men."[29] Questions remained as to who would command the respective forces. General

Smedley Darlington Butler, John Lejeune, and Logan Feland confer. (Library of Congress)

Butler had already served in Nicaragua, three times leading his Panama battalion and dealing with disturbances there from 1909 to 1912. During his time in Nicaragua, Butler had created a fearsome reputation in the country, such that a decade later, Nicaraguan mothers still used the specter of Butler's appearance to quiet intransigent children: "Hush, Major Butler will get you!"[30]

Given his experience in the country and his status as the Corps's senior brigadier general, it would have made sense to send Butler to Nicaragua to command the brigade being formed out of two regiments, the Fifth and Eleventh Marines. Butler had not accompanied the Fourth Regiment when it embarked for China in mid-February 1927 because, initially, there were no plans to send a brigade there. As he noted in a personal letter to Butler, Lejeune believed that sending a brigadier general to China would "unduly magnify the importance of the movement of men and would be an indication that another regiment was to immediately follow the 4th. It was believed that this would have an undesirable effect on public opinion both at home and abroad."[31]

Nevertheless, Lejeune decided to send Feland to Nicaragua instead of Butler. In a letter to Butler, the Commandant noted that Feland had "made no application, either officially or unofficially, to go, in fact, did not come up to Headquarters while the Regiment was being organized. However, it is a wise thing to do from a Marine Corps standpoint. He is not much fonder of me than he is of you. It all dates back to Cole's appointment as Major General [in 1924] and to the incident at Mrs. Reath's in Philadelphia, and was probably accentuated when he was detached from Headquarters and ordered to Quantico."[32]

The incident Lejeune referred to was the culmination of tension that had been brewing for a while. Augusta Roberts Reath was the wife of prominent Philadelphia attorney Theodore Reath. Their son, Thomas Roberts Reath, had been one of the "Fighting Five" Philadelphians, a group of friends and University of Pennsylvania students who had joined the Marine Corps at the start of U.S. involvement in World War I. A Marine in Feland's Fifth Regiment, Reath died at Belleau Wood on June 12, 1918, and was buried in the American cemetery there. When Mrs. Reath visited the site in 1921, she brought back assurances that the American cemeteries in France were well tended and that it was easy to find the graves of the deceased. The Thomas Roberts Reath Marine Post 186, an American Legion post in Philadelphia comprising only Marines, had been formed soon after the war as a tribute to the young man. John Lejeune, Logan Feland, and Ralph Keyser had been guests at a post dinner in December 1920.[33]

In the early 1920s the Reaths were friends with the Felands, as well as with Lejeune and Butler. The incident occurred at a dinner the Reaths hosted in late 1924. Exactly what happened is unclear, but apparently, Feland undiplomatically suggested to the Reaths that they should "narrow their circle of friends," a comment aimed at Butler, who was also in attendance. Butler was contemplating wrapping up his stint as director of public safety in Philadelphia and returning to the Corps, where he would continue to be Feland's chief rival. Feland's actions during the dinner probably stemmed from his frustration at seeing Lejeune and Butler—neither of whom had served at Belleau Wood—linked with the Reaths in promoting remembrances of that battle. Although Lejeune, as Commandant, could be expected to participate in such events, Butler's involvement was suspect in Feland's eyes.[34]

Lejeune's reference to Feland's reaction to the Cole promotion was less mysterious and proved quite accurate. Soon after Cole's promotion to major general was announced in 1924, Feland had written to James Harbord about his "disappointment." Feland was convinced that Butler had influenced Lejeune to promote Cole over him:

> Until the time that Butler insisted that he [Butler] be appointed, General Lejeune was inclined to give me a fair and equal show, to have the matter settled on the records. But from the time that he learned that Butler was seriously an applicant, Lejeune switched over and pressed Cole's name on the Secretary [of the Navy] with all the arguments he could muster. This was because Lejeune knew that under the circumstances, it would be an outrageous thing to back Butler, but that Butler would be less resentful if Cole were named than he would be otherwise. I would not tell you this except that I have already said the same thing to General Lejeune.[35]

Harbord tried to ameliorate Feland's disappointment and sympathized with him, but he noted that Cole was a Naval Academy classmate of Lejeune's. He also pointed out that because Butler's father was still head of the House Naval Affairs Committee, Lejeune probably "felt that he could not afford for the Corps to start anything."[36]

Despite the dynamic tension between them, Lejeune chose Feland to lead the Marines in Nicaragua. On February 19, 1927, Brigadier General Logan Feland received orders to proceed to Norfolk, Virginia, on February 21 to board the USS *Henderson* for transport to Nicaragua. National newspapers carried the story the following day. The *Washington Post* reported that intervention in Nicaragua had taken place the night before and that Feland would command the Marine forces onshore there. Before shipping out, Feland took care of a few personal matters, such as storing Katherine's Steinway piano, as she would be living at her parents' home in Columbus, Ohio, while he was away. Likewise, he arranged for the storage of his duck decoys, boat, and other hunting equipment he would not be needing for a while.[37]

11

Nicaragua, 1927

The United States and the Marine Corps had been involved in Nicaragua since the mid-nineteenth century. In 1855 American soldier of fortune William Walker took a group of men to Nicaragua to support a Liberal Party revolt against the ruling Conservatives. A year later Walker turned coat and accepted the Conservatives' offer to lead the country as president. Fighting continued, so in December 1857 Marines landed in Nicaragua to restore peace, and they eventually captured Walker. In 1860 Walker returned to Central America, where he was subsequently executed in Honduras.

Marines again intervened in Nicaragua at times of perceived necessity. In 1894 Franklin Moses landed with Marines on the east coast to protect American property in Bluefields. The Marines interceded at least three more times before the end of the nineteenth century. Every time they left, the situation deteriorated. Conflict between Liberals and Conservatives continued into the twentieth century.

By 1909, Smedley Darlington Butler was commanding a Marine battalion stationed in Panama. Over the next three years, Butler's Marines sailed to Nicaragua three times, finally staying and fighting in 1912. Additional Marines under Colonel Joseph "Uncle Joe" Pendleton arrived to bolster the U.S. intervention. Fighting eventually died down, but for more than a decade, a small contingent of Marines remained stationed at the U.S. legation in Managua to ensure stability.

In late 1924 the Marines finally withdrew from the legation, but within a month, Liberals and Conservatives were fighting again. The Conservatives seized the government and installed Emiliano Chamorro as president in January 1926. The United States refused to recognize Chamorro's government. In May 1926 fleet Marines again went ashore at Bluefields to protect American lives and property. By the end of the year, the Liberals, under Alfredo Diaz, had regained control; Diaz was slated to be president until a national election could be held in 1928. After one American was killed and other lives and property were threatened, President Calvin Coolidge increased the U.S. military presence in Nicaragua by sending more Marines in early 1927.[1]

Diplomatic efforts to contain the Nicaraguan crisis continued. The Marine Corps's involvement faced strong opposition in Congress, particularly by Democratic senator Burton Wheeler and Republican senator William Borah, who claimed the United States was motivated by a desire to protect its commercial interests in oil and mahogany. Others, such as Secretary of State Frank Kellogg, feared that a "Bolshevik menace" from increasingly leftist Mexico might spread to Nicaragua. Finally, President Coolidge and Secretary Kellogg decided in 1927 to send a peace mission to Nicaragua. They chose former secretary of war and army artillery colonel Henry Stimson to broker an agreement to restore peace and stability.[2]

After being reviewed by Commandant John Lejeune, the Marine Corps Expeditionary Force, with Brigadier General Logan Feland as its commander, set sail on the *Henderson* on February 23, 1927. Major Marion Humphrey served as Feland's chief of staff, and First Lieutenant Arthur Challacombe was his aide-de-camp. Feland's old unit, the Fifth Regiment, comprised most of the 1,200 troops being sent to Nicaragua.

During the voyage, Feland's men watched the movie *Tell It to the Marines*, a silent epic starring Lon Chaney Sr. The Marine Corps had cooperated with the movie's producers during the making of the film, as part of the Corps's strong publicity efforts in the 1920s. The Marines on the *Henderson* thoroughly enjoyed the movie, and it contributed to their high morale.[3]

General Feland and his Marines landed at Corinto, on the west coast of Nicaragua, on March 7, 1927. He assumed command of all Marine Corps forces in the western part of the country—nearly 2,000 men. Feland would report to Rear Admiral Julian Latimer, commander of the U.S. Navy Special Services Squadron since May 1926. Latimer arrived in Corinto a week after the Marines and consulted with several people:

John Lejeune, Eli Kelly Cole, and Logan Feland inspect Marines at Quantico in 1927, just before their departure to Nicaragua. Smedley Butler is in the background, just behind Cole.

Feland, U.S. Minister Charles Eberhardt, and Nicaraguan government and rebel leaders. Feland and Latimer already knew each other: they had both served in 1923 on a committee established by Secretary of the Navy Edwin Denby.[4]

The navy had created the Special Services Squadron in September 1920 to patrol the waters of the Caribbean and the Pacific. Based in the Panama Canal Zone, the squadron's mission was to "promote friendly relations and to contribute to a growth of better understanding in all respects between the United States and other republics in the western hemisphere."[5] Communicating directly with State Department personnel throughout Central and South America, the squadron could act quickly as a mobile protection force when disturbances arose. In the Nicaraguan crisis, Latimer would oversee all navy personnel and Marines in the area.

As the Marine Corps units took up their positions, Liberal forces under the command of General José María Moncada attacked the forces of President Diaz in the central mountains of Nicaragua, threatening the capital of Managua. The Marines initially tried to remain nonaligned, flying only over the neutral zones designated by Latimer. At one point, Marine airplanes under the command of Major Ross "Rusty" Rowell received fire as they flew reconnaissance over Liberal lines.[6] Feland's Marines walked a delicate tightrope and managed to stay out of the battle between Conservatives and Liberals.

After arriving in Nicaragua, Feland initiated a series of confidential letters to Commandant Lejeune. These letters indicated that he was intent on proceeding carefully, but assertively, in Nicaragua. They also revealed his views on the Marine Corps in general. Despite some previous tension with Lejeune, Feland's correspondence was cordial and friendly. He kept Lejeune apprised of the situation by relaying his own experiences and assessments. For instance, on March 21 Feland wrote that he feared the incumbent government would ask the Marines to use force instead of relying on their mere presence to maintain stability, perhaps causing a "campaign" to begin. He did not believe the rebel Liberals would disarm, as demanded by the Conservative government; therefore, the Marines would "have to go out against them [the Liberals]." If so, they would need to act before the rainy season began, around mid-May. Feland made sure that Lejeune understood the practicalities of the situation, including how difficult it would be to move men and supplies into the north, where most of the fighting was taking place. The "automobile road" was inadequate and rough on trucks.[7]

Two weeks later Feland wrote another lengthy letter to Lejeune, detailing his efforts to move sufficient supplies north to carry the Marines through the approximately six-month-long rainy season. He stated that "all thoughtful people" believed the Marines would have to take a more active role eventually. He also addressed the reorganization of the national constabulary, the *Guardia Nacional*. He noted that Colonel James Meade, who would soon return Stateside from Nicaragua, was "interested in the 'mission' to instruct the Nicaraguan Guard." Feland knew that Lejeune wanted the Marines to provide the *Guardia* with guidance and training, but the Kentuckian did not believe the time was right to do so. Feland asserted that he and Admiral Latimer "were in agreement on this, as we are closely on every other matter."[8]

The *Guardia* issue would eventually become a problem for Brigadier

General Feland. Writing decades later, Dana Munro, the U.S. chargé d'affaires in Nicaragua during much of Feland's service there, explained why the United States wanted to train the Nicaraguan constabulary: "Establishment of non-partisan constabularies in the Caribbean states was one of the chief objectives of our policy from the time it became clear that the customs collectorships wouldn't assure stability by themselves." These constabularies were meant to replace corrupt, oppressive local military and police forces. Munro noted that creating disciplined forces, trained by Americans, would "do away with petty local oppression" and "would be an important step toward better financial administration and economic progress generally."[9]

Feland had previous experience with a similar organization in the Dominican Republic. There, the commander of the *Guardia Nacional Dominicana* had been a Marine Corps officer, James Carson Breckinridge, who reported to Feland. After Feland left Santo Domingo, control of the *Guardia* passed over to the Dominicans, prompting Breckinridge to request reassignment.[10] In Nicaragua, control of the *Guardia* would become a contentious issue, with Feland believing that the Marine Brigade commander should have full control, and others taking a different position.

Henry Stimson arrived in Corinto on April 17, 1927, and was greeted by Admiral Latimer and Minister Eberhardt. Accompanied by a Marine guard, Stimson and his wife then took a train to Managua to meet with various officials. At a meeting at the U.S. legation on April 22, Feland brought up the idea of reorganizing the *Guardia*. However, not all their time was spent discussing serious matters. In his diary entry for that day, Stimson noted that after maintaining a hectic pace, he managed to relax and "enjoy a dove shoot" with Feland.[11]

Stimson spent most of his time meeting with key Nicaraguans. On April 22 Stimson got President Diaz to agree to several concessions: that he would give up the presidency after the national election scheduled for November 1928; that the old *Guardia* constabulary would be dissolved and a new one created, under the control of Marine Corps officers; that there would be a general amnesty, and all Liberal and Conservative forces would turn their arms over to the Marines; and that the Marines would remain in the country until after the national election. Having received these concessions from the Conservatives and developed a basic plan, Stimson, Eberhardt, and Latimer met with Liberal general Moncada at Tipitapa on May 4, but they could not conclude a peace settlement. Moncada insisted that Diaz leave office immediately, and Stimson would not agree. Instead, as an act of good faith, Diaz announced a general amnesty and appointed some of Moncada's followers to government positions. Given these concessions, Moncada and most of the other Liberal generals agreed to the terms worked out by Stimson, resulting in the Treaty of Tipitapa. At this point, the State Department, the U.S. Navy, and the Marines Corps thought that progress was finally being made. In an after-visit report, Stimson noted that Latimer and Feland believed that "pacification of the country would be more rapid than we had anticipated and would probably be accomplished without any serious disturbances."[12]

During this period of diplomatic negotiations, Feland continued to keep Commandant Lejeune apprised through a series of confidential and quite lengthy letters. Feland found Stimson to be "a very agreeable man" but noted that he would probably report his conclusions directly to President Coolidge, without apprising the folks in Nicaragua. Feland believed it was simply a matter of time before the *Guardia Nacional* would be organized, and he encouraged Lejeune to ensure that the State Department did not change its mind about the Marines leading the *Guardia*.

On another matter, Feland agreed with Lejeune's previously expressed sentiment that Marine Corps officers should conduct themselves in such a way that they maintain the "high esteem in which we are held by the people at home." Feland noted a sort of "slackness" among officers, who would do anything "they could get away with, without regard to its general effect on the morale of the Corps." He agreed with Lejeune that this attitude was reflected in the "failure of courts martial to dismiss officers when the offense proven clearly justifies it." The Kentuckian wrote that he was trying to initiate in Nicaragua a "general tightening up, without being too nagging or inquisitorial." Feland assured Lejeune that the Commandant could count on him to do "everything I can to restore the before-the-war spirit of the Marine Corps." He observed that the Marine Corps expeditions to China and Nicaragua were good opportunities to teach young officers to think of something "besides their own comfort and personal ease." Overall, Feland concluded that his young officers were "conducting themselves extremely well" and that morale was high.[13]

Feland also raised the possibility of the appointment of a high commissioner to rule Nicaragua, similar to the situation in Haiti. A Marine Corps officer, Brigadier General John Russell, had served since 1922 as the chief official in Haiti, running both military and civil affairs. Feland noted that the appointment of a high commissioner in Nicaragua would "lead not only to peace, but to prosperity and progress of the country. Peace is not quite enough." He believed that putting everything under the control of a high commissioner would "cut out poor government, graft, and the resulting lack of progress." Feland offered to take the position, if Lejeune "wanted it for the Marine Corps," but coyly tergiversated, adding: "if it were offered me tonight I would want to think a long time before taking it." He believed that the position of high commissioner in Nicaragua "would have to be on as good a status as Russell's place in Haiti, and ought to be better, considering the importance of the work to be done, as it will affect our future relations in other countries in Central America."[14] Feland continued to have high aspirations, and the idea of him serving in this special capacity in Nicaragua continued to be bandied about.

One of the key tasks for General Feland was disarming the fighting factions. To this end, he appointed a three-man "arms commission": Captain Julian Brown headed the group, assisted by First Lieutenant Arthur Challacombe and Second Lieutenant Robert Hogaboom. The commission oversaw the collection of all serviceable weapons, paying ten dollars for each weapon surrendered.[15]

When Stimson and his wife returned to the United States in mid-May 1927, he believed that the Treaty of Tipitapa provided a plan for peace and stability in Nicaragua. Stimson wrote to Secretary of the Navy Curtis Wilbur, praising the naval forces on land and sea and the help they had provided during his mission. After lauding Rear Admiral Latimer, Stimson noted that he had "formed a high opinion of Brigadier General Feland of the Marine Corps." Feland's "plans and dispositions were made with judgment and success. The vital question of whether we should succeed in compelling the insurgent army to disarm without provoking a clash with the American forces depended in large measure upon the tact and skill with which the latter were handled. In these delicate operations General Feland was quiet, prompt, and effective, and his general judgment and appraisal of the entire situation seemed to me adequate and sound."[16]

In a separate assessment of General Feland, Katherine MacVeagh, the wife of U.S. diplomat John MacVeagh, wrote to Mrs. Stimson that the general had been "cross" when he learned that some rifles had been stolen from the government armory. But otherwise she praised his performance:

> General Feland has done wonders since you [the Stimsons] took the Admiral down to Corinto with you, the officers all say when the Admiral is here they don't know whether they are on their head or their heels as Admiral and General give different orders at the same time, which accounted for the mix-up the day the first Liberals came in. But left alone the General has made a splendid job of it, patrolled all the streets with Marines, put Marines in the police stations, got thirty or forty of Moncada's men that local authorities had jailed out of jail and sent them on their way.[17]

The U.S. minister to Nicaragua, Charles Eberhardt, also lauded Latimer and Feland in carrying out the disarmament, writing to Secretary of State Frank Kellogg: "Admiral Latimer, General Feland and the American forces in Nicaragua deserve highest praise for having effected a wonderful disarmament with minimum of friction or bloodshed." Eberhardt noted that more than 11,000 weapons had been turned in and that "General Sandino is the only remaining revolutionary leader of consequence who has refused to lay down his arms."[18]

Feland and Stimson stayed in contact. In June, Stimson forwarded a letter to Feland from someone inquiring about a position in the Nicaraguan constabulary. Stimson wrote that he hoped all was well with Feland and asked the general to send him a line "now and then" to keep him apprised of events in Nicaragua. Stimson noted that with the exception of Katherine MacVeagh's letter to his wife, he had heard nothing of affairs in Managua. In closing, Stimson wrote that he was sending Feland "Winston Churchill's two volumes on the World Crisis." In reply, Feland thanked Stimson for the gift and expressed his hope that the two of them might get to do some winter hunting on the Potomac, given that Feland expected "to get out of this [Nicaragua] soon." He also promised to pass along the letter regarding the *Guardia* position to its new commander, Lieutenant Colonel Elias R. Beadle, whom Feland described as "one of the best men I know and I expect he will achieve a great deal of success."[19]

After the successful Treaty of Tipitapa (often called the Stimson agreement), additional Marines from the Eleventh Regiment landed in mid-May to augment Feland's forces. Although the Marines collected many weapons during the disarmament, the pacification effort was not going to be as easy as everyone believed. For instance, in the town of La Paz Centro, Marines under Captain Richard Bell Buchanan were attacked by a band of Liberal fighters. In the effort to repulse the Nicaraguans, Captain Buchanan and Private Marvin Jackson died in a hail of bullets. They were both posthumously awarded the Navy Cross.[20]

Although the Marines suspected that the Liberal band that killed Buchanan and Jackson belonged to rebel leader Francisco Sequeira—better known as "General Cabulla"—Feland apparently did not order any reprisal. Instead, he had the Marines prepare for increasing street violence that he feared would spread from Leon to Managua. Feland also met with General Moncada and Cabulla's secretary to arrange for their groups' disarmament. Within a week, however, Captain William Richards shot Cabulla when the Nicaraguan pulled a gun on him.[21]

Although U.S. officials believed they had brokered a peaceful solution, one Liberal general disagreed with the terms of the Treaty of Tipitapa: Augusto Sandino. Disavowing the peace settlement, Sandino and his forces kept their arms, resisted the Conservative Diaz government, and opposed the presence of the perceived imperialist U.S. Marine Corps. In mid-May Sandino wrote to General Feland, suggesting that Nicaragua be put in the hands of an American governor until a free election could be held. This had not been agreed to in the treaty, and Feland "ordered the Fifth Marine Regiment into northern Nicaragua, to disarm Sandino or force him across the border into Honduras." The Kentuckian sent Colonel Louis Gulick north to oversee the operation, instructing Gulick to disarm Sandino by force, if necessary. However, Feland told Commandant Lejeune that he did not think a recourse to force would be necessary.[22] He would be wrong.

As part of the Tipitapa agreement, President Diaz had appointed Liberal politician Arnaldo Ramirez Abaunza as governor of the northwestern department of Nueva Segovia. General Feland sent Major Harold Pierce and fifty Marines to escort Ramirez to the capital of Ocotal to take his post. Pierce had orders to disarm the rebels but to avoid combat if possible. The Marines traveled by truck to Matagalpa, where they purchased mules and other supplies necessary to continue the trip. On the

Augusto Sandino. Leader of the opposition to Marine Corps intervention in Nicaragua, Sandino was considered either a bandit or a patriot, depending on one's point of view.

way to Ocotal, Major Pierce heard rumors that Sandino and his forces were in the vicinity, near Quilali. After arriving in Ocotal on June 9, the Marines collected weapons from both Conservatives and Liberals. Then Pierce informed brigade headquarters that he had received word that Sandino was keeping two foreigners hostage in Telpaneca, about thirty miles away. Pierce was ordered to proceed to Telpaneca, and he did so, leaving ten Marines under the command of Captain Gilbert Hatfield in Ocotal. Once he got to Telpaneca, Pierce learned that the information about the hostages was wrong, but Sandino had been there. Eventually, Pierce made his way back to Managua, but the stage was set for a battle at Ocotal.[23]

At the beginning of June, Feland explained his philosophy on establishing order in Nicaragua in a letter to Lejeune. Feland's policy had been to send garrisons to the larger cities and then "radiate out, through the country, our influence." The general "very rigidly restricted patrolling," sending men only to areas where reliable information indicated the existence of problems; there was no "indiscriminate patrolling." Feland had balked at Stimson's idea to send U.S. Army cavalry out into the country, and Admiral Latimer had agreed with the Marine Corps commander. As an alternative, Stimson had suggested sending Marines out on horseback, but again Feland demurred, believing that such action would incur "formidable resistance" by "unwarranted charging about the country and shooting people on suspicion."[24] Feland was proceeding firmly but carefully, using Marines only as necessary in important places. He understood that the Marines were not universally liked or appreciated by the Nicaraguans.

By the end of June, the defiant Augusto Sandino had turned up again. Feland received word that the San Albino mine, owned by American Charles Butters, had been seized by Sandino forces. Butters appealed to Feland and to the U.S. legation for help. Subsequently, Feland notified Admiral Latimer that he was planning to send another force northward to occupy towns controlled by Sandino and take back the mine. Latimer ordered Feland to "inaugurate operations as soon as possible to disarm Sandino and his band," but he warned the general to be sure he could trust the *Guardia Nacional*, which Feland wanted to lead the campaign, with advice and guidance from the Marines.[25]

In accordance with the Treaty of Tipitapa, recruiting for the reconstituted *Guardia Nacional*, under the command of Colonel Robert Rhea, USMC, had begun at the end of May. The reconstitution of the *Guardia* was a primary concern for Feland because he wanted its cooperation. The citizens of the country might see the Nicaraguans in the *Guardia* as less threatening than the Americans; they would certainly not see them as foreign invaders. With his characteristic optimism, and perhaps forgetting (or at least glossing over) earlier attempts to remake the constabulary in the Dominican Republic, Feland informed Lejeune that he thought it would not take "more than a few months to get a few men in such condition that they will be of great assistance to the Brigade in maintaining order throughout the Republic."[26] Feland was hoping to send a *Guardia* group to the key northern city of Ocotal in July.

Because of Colonel Rhea's ongoing illness, Feland mentioned five other Marine Corps colonels who would be good candidates to replace Rhea, if necessary: Robert Dunlap, Richard Cutts, Douglas McDougal, Hamilton Disston South, and Elias Beadle. All were contemporaries of Feland's and seasoned campaigners. After World War I, Dunlap had served in China and was commander of the Marine Corps Schools at Quantico. Cutts had commanded the national police in Santo Domingo after Feland left and then served in Haiti. McDougal had served as chief of the *Gendarmerie d'Haiti,* a constabulary force. South had served as aide to High Commissioner John Russell in Haiti and had commanded a *Gendarmerie d'Haiti* detachment. Beadle had served in Haiti earlier in the decade and was currently the chief of staff at the Marine Corps base at Parris Island.[27]

In June, *Guardia* command passed to Colonel Elias Beadle, who was given a Nicaraguan rank of brigadier general and appointed chief director of the *Guardia Nacional de Nicaragua.* Feland approved, writing to Lejeune that he was "delighted that you are sending Colonel Beadle to take command of the Guardia. There is no more important work to be done for this country than the upbuilding of a thoroughly good Constabulary, and it seems to me that Beadle is exactly the right man to do it."[28]

Although he was a Marine Corps officer, Beadle was supposed to report directly to the Nicaraguan president. Feland was unhappy with this plan, however. He had assumed that, similar to the Dominican Republic experience, the *Guardia* commander would report to the brigade commander. Whereas Feland saw the *Guardia* as an adjunct to the Marine Corps mission in Nicaragua, others saw it as an arm of the Nicaraguan government. This would lead to a dispute over control of the *Guardia.*

In the meantime, on July 8 Rear Admiral Latimer relinquished command of the Special Services Squadron to Rear Admiral David Foote Sellers, a former battleship commander and aide to Secretary Denby. In a letter to Commandant Lejeune, Latimer praised General Feland and outlined his mission: to protect American lives and property; maintain open lines of communication between cities; preserve order in the cities and along the railways; disarm the forces of the contending factions "peacefully if possible, but forcefully if necessary"; and maintain and establish order. Latimer believed Feland had "performed these important, difficult and delicate duties most successfully. He displayed at all times excellent judgment, great tact and high ability. Due to his splendid handling of the situation about 14,000 men of both sides were disarmed and despatched to their homes, and good order was restored throughout the country with practically no bloodshed in an incredibly short time." Latimer concluded by recommending that Feland receive the Distinguished Service Medal (DSM). Feland subsequently received a DSM Star to be worn with the DSM he had received on November 11, 1920, for his service in the Dominican Republic.[29]

In mid-May, Feland had expressed the hope that because disarmament was proceeding so well, within three months the Marine presence in western Nicaragua could be reduced to a couple of battalions. In June, he had predicted that by mid-August the force could be cut in half—down to 1,200 men, if not lower. By mid-July, Feland still remained extremely optimistic that "the outlaw movement is on its last legs." He recognized that Sandino was still on many people's minds but argued that they "cannot understand the difficulties in eliminating him."[30]

By the end of June, three *Guardia* companies had been formed. On July 1 the First *Guardia* Company, under First Lieutenant Grover Darnell, left for Ocotal, the capital of Nueva Segovia, and arrived on July 11.[31] Meanwhile, Feland had created the Nueva Segovia expedition, a force of 75 Marines and 150 *Guardia* members under the command of Major Oliver Floyd. Feland had picked Floyd, the Second Brigade's former executive officer, because he "was more familiar with the policy to be pursued and was more imbued with the idea of avoiding combat as far as possible, of depriving Sandino of his territory by pressure of occupying the towns successively which were controlled by Sandino, in short, Major Floyd was thoroughly and entirely in accord with the policy of arriving at a peaceable disarmament of the Sandino forces, if in any way possible, and was selected for that reason."[32] Feland believed that he and Floyd understood the Marine Corps's goals.

Floyd gathered his Marines and his *Guardia* contingent, under the command of Major Victor Bleasdale, at Matagalpa. Normally, Marines serving in the *Guardia* received an increase in rank; thus, Major Bleasdale was actually Captain Bleasdale, USMC. He served as executive officer of the expedition. On July 15 the Floyd expedition left Matagalpa bound for Telpaneca, a key town in Sandino territory. But before they could get into position, Sandino struck at Ocotal on July 16.[33]

In command at Ocotal, Major Gilbert Hatfield had exchanged notes with Sandino, suggesting that the rebel leader and his followers lay down their arms. Sandino refused. Instead, at around 1:00 a.m. on July 16, Sandino and his men attacked. Although Hatfield's forces were outnumbered approximately five to one, they had good defensive positions within the town and managed to hold on throughout the night. In the morning, Sandino called for Hatfield to surrender, but he refused to do so.[34]

At approximately 10:00 a.m., two planes on a scouting patrol observed the fighting in Ocotal and returned to Managua to report to Major Ross "Rusty" Rowell, commander of the air squadron. Rowell relayed the news to General Feland, who had not been informed because telegraph lines from Ocotal had been cut. Feland believed the Marines in Ocotal, who had limited water and ammunition, were in a hopeless situation and faced certain destruction. Convinced that the aviation unit represented the Ocotal garrison's only possible salvation, Feland gave Rowell "a very general directive . . . to take such steps as would be most effective in succoring the besieged Marines." In contrast with previous orders, which had demanded restraint when flying missions, Feland now gave Rowell carte blanche to launch a bombing attack. Consequently, Rowell led a five-plane squadron to Ocotal to bomb the Sandino forces. Rowell's squadron flew over Ocotal in midafternoon and carried out repeated air attacks, using dive-bombing tactics developed by Marine Corps aviator Lawson Sanderson but never before used in war. Feland's order resulted in what was apparently the first instance of Marine Corps close air bombing support in defense of Corps ground units.[35]

Rowell's aerial bombardment broke the back of the Sandino attack. The Marines suffered one man killed and one wounded; three *Guardia* members were wounded. Sandino's forces experienced considerably more casualties because they had been caught out in the open by Rowell's planes. In a handwritten letter to Major Hatfield the day after the battle, General Feland expressed regret for the loss of Private Obleski

Ross "Rusty" Rowell. Rowell led the Marine Corps aviators whose bombing broke the back of the Sandino attack on Ocotal, Nicaragua, in July 1927.

but praised Hatfield's "skill and watchfulness," as well as the "gallantry and devotion of all your officers and men, both of the Marines and the Guardia." Feland thanked Hatfield and his men for their "valor and steadfastness."[36]

President Diaz sent a congratulatory letter to General Feland; he too praised Hatfield and his men and eventually awarded them Nicaraguan medals. Feland passed along Diaz's praise to the entire brigade, reproducing the president's letter in a brigade memorandum, and he also sent a copy to Commandant Lejeune. For their actions at Ocotal, Major Hatfield received the Navy Cross, and Rowell received the Marine Corps's first Distinguished Flying Cross awarded to a pilot for action against an armed enemy.[37]

Stateside, not everyone cheered the victory at Ocotal. Former Illinois governor and Chicago mayor Edward F. Dunne wrote to President Coolidge and decried U.S. intervention in Nicaragua as a "most shocking exhibition of national impertinence and national indecency"; he "declared that instead of a medal for bravery being awarded to Major Rowell of the Marine Corps, the Government should 'degrade and punish' General Feland."[38] Minister Eberhardt defended Feland against the bad publicity. In his report on the battle to Secretary of State Kellogg, Eberhardt noted, "It should be remembered that for weeks, General Feland had given Sandino every opportunity to surrender or leave the country and had brought upon himself much blame for not having dealt with the bandit more severely. Furthermore, Feland had ordered his men to make no advances against Sandino and to only fire on the enemy if they should be attacked."[39]

After the Battle of Ocotal, Major Floyd continued the Nueva Segovia expedition. His troops stopped briefly at Ocotal before moving farther into Sandino country. After a skirmish with Sandino forces at San Fernando, the expedition pushed on to the San Albino mine, which it secured by the end of July. By mid-August, the Nueva Segovia expedition had ended. Floyd and Bleasdale received the Navy Cross for their efforts.

Soon after the Battle of Ocotal, Feland's new commander, Rear Admiral Sellers, traveled to Nicaragua from his command post in the Canal Zone to meet with Feland, Minister Eberhardt, and President Diaz. After this visit, Sellers assured the chief of naval operations, Admiral Eberle, that Nicaragua was "returning to normalcy, crops flourishing, business is being resumed."[40]

On August 9 Feland announced a policy that would encourage the stationing of more *Guardia Nacional* troops in the Nueva Segovia region. The role of Marine Corps officers there would be to assist the *Guardia* by sending out patrols to deny resources to the Sandino forces. The Marines would continue to avoid combat whenever possible. The Americans were in a tenuous position in the country, and Feland recognized it.[41]

In mid-August the *Washington Post* reported that General Feland had offered amnesty to all Sandino followers who would put down their arms. The *Post* also noted Feland's opinion that "conditions in Nicaragua are rapidly approaching normal." A day later the *Post* reported that Feland would be returning home, first to Quantico and then to his next position: commander of the Marine Barracks at Parris Island, South Carolina. Brigadier General Harry Lee had been at Parris Island for three years, and Commandant Lejeune wanted to make a change.[42]

On the eve of Feland's departure from Nicaragua, President Diaz threw him a party attended by more than 200 people, including Eberhardt and other members of the diplomatic corps. In his parting words, Feland asserted that the *Guardia Nacional* would take over the policing of the country as soon as possible. The general continued to have an optimistic view of Nicaragua's future, as did others in attendance.[43] Sandino and his forces had kept a low profile since their defeat at Ocotal. Marine records reveal only a couple of engagements in August. By mid-August, an intelligence report by Lieutenant Julian Frisbie, the acting B-2 intelligence officer, asserted that the "occupied zone" was quiet, the economic situation was improving, and there had been "no trouble between troops and civilians." Police were being replaced by the *Guardia*, "who were doing their work efficiently and well." Frisbie concluded: "Sandino's whereabouts [are] absolutely unknown, no doubt Sandino is endeavoring to flee to Mexico where he hopes to be received by his friends, and thru their aid spread malicious propaganda concerning the activities of the Marines in Nicaragua."[44]

On August 25, 1927, Brigadier General Logan Feland transferred command of Marine Corps forces in Nicaragua to Colonel Louis Gulick and boarded the USS *Argonne* for the journey back to the United States. The new commander of the *Guardia Nacional*, Elias Beadle, wrote to Commandant Lejeune that he was sorry to see Feland leave. The Kentuckian had "understood my problems," Beadle wrote, "and it was very encouraging to be able to consult freely with him [in] all matters as they arose."[45]

The U.S. Navy, the State Department, Marine Corps intelligence, Beadle, and Feland all believed that the situation in Nicaragua was under control and improving. That assessment would change rapidly, however, as the monsoon season ended and Sandino regrouped, necessitating another increase in Marine Corps forces in Nicaragua. Brigadier General Feland would not have long to enjoy his new post at Parris Island.

12

Back to Nicaragua, 1928

While Logan and Katherine Feland were moving to the general's new command at Parris Island, the Marine Corps was still dealing with two difficult situations in China and Nicaragua. Throughout the summer of 1927 the Corps had been withdrawing troops from Nicaragua to sustain an increasing buildup in China. As the Chinese Communists and Nationalists continued to fight, the Marine Corps established a garrison in Shanghai, home to many thousands of foreigners. Another detachment went to Tientsin, commanded by Smedley Darlington Butler.

Back in Nicaragua, Colonel Louis Gulick took over the hunt for Augusto Sandino, who, despite the defeat at Ocotal, simply would not go away. The consensus about the decline of Sandino's forces proved overly optimistic. Learning from his experience at Ocotal, Sandino changed tactics, switching to guerrilla warfare against the Marines and the *Guardia Nacional.* Soon after Ocotal, the ever-defiant Sandino issued a proclamation underscoring his continued resistance to the Treaty of Tipitapa and to the U.S. occupation of Nicaragua.

Debate raged both in the United States and abroad about whether Sandino was a bandit or a freedom fighter. The U.S. State Department, Nicaraguan Liberal leader General Moncada, and Brigadier General Logan Feland regarded Sandino as nothing more than a bandit. Nevertheless, Sandino's increasingly strong guerrilla movement after Ocotal belied that analysis. The Battle of Ocotal increased Sandino's stature in the eyes of many throughout Central and Latin America, who saw his resistance as a worthwhile fight against U.S. imperialism.[1]

In the last quarter of 1927, Sandino and the Marines engaged in several skirmishes. One particularly notable incident occurred when Sandino forces shot down a Marine Corps plane. The pilot and observer, Lieutenant Earl Thomas and Sergeant Frank Dowdell, managed to elude Sandino forces for a while, but they were eventually either killed outright or captured, tried, and hung. A photograph purported to be Lieutenant Thomas hanging from a tree appeared in Mexican and Honduran newspapers, inflaming the Marines. A large-scale recovery effort failed to find the men's bodies and ran into fierce resistance from Sandino forces. The Marines continued to send patrols and flights to El Chipote, Sandino's mountain retreat, but to no avail.[2]

Also in the last quarter of 1927, plans began to jell for a U.S. representative to oversee the Nicaraguan national election in November 1928. Henry Stimson had been sent to the Philippines as governor-general and was not available to return to Nicaragua. In June 1927 President Coolidge announced that Brigadier General Frank McCoy of the U.S. Army would be his personal representative to Nicaragua and oversee an electoral commission there. McCoy had a distinguished military and diplomatic career; he was a veteran of the Philippines insurrection and World War I and had served on the 1920 U.S. military mission to Armenia under the command of James Harbord. McCoy arrived in Managua in late August, along with the new chargé d'affaires of the U.S. legation, Dana G. Munro. The army general evaluated the political and military situation and started planning for a peaceful election. He concluded in a report to Secretary of State Frank Kellogg that the Marines should not be reduced in number and that more should be done to finance and provide officers for the *Guardia Nacional.* At the beginning of October 1927, McCoy returned to the United States and started choosing a team to go to Nicaragua to oversee the national election scheduled for the following year. He and the mission's chief technical adviser, political scientist Harold Dodds, drew up a law that would govern the Nicaraguan national election.[3] McCoy would soon return to Nicaragua, as would Feland.

The Felands had little time to settle at Parris Island before the word came that, given the continued resistance by Sandino, more Marines would be sent to Nicaragua. The *New York Times* reported on January 4, 1928, that, after consultation with President Coolidge, Secretary of the Navy Curtis Wilbur had decided that Feland would return to Nicaragua. His force would be bolstered by another 1,000 men, bringing the total number of Marines in the country to approximately 2,500. The intent was to put more Marines at the front to chase Sandino. In effect, the Eleventh Regiment would be sent back to Nicaragua, this time under the command of Feland's longtime colleague Colonel Robert "Hal" Dunlap. In addition, Commandant John Lejeune would visit Nicaragua on his way to the West Coast by naval ship. Concurrently, anticipating that Sandino and his followers might be driven northward across the border into Honduras, the State Department asked its minister in Honduras, Charles Summerlin, to work with the Honduran government to prevent such crossings or to intern any Sandino followers who escaped into Honduras.[4]

As General Feland prepared to return to command the Second Brigade in Managua, the Marines continued their search for Sandino, encountering fierce resistance at times. In mid-December Colonel Gulick sent out two patrols to converge on Sandino's hideout at El Chipote. On December 30 Sandino forces ambushed one of the columns, killing five Marines and wounding twenty-three. Then on January 1, 1928, Sandino forces ambushed the other column, killing and wounding more Marines. The Americans gathered their wounded at the town of Quilali, where Marine Corps aviator First Lieutenant Christian Schilt landed his plane ten times in three days to carry off the wounded. For this feat, Schilt later received the Medal of Honor. After the Marines withdrew from Quilali, they focused on air patrols to bomb El Chipote. By the end of January it appeared that the Marines had succeeded: Sandino and his forces had abandoned El Chipote.[5] But where had they gone?

Brigadier General Logan Feland arrived in Corinto on January 15, 1928, along with the Marine Corps reinforcements and Commandant Lejeune. While Lejeune stayed in Corinto, Feland traveled to Managua to resume command at Second Brigade headquarters, and Dunlap's Eleventh Regiment moved north to a base of operations in Ocotal. Feland immediately addressed the confused military situation by creating three districts in Nicaragua: Eastern, Northern, and Southern. The Eastern District would be headquartered at the northeastern port of Puerto Cabezas under the command of Major Harold Utley. Dunlap at Ocotal would head the Northern District, and Colonel Rush R. Wallace at Managua would head the Southern District.[6]

With the two other districts quieter, the preponderance of Marines went to the Northern District, so Dunlap could expand the search for

Sandino. Unfortunately, as events at El Chipote had revealed, finding the guerrilla leader was like finding a needle in a haystack. There was a large area to cover and far too few men to garrison all the towns and still send out patrols to look for Sandino.

Soon after Feland and Lejeune arrived, Rear Admiral David Sellers also sailed to Nicaragua. As commander of the Special Services Squadron, he would again oversee Feland. Sellers consulted with Feland, Lejeune, Munro, and Nicaraguan authorities and, as a result of those discussions, agreed to send a letter to Sandino, asking him to discontinue his armed resistance. Once again the United States took the high moral position and tried to obtain a peaceful settlement.[7]

Brigadier General McCoy returned to Nicaragua at the end of January. The U.S. minister to Nicaragua, Charles Eberhardt, also returned after a leave of several months. Thus, the four main U.S. officials had arrived: Feland, McCoy, Sellers, and Eberhardt. Feland and Sellers led the military involvement, along with *Guardia Nacional* commander Elias Beadle, while McCoy and Eberhardt led diplomatic efforts. The relationships among the men would change as they settled in for what some thought would be a tumultuous year, depending on whether they could defeat Sandino and pull off a successful election in November.

Despite the complex diplomatic and political situation, Commandant Lejeune left Nicaragua at the end of January confident the Second Brigade could accomplish its mission. He especially commended the efforts of the aviation service. He was aware of the difficulties involved in keeping the peace and maintaining order in the country. Writing in the Marine Corps's *Leatherneck* magazine shortly after his return to the United States, Lejeune reported that Nicaragua remained peaceful with the exception of the northern province of Nueva Segovia, where Sandino's forces operated. Lejeune acknowledged that this was a scarcely populated, "wild, mountainous country" with no roads and trails that became impassable during the rainy season.[8]

Feland recognized the difficulties of fighting a guerrilla war in such a remote area. Therefore, in late February 1928 he sent a directive advising his area commanders how to conduct a campaign. First, he noted that small, platoon-sized groups marching in daylight would prove ineffective. "Against outlaws familiar with the country and in territory infested with their spies and sympathizers, daylight movements will lack the *essen-*

The "Big Four" in Nicaragua—U.S. Minister Charles Eberhardt, Brigadier General Frank McCoy, Rear Admiral David Foote Sellers, and Brigadier General Logan Feland.

tial elements, surprise and *secrecy.*" Feland touted superior intelligence and training as the key to success. Though recognizing that some detachments had to remain in place to guard the citizenry, Feland believed that the bulk of Marines should be used for reconnaissance and patrolling. "Patrols should travel light, live off the country as far as possible, have definite orders as to territory to be covered, places to go, and time and place to return. Private property must be respected and patrols should be furnished cash with which to obtain supplies." Patrols should move only at night and over familiar trails, with an emphasis on ambushing outlaws.[9]

General Feland reorganized his Second Brigade staff to meet the guerrilla challenge, focusing on intelligence, operations, and supply. He established several B-2 intelligence offices to compile data ranging from communications to mapping. The B-3 operations and training section oversaw the establishment of more landing fields for aviation. The B-4 supply section focused on placing more supplies directly in the Northern District commanded by Colonel Dunlap. Although Feland was leading the military effort, he recognized that other issues affected the Marines' ability to succeed in guerrilla warfare. Therefore, he wanted weekly reports not only on military matters but also on the economic and social situation. In sum, Feland took steps to carry out an aggressive campaign against Sandino. After receiving copies of the brigade staff reports, Admiral Sellers wrote to Feland, "[Your] conduct of the military operations and your plans for the continuance thereof, meet with my full approval."[10]

Feland and Sellers met in mid-February 1928 when the admiral visited Nicaragua. From this trip, Sellers gained a better understanding of the difficulties Feland faced. He ascertained that Feland "constantly receives all kinds of conflicting reports as to the whereabouts and activities of Sandino." Sellers blamed this confusion not on the general and his men but on Nicaraguan authorities, who were "not co-operating with the Marines as they should." Sellers realized the difficulties of "conducting guerrilla warfare in a wild country" and noted the problems related to transportation, the rapid movement of troops, and inadequate maps. Despite these challenges, Sellers approved Feland's plans and remained optimistic that the Marines would be successful.[11]

While Sellers was visiting Managua, radical journalist Carleton Beals delivered to him Sandino's reply to the admiral's letter requesting the rebel leader's surrender. The only American journalist to meet with Sandino, Beals wrote several articles for *The Nation* about his trip to Nicaragua. The first article appeared on February 22, 1928; successive articles appeared over the next eight weeks. These articles generally portrayed Sandino in a favorable light, and one article in particular described purported "Marine atrocities" against the Nicaraguan people. Sandino refused to give up. He called for the "withdrawal of invading forces," for the replacement of President Diaz with someone who would not be a candidate in the national election, and for Latin Americans, not Marines, to supervise that election.[12]

While in Managua, Beals met with both General McCoy and General Feland. In his book *Banana Gold*, published in 1932, Beals wrote of his contentious meeting with the Marine Corps general: "General Feland, a powerful man with bushy eyebrows, took the cake for apathy.

His drawling voice, his apparent lack of interest in everything, his completely bored air with his present job, the way he sat on the end of his spine in most unmilitary fashion—all betokened a supreme indifference to existence which placed him at once in quite a remote realm. I really wondered why he wanted to see me. To all my inquiries he droned: 'You can get that information from Major Glass.'"

Beals asked, "And how will all this terminate?"

In reply, Feland drawled, "Oh, the bird will fall sometime . . . they all do sooner or later." Feland then asked Beals, "What do you think of Sandino?"

The journalist replied, "He is not a bandit, call him a fool, a fanatic, an idealist, a patriot—according to your point of view; but certainly he is not a bandit."

Drawled the general, "Of course, in the army, we use the word 'bandit' in a technical sense, meaning the member of a band."

Beals cleverly asked, "Then [John Philip] Sousa is also a bandit?" Feland "did not deign to smile." Beals followed up: "In the publicity which you give out to the United States of course, you explain to the dear public that you use the word 'bandit' in its technical sense; you have no ulterior motive in your reports?"

"Guess you've got us on the hip there," Feland replied in the same indifferent tone.

Beals asked, "Can you give me details of the supply convoys Sandino has captured, or should I get that information from Major Glass?"

"For the one and only time Feland threw off his apathy. He jerked upright. 'That's a lie,' he cried. 'We haven't lost a single convoy, not one.'"

Beals pressed: "How did Sandino get hold of American supplies, then—uniforms, guns, foodstuffs?"

"'We lost no convoys,' repeated Feland, and subsided to the end of his spine."

When Beals left, "the General pulled himself painfully from his lounging position. 'Come and see me again, any time while you are here,' he said with a show of cordiality, 'and I will tell Major Glass to give you all the information that it is possible to give out.'" Beals was "convinced that the only reason Feland wished to see me was to try to pin the Logan act on me." (The Logan Act prohibited Americans from acting as unauthorized private citizens in negotiations with foreign governments.)[13]

Logan Feland and Second Brigade officers consult at Jinotega.

Beals may have left with the impression that Feland was unconcerned about Sandino, but Feland was very concerned. The Kentuckian's laconic style was simply part of his character; he did not excite easily. The general believed he was implementing sound policies for fighting a guerrilla war.

Feland was not content to sit around at brigade headquarters. To get a better idea of how Marines were operating in the field against Sandino, he flew up to Dunlap's headquarters in Ocotal at the end of February. *New York Times* staff correspondent Harold Denny reported that after visiting with Nicaraguans in the area, Feland concluded that they "laugh at his [Sandino's] pretense for trying to do something for Nicaragua." According to Feland, the Nicaraguans referred to Sandino as a bandit, "a plain, ordinary robber." Denny noted that Feland believed the locals were "more favorable to this pacification than they had been before." Feland repeated this optimistic view in his report to Admiral Sellers, noting that he was "especially glad to find that it is getting easier for us to get some information from the people up there which can be relied upon."[14]

President Coolidge's envoy, General McCoy, was not as optimistic as Feland about the military situation. As head of the electoral commission, he worried that Sandino's forces would upset plans for a peaceful national election. Soon after arriving back in Nicaragua, McCoy sent his deputy, Colonel Francis Parker, to Ocotal to scout out the situation. Reporting that "lawless violence was not uncommon," Parker blamed both sides and noted the ineffectiveness of civil authorities in places that were not manned by *Guardia* and Marines.[15] Sellers resented McCoy's intrusion into the admiral's area of responsibility—that is, command of the military situation in Nicaragua. Tension between the military men in charge—Sellers and Feland—and those tasked with diplomatic missions—McCoy and Eberhardt—was developing.[16]

Secretary of State Frank Kellogg remained especially leery of the military situation in Nicaragua. In a personal and confidential letter to McCoy, Kellogg asked the general's opinion about the Marines' efficiency in terms of leadership, discipline, morale, equipment, and adequacy. Kellogg wrote that people were questioning the sacrifice of American lives with no apparent result. "People can not see why the job cannot be done and frankly I do not understand myself. There is an uneasy feeling that there may be something wrong with the plan of campaign or the leadership."[17]

In his reply to Kellogg, McCoy noted that he had expressed his concern at daily conferences with General Feland as well as with Admiral Sellers. However, McCoy recognized his delicate position in these matters and, in an attempt to maintain "cordial relations," had refrained from commenting on the military situation, but since Kellogg specifically asked, McCoy analyzed the situation. The general acknowledged the "more than ordinary difficulties" the Marines faced, including rough terrain, lack of food and supplies, and deficient roads and means of communication. McCoy also recognized Sandino's advantages, including speaking the local language, knowing the terrain, and having the assistance of sympathizers. McCoy decried support for Sandino in the United States, which, he said, was stiffening the insurgent's resolve. He believed the Marines needed to undertake more vigorous military operations before the start of the rainy season two months hence. Because Nicaraguan authorities had failed to pass legislation that would have allowed the *Guardia Nacional* to take over police functions, the Marines were forced to carry out police activities when they should be conducting field operations against Sandino. To be successful within the time limit—that is, before the Nicaraguan election—the military campaign demanded "exceptional qualities of leadership activity and persistence" as well as "vigorous attack" and "relentless pursuit." McCoy criticized the Marines' military operations thus far, which had been characterized by a "lack of effective information service, tardiness in using information obtained, and failure to maintain continuous contact with Sandino forces." McCoy even stated that he had tried to convince Feland and Sellers that Sandino had to be eliminated.[18]

McCoy went on to assess General Feland and Admiral Sellers. He acknowledged Sellers's cooperation and noted that the admiral had delegated to Feland the conduct of operations ashore, which McCoy considered a wise move. McCoy wrote that Feland "appears to have [a] cool head and generally good judgment and has cooperated within the limits of his abilities." Nevertheless, McCoy candidly admitted that Feland's "average" leadership "has lacked a certain vigorous and compelling quality needed under the present difficult conditions to energize the operations everywhere." McCoy reported that morale and discipline were good, leadership and performance in the aviation section had been superior, and the equipment and supply situation was improving. In sum, McCoy concluded: "I do not recommend the relief of the present Marine Commander unless [an] exceptionally better replacement can be assured." However, he wanted Kellogg to apprise Commandant Lejeune of the need to have "decisive results [with regard to eliminating Sandino] before the rainy season begins."[19]

Although the politicians and diplomats would have liked faster results, the Marines were not idle. The Brigade B-2 Intelligence Office continually sought and received information from Marine Corps outposts. For example, the brigade intelligence journal for the week of February 5, 1928, noted that Lieutenant Colonel Beadle had given a verbal report regarding Sandino's supposed whereabouts. Various officers, ranging from lieutenants in the field to Colonel Dunlap, filed reports of sightings and skirmishes with "bandits."[20]

Major Harry Schmidt had arrived at the beginning of February 1928 to take over as brigade intelligence officer. He immediately reminded all units that "more energetic measures must be taken to secure information." He also decided that while all "subordinate" units should gather information, "higher" units would evaluate it. He instructed the subordinate units not to downplay any information, because it might make sense to the higher units when they considered the "big picture." Schmidt continued the procedure of writing weekly intelligence reports assessing the situation in Nicaragua, and he provided complete and nuanced appraisals. In his second report, Schmidt summarized the major problem: "There are so many reports coming in that it is difficult to determine any of his [Sandino's] groups." Nevertheless, "the mounting of [a] great many men, night operations and air service reconnaissance all have been a factor in making Sandino and his principal leaders impotent for another week." Schmidt quickly and correctly analyzed that "mobility continues to [be] the enemy's chief asset. He continues to avoid us. It is believed he will [not] attack unless he can ambush us and get away quickly." Schmidt surmised that many of the reports of Sandino sightings were "pure fabrications sent in as counter espionage material by Sandino spies. Also that a great many reports are grossly exaggerated."[21]

To address some of McCoy's concerns, Feland asked for more Marines, and Sellers concurred. More men were needed to carry out operations, but it was also becoming apparent that Marines fluent in Spanish would be needed to oversee the election in the towns throughout the country. In addition, the general wanted enough men to form a reserve that could immediately be sent wherever it was needed. Sellers requested two additional Marine battalions, and with these reinforcements, he believed the "military situation can be successfully handled."[22]

Meanwhile, controversy was brewing on another issue. When the Nicaraguan Congress could not agree on the election law presented by General McCoy, President Diaz simply decreed that a National Election Board headed by McCoy would oversee the 1928 election. The decree also gave McCoy command of the *Guardia Nacional* to maintain order. When Feland learned of this, he pointed out that it conflicted with a Navy Department letter of December 9, 1927, stating that during emergency combined operations involving the *Guardia* and the Marine Corps, the senior naval officer—that is, the brigade commander—would be in charge.[23]

The supervision of the election was considered a combined operation between military and diplomatic representatives. McCoy considered it essential that he have authority over the *Guardia*; usually, he would have delegated this authority to Feland. The day after the decree, McCoy stopped by Feland's office to assure him that "in working out the plans for use of Marines in the election," he had ordered Colonel Parker that

Rear Admiral David Foote Sellers and
Brigadier General Logan Feland.

"the carrying out of [Feland's] military mission is not to be interfered with
and is to remain supreme." McCoy suggested that "in a general way" he
wanted to turn over control of the *Guardia* to Feland.[24]

Feland found himself in a complex and confusing situation. Because
overseeing the election was a combined operation, he believed the navy letter should apply and he should have complete control of both the Marines
and the *Guardia*. Now he was seemingly being directed by an army officer
acting in a diplomatic role. Feland wrote to Sellers that "this matter can
and will be arranged but it ought to be carefully thought out. I do not see
how I can exercise any command, the authority for which is derived from
an Army officer, acting under direction of the Department of State."[25]

Admiral Sellers supported Feland and wrote to the Navy Department
that he agreed "with [the] Brigade Commander that command of the military forces in Nicaragua should not pass out of the hands of the Navy."
After McCoy assured both Feland and Sellers that he would cooperate
with the Marine Corps commander so that "appropriate action may be
taken," the controversy subsided temporarily.[26] Nevertheless, the issue of
Guardia control increased the tension between General McCoy, on the
one hand, and General Feland and Admiral Sellers, on the other.

Sellers visited Managua again at the end of March 1928. It had come
to his attention that *New York Times* correspondent Harold Denny had
reported that the Marines would cease their efforts against Sandino with
the start of the rainy season. Feland later had a talk with Denny to set
him straight: the Marines would not stop or slacken their attempts to
combat Sandino after the rainy season began. Although Feland had
impressed upon his Marines the importance of doing everything they
could before the rainy season, when conditions would be more difficult,

he was certainly not going to suspend the search for Sandino because of the weather.[27]

Denny generally supported the Marine Corps, especially in denying alleged atrocities. But this episode with him reflected the difficulties faced by American diplomats and military men when dealing with the press. Back in July 1927, after Ocotal, Minister Eberhardt had received a communication from Secretary of State Kellogg expressing the State Department's embarrassment at reading press reports about engagements with Sandino forces before it received official reports from the legation. Eberhardt replied that neither he nor General Feland could keep such articles from appearing; as soon as "any activity occurs or seems imminent in any part of the country local telegraph operators submit guesses or true, false, or manufactured accounts to correspondents here at Managua who immediately send [them] to the United States." This sometimes occurred a day or two before Feland and Eberhardt received information about such events. Eberhardt noted that the reporters often "guessed right," whereas he and Feland, not wishing to report rumors, waited for confirmation. However, the minister regretted any information that had been inaccurate or misleading.[28]

A year later, the situation had not changed dramatically. In his reporting on various skirmishes, Denny sometimes noted that Feland's headquarters had not yet heard about certain events. In reality, Feland may have heard the news but was simply keeping quiet about it. He was never one to publicize bad news. He took a personal interest in news reports, apparently censoring, when necessary, the intelligence section's press releases for local Nicaraguan newspapers.[29]

One particularly thorny issue involved accusations that the Marines committed atrocities during Feland's command in Nicaragua. Both the U.S. and the international press accused the Marines of bad conduct, brutality, and indiscriminate aerial bombing of civilians. One of Beals's articles in *The Nation* claimed that the Marines punished alleged followers of Sandino by bombing their homes and burning their towns. Beals asserted: "Even in places remote from the war zone, as on the Atlantic coast, the Marine policing has been frequently carried on with highhanded brutality."[30]

Certainly there was some bad conduct by Marines, such as the case of one Marine who got drunk and killed a Nicaraguan. But General Feland asserted that all charges against his Marines were investigated thoroughly, and punishments meted out as necessary. Major Ross Rowell supported Feland's statements. Rowell, of Ocotal fame, noted that he had forgone an opportunity to bomb the town of San Rafael del Norte while Sandino was there (being interviewed by Beals, unbeknownst to the Marines). This restraint proved to be a missed opportunity, but it had been exercised because of the "policy of the Commanding General to avoid the possibility of injury to the lives and property of innocent persons by refraining from attacks on towns."[31] Feland's intelligence officer, Major Schmidt, later asserted that Feland possessed "foresight and keen knowledge of the native psychology," and "his often reiterated policy that no harsh, cruel or inhuman treatment of natives suspected of having information which we needed, produced more and lasting results than would have been the case otherwise."[32]

The hunt for Sandino continued unabated from February through April 1928. Marine planes continued to search for Sandino's forces, bombing and strafing where possible. Although still rather modest, American casualties increased. Colonel Dunlap's Eleventh Regiment continued to harass Sandino's followers in the northwest, prompting the guerrilla leader to shift his operations into the mining region around Pis Pis, nearer the eastern coast.

On February 24, 1928, the Eastern District commander, Major Harold Utley, moved his headquarters from the southeastern port of Bluefields up to Puerto Cabezas, in the northeast. That month, Marines from the USS *Denver*, under the command of Captain Merritt "Red Mike" Edson, disembarked at Puerto Cabezas to augment the small contingent there. Even more Marines arrived at Puerto Cabezas in April. The Eastern District had been rather quiet during the Sandino rebellion, but after the Sandinistas seized American mines inland, it would become the focus of the conflict. The stage was set for a major effort against Sandino in the east.[33]

In the meantime, the Marines' inability to kill, capture, or even pin down Sandino created increasing tension among the U.S. officials in Managua. General McCoy sent a civilian adviser, William Howe, to question General Feland and General Beadle about the conduct of operations and the investigation of incidents involving Nicaraguans.[34]

On April 19 Eberhardt, Munro, McCoy, Beadle, and Feland met at the legation. After discussing the forthcoming election, General McCoy turned his attention to the military situation and expressed his unhappiness: "It is NOT satisfactory to me; you are making NO progress and I am not satisfied." When Feland suggested that McCoy put his concerns in writing, the army general refused; he wanted to address the matter then and there. McCoy wanted to know where Sandino was located and railed against the poor intelligence: "You ought to have spies with Sandino all the time to tell you where he is." McCoy tried to temper his message by claiming that he was speaking in a friendly manner and just wanted to let Feland know what was on his mind. Noting that he was the "Special Representative of the President," McCoy continued: "The rainy season is coming on, if you haven't gotten Sandino in a month from now I feel that you will have failed and I shall so report to the state department." Then McCoy blamed both Feland and Beadle for not getting out of Managua long enough to understand the situation for themselves.[35]

After the meeting, McCoy visited Feland at the latter's quarters to continue the conversation, and Feland tried to explain recent operations. McCoy was called away for another appointment but returned to Feland's office the next morning, and after hearing a further explanation of Colonel Dunlap's work, he seemed to be mollified. The army general reiterated that he was speaking in a "friendly spirit of cooperation" and revealed that he had told the State Department that Feland had good judgment and a cool head. Feland believed his private conversations with McCoy had been more constructive than the legation meeting, but he concluded in a secret report to Admiral Sellers: "McCoy intends me to be warned by and to take in the fullest significance, the statements made by him at the Legation on April 18. I do not fell [sic] that General McCoy is animated by any feeling against me personally, but that when he spoke of 'your failure' and 'your intelligence service falling down' that he was speaking of the Naval Forces on shore in Nicaragua."[36]

When apprised by Feland of McCoy's outburst, Sellers replied that it was not "wholly unexpected as you may recall that you and I have conversed on the possibility of such a thing before." Sellers decided to pass along Feland's secret communication to the chief of naval operations. Sellers also noted that in March, General McCoy had tried to pin him down on whether he could "guarantee that the Marines would catch Sandino in two months." Sellers had replied that it was "not sound military policy to attempt to predict the date upon which a campaign against an enemy who was conducting guerrilla warfare in the wild, unexplored mountains of Nicaragua would terminate." Sellers concluded that he "could not understand how, in the light of many historical instances, General McCoy can make this statement that our military campaign in Nicaragua is to be classed as a failure if Sandino is not captured in one month."[37] The truth is, few military men would or could have made the unrealistic guarantees demanded by McCoy. Even more than seventy years later, with twenty-first-century communications and technology, it took U.S. authorities ten years to find and eliminate the world's most wanted terrorist: Osama bin Laden. Although Augusto Sandino could not be found and eliminated, he might be contained.

Sellers continued to support Feland in his communications with the Navy Department, stating that McCoy, "both by his actions and his language, placed General Feland in a very embarrassing position and that the latter displayed a considerable amount of patience and tact in a trying situation." In turn, Feland thanked Sellers "with all [his] heart for [Sellers's] understanding and support.[38] They were in agreement in their assessment of the situation.

In a letter to Commandant Lejeune on May 19, Feland explained what had been happening in the Eastern District, where Sandino had gone to raid American-owned mines. Feland believed that Sandino's "harsh treatment of the native population," the Miskito Indians, was "evidence that the leaders under Sandino are more or less desperate." The Kentuckian asserted that the Marines would "carry out their military mission" and "reduce the Sandino forces, long before the period of the election, to such a state that they will be impotent to exercise any effect on the elections." He predicted that "the Sandinistas as an armed force will not appreciably affect the elections."[39] Feland was correct about that.

Despite the unpleasantness with McCoy, Feland continued to work to ensure that the Marines Corps would play an important role in providing security for the national election in November. However, he worried that General McCoy's call for 500 Marines to oversee polling would take too many men away from the hunt for Sandino in the Eastern District. Feland also continued to cultivate a proper image for the Marines in Nicaragua. He reissued orders that his men should avoid excessive physical force or mental suffering when dealing with the Nicaraguans. Conciliatory methods would help the Marines; harsh methods would injure their mission.[40]

Feland troubled himself with other matters that might affect the military situation. He realized that opposition to the intervention in Nicaragua remained strong in the United States. Even the former assistant secretary of the navy, Franklin Roosevelt, eventually questioned the policy of unilaterally sending Marines into Central America. He wrote to Feland: "I am very sure that the Marines are doing a splendid piece of work, although frankly from the point of view of sound government, I do not like this expedition which has been sent down to carry out an agreement which has never had the sanction of Congress. It must be interesting but very difficult work and I hope that the health of the Brigade is holding up well."[41]

Demonstrating more overt opposition, various groups in the United States raised funds for the Sandinistas. General Feland and Minister Eberhardt were concerned that this money would be used to buy ammunition and guns for Sandino's forces. Representatives of the All-America Anti-Imperialist League denied that the funds were being used for arms and asserted that they were being used by the Hands-Off Nicaragua Committee to purchase medical supplies.[42]

Brigadier General Feland cultivated the Nicaraguan press and met with the editors of several Nicaraguan newspapers, both Conservative and Liberal. At the beginning of June they discussed an incident in which a group of men had attacked a police station in Masaya. Both Liberals and Conservatives denied complicity. Feland spoke in slow, concise Spanish, with little help from an interpreter, and tried to mollify both groups. He did not want to pin the blame on either side, he said, and he asked both to consider their duties as Nicaraguans. After this meeting, Feland noted that he had been able to get Conservative leader and former president Emiliano Chamorro "publicly committed to the policy of aiding in upholding law and order and in backing pacification." Feland acknowledged to Admiral Sellers that he would have to be very careful in dealing with the newspapers and use them only "when I feel assured of getting some results which will be beneficial." In a follow-up letter to Sellers, enclosing copies of the resulting newspaper articles, Feland asserted that "by talking to the editors very occasionally and on selected subjects, something can be accomplished. I have in mind, if things get just right, to line them all up to tell just how little the whole Sandino business now amounts to and just how he is doing great harm to this country."[43]

The military action had shifted primarily to the east, where Sandino and his followers had destroyed American-owned mines. Brigadier General Feland and Rear Admiral Sellers traveled at the end of June to Puerto Cabezas on the northeast coast and to Bluefields on the southeast coast to discuss tactics and strategy with Marine Corps officers.[44]

At Puerto Cabezas, Feland and Sellers met with the Eastern District commander, Major Utley, and with Captain Edson (a future major general and Medal of Honor recipient for his leadership on Guadalcanal in World War II). Soon after Edson had arrived in February with fifty-seven enlisted men, he had started leading patrols into the interior, using the rivers that crossed the region. Primarily he patrolled on the Coco River, near the northern border with Honduras, and had pushed all the way up the river to Poteca, a center of Sandinista activity. With the onslaught of the rainy season, however, Edson was scheduled to move to Managua and take on other duties. Those plans changed with the arrival of Feland and Sellers on the USS *Rochester* on June 28, 1928. After meeting aboard the ship with Major Utley, Sellers and Feland disembarked. Immediately upon meeting Edson, Feland said to the young captain, "Major Utley tells me you would like to go to Poteca. Can you get there from this coast?" Edson replied, "Yes, sir; it can be done." And Feland said, "Well I am going to give you the chance to do it." Feland noted that airplane reconnaissance and other sources indicated a concentration of Sandinistas around Poteca, and they had raided a nearby lumber camp. Marines from the northern area could not reach Poteca from the west. Thus, it was left to Edson's Marines to gain access from the east.[45] With this conversation began one of the most famous patrols and exercises in jungle warfare ever undertaken by the Marine Corps. Edson and his men pushed 470 miles up the Coco River, reaching Poteca on August 17, 1928, and dispersing Sandino's forces as they tried to avoid the Marines.[46]

Having given Edson permission to carry out the Coco River patrol, Feland and Sellers sailed on the *Rochester* to Bluefields to inspect the Marines and the *Guardia* detachment there. Then they sailed back through the Canal Zone and up the west coast of Nicaragua to Corinto, where they proceeded by special train to Managua. Sellers cabled the

Navy Department that the "military situation in Nicaragua has improved steadily and is now in a very satisfactory condition despite the fact that Sandino is still at large."[47]

In Managua, Feland resumed his duties, and again the issue of the *Guardia*'s reporting structure arose. *Guardia* commander Elias Beadle reported that a new *Guardia* agreement would have to be negotiated with the Nicaraguan government, and General McCoy and Minister Eberhardt were maneuvering to make a change: rather than reporting to Marine Corps officers, they wanted the *Guardia* to report to "American" officers. This wording implied that the *Guardia* might report to U.S. Army officers or to the State Department. Feland believed that he and Sellers might have to intercede to maintain the status quo so that the Marine Corps could retain the simple, efficient operating structure it needed.[48]

Feland continued to monitor the Eastern District situation. Whereas he was comfortable leaving the now calmer Northern District in the capable hands of Colonel Dunlap, Feland communicated more directly with Major Utley. Many cables passed between them. In late August, Feland counseled Utley to maintain control of the Coco River to serve as a barrier against the Sandinistas going to Honduras and returning "recuperated, re-supplied and reenforced." He concluded, "Our line along the border ought to be shooting both ways and prevent crossing in either direction."[49]

Brigadier General Feland also attended to morale matters in Nicaragua. In August he pinned the Navy Cross on several men, including two Kentuckians: Sergeant Alva Eadens of Bowling Green and Corporal Herbert D. Lester of Rose Hill. A photograph of Feland pinning the medal on Lester appeared in many Kentucky newspapers several months later. The day before the medal ceremony, Feland's men threw him a birthday party, replete with music by the regional orchestra. Morale seemed to be high among the Marines, who were being lauded for taking the fight to Sandino and negating his potential influence over the election in November.[50]

Even General McCoy had to admit that, since his initial criticisms in February, "command and staff work of the Marine forces have improved." This improvement was reflected in "better information service, patrol activity during the rainy season, daily and effective air reconnaissance, and the acceptance of amnesty by some six hundred more bandits." Consequently, McCoy believed that Sandino would not be "in a position to affect materially the registration or voting in the elections."[51]

General Feland continued to monitor all aspects of the fight against Sandino, and he remained confident that the situation in Nicaragua was well in hand. Feland also knew that much was riding on his shoulders. In early July, Feland's new chief of staff, Randolph Berkeley, shared some comments made by Commandant Lejeune at the end of May. According to Berkeley, Lejeune "considered the duty being performed by the Second Brigade the most important duty now entrusted to the Marine Corps and that the future of the Corps depended very much upon the outcome in Nicaragua." The results accomplished by the Second Brigade would mean the "making or breaking of the Marine Corps."[52]

Given the improved situation in Nicaragua, Feland began to contemplate his future. In early August 1928 he wrote to his mentor, James Harbord, and asked for his advice and assistance. Anticipating that he would return to the United States in early 1929, Feland knew that a new Marine Corps Commandant would probably be appointed around that time. He assumed that his former commander, Buck Neville, would be the logical choice and would encounter little or no resistance. Feland also believed that Neville would rely for advice on John Lejeune, who in turn would rely on Smedley Darlington Butler and Cyrus Radford, "who always work as one, the former furnishing the impulses and the latter doing the scheming." Radford, a Marine Corps colonel from Christian County, Kentucky (also Feland's home county), was a U.S. Naval Academy classmate of Neville's. Radford had spent much of his career at the Marine Corps supply depot in Philadelphia, serving as assistant quartermaster. Feland figured Neville would listen to Radford because he "was a power with the Democrats and [presidential candidate Al] Smith may win"; he would listen to Butler "for the sake of keeping him quiet and using any influence inherited from his father." Feland also believed that Butler and Radford would encourage Neville to make Feland's life in the Corps "as uncomfortable as possible. They would want me to have the last choice of stations, the least credit for anything I might have done." Feland asserted that Butler's and Radford's influence had "worked against me in the past," referring to Cole's promotion to major general in 1924. But Feland was also sure that, if left to his own devices, Neville would not do anything to hurt him. He asked Harbord to talk to Neville so that Feland might be given a "square deal."[53]

In writing to Harbord, Feland poured out his anguish to his friend.

He noted that after Lejeune had supported Cole for the major general's slot in 1924, his relationship with the Commandant had been strained. After Feland returned to Nicaragua, the relationship had changed, and Lejeune's letters had become more friendly and cordial in tone. Lejeune had also written to Feland about important matters, indicating his confidence in his commander in Nicaragua. Obviously referring to Berkeley's memo, Feland noted that Lejeune considered their work in Nicaragua the most important thing ever handled by the Corps. Despite this apparent thawing in relations, Feland remained a bit wary, noting that Lejeune had said little about Feland in his Senate testimony about Nicaragua earlier in the year.

On the subject of Nicaragua, Feland remained optimistic in his letter to Harbord. He believed the work there would be "finished in good time and in [a] creditable manner." Feland noted that previous U.S. campaigns in the Philippines, Haiti, Santo Domingo, and Mexico had lasted longer. Therefore, he did not understand how any "reasonably informed man expected to get a guerilla leader in a country bigger and rougher than Luzon within a few weeks. We are going to finish him [Sandino] and the time is going to set a record, shorter than for any comparable affair."[54]

In August 1928 Harbord was deciding whether to take a leave of absence from RCA to work on the campaign of Republican presidential candidate Herbert Hoover. Nevertheless, he took the time to reply to Feland and said he would try to talk to Major General Neville on Feland's behalf. Harbord finally met Neville in September and tried to assuage Feland's fears, writing that Neville had been glad to hear of Feland's "friendship." Harbord added his own realistic view of the future, reminding Feland that Butler was still senior and would likely be promoted first. Feland's promotion would probably have to wait until Cole retired. Harbord acknowledged that Feland's war record had been achieved in a "greater war than General Butler ever participated in," but he reiterated that Butler was senior, and it would be difficult to promote anyone over the holder of two Medals of Honor.[55]

Actually, earlier that spring, Commandant Lejeune had thought about sending Dion Williams to China to replace Butler and transferring Feland to the base in San Diego to replace Williams. That would have allowed Butler to return to Quantico and be near his ailing father. Thomas Butler died, however, on May 26, 1928. General Lejeune and

Colonel Radford were among the notables spotted at his funeral. Butler would miss his father's funeral and would not return to the United States until early 1929.[56]

Feland was probably glad to get Harbord's letter, but for the time being, his focus remained on Nicaragua. Feland sought ways to promote order in the country, and at the end of September 1928 he announced a "general clean-up week" during which the Marines would "endeavor to induce the inhabitants as a matter of civic pride to devote this week to making a general clean up of their towns," especially those without proper sanitation. Feland warned, however, that this should be a voluntary, not a coercive, campaign. He envisioned this effort continuing after the November election and including the digging of ditches to draw off standing water, thus decreasing malaria outbreaks. In a follow-up memo to the area commanders, Colonel Berkeley noted, "The general thinks that if you can get the people interested in something of this kind during the periods immediately following the registration and the election respectively, that it may prevent some disorders that might arise during these periods, and at the same time prove beneficial to our command [in] Nicaragua as a whole." Berkeley also reminded the commanders not to use force or duress.[57] Feland recognized that the key to ensuring a better situation in Nicaragua involved not only military action but also appropriate civic action. In this manner, he foreshadowed future Marine Corps efforts at counterinsurgency in places such as Vietnam and Afghanistan.

Because of the national and international attention on the Nicaraguan situation, Headquarters Marine Corps realized that Feland and the Second Brigade needed help with publicity. In mid-October Major Edwin McClellan arrived in Managua on temporary duty as "Officer in Charge of Photographic Party to procure photographs of Marine Corps activities in Nicaragua." Having been appointed the Corps's first historical officer, McClellan had produced in 1920 the first official history of Marine Corps activities in World War I. McClellan and Feland had known each other when they both worked in Washington in the early 1920s—McClellan in the Historical Section, and Feland as DOT director and Assistant to the Commandant. They had also exchanged communications regarding Belleau Wood.[58]

Perhaps because he simply valued learning, or perhaps because his engineering background had taught him to analyze situations before seek-

Major Edwin McClellan and his
photographer, Private Charles Palmer.

ing solutions, Feland supported historical studies by the Corps. While
commanding Marines in the Dominican Republic, he had written to
General Pendleton, seeking information for a history of the Marine Corps
in the country. Feland believed the Second Brigade had a "long and very
creditable history which in the interest of morale and esprit should be
recorded and preserved." To this end, Feland had appointed a board to
write a draft history that he hoped Pendleton would review and comment
on. Pendleton had agreed to cooperate, believing that "a lot of the good
work done by the Brigade was never appreciated."[59]

McClellan arrived in Nicaragua accompanied by a photographer,
Private Charles Palmer. The two men spent a couple of weeks traveling
throughout Nicaragua, taking more than 600 photographs and making
several films. McClellan sent the materials back to Joe Fegan and John
Craige at the Marine Corps Publicity Bureau, headquartered in Philadelphia, to use in disseminating news about the Corps. McClellan believed

the Marine Corps's story in Nicaragua had been underreported and that Feland was "doing wonderful work." He wrote, "Every day there is a publicity item that would read well." Nevertheless, in McClellan's opinion, there was one possible obstacle: Feland was "a military man & inwardly resents publicity and exploitation."[60] Although he understood the value of working with the press, Feland did not enjoy or seek publicity.

In October, as the national election approached, General Feland reiterated his Marines' mission: to facilitate a fair, supervised Nicaraguan election. He instructed his officers to continue patrolling aggressively but also to prepare defensive plans, especially for those small polling stations that would be manned by Marines. Two weeks later, the general counseled "patience and care" but added: "If violence is attempted, strike hard at those guilty, while doing all in your power to protect and reassure the innocent." In so ordering, Feland presaged a popular motto of the Marine Corps in the twenty-first century, as articulated by General James N. Mattis: "No greater friend, no worse enemy."[61]

13

Postelection Nicaragua, 1929

Nicaraguan voters turned out in large numbers on Sunday, November 4, 1928. The day before, believing the situation was well in hand, General Feland had gone deer hunting. Throughout the difficult year, he had tried to relieve the stress of command by pursuing his hobbies of hunting and fishing. Aide-de-camp James Riseley accompanied the general on some of those trips. He later recalled that if Feland shot at fifty doves, he would hit forty-four of them, while Riseley could barely manage to bring down twelve. Riseley claimed that when hunting ducks, the general never missed.[1]

The day of the election, Major McClellan wrote to his friend John Craige at the Marine Corps Publicity Bureau and remarked that "this is a damn peaceful election." McClellan lamented, however, that "we have not put over to the public the BIG STUFF that the Marines have done down here." The Marines had "performed miracles down here," he observed, "and nobody actually knows it." Although McClellan was sending the Publicity Bureau pictures of Sandino, the major advised against "making him [Sandino] a patriot or a hero, for he is neither." McClellan also stated that "no publicity of the Marine Corps should make Sandino more important than he is." Craige was delighted with McClellan's contributions and said he would suggest to Commandant Lejeune the idea of sending an officer and a photographer on all Marine Corps expeditions.[2]

The election was a grand success, with little disruption. Certainly the Electoral Commission's chief worry, Augusto Sandino, had not prevented record numbers of Nicaraguans from going to the polls. More than 400 Marines and navy bluejackets had served as polling officials, supervising the voting process. In the presidential election, Liberal Party candidate José María Moncada beat Conservative Party candidate Adolfo Bénard. Moncada would be inaugurated on January 1, 1929.

The Marines had succeeded in their task of enabling a free election, but General Feland spent little time celebrating. He wanted to ensure that the Marine Corps learned from the campaign in Nicaragua. Toward that end, on November 9, 1928, he sent a memorandum to each of his officers, asking them to provide "constructive criticism, suggestions or recommendations" that could be combined in a pamphlet to guide similar expeditions in the future. To steer their thinking, the memorandum listed twenty issues for consideration, ranging from "combat in bush warfare in conjunction with planes" to "reduction of paperwork."[3]

Many of Feland's officers took the survey seriously, typing multi-page responses. Major John Gray, who had served with Feland in the 1912 Cuban expedition, suggested that thirty-two-man patrols of four squads each, armed with two Thompson submachine guns, a Browning automatic rifle, and a grenade rifle, would do well in bush warfare. He believed rifle grenades had an especially strong "psychological" effect on the Nicaraguans. Gray would continue to be very interested in Marine Corps training; his "Plea for Revision of the Field Officers' Course" would be published in the *Marine Corps Gazette* in February 1931.[4]

The commander of the Eastern District, Major Utley, replied that two things were necessary: a greater focus on communications and supply, including better radios, and a headquarters company that was organized permanently, not just on an ad hoc basis for expeditions. Utley later encountered difficulties with civilian businessmen in the Eastern District, who complained about Utley's alleged womanizing and drunkenness; these complaints led to his relief as commander. He avoided a court-martial, and "General Feland intervened from his position at HQMC to put the matter completely to rest." Utley eventually returned to the United States and became an instructor and then director of the field officers' course at Quantico.[5]

The Northern District commander, Colonel Dunlap, was more expansive. In his usual thorough manner, he wrote a seven-page, single-spaced response to Feland's memorandum, addressing most of the points raised; he had his appropriate subordinates file separate reports on matters such as medical and supply issues. Dunlap also addressed other, larger concerns. For example, he criticized Headquarters Marine Corps for not counterbalancing "communistic societies" that made Sandino seem like the "George Washington of Nicaragua." The Marine Corps continued to struggle with its public image, and Dunlap thought headquarters should have done more to expose the true nature of Sandino and his followers, who had consistently been characterized simply as "bandits." Dunlap also criticized the lack of unity of command. He noted that at times there appeared to be two or even three centers of command represented by Feland, McCoy, and *Guardia* commander Beadle. Dunlap concluded, "That failure did not result is a miracle." In the future, if a special envoy were appointed, Dunlap believed that envoy should have the entire command responsibility and "take the blame for the whole, should that occur." On the plus side, Dunlap credited the "marvelous exhibition of tact, cooperation, and the sinking of all ideas of personal dignity, etc., on the part of everyone" for the overall success in Nicaragua.[6]

By the time most of the responses to his survey arrived in Managua, General Feland was already in the process of giving up his command. His memorandum, however, would eventually help set in motion an intensive, introspective review of Marine Corps doctrine and training. The real impetus for better Corps education and training would come in the early 1930s, as officers who had served under Feland in Nicaragua and the Dominican Republic, such as James Carson Breckinridge and Randolph Berkeley, analyzed and documented lessons from their experiences in the latest of the Marine Corps's "small wars"—a term Feland had used when commanding in the Dominican Republic. As commanders of Marine Corps schools, these men pushed forward, conceptualizing and advising on the operations of small wars. These efforts would result in the *Manual for Small Wars Operations* in 1935 and the *Small Wars Manual* in 1940.[7] In the twenty-first century, U.S. military commanders would use the 1940 manual to develop strategies for counterinsurgency and so-called asymmetric warfare in Iraq and Afghanistan.

On November 10, 1928—a date deliberately chosen because it was the celebrated birthday of the U.S. Marine Corps—U.S. Army brigadier general Frank McCoy sent a letter to Marine Corps brigadier general Logan Feland, congratulating the Kentucky Marine on the successful conduct of the Nicaraguan election. McCoy wrote: "We have reason to be more than satisfied at the peace and good order which prevailed throughout the country. To a large extent this responsibility rested on you and you are to be congratulated on the results."[8] Although the two men had differed, the successful election had seemingly dispelled any problems. Unfortunately, the détente between them would not last long, and Feland's relationships with Minister Charles Eberhardt and *Guardia Nacional* general Elias Beadle would worsen.

After the election, General McCoy asked his chief of staff, Colonel Gordon Johnston, to prepare a memorandum on the military situation in Nicaragua. Johnston asserted that Sandino's prestige as a patriot would grow until he was either captured or destroyed. He also foresaw that the *Guardia* would not be fully prepared to take over the country's policing tasks for approximately a year after Moncada's inauguration in January 1929. Navy bluejackets and fleet Marines had been pulled ashore to help during the election, but Johnston argued, "from a psychological point of view all Marines should be held until the primary mission of eliminating Sandino and other organized armed bands has been fulfilled." As soon as he received a draft of Johnston's memorandum, General Feland sent a copy to Admiral Sellers. Feland apparently resented this independent analysis of the military situation and believed that he had a better understanding of it. In a follow-up communication to Sellers later in November, he opined that McCoy had misconstrued some *Guardia* figures on hostile engagements and that the error confirmed Feland's previously expressed concern that McCoy was "not in a position to know, can not know, and does not know the military situation in Nicaragua."[9]

For his part, Sellers seemed quite satisfied with the successful election, acknowledging that "great credit is due to General Feland, who, by good organization and an active campaign against the bandit groups, had the country in such a state that the election could be conducted in a perfectly peaceful manner." Sellers and Feland agreed that the naval troops and fleet Marines should be returned to their vessels but that the nearly 4,000 Marines in Nicaragua should be kept at that level, at least until after Moncada's inauguration and the strengthening of the *Guardia*.[10]

Even though Augusto Sandino and his followers had been reasonably quiet in the months immediately preceding the election, he remained on General McCoy's mind. In a meeting with Sellers and Feland on November 8, McCoy strenuously objected to the reduction of any military forces

Logan Feland (left), Nicaraguan president-elect José Moncada (center), and future president Anastasio Somoza (right) at Thanksgiving dinner, 1928.

in Nicaragua, maintaining that the Marines had utterly failed in an important part of their mission as long as Sandino and other bandit leaders remained at large. Actually, General Feland and his Marines continued to gather intelligence to plan their operations against the so-called bandits, primarily in the Northern District. They asserted that the military situation was "the best it has ever been" and that "banditry in Nicaragua is no longer a lucrative profession." Feland preferred to maintain a relatively high number of Marines in country, alleging that the *Guardia* "had not undertaken any constabulary duty" in the north.[11]

At the beginning of December, Major McClellan sent Commandant Lejeune a six-page, single-spaced letter decrying previous Marine Corps publicity efforts with regard to Nicaragua. McClellan professed to be "overwhelmed" as he "contemplated the magnificent work that had been accomplished [by the Marines]" and stated that it was "no trouble at all" for him to "burst into superlatives." However, the Marine Corps had "fallen down" in its publicity efforts, especially in contrast to the fine job done by the U.S. Army—presumably by highlighting General McCoy and the army officers on his Electoral Commission. Publicity had to be planned in detail, he advised, and he believed that first-rate publicity was good for general Corps morale. Army publicity was better, McClellan argued, and "due to the presence of the Army here the whole problem has been an unusually delicate and difficult one for General Feland to solve." Regarding Feland, McClellan asserted: "One of our best bets for publicity is General Feland. He is rather 'shy' when it comes to stunting for publicity but I have hopes that he will shake off some of this reserve." McClellan went on to "urge strongly" that Lejeune "make it an *express* part of publicity policy to feature General Feland."[12]

McClellan would get an opportunity to improve publicity for the Marine Corps in Nicaragua when he stayed on at Second Brigade headquarters as publicity officer after his photographic assignment. He and Feland would have an odd but increasingly better relationship. The Kentucky Marine found publicity tiresome, but he recognized that McClellan's efforts and expertise would help in the overall cause. One day when McClellan wanted to take a picture, General Feland said, in a "not very nice way": "McClellan, I've got too many things to think about." McClellan started to back off, but then Feland changed his mind and said, "Take a picture if you feel like it." The publicity officer thought the general considered him a "nuisance," but a week later McClellan wrote of Feland: "Gracious he was not, but he is a fine thinker and efficient for this job down here. Probably no man who drives ahead for an objective known completely only to himself has time to be happy and pleasant."[13]

McClellan wrote these comments during a period when Feland was involved in several controversies. When he was less busy, Feland could appreciate Major McClellan's efforts. For example, McClellan helped Feland write a letter to the general's friend Senator Walter Edge about a proposed canal across Nicaragua. The project appealed to the civil engineering–trained Feland and was championed by Edge as head of the Senate Committee on Interoceanic Canals. One morning when McClellan walked into Feland's office, the general said he had a compliment to pass along. Feland explained that Senator Edge had responded to their letter and had lauded General Feland not only as a fine soldier but also as a "wonderfully graphic writer," praising "the style and interest of the letter" actually cowritten by McClellan.[14]

Feland could be demanding and irascible at times, but he often recognized his impatience and made an effort to be nicer. The general obviously recognized McClellan's talent and valued what the major had done. A few days after mentioning the Edge letter, and just before leaving Nicaragua, Feland asked McClellan if he would like to collaborate on a book. McClellan agreed, knowing that Feland had started writing a book about Belleau Wood.[15]

In addition to recognizing individual achievements, Feland lauded his Marines' group effort in his Christmas 1928 message. He acknowledged that "duty here in practically all cases has been most trying, perhaps never before had any military organization been so widely dispersed and yet required to perform any more exacting and difficult tasks."[16] Despite the possible hyperbole of Feland's message, his Marines had done a fine job. Foremost, their mission had been to oversee a peaceful election, and they had succeeded brilliantly. Although Sandino continued to elude the Marines, their constant pursuit of him had negated his influence over the election. The Marines had pushed their search in some of the world's most inhospitable terrain, including Edson's trip up the Coco River. Sandino had not gone away, but his tactical significance had been diminished.

To deal with threats from Sandino and his followers, President-elect Moncada, like Feland, wanted the Marines to remain in Nicaragua, at least until the *Guardia* had been strengthened. He acknowledged in a meeting with Admiral Sellers that he wanted to appoint *Guardia* head Elias Beadle as director general of police in his new administration, and he also hoped to appoint a general from the American military forces to act as his military adviser. In fact, in a follow-up letter to Sellers, Moncada suggested Feland for the position. Feland appeared to be amenable to this assignment, having mentioned the possibility in a letter to Commandant Lejeune in December. In a personal and confidential letter to Lejeune on January 3, 1929, Feland asked whether the Commandant had been able to speak to Assistant Secretary of State Francis White about the appointment of an adviser to Moncada.[17]

The idea of appointing an American military adviser to the president was not a new one. Feland told Lejeune that as early as April 1927 the idea had been discussed among Feland, Henry Stimson, and Eberhardt. Feland averred that he had never approached Moncada about the possibility. Furthermore, Feland told Lejeune that Admiral Sellers had consulted with chargé d'affaires Dana Munro of the U.S. legation and Eberhardt

Colonel Elias Beadle and his *Guardia Nacional* officers.

about the idea. Feland realized that the State Department would have to concur because the position entailed diplomatic status. The Kentuckian told Lejeune that Moncada had requested Feland personally and asserted, "It may sound like boasting, but what I have done down here through the Brigade of Marines has given me the confidence of all well-intentioned Nicaraguans." Although Feland thought Munro and Eberhardt supported the idea, he warned Lejeune that McCoy might not like it. Finally, Feland reported that he and Admiral Sellers agreed that his appointment "will be the best consolidation of our position." Feland asserted that the Navy Department, with the Marine Corps as its active agent, was most concerned with carrying out U.S. policies in Latin America, particularly in Central America. Feland believed that Lejeune and Chief of Naval Operations Hughes would "see the advantage in such consolidation of our position."[18]

Sellers traveled to Managua at the end of December for Moncada's inauguration. On December 31, 1928, the president-elect gave Sellers the letter in which he asked for Feland as his adviser. Moncada stated that the Marine Corps general "knows the country and the people well"; he considered Feland "a good friend" personally, as well as a friend of his government and "all Nicaraguans." Moncada requested three additional U.S. military officers—an auditor skilled in accounting, an engineer, and a medical officer—who would be under Feland's supervision. Sellers forwarded Moncada's letter to Chief of Naval Operations Charles Hughes, noting that he had already discussed it with Munro and Eberhardt. Sellers opined that the letter contained "a very important request and several suggestions of a constructive nature." He believed Moncada's high esteem for Feland was a "very valuable asset" that should be used to "full advantage" in "future relations with the new Government of Nicaragua." Sellers considered Moncada's request for Feland a "very eloquent tribute to the manner in which the campaign has been conducted and makes an excellent answer to those who have adversely criticized the activities of the Marines." Sellers also noted that Moncada's letter was an "unofficial" communication and that future official communications would be conducted by Minister Eberhardt.[19] In short, President Moncada's request for Feland's services received support from the general's in-country supervisor, Admiral Sellers.

While the idea of Feland becoming Moncada's adviser was being discussed, the general's future was uncertain: would he return home or stay in Nicaragua? Despite this ambiguity, Feland continued to command efforts to deal with Augusto Sandino. Still looking for a way to defuse the difficult situation, in November 1928 Feland had appealed to Sandino's family. He had arranged for Sandino's father, Don Gregorio Sandino, to fly to San Rafael del Norte on a Marine Corps plane to meet with Augusto's wife, Blanca, who was a telephone operator in the town. Blanca Sandino suggested that Don Gregorio write to Augusto and ask the insurgent leader what it would take to bring about peace. Don Gregorio did so and asked his son to reply directly to General Feland and Admiral Sellers. Feland also asked Sandino's mother, Margarita Calderon, to write a letter to Blanca, passing along the general's personal assurances; Marines delivered the letter to Blanca. In addition to appealing to Sandino through his family, Feland sent Sandino a letter from Sellers, who asked the Nicaraguan insurgent to "terminate the armed resistance." If Sandino were so inclined, Sellers indicated that he would be happy to give careful attention and consideration to efforts to cease hostilities.[20]

Meanwhile, a portent of the future had arrived in Corinto on November 27, 1928, in the person of President-elect Herbert Hoover. On a goodwill tour of Central and Latin America, Hoover stopped for a day in Nicaragua to meet with various U.S. and Nicaraguan officials, including

Admiral Sellers, Generals Feland and McCoy, Minister Eberhardt, chargé d'affaires Munro, President Diaz, and President-elect Moncada. A World Wide Photos picture of Hoover and Feland shaking hands appeared in national newspapers. Feland is dressed in his military finery, with polished knee-high riding boots and sword, a chest full of medals, and his Fifth Regiment fourragère on his left shoulder. Eberhardt appears behind the U.S. president-elect as McCoy looks on, while Sellers chats with Mrs. Hoover. Hoover later feted the large greeting party on board the USS *Maryland*, which was carrying the president-elect on his trip.[21]

Feland's Marines continued to focus on Sandino. In December 1928 Feland himself flew north to Jinotega to reconnoiter the situation, determined to do "everything possible to continue pressure on small groups of bandits." After his visit, Feland concluded that "things were going very good in the north." Sporadic contact with "bandits" continued, and as a result, some were quitting their resistance and going home. During that trip he learned that Sellers's letter had been delivered to Sandino, and he hoped for positive results. Feland was not naïve, however; he did not believe the Nicaraguan would surrender, and he opposed the idea of Sandino participating in national politics as a leader in the Liberal Party—a stance supported by Moncada. Feland believed Sandino's behavior would remain unsettling and that the Marines would "have to go on until [Sandino] has practically no followers left and is forced to flee the country."[22]

While Feland was dealing with the Sandino situation, meeting Hoover, and wondering whether he would become Moncada's military adviser, General McCoy was wrapping up his part of the American mission to Nicaragua. McCoy's Electoral Commission wound up its work in mid-December 1928, when McCoy delivered the results of the election to the Nicaraguan Congress, which approved the outcome later that month. His work complete, General McCoy and his wife left Managua on December 17; General Feland assigned a Marine Corps battalion to give the army general "the full honors of a minister on his departure."[23] The two men may have disagreed on some issues, but Feland made sure the president's envoy received an appropriate farewell.

Controversy, however, did not disappear with McCoy's departure. Admiral Sellers arrived in Managua on December 31, just in time for Moncada's inauguration on January 1. The day before, the Nicaraguan House of Deputies had passed a resolution giving General Feland and

Admiral Sellers the status of ministers plenipotentiary. Feland termed the resolution "purely an act of courtesy." The full Nicaraguan Congress then passed a law granting this status, which went into effect on January 4, 1929. Unfortunately, this seemingly simple act raised a firestorm of diplomatic protest, chiefly from Minister Eberhardt of the U.S. legation. According to Eberhardt, the law was "the result of several recent painful incidents caused by General Feland's insistence that he be placed ahead of the British, the Italian and other chargés des affaires at official functions." Eberhardt noted that the Nicaraguan Congress's action "naturally aroused resentment among the members of the Diplomatic Corps," and he pointed out the undesirable complications of the law, which could give the wrong impression that the U.S. military dominated Nicaragua.[24]

Admiral Sellers and General Feland did not agree with Eberhardt's conclusions. In a letter to Munro, Sellers noted that initially, he had given the matter little thought. He pointed out that General McCoy had been given the rank of minister plenipotentiary, and Sellers believed that he, as commander of the Special Services Squadron, deserved the same honor. Like Feland, Sellers considered the act of the Nicaraguan Congress a mere courtesy, with little practical importance: Sellers was rarely in Nicaragua, and since the Nicaraguan government seldom entertained officially, the title had little relevance for Feland. The other foreign legations refrained from making formal protests, and eventually the controversy died out because it became apparent that changes were in the making.[25]

This conflict was not the only one Feland had with other U.S. representatives in Nicaragua in January 1929. Another problem—this time with fellow Marine Elias Beadle—also came to a head that month. In early November 1928 chargé d'affaires Munro had written to his friend Francis White, assistant secretary of state for Latin American affairs, stating, there "is a strong probability that there will be an effort to have the *Guardia* placed under the control of the Marine Brigade again after the electoral period is over. It was under the brigade for a time, and the arrangement worked rather badly." Munro believed that since the *Guardia* was "an instrument of the State Department's policy" in Nicaragua, it should take steps to ensure that the *Guardia* remained independent, reporting to the Nicaraguan president, before the Navy Department considered it a strictly military matter and issued orders without informing the State Department. White passed the issue up the ladder to Secretary of State Frank Kellogg. Kellogg spoke to Secretary of the Navy Curtis Wilbur, expressing his hope that the Navy Department would not try to place the *Guardia* under Marine Corps control. Kellogg received assurances that the navy had no such thing in mind.[26]

When the *Guardia* had first been reconstituted, Feland had initially believed the *Guardia* commander would report to him, as the Marine Brigade commander. This had been the case in the Dominican Republic. Then, when General McCoy arrived, *he* seemingly had control of the *Guardia*. In reality, the final agreement establishing the *Guardia* acknowledged that the constabulary commander reported directly to the Nicaraguan president. Nevertheless, control of the *Guardia* became a contentious issue between Feland and *Guardia* commander Beadle, and it devolved into personal animosity between the two men.

Other issues added to their antagonism. Right before the start of 1929, Feland had asked Beadle to appoint Feland's aide-de-camp, Lieutenant Arthur Challacombe, to the rank of *Guardia* major and assign him as Moncada's aide-de-camp. Beadle had declined, for three reasons: he thought Challacombe was too friendly with Moncada; he believed the rank was inappropriate, given that of other Marine Corps officers assigned to the *Guardia*; and he did not want Challacombe in his organization. A recipient of the Navy Cross for his work in 1927 on the Nicaraguan arms commission, Challacombe had become close to Moncada. Some Nicaraguan Conservatives perceived this friendship as proof that the Marines had not been impartial during the run-up to the national election. After his inauguration, President Moncada himself insisted on Challacombe's appointment as his aide-de-camp, and Beadle was forced to acquiesce. The incident soured Moncada's relationship with Beadle, and it also strained relations between Feland and Munro. Munro believed Feland had "deliberately incited the President's hostility toward the Chief of the *Guardia*" because Beadle had managed to keep the *Guardia* from being under Feland's command.[27]

Feland's problems with State Department representatives—with Munro regarding Challacombe and with Eberhardt regarding the plenipotentiary honor—resulted in the buildup of serious tensions. To make matters worse, in the eyes of the State Department, Challacombe and Feland had conspired to bring A. E. French—Challacombe's father-in-law and Feland's MIT classmate—to Nicaragua to manage the Pacific Railroad for the J. G. White Management Corporation. The Nicaraguan government owned the railroad, but White Management was responsible for its daily operations. Eventually, another manager was chosen. Although the State Department declined to intervene in this matter, the perceived collusion increased the diplomats' animosity toward General Feland.[28]

In the midst of this turmoil, Feland and Beadle continued to disagree. On January 22, 1929, Minister Eberhardt reported to Secretary of State Kellogg that the friction between Feland and Beadle had become "very serious." Eberhardt asserted that in the weeks since Moncada's inauguration, Feland had become the virtual minister of war. He had written directly to Headquarters Marine Corps, requesting that an audit of *Guardia* accounts be conducted under his supervision. Feland claimed that Moncada had asked for the audit, since the Nicaraguan president did "not know prior costs of the *Guardia* nor how and by what authority money has been spent." This audit request exacerbated the tension between Feland and Beadle. Beadle did not object to the audit, but he preferred that it be conducted under the direct supervision of headquarters. Eberhardt clearly supported Beadle, noting that the *Guardia* chief was "a most popular official among both natives and foreigners." Feland disagreed with that assessment, avowing that Nicaraguan newspapers contained "many and detailed complaints of improper conduct by enlisted *Guardia*." Ultimately, Beadle asked to be relieved. Feland told Sellers that ordinarily, he would have suggested that Beadle remain in his post until the "bad conditions" of the *Guardia* were cleared up, but in this case, he believed Beadle should be relieved immediately, before the audit. However, he recommended that Beadle stay in Nicaragua to assist the auditor and "for [the] protection of his own interest."[29]

Admiral Sellers was not happy that General Feland had written directly to Headquarters Marine Corps rather than requesting the audit through him, and he chided Feland for doing so. Nevertheless, Sellers authorized Feland's Second Brigade officers to carry out the audit, rather than someone from the Marine Corps Adjutant and Inspector's Office, as Beadle had requested.[30]

In addition to the conflicts over the *Guardia*, another issue arose. President Moncada decided to create a force of about 500 men, the *Voluntarios*, who would be loyal to him and would take the fight directly to Sandino. Moncada believed this new group would enable the United States to reduce the Marine Corps presence in his country. Feland supported the idea; Beadle opposed it. In a long confidential letter to Commandant Lejeune, Feland noted that Moncada had brought up the *Voluntarios* idea at a meeting with Sellers, Feland, Beadle, Munro, and Eberhardt on January 3. Moncada had expressed dissatisfaction with the *Guardia*, which had been hurriedly thrown into service, was untrained for fieldwork, and harbored "unsuitable, even criminal, members." Feland noted that the *Voluntarios* would be under his own general direction and under the direct command of Colonel Dunlap in the Northern District. He told Lejeune that a *Voluntarios* column was already in the field and doing well. Feland had placed the Northern District under combined operations status, commensurate with a December 1927 order by the secretary of the navy, which meant that Marines and *Guardia* soldiers would accompany the *Voluntarios*. Feland noted that the entire command of Marines, *Guardia*, and *Voluntarios* in the field would remain under his control, which was what President Moncada wanted.[31]

In the same letter, Feland relayed to Lejeune that Moncada wanted to establish martial law in the four northern provinces most threatened by Sandino and other insurgents. Moncada and Feland believed this would enable the arrest and detention of "outlaw agents and spies" and give the Marines and *Guardia* a legal basis for holding prisoners. Enforcement of martial law would be the duty of the *Guardia*; the Marines would simply hand prisoners over to the *Guardia*. Minister Eberhardt supported this idea, but Secretary of State Kellogg advised that this was a Nicaraguan issue that should be handled internally, and only Nicaraguan authorities should enforce martial law.[32]

The ongoing tension between Beadle and Feland became so serious that on January 30 Kellogg reported to Eberhardt that the Navy Department was contemplating the early replacement of both Feland and Beadle, "apparently because of the recent actions of the former." Kellogg asked for Eberhardt's personal opinion on whether replacing one or both men would "improve the situation and solve the existing difficulties or not." Eberhardt replied that the friction between the two Marines warranted the replacement of both, and he noted that Beadle would probably like to be relieved from command of the *Guardia*. Eberhardt had spoken to Moncada and concluded that it would be useless for Beadle to remain: "There are many indications that Feland had prejudiced Moncada's mind against Beadle and he so intrigued in various ways for his own personal satisfaction and advancement as to have actually imperiled the success of the *Guardia Nacional*." Eberhardt surmised that Moncada would soon ask for Beadle's resignation as *Guardia* chief, at Feland's instigation, and that Feland would have Beadle reassigned to the Second Brigade. In Eberhardt's opinion, Beadle's resignation and demotion would harm the *Guardia*'s prestige as well as the legation's. Eberhardt therefore requested that the State Department take steps to facilitate Beadle's return to the United States.[33]

Beadle had, in fact, requested relief from his position, and Secretary of the Navy Wilbur informed Secretary of State Kellogg that the *Guardia* chief would be returned to the United States. Colonel Douglas McDougal would take Beadle's place if Moncada approved, which he eventually did. McDougal had initially enlisted in the navy but joined the Marine Corps in 1900; he had previously served as head of the *Gendarmerie d'Haiti*. Headquarters Marine Corps informed Admiral Sellers of Beadle's replacement on January 31, and the news was relayed to General Feland the following day. However, Beadle would not be the only one going home. Kellogg informed Eberhardt on February 2 that Feland would also be replaced, by Brigadier General Dion Williams. Williams had succeeded Feland as director of operations and training and then as Assistant to the Commandant.[34]

The disturbing situation between Feland and Beadle had caused Sellers to cancel a trip to Havana in late January and schedule one to Nicaragua instead. On February 5 Sellers, Feland, and Eberhardt met with President Moncada, who asked that Feland be allowed to remain in Nicaragua for three months, a request that met with the approval of both Feland and Sellers.[35]

Before leaving Nicaragua, Sellers suggested that Beadle and Feland get together with some of their respective officers to talk over their differences and resolve their issues, for the benefit of the Marine Corps. Feland subsequently reported that he had sat down with Beadle and two of his officers and gone "over everything in a calm manner." In his usual optimistic fashion, Feland expected that "the result will be wholly good." He also noted that he had addressed a memorandum to his brigade officers, reminding them to keep good relations with the *Guardia*, as they were "all working to the same end." Feland concluded that although Moncada still seemed bitter about Beadle, if no further irritants arose, the situation should remain stable until McDougal's arrival in March.[36]

Feland wrote the aforementioned brigade memorandum on February 6, in which he asserted that it was "most essential that this Brigade work harmoniously with all military forces of this [Nicaraguan] Government," including the *Guardia* and the *Voluntarios*. He counseled the officers to maintain a "spirit of encouragement" and underscored the need to "gain and hold the confidence of all the people." As soon as the Nicaraguans themselves could control the cities and the countryside, he believed, there would be no need for the Marines; their mission would have been fulfilled.[37]

Sellers filed a detailed report on his trip to Nicaragua in February. In his communication to CNO Hughes, Sellers noted that he had had a lengthy conversation with Beadle and had been "unable to find that the Chief of the *Guardia Nacional* had any legitimate [*sic*] cause for complaint against the Marine Brigade." In contrast, he believed Beadle had "displayed a lamentable lack of tact" when dealing with President Moncada and General Feland. Sellers enumerated several episodes in which Beadle had acted inappropriately, especially in agitating Moncada, but he could find no fault with Feland. Two days later, Sellers wrote privately to Hughes, reiterating his findings. He included Feland's earlier letter describing his attempts to establish better relations with Beadle and the *Guardia* officers. Regarding the military situation, Sellers observed that Feland had "conducted the campaign against the bandits in a very thorough and soldierly manner." The admiral pointed out the "immense influence" the United States had in Nicaragua "due to the fact that President Moncada reposes great confidence in General Feland and in addition, has a great personal regard for him." In Sellers's opinion, the State Department did not fully appreciate this "great asset."[38] Once again, Feland's commanding officer supported him fully. Despite Feland's missteps (such as going over Sellers's head when requesting the *Guardia* audit), Sellers remained loyal to the general and truly believed that Feland had conducted himself appropriately.

Also in February, more controversy developed over the new proposed *Guardia* agreement that was being debated by the Nicaraguan Congress. Eberhardt and Beadle were against the proposal. They believed its provisions opened the door for another military and police organization, and they thought the *Guardia* should be the sole entity with such responsibilities. They also believed the *Guardia* chief should retain authority over all recruiting, appointments, and promotions, to keep the *Guardia* from being politicized. After a meeting in early February, Eberhardt reported to the State Department that Feland and Sellers had no objections to the proposed agreement, and he claimed their attitude had undermined the State Department's position, encouraging President Moncada to ignore Eberhardt's protestations.[39]

Sellers took great offense at Eberhardt's statement. The admiral claimed he was unaware of some of the proposed changes to the agreement and could not support or oppose something he did not know about. In a cable to the chief of naval operations, with a copy to General Feland, Sellers called Eberhardt's assertion that he and Feland had undermined the State Department "not true," and Sellers pointed out that he had immediately sent Eberhardt a letter denying the charge. Sellers told the CNO that Eberhardt had misrepresented his position, and he was "at a complete loss to understand the action of the American Minister in furnishing Department of State with such gross misinformation." He also disliked Eberhardt's veiled reference to the "independent political activities of the officers of American armed forces in Nicaragua." Sellers wanted the names of any officers engaging in such activities so that appropriate action could be taken. In his reply to Sellers, Feland asserted that he had kept Eberhardt informed of any discussions regarding the new *Guardia* law that he had been involved in outside of Eberhardt's presence. Feland believed Eberhardt's charges were based on "a single piece of underhand gossip which [w]as imparted to the informant by another person at one of the Managua clubs."[40]

In a private latter to General Feland on February 27, 1929, Sellers stated that to say he was "indignant" would be "very mildly expressing it." The admiral could only conclude that Eberhardt "was deliberately trying to discredit both of us." He believed, however, that the Navy Department fully understood the "true situation." Along with this letter, Sellers included excerpts of his communications to the Navy Department that lauded Feland's work. The admiral also noted that with Commandant Lejeune's imminent departure from the Marine Corps to assume the presidency of the Virginia Military Institute, a major general's slot would open up, and he hoped Feland would get the promotion. Sellers's letter revealed that the admiral's own replacement would probably be arriving in May.[41] Sellers had known for a long time that he had been recommended to become the navy's next judge advocate general, a position he would hold until 1931. He would later become commander of the U.S. Fleet, and his last assignment, before retiring in 1939, was superintendent of the U.S. Naval Academy.

For his part, General Feland was also preparing to leave Nicaragua. Despite assurances that Feland would be retained in Nicaragua until May, as requested by President Moncada, the Marine Corps commander was scheduled to leave around mid-April. Katherine Feland traveled to Nicaragua to accompany her husband home. In anticipation of Feland's departure, his chief of staff, Colonel Randolph Berkeley, hosted a farewell party, as did Moncada.[42]

Meanwhile, Managua was a busy place. Douglas McDougal arrived to replace *Guardia* chief Beadle, and Brigadier General George Richards, the Marine Corps paymaster, visited to carry out an inspection. Colonel Dunlap traveled down from the north to take over temporary command of the Second Brigade, pending the arrival of Brigadier General Dion Williams. On March 19 Senator Burton Wheeler, an outspoken opponent of U.S. intervention in Latin America, paid a visit and was greeted by General Feland. Wheeler had traveled to Nicaragua to investigate the need for a canal. While in Managua, he reiterated his opposition to U.S. military intervention but grudgingly admitted that the Marines had "conducted themselves very creditably."[43]

On March 23 General Feland suddenly received orders to return to the United States as soon as possible and report to Headquarters Marine Corps. That same day, Sellers had invited Feland and his wife to stay with Admiral and Mrs. Sellers while in the Canal Zone awaiting departure on a steamer to the United States.[44]

Three days later, Feland turned over temporary command of the Second Brigade to Dunlap. On March 27 General and Mrs. Feland arrived at the Marine Corps airfield in Managua to fly to the Canal Zone. Feland's officers staged a large send-off at the airfield, complete with a band and presentations. Pictures of the event show the Felands in the company of his officers and several Nicaraguans, including Vice President Enoc Aguado. A guard of honor paraded, and the officers presented Katherine Feland with a large bouquet of flowers. Katherine donned a leather avia-

Logan and Katherine Feland prepare to leave Nicaragua.

tor's cap, and then the Felands boarded the Marine Corps Fokker airplane and departed.[45]

Brigadier General Logan Feland left Nicaragua believing that the Marines had accomplished their main mission: to help the Nicaraguans conduct a successful, peaceful national election. Augusto Sandino remained at large; his forces were weakened, but he remained persistent. His international reputation may have been more robust than his reputation in his own country. Sandino would continue to be the subject of Marine Corps and *Guardia* hunts until 1933, when he was lured to a meeting at Managua and summarily shot by *Guardia* forces under Anastasio Somoza, the future Nicaraguan dictator.[46]

Of the five major American figures playing important roles in Nicaragua, all would be gone by July 1929. McCoy had left in December, and Beadle and Feland were gone by the end of March. Beadle would serve in the Adjutant and Inspector's Office before retiring in 1930, after thirty-one years of service. He received the navy's second highest decoration, the Navy Cross, for his service in Nicaragua. Eberhardt, who had been requesting reassignment for many months, owing to his declining health, also departed in March; his next assignment would be in Costa Rica. Admiral Sellers soon joined the exodus from Nicaragua.[47]

After a brief stay in the Panama Canal Zone with Admiral and Mrs.

Logan and Katherine Feland arrive in New York City from Nicaragua. (Author's collection)

Sellers, the Felands boarded the steamer SS *Calamares,* bound for New York City. When they arrived on April 7, 1929, they were met by the commander of the Marine Barracks, Brooklyn Navy Yard, and escorted to Penn Station, where they boarded a train for Washington, D.C. The Felands' arrival in the United States received press coverage, including photographs of the general and his wife.[48]

Two days after arriving in the United States, Brigadier General Feland met with Francis White, the assistant secretary of state for Latin American affairs, at the State Department. During their extensive conversation, White queried Feland about several aspects of the Nicaraguan situation. Feland told him the military situation was "well in hand," although he did not know how long it would take to clean up the "bandit situation." White mentioned the State Department's worry that the *Guardia Nacional* would become partisan under President Moncada, to which Feland replied there was no way the *Guardia* could *not* be partisan. Feland emphatically defended the audit of the *Guardia,* as well as his appointment as a minister plenipotentiary. Feland was especially chagrined that Eberhardt had not helped him acquire the recognition that would place him above the U.S. chargé d'affaires, despite his promise to do so. Regarding the incident involving Challacombe's father-in-law, Mr. French, Feland acknowledged that although there had been a man by the same name in his MIT class, he did not think it was the same person. When asked by White if he had anything else to add to the conversation, Feland said he believed Eberhardt had misrepresented Moncada's attitude. The Nicaraguan president was very friendly to the United States, according to Feland, and the State Department "should not be misled on this score."[49]

General Feland received various encomiums for his work in Nicaragua. In April 1929 the *New York Times* reported on a letter from President Moncada in which the Nicaraguan president expressed his deep appreciation and esteem for Feland's conduct and handling of the situation in Nicaragua. The letter, which Moncada had made public, praised the Kentucky Marine for his "gentlemanliness, humane and generous manner, ideals in performance of duty, impartial conduct and self-control."[50]

In May 1929 the Marine Corps's *Leatherneck* magazine translated an article from the Nicaraguan newspaper *Diario Moderno* that called Feland a "friend of justice" and a "sincere friend of Nicaragua and of all the Nicaraguans, without distinction of class." Feland was also notified by the secretary of the navy that he would receive his third Distinguished Service Medal, adding to his previous awards in 1920 for his service in Santo Domingo and in 1927 for his first stint in Nicaragua.[51]

So ended Brigadier General Logan Feland's official connection with Nicaraguan affairs. He would remain interested in the country and occasionally spoke about it. In 1930 and 1932 he would even investigate the possibility of returning to oversee another Nicaraguan national election. But in the spring of 1929, it was time for Feland to move on to new challenges.

14

Returning Home

After nearly two years in Nicaragua, Brigadier General Logan Feland returned Stateside to find that the Corps had changed dramatically. After eight years as Commandant, Major General John Lejeune had decided not to seek another four-year term. Consequently, on February 7, 1929, he announced that he would step down the day after Herbert Hoover was inaugurated as president in March. Wendell Neville's appointment as the new Commandant was made public the next day, to no one's great surprise. Then, toward the end of March, Lejeune surprised everyone and accepted a position as president of the Virginia Military Institute (VMI). Lejeune would officially retire from the Corps in November 1929.[1]

Feland seemed pleased that his old Fifth Regiment and Fourth Brigade commander had been chosen to succeed Lejeune. Just before leaving Nicaragua, Feland had written to James Harbord, noting that "the appointment of Neville to Major General Commandant was exactly what I wished and nobody was more pleased to congratulate him than I was." He also mentioned that a major general's slot would open up when Lejeune retired, and he hoped Harbord would once again assist him in seeking the position.[2]

Although their correspondence had been reasonably friendly during his time in Nicaragua, Feland would certainly not miss working with Lejeune, which he considered "hell." Feland had found fault with several things Lejeune had or had not done during the Kentuckian's command in Nicaragua. For example, the Commandant had barely mentioned Feland in an appearance before Congress to report on the Nicaraguan inspection trip in January 1928. Feland also believed that Lejeune had not defended

Commandant Wendell Neville.

the Marines vigorously enough against false charges of committing atrocities. Nor had he responded strongly when newspapers incorrectly reported that the Marines had lost a battle flag to the Sandinistas, a charge that insulted Feland's brigade.[3]

In February there was rampant speculation as to how the generals would be moved around, given Lejeune's decision not to seek another term as Commandant and the return of Smedley Butler and Logan Feland from abroad. Initial rumors had Lejeune going to the Department of the Pacific in San Francisco, Butler to Quantico, and Feland to the Assistant to the Commandant position or back to Parris Island. The latter prospect apparently made Feland very unhappy, but as of mid-March, that seemed the most likely posting for the general.[4]

Feland's next assignment remained in limbo while he took leave and Neville wrestled with command assignments. Fortunately for Neville, Lejeune's March announcement of his retirement meant there would be an opening as commanding general of the Department of the Pacific. As Commandant, Lejeune had created this post in San Francisco for George Barnett, who had refused to retire from the Corps after his removal as Commandant in 1920. Neville had replaced Barnett when he retired in 1923, and when Neville returned to Quantico in 1927, Eli Kelly Cole had succeeded him in San Francisco. Cole was in poor health and awaiting retirement when he died of a heart attack on July 4, 1929.[5] Neville therefore had a position available for Feland as head of the Department of the Pacific.

At the end of July the Felands moved to San Francisco and assumed their various official and social obligations. General Feland's duties revolved around periodic visits to various Marine Corps outposts on the West Coast from San Diego to Bremerton, Washington. He inspected the Marine posts and dealt with assorted administrative matters. After nearly two years in Nicaragua, duty in San Francisco proved to be much more comfortable, if not so meaningful.

In November 1929 Feland and Butler received their long-awaited temporary promotions to major general. Veteran Marine Corps officers John Twiggs "Handsome Jack" Myers and Robert "Hal" Dunlap became brigadier generals, assigned to Headquarters Marine Corps. Brigadier General Ben Fuller served as Assistant to the Commandant, while Brigadier General John Russell remained in Haiti as high commissioner. The other brigadier general, former Sixth Regiment commander Harry Lee, was in charge at Parris Island.[6]

As the Great Depression settled over the country, the Marine Corps struggled to maintain its strength and its good reputation. Unfortunately, bad publicity sometimes intervened. For example, in December 1929 a speech by the Marine Corps's "stormy petrel," Major General Smedley Darlington Butler, criticized the Marine Corps's missions overseas. Butler eventually summed up this theme in a book in which he decried his role as "a gangster for capitalism." Butler criticized U.S. foreign policy and the use of the Marine Corps as "State Department troops."[7]

Butler's chief rival, Major General Logan Feland, believed otherwise. In a speech to former secretary of the navy Curtis Wilbur's Sunday school class, Feland disagreed with Butler's analysis. As reported in the newspapers, Feland directly contradicted Butler's assertion that "the Marines so manipulated the elections in Nicaragua as to make sure their candidate was elected." Instead, Feland insisted, "The Marines gave Nicaragua a free and fair election." To Butler's suggestion that the Marines had simply found voters who favored their candidates and then closed the polls after their ballots had been cast, Feland countered that every man who wanted to vote had been allowed to do so. He added that President Moncada was "anxious for peace and a free election."[8]

Commandant Neville had little time to worry about the dispute between his new major generals. On March 27, 1930, Neville suffered a stroke. His assistant, Brigadier General Ben Fuller, temporarily took over the Commandant's duties. Neville himself thought he was fine. He wrote to Lejeune on April 12 that he was "getting along famously," able to sit up in bed and getting over his weakness. Only his right foot had been impaired, and that was improving. Neville was aware of the talk regarding his illness. He told Lejeune: "I fear the rumor has gotten around that I am down and out for good, particularly at that nest of rumors—Quantico." Neville was right: speculation about a potential successor was growing, and the major candidates started lining up support.[9]

In April 1929 Feland had called on his Republican friends to assist in his quest for the major general's slot that would become available when Lejeune retired in November. One of the most influential was Mark Requa, whose father had made a fortune in railroads and mining. A mining engineer himself, Requa had first met Herbert Hoover before World War I;

during the war he had served with Hoover in the U.S. Food Administration and then as head of the Oil Division of the U.S. Fuel Administration. Requa had also played an important role in Hoover's 1928 presidential campaign. In April 1929 Requa wrote to the White House regarding Feland's desire to become a major general. He followed up in May with a reminder to Hoover's personal secretary, Lawrence Ritchey, not to overlook the matter. Requa noted: "I have set out to get this promotion for Feland and I don't want to fall down on it." He asked Ritchey to take up the matter with Secretary of the Navy Charles Adams.[10]

Feland called on Requa again when Commandant Neville became ill. In April 1930 Requa forwarded to Ritchey a letter from Feland expressing his interest in the Commandant's position, should it become available. In late June Feland wrote to Requa, citing a confidential letter he had received from a "reliable man" who believed that the contest for Commandant would be between Butler and Russell. The speculation was that if he recovered, Neville would take a three-month leave of absence to recuperate and then serve another year before retiring. Feland believed the Navy Department would split over the choice of Neville's successor, and although he had good friends in the department, he had not contacted them because he did not want to make a "false move." Requa promptly forwarded Feland's letter to Ritchey, admitting, "I am for Feland because it seems to me that he is entitled to the job." There the matter rested until Neville died on July 8, 1930. The next day Requa sent a telegram to Ritchey again asking that Feland be considered, noting that the much younger Butler still had time to become Commandant, but "so far as Feland is concerned, it seems to be now or never."[11]

Immediately after Neville's death, newspapers reported that four primary candidates had emerged to succeed him. The *Washington Post* pointed out that as the "senior ranking officer," Major General Smedley Butler was the putative next in line to the throne. Three days later the *Post* reported that the State Department favored Brigadier General John Russell, who had been working for the department as the high commissioner in Haiti for ten years. Russell was fourth in seniority, behind Major Generals Butler and Feland and Brigadier General Harry Lee, who had commanded the Sixth Regiment during much of World War I. Lee, however, was never a real candidate. The fourth contender proved to be Brigadier General Ben Fuller, who was serving as Acting Commandant.[12] Thus, it came down to a four-horse race, and this time, Major General Feland would vigorously pursue the Commandant's position.

Feland had Requa working for his candidacy, and he somewhat belatedly asked James Harbord for assistance as well. In a telegram on July 27, Feland noted that the contest was between himself and Butler, who had allegedly said he would "rid the Corps of all Second Division men." According to Feland, this sentiment was already hampering the promotion of Julius Turrill, one of his key Fifth Regiment battalion commanders who had received the Distinguished Service Cross for his actions at Belleau Wood on the same day as Feland. Feland asked for Harbord's immediate intercession with Hoover (Harbord had led Hoover's 1928 presidential campaign while on a leave of absence from RCA).[13]

Harbord immediately sent a telegram to the White House and a long follow-up letter touting Feland's candidacy. Harbord's letter focused on Feland's World War I service. The former army general noted that during Belleau Wood, "whenever there was a special difficulty to be overcome or an Officer of experience needed to supervise the command of the units that might, at the time, be operating in the Wood, Lieutenant Colonel Feland was the Officer invariably sent. There was no Officer in the command who had a more intimate and varied experience, under great responsibility, during that time than Colonel Feland. He repeatedly demonstrated personal valor and high capacity for command." Harbord noted that Feland was "considerably older" than the other candidates and that if Feland was not appointed this time, "his career will lack the final reward of the command of his Corps." Hence Harbord "strongly recommended" Feland's appointment.[14]

Harbord also tried to enlist the help of others. He asked General Frank McCoy and Colonel John Callan O'Laughlin to write letters on Feland's behalf. Among other things, O'Laughlin had been an Associated Press correspondent in St. Petersburg, a personal assistant to President Theodore Roosevelt, an assistant secretary of state, and a good friend of John J. Pershing. In 1925 O'Laughlin had become publisher of the influential *Army and Navy Journal*, and he was an adviser to President Hoover. In a follow-up letter to Feland, Harbord noted that he had written to McCoy, O'Laughlin, and Lejeune, from whom he had not received responses. Harbord chided Feland for not attending the Second Division reunion in Los Angeles. Only General Dunlap and Colonels Harry

Lay and Burton Sibley had been there to represent the upper echelons of the Corps. If Feland had attended, Harbord believed he would have been elected president of the Second Division Association. In any case, if Feland needed anything else, Harbord volunteered his assistance. He noted that the announcement of Neville's successor had not yet been made, and he hoped Feland would get the position.[15]

Feland remained optimistic regarding his candidacy. On August 4 he telegraphed Harbord and suggested that he write to Secretary of the Navy Adams to "counteract representations made to Adams by [a] small group at headquarters that all [the] Marine Corps favors Fuller which is not true." Harbord immediately did so, noting that he had recommended Feland to the president. Harbord once again cited Feland's World War I record. He also quoted McCoy's telegram saying that he would be glad to state his opinion of "Feland's good work" in Nicaragua. Harbord acknowledged Butler's candidacy but stated, "the weight of age and record calls for the appointment of General Feland." Three days later Secretary Adams replied to Harbord, thanking him for his letter but stating that "there were reasons which seemed to us good which led to the appointment of someone else." Adams had nominated the Acting Commandant, Brigadier General Ben Fuller, to be the next Marine Corps Commandant. The announcement had appeared in the *New York Times* the previous day.[16]

In the meantime, Butler had also vigorously sought the Commandant's position, but he acknowledged that navy admirals disliked him. Nevertheless, Butler believed he had strong congressional support. He had been assured that "Feland's name was not being considered anymore as he has but three years to do," a reference to the fact that because the mandatory retirement age was sixty-four, Feland would not be able to complete a four-year term as Commandant.[17] Both Butler and Feland lacked support from former Commandant Lejeune. Having moved to Lexington, Virginia, to be VMI president, Lejeune could claim to be a distant bystander during the Neville succession maneuvers. He gave only lukewarm support to Butler and did not support Feland at all. Historian Merrill Bartlett believes that Lejeune "harbored grave concerns over Feland's own dependence on alcohol."[18]

If Feland's alleged dependence on alcohol had been an issue beforehand, it certainly had not prevented him from getting important commands and completing important tasks. His fitness reports and health

Ben Fuller. Fuller became Commandant of the Marine Corps in 1930, prevailing over Logan Feland, Smedley Butler, and John Russell.

records do not indicate any serious alcohol debilitation, unlike his protégé Earl Ellis, who had a well-documented drinking problem. As for his age, Feland was only a few months older than Fuller, the man selected to be the next Commandant. If anything, Feland's major liability was most likely his lack of a Naval Academy degree.[19]

Actually, the die had been cast early in Fuller's favor. On July 21, 1930, President Hoover's naval aide, Commander Charles R. Train, had prepared a memo on the Commandant candidates after speaking with his Navy Department contacts. Train concluded that "both services (Navy and Marine Corps) seem to be unanimous for General Fuller." Although junior in rank, Fuller was senior in service to the other three contenders. He was also an Annapolis classmate of the new chief of naval operations, Admiral William Veazie Pratt, which, in Train's opinion, could "only tend to good results." Train could find no support for Butler; as for Feland, Train thought he was "probably the second choice." Train noted that Feland was "a fine soldier and had always cooperated with the Navy to a high degree."[20]

In analyzing his prospects for the Commandant's position, Feland had rightly dismissed Russell as being too far distanced from mainstream military activities after serving for a decade as the State Department's high commissioner in Haiti. Feland mistakenly focused his attention on Butler, who was the senior major general, the youngest of the candidates, and the general most well known to the public. Feland failed to grasp how much Butler had alienated navy officials with his constant criticism; there was no way they would accept Butler as Commandant, especially after his influential father had died.

Feland also mistakenly dismissed Fuller, who lacked combat experience. But Fuller proved to be the right person in the right place at the right time. He had been Assistant to the Commandant when Neville had his stroke and then Acting Commandant after Neville died. He did not engender controversy. Although junior in rank to Feland and Butler, Fuller had more service time in the Corps. Probably most important, he "wore the ring," the mark of the Annapolis graduate, and had been a classmate of the chief of naval operations.

With great anguish, Feland sat down at his typewriter on August 22, 1930, and wrote to Harbord, expressing his bitter disappointment at being passed over for the Commandant's position. He ascribed Fuller's appointment to the personal efforts of Assistant Secretary of the Navy Ernest Lee Jahncke. Uncharacteristically, Feland's emotions poured out. He called Fuller "one of the most worthless men" ever in the Corps. Feland thanked Harbord for all his efforts and noted that he had also sent Frank McCoy a thank-you letter. Feland regretted, however, that Harbord had written to Lejeune on his behalf. Feland scathingly characterized the former Commandant: "He works in an underhand way always. Probably he worked for Butler for a time, then double crossed him and went in for Fuller or anything to beat me. I know him like a book and there is nothing too low for him to do."[21]

Harbord wrote back, asking Feland to help raise money for a Second Division memorial. Back in 1926, at the annual meeting of the Second Division Association in Chicago, Harbord had been appointed chairman of the Second Division Memorial Committee. The committee was in the process of raising $150,000 to create a memorial in Washington, D.C., originally intended to be etched with the names of all the Second Division men who had died in World War I.[22]

Feland had issues with Harbord's request because of Lejeune's involvement in the memorial project. Feland expressed his powerful emotions to Harbord in a return letter, excoriating Lejeune. He believed that Lejeune, "for his own selfish ambitions," had created the impression that "he was the only one who did so very much in the Division." Feland criticized the former Commandant's character, which, he said, had been revealed in an episode during the Nicaraguan conflict. The *New York Times* had published "the lie that Marines in Nicaragua were being killed by machine guns taken away from them," and Lejeune had failed to counter this assertion. That failure "allowed the Corps of which he was head to be traduced because of some reason best known to himself." Feland also believed Lejeune harbored personal animosity toward him because Feland had once told the Commandant that he had made an untrue statement. Feland concluded: "I am by no means alone in my opinion that Lejeune is what is known as an S.O.B."[23]

Feland also believed that Lejeune had influenced both Neville and Harbord against him. Yet he was "not inclined to put any blame on anyone except Lejeune" because he had "endured for a long time the results of his [Lejeune's] malice and underhanded methods." Not wanting to break their friendship, Feland nevertheless told Harbord that he could no longer ask for his assistance if he were going to consult with Lejeune, who would find a way to block anything Harbord might do to help Feland. This was a startling statement, given that Feland had trusted Harbord so completely for more than fifteen years. As for supporting the Second Division memorial project, Feland believed Lejeune had "manipulated" not only the Second Division but also the Belleau Wood Association, the Marine Corps League, and other groups "for his own glorification." Hence Feland "did not go to Los Angeles [for the Second Division Association meeting] for fear this man would be there and it is my sincere hope never to see him again as long as I live." Despite these misgivings, Feland concluded that perhaps he could assist Harbord in the memorial project "without taking part in a public way," because he really wanted to do something for Harbord and the Second Division.[24]

In a reply letter, Harbord expressed surprise that Feland had such feelings about Lejeune. He denied consulting Lejeune on the matter of Feland's appointment; he had simply written to Lejeune and asked him to support Feland. Harbord proclaimed his continuing support for Feland: "I am as devoted to you as I was in 1918, and I think you know I considered you the strongest man in the Marine Brigade. I loved Neville and I think he was a very fine Officer, but I was always conscious of the fact that, as his Lieutenant Colonel, you were a mainstay on whom he constantly leaned." Then Harbord turned his attention to the Second Division memorial and asked Feland to "please go ahead and see what you can do in the way of getting us some money, and please also be sure that I stand by you, behind you, and with you just as strongly as I did in those days in which I depended on you at the Belleau Wood, and I will always be willing to do anything I can for your welfare."[25]

Shockingly candid, Feland's letters to Harbord offer a strong insight into his personality. The distress reflected in those letters and his exceedingly sharp tone underscore Feland's competitiveness and ambition. The anguished exchange of correspondence with his mentor reveals how desperately Feland wanted to become Commandant of the Marine Corps. He had served the Corps well for thirty years. He had proved himself intelligent, brave, and competent to command at the highest levels. He also knew that his last opportunity to become Commandant had come and gone.

The question remains as to what sort of Commandant Feland might have been. Absent any specific policy paper outlining his plans for the Corps, some clues reveal what he might have done. Without doubt, he would have valued loyalty to the Corps, along with discipline, hard work, and propriety. Writing to mining company officer Julian Smith back in 1920, Feland had noted that things were "going along good" down in the Dominican Republic, but it was "a hard thing to imbue a whole brigade with 2nd company [mining company] ideas." Nevertheless, Feland claimed he "did it in the 5th Regiment and we are progressing all the time here." In an oral history interview many years later, Smith related what Feland meant by mining company values: "you had to be on the job all the time with him." Smith added that he had learned more from Feland than from any other Marine Corps officer.[26]

Given his intelligence, experience, and proven adaptability, it is highly likely that Feland would have been successful in balancing the conflicting needs and missions of the Marine Corps. He had been one of the first instructors at the Advanced Base School, head of the Philadelphia Military Training Camp, and the first director of operations and training. He had extensive experience in expeditionary conflicts and major wars. He deeply believed in the importance of learning from experience and training to meet developing needs. For example, his subordinate officers were already attempting to create a doctrine to govern the Marine Corps in small wars. In addition, he had served as Assistant to the Commandant during a crucial transitional period in the 1920s under Commandant Lejeune.

Given this experience, Feland recognized that the Marine Corps had to adapt to an evolving situation with regard to amphibious warfare. This required a transition from a defensive, advanced base concept to a more offensive, amphibious mission to take over islands in the Pacific. With his engineering background and interest in technology, Feland most likely would have embraced the challenges involved in getting large numbers of Marines ashore quickly. However, the task of formulating the Marine Corps's dual lines of small wars doctrine and amphibious warfare would devolve to younger officers trained by Feland: men such as James Carson Breckinridge and Harold Utley. After his appointment to head the Department of the Pacific and his failure to become Commandant, Feland would settle into a comfortable sinecure in San Francisco.

During his last years in the Marine Corps, Feland turned his attention to other personal and professional matters. His relationship with Harbord proved strong, and the two men would remain friends and collaborate on various projects during the 1930s, as the nation faced the economic crisis of the Great Depression.

Feland's official duties kept him traveling up and down the West Coast, inspecting Marine Corps units. In San Diego he saw his old colleague Robert Dunlap, newly promoted to brigadier general and commanding the Marine base there; Dunlap was assisted by Colonel Harry Lay, who had been General Harbord's adjutant at Fourth Brigade headquarters during World War I. Feland also got to visit with the hero of Ocotal, Major Ross Rowell, who was commanding the Aviation Squadron of the West Coast Expeditionary Force at San Diego.

During his command at San Francisco, General Feland helped nur-

Logan Feland and Ross "Rusty" Rowell, San Diego, 1931.

ture the newly formed Marine Corps Reserve units on the West Coast. On one occasion he rushed down to Los Angeles to help sort out a problem when the 307th Reserve Company proved unable to muster the forty men required by headquarters to attend the annual summer training camp at San Diego. Feland met with the company officers and men for a "skull session," then interceded with headquarters to reduce the minimum requirement to twenty-five men. The 307th Reserve Company attended summer camp in San Diego, under the watchful eyes of General Dunlap and Colonel Lay.[27]

General Feland also participated in several celebrations. For example, in November 1930 in Vallejo, California, he presided over the formation of a new Marine Corps League detachment named after his old commander, Buck Neville.[28]

In the 1930s the Corps started to lose more of its older World War I and prewar officers. Neville had died in 1930. In June 1931 Feland traveled east to Washington for the burial of his old colleague Robert Dunlap. Touted as a future Marine Corps Commandant, Dunlap had gone to France, where he was scheduled to attend the *École de Guerre* in Paris. While walking with his wife in the countryside south of Tours, Dunlap had gone to the rescue of a French woman trapped in a cave. The woman survived; Dunlap, however, became trapped himself and perished on May 19, 1931. After funeral ceremonies in Paris, Dunlap's body was ferried home and interred in Arlington National Cemetery on June 13, 1931. Major General Feland served as an honorary pallbearer, along with other Marine Corps luminaries that included Commandant Ben Fuller, Major General Smedley Butler, Brigadier General Dion Williams, his old friend Fritz Wise, and General Frank McCoy.[29]

In October of the same year Feland's old hunting friend, Thomas Turner, died in a freak accident when he was hit in the head by a plane propeller while in Haiti. Turner was buried at Arlington National Cemetery. His honorary pallbearers included several men who had served under Feland in Nicaragua, including Lieutenant Colonels Charles "Sandy" Sanderson and Phil Torrey and Major Clyde Metcalf, who would become Marine Corps historian.[30]

In July 1932 Harry Lay died. Feland had known Lay since their early careers, and Lay and Feland had served as ushers at Dunlap's wedding in 1905. Lay's death prompted Feland to write to Harbord, "We received the sad news this morning of Harry Lay's death." Feland noted that Lay had died of apoplexy and surmised that he would be buried in Washington. Feland concluded about his longtime colleague: "Poor Lay had a right bad time, but has always remained a steadfast friend to all of us."[31]

During this time, Feland (whose promotion to the permanent rank of major general had been granted in December 1931) was still carrying on his duties on the West Coast. In April 1932 he visited San Diego to inspect Marines under the command of Brigadier General Frederick Bradman. While there, Feland presented the Marines with a maneuver problem with a twist: a new brigade and organization had to be created temporarily to carry out the maneuver. Bradman's Marines were successful, and General Feland proclaimed "his satisfaction at the splendid manner in which the games were carried on."[32]

Even though he was back in the States, Nicaragua continued to weigh on Feland's mind. Milly Bennett, a well-known reporter for the *San Francisco Daily News*, wrote about Nicaragua and quoted Feland as saying, "with a note of bitterness in his voice": "'There weren't any battles. . . . It was ambushing, bushwacking, the dirtiest kind of fighting.'" She added, "General Feland insists that Sandino has never been a power, a dangerous challenge to the United States." The general cautioned against giving money to organizations sympathetic to Sandino, however. Despite claims that the money would be used for hospitals, in reality, it would buy "'guns and bullets to fight American Marines.'"[33]

Feland continued to worry about the Marines who had fought in Nicaragua. In the summer of 1930 he wrote to radical journalist Carleton Beals, searching for information about Lieutenant Thomas and Sergeant Dowdell, the two aviators who had been shot down and killed by Sandino forces in October 1927. Feland's first letter asked Beals to let him know when the journalist returned to the Berkeley area; Feland wanted to "look [him] up," in the hope that Beals could provide "some information which will be of value or comfort to families of some of our men who died in Nicaragua." Beals replied from Mexico, where he was doing research for a book on former Mexican dictator Porfirio Díaz. Beals wrote that he would not be returning to California anytime soon, but if Feland had some specific questions, he would try to answer them. He also noted that a Dr. Cepeda, Sandino's representative in Mexico, had told him that the dog tags and documents of U.S. troops killed by the Sandinistas had been preserved.

Feland had recently learned, during a conversation with aviator Ross Rowell, that Thomas and Dowdell had never been officially recognized for their service. The Marine Corps lacked the specific information about the circumstances of their deaths on which to base a citation, and Rowell had told Feland that Beals knew more details. Feland therefore wrote to the journalist, hoping that he could provide enough information to take to the Navy Department so that "their valor may be recognized." Beals replied that he had no notes on the subject, but to the best of his recollection, Sandino had told him that the two aviators were forced down by a gasoline tank leak. The Marines then encountered two native guides and set out for Ocotal, but their guides turned on them, killing Dowdell with a machete and seriously wounding Thomas. While holed up in a cave or in some rocks, Thomas killed four Sandinistas before succumbing. Beals thus clarified the mystery of how they died. Supported by Rowell and Dunlap, Feland then tried to get Medals of Honor awarded posthumously to the two aviators, but he was unsuccessful.[34]

Feland also attempted to obtain additional military awards for some of the men who had served him well in Nicaragua. He tried to get Distinguished Service Medals for Harry Schmidt and Oliver Floyd to supplement the Navy Crosses they had already received. Although his efforts were much appreciated by the two men, Feland was again unsuccessful.[35]

As he tended to Marine Corps matters, General Feland was aware that his service in the Corps would soon end. He was scheduled to retire on September 1, 1933. As his official duties became routine, he turned his attention primarily to personal projects.

15

Retirement

Major General Logan Feland undertook some major personal projects during his time on the West Coast. Although he had started writing a book about Belleau Wood before leaving Nicaragua, in San Francisco he turned his attention to writing a movie script about the battle.

During the 1920s, a few Marines wrote successful novels, plays, and short stories about the Corps in World War I. In 1923 the first major artistic work about the Marine Corps in World War I appeared: the novel *Through the Wheat*, by Thomas Boyd. Boyd had served with the Sixth Regiment at Belleau Wood, Soissons, and Saint-Mihiel before being gassed at Blanc Mont. Invalided out of the Marines, Boyd eventually landed in St. Paul, Minnesota. While working in a bookstore there, Boyd met up-and-coming author F. Scott Fitzgerald and gave him a draft of a novel based on his World War I experiences. Fitzgerald convinced famed Scribner's editor Maxwell Perkins to publish Boyd's novel, which received critical acclaim in the *New York Times* and other publications. Boyd sent a copy of the book to General Feland, which the Kentuckian acknowledged in a thank-you note.[1]

In 1924 Maxwell Anderson and Laurence Stallings wrote a play, *What Price Glory?* that became a big success on Broadway. In 1926 the play was made into a movie starring noted actors Victor McLaglen and Dolores Del Rio. Stallings, who had served in Feland's Fifth Regiment, had been severely wounded in the leg at Belleau Wood, requiring its amputation in 1922. Another Fifth Regiment veteran, John Thomason, the "Kipling of the Corps," wrote three books of war stories published by Scribner's: *Fix*

Bayonets! in 1925, *Red Pants and Other Stories* in 1927, and *Marines and Others* in 1929.[2]

Although not specifically about World War I, the 1926 film *Tell It to the Marines,* starring Lon Chaney Sr., boosted the image of the Corps. The film version of Erich Maria Remarque's famous World War I novel, *All Quiet on the Western Front,* was released in 1930.

Major General Feland believed the time was right for a realistic film depiction of the Battle of Belleau Wood. While stationed in San Francisco, he used his personal contacts to approach the RKO Company about producing the script he had written. (Created by RCA executive David Sarnoff and Boston millionaire Joseph P. Kennedy, RKO had been formed in 1928 to take advantage of new technology and produce sound movies.) Feland had read Boyd's *Through the Wheat* and had complimented the author on its realism, so he suggested that RKO contact Boyd's agent about the possibility of him working on the screenplay. In March 1931 Boyd traveled to California to meet with Feland and RKO officials. The meeting with Feland proved frustrating; Boyd felt that the general simply wanted to reminisce about the war and had no idea how to make a movie. Boyd was further disillusioned when RKO officials told him the picture needed "glamour." Nevertheless, during the summer of 1931 Boyd worked on a script, but it was eventually rejected by RKO.[3]

Ever optimistic, Feland reported to James Harbord in late August 1931 that a "fresh start" was being made. RKO's president of production, Joseph Schnitzer, was committed to the film, and Feland was encouraged about its "final success." Unfortunately, Schnitzer was replaced in 1932 when RKO underwent a major reorganization. Feland lamented this change to Harbord, ascribing it to "jealousy and self-seeking" among Schnitzer's subordinates. He described Schnitzer as a "fine, decent man" who had worked hard to get the Belleau Wood picture made.[4]

After the failed RKO experience, Feland continued to shop around his film script. In this endeavor he enlisted the aid of Major Adolph B. Miller, a Marine Corps recruiter in Los Angeles. Miller, who had good connections to the film industry, acted as a conduit for Feland's efforts to get his film produced. They gave the script to Melville Shauer at Paramount, where his father was a vice president. Shauer critiqued the script, noting that it was more fact than fiction; it contained "narrative incident but lacks thread for story purposes." He suggested that Feland might want to turn it into a book instead.[5]

Thwarted at RKO and Paramount, Feland next turned to famous Metro-Goldwyn-Mayer director W. S. Van Dyke. Having directed half a dozen films in the 1920s, Van Dyke had recently directed the 1932 hit *Tarzan the Ape Man*, starring Johnny Weissmuller and Maureen O'Sullivan. He would go on to direct a series of films featuring Myrna Loy and William Powell and another series starring Jeanette MacDonald and Nelson Eddy. Van Dyke also sought and eventually received a commission in a newly formed Marine Corps Reserve unit in Los Angeles, for which Major Miller served as inspector and instructor.[6] Following Van Dyke's return from a trip to Alaska, Miller gave the director the Belleau Wood script.

In May 1933 Van Dyke sent Feland his comments about the script, noting that "as picture material, it represents a wealth of valuable and picturesque incident, but lacks entirely in story thread, particularly the romantic thread which is so necessary to pictures of this sort." Van Dyke wondered whether Feland's script could be revised to include a female character, such as "Cigarette" in Marie Louise Ramé's book *Under Two Flags*, a late-nineteenth-century swashbuckling romance set in Algeria. "Otherwise," Van Dyke concluded, "very frankly, the studios will not touch war dramas unless they possess [an] unusual romantic sex incident." Given this advice by a major Hollywood director, Feland moderated his quest to have the Belleau Wood script produced, although he did not give up the idea completely. He toyed with hiring a woman to inject a feminine viewpoint into the script, and he considered putting the script in the hands of an agent.[7]

Feland also remained interested in international affairs, especially pertaining to countries in Latin America. In November 1930 Feland spoke before the venerable Commonwealth Club of California on the subject of "Reconstruction in Nicaragua." Founded in 1903 as a public affairs forum, the Commonwealth Club in San Francisco hosted a diverse group of speakers, including former president Theodore Roosevelt in 1911. Noting that he was "not talking for publication," Feland stated his belief that the United States had refrained from aggressive military action in Nicaragua so President Coolidge could "show to the outside world" that Americans "had no desire to intervene in the affairs of Nicaragua to a larger extent than necessary." Regarding the Marines' task of ensuring free and fair elections, Feland asserted, "There was no motive of imperialism or territorial aggrandizement actuating the naval and military forces." Feland cited the conduct of successful elections as proof of the wisdom of the U.S. policy. There had been no infringement of rights, no martial law, no atrocities, and no press censorship. As soon as the *Guardia Nacional* could ensure order, the Marines would be "diminished to a minimum." In response to a follow-up question after the speech, Feland claimed "there was no dollar diplomacy" in Nicaragua.[8]

In a lengthy article in the *Los Angeles Times* published in January 1931, General Feland called for better relations with Mexico and Central America as a way to improve relations with South American countries that were "growing in strength and influence." He reminded readers of the three great cultures of the region: Aztec, Maya, and Inca. He believed the traits of all Central Americans, regardless of class, included "courtesy and kindliness, hospitality, artistic perception, taste and skill and a habit of taking enough leisure to be kind and considerate." He underscored that the economic situation was "very bad, deplorably so, as far as the lower classes are concerned." Due to a lack of education, sanitary conditions were bad and disease was prevalent. Feland believed that, above all, Central America needed "good roads and primary schools," and the best way to help Central Americans was by "breaking down the barriers of race and language and thus learning to know and appreciate their good qualities, their weaknesses and their difficulties."

Feland went on to say that American business, "in invading Central America," seemed intent "on getting all possible and giving as little as possible." Given its wealth, the United States "could afford to see that in financial matters these poorer neighbors are not unjustly treated." Feland also noted that the essence of the 1927 Stimson agreement had been to carry out free elections in 1928—a task he had originally considered impossible (a surprising admission from the general). He credited his Marines with keeping the peace and discounted stories of violence and atrocities. He believed the Central Americans would attest that the campaign had been carried out "with respect for citizens' rights and the sovereignty of Nicaragua." Although Feland's article leveled some criticism at American businesses in Latin America, he refrained from the strong position taken by Smedley Butler.[9]

This long article by Feland was uncharacteristic, in the sense that he was not known to write much for publication. Previously, he had written only a few short articles for the *Marine Corps Gazette*. The *Los Angeles Times* article underscored his great concern for Nicaragua; it displayed the general's knowledgeable perspective and his kindhearted empathy for the people. Above all, it indicated Feland's belief that the Marine Corps had been helpful in Nicaragua.

Feland lobbied to return to Nicaragua in 1932 as head of the Electoral Supervision Commission. Pennsylvania congressman William Coyle, a former Marine and an old friend of Feland's, had visited Secretary of State Henry Stimson in December 1930 "to ask about the future possibilities of General Feland of the Marines in whom he was interested as a brother Marine." Stimson replied that although he had personal friendship with Feland, "the feeling in the [State] Department was that Feland 'had not quite played the game' in Nicaragua" after Stimson had left in 1927.[10]

Once again, Feland asked James Harbord for support in gaining a position he coveted. After attending Robert Dunlap's burial in Arlington in June 1931, he had visited Harbord in New York City, where they discussed the possibility of Feland serving as supervisor of the next Nicaraguan elections. Feland noted that in conversations at the State Department, he had detected some opposition to his candidacy, allegedly based on his lack of cooperation with General McCoy in Nicaragua in 1928. Harbord wrote to McCoy on Feland's behalf, hoping that the army general would assist in countering that perception. McCoy promised to take up Feland's candidacy with officials at the State Department the next time he visited Washington. McCoy noted that he "had got along with Feland as well as could be expected," and the Marine Corps general had extended his "most thorough cooperation" in supervising the 1928 elections. Although McCoy expressed his "very high personal regard" for Feland, he did not want to commit himself to Feland's candidacy until he determined how Nicaraguan officials might react to someone who had played such an "intimate part in the previous troublesome times." McCoy acknowledged that Feland was very experienced in Nicaraguan affairs, but he thought someone without a history there might be more desirable.[11]

Harbord apprised Feland of McCoy's stance; Feland appreciated the kind words and favorable tone of McCoy's letter. Later in July Feland telegraphed Harbord, pressing him to ask McCoy to "make [a] strong recommendation at once," given that the secretaries of state and the navy were currently considering the supervisory position. Harbord complied immediately, sending McCoy a copy of Feland's telegram along with a letter noting that the position meant a great deal to Feland. A few days later, Feland reported to Harbord that although Secretary of the Navy Charles Adams wanted to nominate Feland, the Kentucky Marine's close ties to President Moncada might make such a nomination inadvisable. Feland believed McCoy's intercession would overcome this "trumped up" objection put forth by "some subordinate in the State Department"— perhaps Francis White, who had questioned Feland so thoroughly after his return to the States. Feland denied favoring Moncada during the 1928 campaign, asserting that he had interacted more often with the Conservative candidate. If Feland had shown any partiality to either candidate, he pointed out that McCoy would have said something to him about it. Feland concluded: "Everybody in Nicaragua knows I would give all hands a square deal."[12]

In replying to Harbord, McCoy remained "somewhat nonplussed about how best to handle our friend Feland's prospects." He had contacted State Department officials about Feland's candidacy but could "not urge [Feland's] claims very strongly." The problem "might not be summed up in what Feland did, because his record in Nicaragua is well known, nor would he be partial to any candidate; but any one of us who was there would, in a sense, be charged with favoritism."[13] In other words, McCoy believed that the resistance to Feland's appointment came not from the State Department but from Nicaragua. No one from 1928 would be welcomed back because the Nicaraguans wanted to move forward. Hence the State Department's inclination to nominate someone without close ties to the country, someone who would be perceived as impartial.

Harbord communicated the gist of McCoy's letter to Feland, warning that McCoy was "not very sanguine" about Feland's prospects. Harbord underscored the army general's friendly but frank statement and advised Feland to accept McCoy's judgment as to what the State Department would do. Feland acquiesced to both McCoy's and Harbord's reading of the matter, noting that he "only wanted the place because I thought I could do some good for the administration in the way of bringing about better conditions" in Nicaragua. On the downside, it would have been "a mean job and involve another year in the tropics which I do not care for very much." In the end, President Hoover appointed Rear Admiral Clark

Woodward as chief of the Electoral Commission. So ended Feland's quest to return to Nicaragua.[14]

Despite the prospect of a good pension as a retired Marine Corps major general, Feland worried as the Depression deepened. In a letter to Harbord, he mentioned that he had "hoped to make a little money on the Belleau Wood movie," which, unfortunately, never happened. Nevertheless, he was "in fine health and would be willing to go to work." Feland recognized, however, that jobs were scarce; thus, he and Katherine were "planning now to live in the most economical way possible for us. This involves getting away from centers of activity." After the general's retirement, they would live at their summer camp in remote northeastern Pennsylvania and then move to Columbus, Ohio, where they would live in Katherine Feland's family home. Still worried about money, Feland even asked Harbord to try to get him a discount on a particular brand of RCA Victor radio that would be useful at the Felands' summer camp.[15]

In his correspondence with Harbord, Feland also expressed his opinions about the Depression and the overall national situation. He supported the adoption of a thirty-hour workweek, which the press reported was favored by the American Legion, of which Harbord was a key leader. (At the time, some people believed that limiting workers to thirty hours per week would result in the employment of more people, thus ameliorating the effects of the Depression.) Feland also wondered why RCA and other large companies did not detail people from their research departments "to make a report as to what is necessary to be done to develop the best industrial system for the country. Such a report would 'not be in restraint of trade' and ought to command respect." Feland also opposed a scheme to tax machines instead of land and personal property. An economist friend of Harbord's had suggested this method as a proper way to "speedily restore the equilibrium between man and the machine." Feland countered that when production was proceeding too rapidly, it was better to "go around with a sledge hammer and break up a percentage of machines. Taxation always has an unexpected result on the side."[16]

Knowing that he would soon be retiring, Feland sent letters, along with his picture, to several officers who had served under his command in World War I and Nicaragua. Their replies revealed genuine affection for the general. Past and future Marine Corps leaders wrote their thanks, including Dulty Smith, Phil Torrey, Charles "Sandy" Sanderson, Gilder

Jackson, Oliver Floyd, Ross Rowell, Marion Humphrey, Henry Larsen, David L. S. Brewster, and Merritt Edson. Somewhat embarrassed that his reply to Feland had inadvertently been set aside, Edson took the trouble to send a thank-you letter after a hiatus of two years. Major Marion Humphrey, who had helped assure General Moncada's safety in the days leading up to the Treaty of Tipitapa in 1927 and had served as Feland's chief of staff in 1928, wrote: "I deeply appreciate the interest you have taken in me, and your characteristics are much like my father's which made you seem closer to me than my elder brothers." Humphrey wrote he regretted Feland's failure to make Commandant but hoped the general would enjoy much hunting and fishing in his retirement.[17]

Henry Larsen, one of Feland's old Fifth Regiment battalion commanders who had also served with him in Nicaragua, wrote a meaningful letter to the general. Larsen expressed his disappointment at Feland's retirement, which was not only a loss for the Corps but also a significant personal loss of "one whom I have for so many years looked upon as a personal friend and a champion." The example set by Feland spurred his subordinates to their best efforts. Larsen wrote: "While you had the respect and loyalty of your subordinates in full measure, you demonstrated that this cooperation is a reciprocal sort of action or relation in true leadership and in turn supported and respected your subordinates in their worthy endeavors." Larsen observed that Feland's understanding and personality permeated down to "the last buck-private out in the listening post."[18]

In his retirement, General Feland would take pride in seeing the men who had served with him become senior leaders in the Marine Corps. In 1934 Phil Torrey became a colonel, as did Ralph Stover Keyser; Marion Humphrey, Keller Rockey, Oliver Floyd, Henry Larsen, Alphonse de Carre, and Harry Schmidt were all promoted to lieutenant colonel. Larsen, Torrey, Rockey, de Carre, Schmidt, Edson, and aviators Ross Rowell and David L. S. Brewster would all go on to become general officers.[19] Feland thus left his stamp on the Marine Corps leadership that would carry through World War II.

In February 1933 Logan and Katherine Feland traveled east to take up the general's final preretirement post at the Marine Corps Department of Supplies at Philadelphia. While awaiting his mustering out, Feland spent the few months remaining of his official service presenting awards and presiding over other ceremonial duties. In April he had the pleasure of giving out medals to four men for their service in World War I and Nicaragua. During the summer of 1933 the Felands spent time at their cabin in Pennsylvania.[20]

Major General Logan Feland officially retired from the Marine Corps on September 1, 1933, as reported in newspapers across the United States. Associated Press articles described him as a "famous Kentucky Marine" with one of the most distinguished records in the Corps.[21] After Feland's retirement was announced in the *Army and Navy Journal*, Harbord wrote to his old friend, extending his "affectionate good wishes" and once again praising Feland's World War I service. The RCA chairman also expressed his happiness that Feland had finally received his major general's stars but regretted that he had never been appointed Commandant.[22]

Even the "last buck-privates" weighed in on Feland's retirement. For example, John Calahan from Stockbridge, Massachusetts, had seen the notice of General Feland's retirement in the newspaper. He reminded the general that they had both served in the old advanced base mining company, and Calahan had been with Feland at Vera Cruz. He had also run into Feland in France during World War I, where Calahan "got shot up pretty bad." Calahan remembered the general fondly and wrote that all Feland's men "loved you, for your kindness, squareness, and an even break for every body."[23]

In his retirement, Feland would continue to correspond with Harbord, and after the Felands moved to Columbus, Ohio, Harbord expressed his surprise and said he hoped Feland "did not leave [Pennsylvania] on account of Smedley."[24] Feland's rival, Major General Smedley Butler, had retired from the Marine Corps in September 1931 at the young age of fifty. In contrast to Feland, the final years of Butler's career had been turbulent. After his reprimand from Secretary of the Navy Charles Adams for his 1929 speech denouncing U.S. imperialist interventions and his failed candidacy for Commandant in 1930, Butler delivered another speech in January 1931 that got him into trouble. Butler repeated a story told by Cornelius Vanderbilt about Italian dictator Benito Mussolini callously running over a child with his car. The Italians protested, U.S. Secretary of State Stimson apologized, and Butler was nearly court-martialed. As Butler's only Marine Corps peer, Feland could have been detailed to serve at the court-martial. Instead, the secretary of the navy selected six rear admirals and retired Marine Corps major general Joseph Pendleton.

Negotiations ensued before the court-martial, and Butler suffered only a reprimand. Nevertheless, his military career was finished.[25]

Feland's career ended more quietly; he seemed reconciled to retirement and had several projects to keep him busy. One key task involved a memorial for his old Marine Corps mentor, former Commandant George Barnett. Barnett had retired in 1923 and passed away in April 1930. Three years later the Episcopal bishop of Washington, the Right Reverend James E. Freeman, agreed to the placement of a bronze tablet memorial to Barnett in the Washington National Cathedral. Consequently, Feland led a fund-raising committee that included Brigadier General George Richards and Lieutenant Colonel Charles R. "Sandy" Sanderson. The committee drafted a letter and sent it to Marine Corps personnel, hoping to raise $1,200 for the memorial. The fund-raising campaign proved a success, and on June 8, 1934, the memorial tablet was unveiled before a crowd of 700 people. Mrs. Barnett attended, Eleanor Roosevelt represented President Roosevelt, and Commandant John Russell made remarks.[26]

Feland missed the unveiling of the Barnett memorial because of prior commitments to the Baltic Society and the Second Division Association. First, Feland attended the May 1934 meeting of the Baltic Society, comprising the men who had accompanied General Pershing to Europe on the SS *Baltic* in May 1917. Feland had missed the annual meeting for several years but managed to attend this one, along with Harbord and George Patton. Pershing was absent, however; he had gone to France as chairman of the American Battle Monuments Commission to inspect U.S. military cemeteries. Following this meeting, the Felands traveled to New York City, where they visited Radio City Music Hall, courtesy of Harbord. RCA had joined with financier John D. Rockefeller to build the famous entertainment venue, which had opened in 1932.[27]

The Felands stayed in New York to attend the annual reunion of the Second Division Association held at the Hotel Astor on June 7–9. Attending the reunion were many of the men who had helped make the Second Division famous, including Generals James Harbord, Omar Bundy, and Hanson Ely. The event was officially hosted by Feland's former commander in Nicaragua, Admiral David Foote Sellers, who was commander in chief of the U.S. Fleet, which had docked in New York Harbor. A former Sixth Regiment company commander and future Commandant, Clifton Cates, welcomed his old Marine colleagues aboard the USS *Wyo-*

ming, where he commanded the Marine contingent. New York City mayor Fiorello LaGuardia was the guest of honor at the annual reunion dinner.

In a lighter moment at the event, Sergeant Dan Daly, a two-time Medal of Honor recipient and member of Feland's wartime Fifth Regiment, stood up and told a joke on Harbord. This set the tone of the reunion, as the veterans retold and refought the division's famous battles, such as Belleau Wood. In a particularly poignant moment, General Feland asked Gold Star mothers and fathers, whose sons had fallen in battle, to come forward to receive medals for their sons, who were gone but not forgotten. The reunion concluded with the announcement that Feland would serve as Second Division Association president for the next year.[28]

In November 1934 General Feland attended the groundbreaking for the Second Division memorial in Washington. There he joined Commandant John Russell, Brigadier General Thomas Holcomb, James Harbord, Hanson Ely, Frank Mason, and other dignitaries and a thousand attendees. Harbord turned over the first spade of earth for the new memorial, situated between the White House and the Washington Monument.[29]

Feland's presidency of the Second Division Association entailed one possible difficulty: his reacquaintance with former Commandant John Lejeune. Feland wrote to Lejeune and invited him to the next reunion. Lejeune replied that he and his wife would attend, but at the last minute, on July 10, 1935, Lejeune sent his regrets. He explained that, after taking a bad fall while inspecting a water tower in September 1932, he had been "nearly unconscious for a week, and the accident kept him inactive for almost a year." Two years later, Lejeune was not feeling "hale and hearty" enough to join his Second Division comrades for their reunion in Cincinnati.[30]

At the reunion, Feland graciously expressed his regrets that General Lejeune would be unable to attend. The delegates also acknowledged the loss of yet another Feland contemporary, Major General Harry Lee, commander of the Sixth Regiment, Fourth Marine Brigade, after Belleau Wood. Feland then turned the presidency of the association over to Major Frank Mason, who had served in the Ninth Infantry Regiment and was a vice president at the National Broadcasting Corporation (NBC).[31]

Mason and Feland later corresponded about the general's Belleau Wood manuscript, which he now contemplated turning into a book rather than a movie. Feland wrote to Harbord about reviewing it and hoped the RCA chairman might also pass it along to Mason for review. Mason had already shared some information with Feland regarding the German side of the story. Harbord did read the manuscript and encouraged Feland to continue working on it, observing that, "as the individual officer most connected with the [Battle of] Belleau Wood," Feland was "the man to write such a story." Feland subsequently traveled to New York City in early December 1935 to discuss his manuscript with both Harbord and Mason. He looked forward to the trip, admitting to Harbord that he got "a little lonesome out here" in Columbus.[32]

In addition to working on his manuscript, Feland stayed active in the Columbus community, speaking to local organizations on occasion. On July 4, 1934, he addressed the Allied Democratic Clubs of Franklin County at a National Defense Day celebration. In his speech, Feland warned that the "lack of a fixed policy as to what we are to defend" had "confused the problem of national defense." Once the policy was determined, Feland believed it would be "far easier to provide the means of defense." The commander of the U.S. Army's Fifth Corps area, Major General Albert Bowley, followed up with a warning against a "pacifist element which intends to disarm this country and leave us helpless."[33] Given the current world situation—war in East Asia stemming from Japan's 1931 attack on Manchuria, and Adolf Hitler's ascendancy to power in 1933—the two major generals were addressing issues that would continue to be debated in the United States throughout the 1930s: Should the United States stick with "splendid isolationism," or should it prepare for war in the future in either Asia or Europe?

In October 1935 Feland spoke at a Navy Day celebration at the American Legion's Franklin Post No. 1. According to a newspaper account, the former Marine chided his audience, saying they "'should be ashamed to go around telling the boys' that while war was 'pretty bad' they would go again." Feland reminded the veterans of the horrors of World War I, telling them that if they had served at the front for any length of time, "wild horses could not drag you back." Feland "urged that all 'keep cool,' avoid hysteria at the present time and 'shun talk about national honor being insulted and loss of trade.'"[34] It was interesting and somewhat surprising that Feland would speak so candidly in public, given his dedication and his loyalty. But Feland knew firsthand the horrors of war. He had a level-headed, realistic view, and he supported a strong military presence that would deter belligerence before it got out of control, as it had in World War I.

During his residency in Columbus, Feland apparently met with journalist Carleton Beals, with whom he had sparred in Nicaragua and exchanged correspondence while commanding the Department of the Pacific. When Beals was in Columbus in 1933 to speak at the Foreign Policy Association, Feland stopped by the Athletic Club, where Beals was staying. During this visit, Beals discovered that Feland "was a man with liberal convictions he dare not express [while in the Corps]."[35] Beals alleged that Feland told him things the general could not have said in 1928 in Managua. Specifically, Beals quoted Feland as saying: "We had no business being in Nicaragua at all. Before we sent in troops, no American lives or property were in any danger. After we came, many American lives were lost. It was just a miserable effort to get hold of Nicaraguan property, to satisfy the bankers and the politicians. I could not say so in those days, and can't say so openly even now. I was a soldier obeying orders. But you were wholly right, and I admire you, as I did then." Based on this discussion, Beals was impressed with the general's clear view of reality and concluded, "Feland was greater than the forces which moved him."[36]

On Memorial Day 1936 General Feland attended the annual meeting of the Baltic Society. General Pershing himself hosted the reunion, and famed journalist and fellow *Baltic* passenger Frederick Palmer reported on the event for the *American Legion Monthly*. A photograph in the *Monthly* depicted the head table: General Pershing sat in the middle, glancing to his left at Fox Conner. To the left of Conner sat two men engaged in a seemingly serious conversation—Brigadier General John McAuley Palmer, who had once served as Pershing's assistant chief of staff, and Major General Walter A. Bethel, an eventual U.S. Army judge advocate general. To Pershing's right sat his former chief of staff, James Harbord, who was turned to his right and chatting with Logan Feland, who had a big smile on his face. According to Frederick Palmer, the "Baltic party would never have been complete without a Marine," and since Robert Dunlap had already "met a gallant death," the group "rejoiced that Feland was with us. His smile helps to make any party a success. He never missed a trick under fire in any battles the Marines fought. Even among the Marines there is only one Feland."[37] After the Baltic Society reunion, the next major event on Feland's calendar was the annual Second Division Association reunion, to be held in Washington, D.C., in July 1936.

Unfortunately, General Feland suffered a fatal heart attack on July 17, 1936, at his home in Columbus, Ohio. His wife, Katherine; his sister, Mary Gilmour of Owensboro, Kentucky; and three nieces and two nephews survived him. Katherine Feland telegraphed the news to Harbord, who was already in Washington for the Second Division Association reunion. A few days later, Harbord replied to Katherine, expressing his "warmest sympathy." Noting his reliance on Feland during the war, Harbord concluded: "I have ever since thought of him as one of my best friends. I shall never forget him. He should have been spared for many years." At the dedication of the Second Division memorial on July 18, the division's veterans accepted Harbord's resolution expressing deep regret at Feland's death.

Feland was interred with full military honors in Arlington Cemetery on July 22, 1936. Honorary pallbearers included Major General Louis McCarty Little, future Commandant Brigadier General Thomas Holcomb, Brigadier General Hugh Matthews, Brigadier General Richard Williams, Colonel Frederick Barker, Colonel Ralph Stover Keyser, Colonel Ross Rowell, and Lieutenant Colonel Alphonse de Carre. The burial party included a trumpeter, a section of the Marine Band, a firing party, and a noncommissioned officer bearing the major general's flag. An American flag–draped caisson bore Major General Logan Feland's body to the grave, and the Kentucky Marine was laid to rest before a Marine Corps honor guard.[38]

Epilogue

On November 10, 1942, the observed 167th birthday of the U.S. Marine Corps, Katherine Feland and Mary Gilmour (the general's sister) met in Long Beach, California, for the launching of a new ship that would be vital to the United States in World War II. They were joined at the ceremony by Major General Holland Smith, commanding general of the Amphibious Force, Pacific Fleet, and the Fleet Marine Force, San Diego. Acting as the ship's sponsor, Katherine Feland smashed the traditional bottle of champagne against the hull of the USS *Feland*, which then slipped sideways off the launching ramp. Named after the Kentucky Marine, the navy transport would see extensive service in the Pacific, most notably ferrying Marines to the iconic battle at Tarawa as well as at Saipan, Guam, Leyte Gulf, and Iwo Jima. The *Feland* was eventually decommissioned in March 1946.

Katherine Feland died on February 8, 1946, and was interred in Arlington National Cemetery next to her husband, Major General Logan Feland.[1]

Logan Feland of Hopkinsville, Kentucky, led a momentous life. Though joining the Marine Corps at a later age than most of his colleagues, he almost reached the pinnacle of Marine Corps command: Commandant. His service in the Marine Corps coincided with the United States' expansion as a global power, with territories and responsibilities around the world. In an expanding Marine Corps, which was often the tip of the spear in times of crisis, Feland served as a sea soldier of the new empire.

Katherine Feland and Mary Gilmour at the launching of USS *Feland*, November 10, 1942.

Recognized early for his courage and intelligence, Feland was given increasingly important duties. The Corps relied on his technical skills and his ability to impart those skills to others.

A brief history of General Feland's service generated by the Marine Corps in 1953 noted that he was "known in the Marine Corps as one of its best strategists and technicians."[2] His interests in civil engineering, underwater mines, a rifleman's shooting aid, and aviation were all manifestations of a keen intelligence and a rational approach to dealing with problems. But Feland was not interested in such technical advances in a vacuum; he was no laboratory-bound engineer with little appreciation of the practical uses of technology. Feland used technology to solve problems, such as when he recognized that Ross Rowell's air fleet could save the day at Ocotal.

As a strategist, Feland understood that the larger picture extended beyond simple tactics in the field. He was a hero, racing around the battlefield in World War I. During that war he adapted from being an officer who was tactically involved in Belleau Wood to the leader of a regiment who had to deal with larger strategic issues. His interest in military intelligence and his willingness to work on public relations (albeit sometimes reluctantly) reflected his understanding of the larger issues in warfare.

In writing about another Kentuckian, Harold "Hal" Moore, who led soldiers in the famed Ia Drang Valley battle in 1965, army general H. R. McMaster notes that "philosopher of war Carl von Clausewitz . . . argued that commanders need intellect, courage, and determination—the three principal components of military genius—to penetrate 'the fog of greater or lesser uncertainty' that surrounds combat." During the critical Battle of Belleau Wood, Feland reflected these three traits, thereby setting the stage for his future success and increasing leadership responsibilities.[3]

Major General Feland's greatest test as a Marine Corps leader came in Nicaragua in the late 1920s. He and his Marines faced a difficult task: to negate or eliminate the influence of Augusto Sandino and oversee a national election in Nicaragua. The Marines failed to eliminate Sandino. Given the resources they had and the conditions they faced, they did well to minimize the Nicaraguan's influence and make him a nonissue during the election. Although Feland encountered and even engendered controversy, he understood the local situation and always remained focused on the Marine Corps's mission in Nicaragua: oversight of a successful, peaceful election.

Throughout his Marine Corps career, Feland stressed education and training. He himself was a keen student of military tactics, strategy, and history. When the United States Infantry Association began its *Infantry Journal* in 1906, Feland subscribed within a year. He taught at the Marine Corps School of Application and was one of the first instructors at the Advanced Base School.[4]

Recognizing Feland's interests and skills, in 1920 Commandant Lejeune picked the Kentuckian to be the first leader of the new Division of Operations and Training. Feland was proud of his training efforts in the Dominican Republic. Later, in Nicaragua, Feland sought to bring together the lessons learned there, as reflected in the questionnaire he distributed to his officers, asking them specific questions about their activities and needs in the field.

One problem would continually interrupt the Corps's training efforts, however. Even though the Corps doubled in size at the time Feland joined and would become much larger than its pre–Spanish-American War level, it would often be undermanned, given the scope of its missions. Repeated expeditions into the Caribbean before World War I often necessitated the temporary cessation of training, as Marines gathered into provisional brigades and regiments and sailed off to foreign lands. After severe reductions following World War I, Commandant Lejeune tried to emphasize better education, but crises in China and Nicaragua hampered these efforts.

Feland's leadership in Nicaragua led other Marine Corps officers to examine the issue of small wars and how the Corps might better prepare for and conduct these wars in the future, such as by implementing much-needed changes in Marine Corps training. In the 1930s, Marine Corps proponents of preparation for small wars vied with those who viewed amphibious assaults as the wave of the future. Alarmed by increasing Japanese belligerency in East Asia, punctuated by Japan's attack on Manchuria in 1931, Corps leaders sought to build on the knowledge and planning initiated by Feland's protégé Earl Ellis in the early 1920s. Although Feland had observed the amphibious landing exercises at Hawaii in 1925, further development of an amphibious landing doctrine slowed when the Marines became involved in Nicaragua and China. Nevertheless, when John Russell became Commandant, preparing for amphibious assaults once again became a priority. Russell made this clear when he created the Fleet Marine Force in 1933 and ordered the production of a landing manual.

Major General Logan Feland was a transitional figure in the Marine Corps, reflecting its changing nature during the early twentieth century. By the 1930s, the Corps was forced to focus on both small wars and amphibious warfare.[5] Feland stood in both camps. He advocated preparation for small wars and had played a significant role in the Advanced Base Force, a forerunner of the Fleet Marine Force and subsequent amphibious warfare operations. Furthermore, as director of operations and training and Assistant to the Commandant in the 1920s, Feland had worked on the evolution of the Marine Corps Expeditionary Force.

As a result of his responsibilities in the 1920s, General Feland knew that the Marine Corps's budget and personnel would be limited throughout the decade. Nevertheless, thanks in part to his vision, the Corps was able to make the transition in the early 1930s and consider multiple missions. Unlike his rival Smedley Butler, who remained wedded to the idea of the Corps as colonial troops destined for small-scale expeditions to quell unrest in various countries, Feland embraced the concept of multiple missions. With appropriate resources, the Marine Corps could serve in many capacities and adapt as necessary, just as it had when called on to fight a major conventional war in France in 1918. Feland's versatility in expeditionary small wars, large-scale conventional warfare, and planning for amphibious warfare marked him as one of the Marine Corps's most valuable leaders in the first three decades of the twentieth century. Feland, however, was not directly involved in the 1930s discussions of small wars and amphibious warfare. He remained in San Francisco at the Department of the Pacific, far from Headquarters Marine Corps in Washington and the Marine Corps schools at Quantico. Instead, he would be relegated to wondering what might have been if he had become Marine Corps Commandant in 1930.

Logan Feland was recognized throughout his career as one of the Marine Corps's best and brightest. He apparently did not suffer fools easily and could be hard to please, although he sometimes tempered this attitude with a laconic demeanor. He was acerbic and had a sharp wit. He had high standards and expected the same from his subordinates. He was concerned about his men, but he was also highly ambitious.

Despite failing to achieve the ultimate goal of Commandant, Major General Logan Feland could be proud of his service to the Corps and his country. He had proved his bravery and his willingness to take on increasingly important tasks for the Corps. Throughout his service, Feland remained ambitious and always optimistic; he really believed that he could benefit the Corps. Unlike Butler, Feland kept a reasonably low profile after retiring, perhaps questioning but not criticizing the work he had done during his military career.

Given the scarcity of specific references, it is difficult to assess the impact Feland had on the individual officers with whom he served during his thirty-four years in the Marine Corps. In one oral history interview years later, however, the Marine who had commanded at Tarawa, Lieutenant General Julian Smith, said about Feland: "He was one of the best educated officers we had in the Marine Corps. I was in his company and I learned more from him, I think, than any other officer I ever served under, although you had to be on the job all the time with him."[6]

The letters written by Marine Corps officers to General Feland after he retired point to a man who was well respected and liked. Letters written by enlisted men indicate that he always considered the welfare of his men. In any case, the younger officers who served under General Feland, especially in Nicaragua, certainly took some of his command influence with them when they led units in World War II.

The Marine Corps likes its heroes strong and bold. It reveres men such as two-time Medal of Honor recipients Smedley Darlington Butler and Dan Daly and five-time Navy Cross recipient Lewis "Chesty" Puller. But many other types of leaders, such as Logan Feland, have also served the Corps well. The twenty-ninth Commandant of the Marine Corps, General Alfred Gray, had this to say about great Marine Corps leaders:

> These leaders had broad professional knowledge of not just the military but also all other elements of national security, including political, economic, and social factors. They understood the value of training and education to include discipline, particularly self-discipline as essential to develop character, self-control, and effectiveness. . . . The great ones had personal character that shone through in all decisions and judgments. They did what they thought was right, regardless of the consequences. They had a sense of fairness in dealing with people and more than a normal dose of common sense at all times. These leaders willingly shared their knowledge with others, and they took the time to teach, when appropriate. They had strong beliefs and a high moral code. "Service to God, Country, and Corps" was not just an expression, but a way of life.[7]

Logan Feland met these criteria of great leadership. Whether he was teaching in schools or making on-the-spot decisions in battle, Feland stood quiet but strong, striving for whatever was best for Corps and country.

Major General Logan Feland of Hopkinsville, Kentucky, proved to be intelligent, brave, and influential; he was an outstanding Marine Corps officer. He was personally courageous and intellectually versatile, one of the most adaptable and significant officers in the Corps. He should always be remembered as the Kentucky Marine who gave his best to his beloved Marine Corps.

Acknowledgments

If it takes a village to raise a child, it certainly takes at least several people to create a book. Many kind people helped me. First, I wish to thank my wife, Roi-Ann Bettez, for her tremendous support. From our first visit to Quantico in January 2008, she enthusiastically supported my efforts to write a biography of Major General Logan Feland, USMC. She traveled to various archives, discussed with me all aspects of the book, and read the manuscript so many times that she knows more about General Feland than she thought possible when we began this project.

Historians generally depend on archives and their professional staff, and I had the pleasure to encounter some wonderful archivists. From the beginning, director Mike Miller and his staff at the Marine Corps Archives and Special Collections at the Alfred M. Gray Marine Corps Research Center in Quantico enthusiastically supported this project. Mike read and earnestly discussed the manuscript with me; he was a General Feland fan from the outset, and I hope this resulting work satisfies his enthusiasm. Other Marine Corps Archives staff members were always helpful, pleasant, and polite when answering questions and getting materials for me. I am grateful to John Lyles for making suitable copies of photographs to use in this book. I especially enjoyed my discussions with archivist Jim Ginther regarding General Feland's influence in the development of Marine Corps aviation.

Across the way at Quantico, several folks at the Marine Corps History Division, Historical Reference Branch, assisted me, including Danny Crawford, Robert Aquilina, and Kara Newcomer. Kara tracked down information on the Marine Corps mail guards of the 1920s, as well as some of the photographs for this book. My biggest supporter there was historian Annette Amerman, another Feland enthusiast. I spent much time discussing this project with Annette, whose encyclopedic knowledge of Marine Corps history and of the resources in the History Division guided me to sources that had not been used in many years, allowing me a fresh view of Marine Corps history and General Feland's place in it.

Farther down the road at Quantico, the folks at the Marine Corps Association were supportive of the project and granted me permission to use material for this book. I thank *Marine Corps Gazette* editor Colonel John Keenan, USMC (Ret.), and especially *Leatherneck* executive editor and publisher Colonel Walter Ford, USMC (Ret.). When I appeared in Colonel Ford's office one afternoon, he graciously took time out of his busy schedule to help me track down photos in the *Leatherneck*'s collection for use in this book.

At this point I would also like to thank the Marine Corps Heritage Foundation for its financial support of this project, especially the vice president for administration, Susan Hodges. The foundation took a gamble and gave me a grant that proved very beneficial in getting this project under way. I also appreciate the foundation's support of other historians in telling the story of a magnificent organization: the U.S. Marine Corps. In addition, the foundation runs the Museum of the Marine Corps, which even my wife, who has been dragged to far too many military museums, agrees is truly outstanding. Everyone should visit the museum.

Other archives and institutions outside the Quantico area proved helpful as well. These include the National Archives, the Library of Congress, the New-York Historical Society, the Franklin Delano Roosevelt Library, the Herbert Hoover Presidential Library, the Military Heritage Institute, the Cincinnati Public Library, the University of Arizona Special Collections, the Massachusetts Institute of Technology (MIT) Museum, the MIT Archives, the National Personnel Records Center in St. Louis, the Yale University Archives, the Howard Gotlieb Archival Research Center at Boston University, Princeton University's Mudd Manuscript Library, and the University of Kentucky's W. T. Young Library. At the Young Library, Barbara Hale and her staff worked miracles, obtaining rare materials with speed and grace. At the National Archives in downtown Washington, D.C., Charles Johnson proved extremely helpful in tracking down materials on General Feland from the Marine Corps record group.

I would also like to thank editor Nelson Dawson of the *Register of the Kentucky Historical Society*, as well as its anonymous reviewers, for his support in publishing an article on General Feland that gave readers a closer look at this Kentucky Marine. Thank you to the *Register* for permission to use this material in the present book.

Friends were encouraging. University of Kentucky (UK) Professor Emeritus George Herring commented on an early draft of the *Register* article; both George and his wife, Dottie, were very supportive. Bob and Mary Kathryn Tri; Damon Snyder and Janet Cabaniss; Kevin and Melanie Sullivan; Major General Dennis Moran, USA (Ret.), and Cindy Moran; Kathy De Boer; Bill Marshall; "Mac" Coffman; and Bob Stubblefield all suffered through my fixation on General Feland. The late Shearer Davis "Dave" Bowman of the UK History Department enthusiastically encouraged me during the early phases of this project.

Besides my wife, the person who heard the most about General Feland is Captain Mark Pittman, USMCR (Ret.), who served his country in Vietnam in 1970 as a forward air controller with the Eleventh Artillery Regiment. At our weekly breakfasts, lunches, or golf games, he graciously listened, advised, and enthused about this project. Semper Fi, "Pittbull."

I also thank the fine folks at the University Press of Kentucky, starting with acquisitions editor Ashley Runyon. Ashley was most patient and helpful, guiding this neophyte author at every turn. The anonymous reviewers responded enthusiastically to the submitted manuscript, and their critiques resulted in good changes and additions to the final draft. Special thanks to Linda Lotz for her great effort in editing this book.

I give special credit and thanks to others who helped or were inspirational as I worked on this project. I thank Erika Slaymaker for tracking down materials for me at the Temple University Urban Institute archives in Philadelphia, while she was a busy student at Swarthmore College. I thank Dr. Gus Paris of Owensboro, Kentucky, for writing the manuscript that is in the Feland Collection at the Marine Corps Archives; this work made me want to learn more about General Feland and eventually prompted me to write this book. I also enjoyed a personal visit with Dr. Paris, a former Marine of the Fifth Amphibious Tractor Battalion who was twice wounded in World War II while participating in battles at Guadalcanal, Saipan, Tinian, and Iwo Jima. Another person who encouraged this project was Major Rick Spooner, USMC (Ret.), author and proprietor of the famous Globe and Laurel restaurant in Quantico.

Finally, I include the usual disclaimer: Any mistakes in this work are mine alone. The above folks were helpful, but "the buck stops here," with me. I trust that if you spend a buck or two to buy this book about Major General Logan Feland, you will not be disappointed in the story of this dedicated Kentucky Marine.

Appendix

Key Dates in the Life of
Major General Logan Feland, USMC

1869, August 18	Born in Hopkinsville, Kentucky
1892	Graduates from Massachusetts Institute of Technology
1898–1899	Serves in Third Kentucky Regiment during Spanish-American War
1899, July 1	Appointed first lieutenant, USMC
1899, December	Arrives in Manila, Philippines
1902, March	Ordered to Annapolis, Maryland, to oversee construction of Marine Barracks
1903, July	Promoted to captain
1903, December	Sent on expedition to Panama
1904, November	Assigned as instructor at School of Application, Annapolis
1905, May	Posted to study submarine mining at Torpedo School, Narragansett Bay, Rhode Island
1905, December	Assigned to command Marine Guard on USS *Massachusetts*
1906, October–December	Sent on expedition to Cuba
1907, February 14	Marries Katherine Cordner Heath in New York City
1907, March	Assigned to command Marine Guard on USS *Minnesota* and participates in Great White Fleet, sailing around South America to U.S. West Coast

1910, July	Assigned as instructor at Advanced Base School, New London, Connecticut
1911, March	Sent on expedition to Cuba
1911, July	Moves to Advanced Base School's new headquarters in Philadelphia
1912, May	Sent on expedition to Cuba
1913, February	Sent on expedition to Cuba
1914, January	As captain of mining company, participates in advanced base exercise at Culebra, Puerto Rico
1914, April	Participates in occupation of Vera Cruz, Mexico
1915–1916	Serves in Advanced Base Force at Philadelphia
1916, September	Promoted to major and serves as head of Philadelphia Military Training Camp
1917, March	Promoted to lieutenant colonel
1917, May	Sails to France on SS *Baltic* with General Pershing's advance party
1917, June	Becomes second in command of Fifth Regiment in France
1918, June	Participates in Battle of Belleau Wood
1918, July	Promoted to colonel and assumes command of Fifth Regiment in France
1918, July–November	Commands Fifth Regiment in battles at Soissons, Saint-Mihiel, and Blanc Mont and in the Meuse-Argonne offensive
1919, March	Temporarily appointed brigadier general
1919, December	Assumes command of Second Provisional Brigade in Dominican Republic
1920, December	Becomes director of the Division of Operations and Training, Headquarters Marine Corps, Washington, D.C.
1921, March	Appointed permanent brigadier general
1923, July	Appointed Assistant to the Commandant
1925, August	Appointed commander, East Coast Expeditionary Force, Quantico, Virginia
1926	Serves as commander of Eastern Mail Guard
1927, March	Sent to Nicaragua to command Second Brigade

1927, August	Returns to United States to command Marine Barracks, Parris Island, South Carolina
1928, January	Returns to Nicaragua to command Second Brigade
1928, April	Returns to United States from Nicaragua
1929, July	Sent to command Department of the Pacific in San Francisco, California
1929, November	Appointed major general
1930, July	Candidate for Commandant, USMC
1933, September	Retires from USMC
1936, July 17	Dies in Columbus, Ohio

Notes

Abbreviations

CNO	chief of naval operations
COMSECBRIG	Commander, Second Brigade
COMSPERON	Commander, Special Services Squadron
FRUS	U.S. Department of State, *Foreign Relations of the United States* (Washington, DC: U.S. Government Printing Office, 1927, 1928, 1929)
HRB, MCHD	Historical Research Branch, U.S. Marine Corps History Division, Quantico, VA
MCA	Marine Corps Archives and Special Collections, Library of the Marine Corps, General Alfred M. Gray Marine Corps Research Center, Quantico, VA
MD, LOC	Manuscript Division, Library of Congress, Washington, DC
NARA	National Archives and Records Administration, Washington, DC
NARA-CP	National Archives and Records Administration, College Park, MD
NPRC	National Personnel Records Center, St. Louis, MO
NYHS	New-York Historical Society, New York, NY
OPNAV	Office of the Chief of Naval Operations
RG	Record Group
SECNAV	secretary of the navy

Prologue

1. See W. Ekin Birch to John Lejeune, August 9, 1936, reel 7, John Archer Lejeune Papers, MD, LOC, where Birch lumps together "Old Tony" Waller, Logan Feland, John A. "Johnny-the-Hard" Hughes, and Lejeune as "personifications of something the word 'Marine' meant." Feland's description is from Carleton Beals, *Banana Gold* (Philadelphia: J. B. Lippincott, 1932), 306. The caricature of Feland by "Torrealba" can be found in *Report of the Chairman, American Electoral Mission*

in Nicaragua, 1928, Photographic Section, 54, box 17, Individual and Subject File, Francis White Papers, Herbert Hoover Presidential Library, West Branch, IA.

2. Logan Feland to James Harbord, August 22, 1930, file F, James Harbord Papers, NYHS.

3. For the Feland entry, see Mary Young Southard and Ernest C. Miller, *Who's Who in Kentucky: A Biographical Assembly of Notable Kentuckians, 1936* (Louisville, KY: Standard Print Co., 1936), 136. For entries on O'Bannon and Sousley, see John E. Kleber, *The Kentucky Encyclopedia* (Lexington: University Press of Kentucky, 1992), www.kyenc.org.

1. The Early Years

1. The history of the Feland family can be found in Martha Thompson, *Feland and Singleton Families: Virginia, Kentucky, and Missouri* (Redding, CA: Martha Thompson, 1985), 3–6.

2. A short account of John Feland's early life is included in William Henry Perrin, *County of Christian, Kentucky: Historical and Biographical* (Chicago: F. A. Battey, 1884), 366–67.

3. See Thomas Speed, R. M. Kelly, and Alfred Pirtle, *The Union Regiments of Kentucky* (Louisville, KY: Courier-Journal Job Printing Co., 1897), 272–74. Simon Bolivar Buckner later served as Kentucky governor from 1887 to 1891. His son, Simon Bolivar Buckner Jr., was a lieutenant general commanding the Tenth Army when it attacked Okinawa in June 1945. He was killed by Japanese artillery fire and was succeeded in command by aviator Roy Geiger, the first Marine to command an army group. The Buckners are buried in the Frankfort, Kentucky, cemetery.

4. The history of the Kennedy family can be found in J. H. Battle, ed., *County of Todd, Kentucky: Historical and Biographical* (Chicago: F. A. Battey, 1884), 273–75.

5. John Feland's time as a Kentucky state representative is covered in William Henry Perrin, ed., *Counties of Christian and Trigg, Kentucky: Historical and Biographical* (Chicago: F. A. Battey, 1884), 114. Feland's candidacy for Congress is noted in the *Hartford (KY) Herald*, October 27, 1880. According to the May 12, 1887, edition of the *Maysville (KY) Daily Evening Bulletin*, he was a "sure thing for lieutenant governor [as W. O. Bradley's running mate], if he will accept." Feland apparently declined. Though defeated in 1887, Bradley was elected Kentucky's first Republican governor in 1895. For details of John Feland's later life, see his obituary in the *Owensboro Daily Messenger*, January 10, 1899. See also the *Hopkinsville Kentuckian*, January 10, 1899, and the character sketch in Rev. S. E. Smith, ed., *History of the Anti–Separate Coach Movement of Kentucky: Containing Half-Tone Cuts and Biographical Sketches* (Evansville, IN: National Afro-American Journal and Directory, 1895), 153–54.

6. Thompson, *Feland and Singleton Families*, 18.

7. For the development of Hopkinsville and surrounding Christian County, see Charles Mayfield Meacham, *A History of Christian County Kentucky from Oxcart to Airplane* (Nashville, TN: Marshall and Bruce, 1930). Population statistics are from

Lewis Collins and Richard H. Collins, *History of Kentucky*, rev. ed. (Covington, KY: Collins and Company, 1878), 2:124–25, 258.

8. *Kentucky New Era*, February 23, 1883.

9. For Feland's picture as a cadet, see Alejandro M. de Queseda, "The *Carte de Visite* of Cadet Logan Feland: The Making of a Marine Corps General," *Military Collector and Historian* 61, no. 3 (Fall 2009): 225–26.

10. Undated newspaper clipping in the author's possession. For more information about Ferrell and his school, see Meacham, *History of Christian County*, 245–50, 283–90. See also "Hero in Gray Who Is Loved by Hundreds of Ferrell's Boys," *Hopkinsville Kentuckian*, July 17, 1907. Logan Feland was identified as attending Ferrell's School in the *Hopkinsville Kentuckian*, August 19, 1915.

11. *Hopkinsville Kentuckian*, August 24 and 26, 1915.

12. *Kentucky New Era*, June 17, 1886. For Feland's membership in Sigma Alpha Epsilon, see Howard P. Nash, Edward H. Virgin, and William Collin Levere, *The Sixth General Catalogue of Sigma Alpha Epsilon* (Evanston, IL: Sigma Alpha Epsilon, 1904), 140. Information on South Kentucky College can be found in Alfred Fayette Lewis, *History of Higher Education in Kentucky* (Washington, DC: Government Printing Office, 1899), 170–73.

13. Feland's participation in the Latham Light Guards is noted in Meacham's *History of Christian County*, 209, 216. For his return from the Greenwood crisis, see *Kentucky New Era*, March 25, 1886. See also G. Lee McClain, Adjutant General, *Military History of Kentucky* (Frankfort, KY: State Journal, 1939), 151. For more on Logan Feland's early years, see the unpublished manuscript by Gus E. Paris, "Hold Every Inch of Ground," 1–3, MCA.

14. For Feland's work on the railroad, see the *Sigma Alpha Epsilon Record* 8, no. 3 (November 1888): 142. Feland's fraternity continued to keep track of him; his receipt of a Distinguished Service Cross and other medals was reported in William Collin Levere, *The History of Sigma Alpha Epsilon in the World War* (Menasha, WI: George Banta, 1928), 148. Feland's work in Kuttawa and his appearance in town were reported in *Kentucky New Era*, November 2 and 8, 1886. On April 26, 1887, the newspaper noted that "Logan Spot Feland spent Sunday and Monday in the city" and identified him as the "assistant resident engineer on the O. V. road." The nickname "Spot" derived from Feland's childhood hero, Chief Spotted Tail of the Lakota tribe (*Louisville Courier-Journal*, November 19, 1922); it apparently did not carry over to his later professional life.

15. John Feland Sr. and William S. Feland are listed as collector and deputy collector of internal revenue, respectively, along with their salaries, in *Official Register of the United States, Containing a List of Officers and Employees in the Civil, Military, and Naval Service* (Washington, DC: Government Printing Office, 1892), 188. Collector Feland's appointment was reported in the *Owensboro Daily Messenger*, June 18, 1889.

16. For the controversy involving "Judge" Feland, see "Down on Feland: Owensboro Republicans Adopt Resolutions Rebuking Honest John," *Kentucky New Era*, April 21, 1891. The *New York Times* covered the story, reporting the accusations

against Feland and other revenue officials in Kentucky on May 5, 1892, and the guilty verdict for Feland's deputy, Eugene McAdams, on January 23, 1893. William Feland was later acquitted of similar charges. See *Hopkinsville Kentuckian*, July 4, 1893.

17. Feland and several other USMC officers are listed as former St. John's students in "Schools," *Marine Corps Gazette* 14, no. 8 (August 1931): 20.

18. See Ira Reeves, *Military Education in the United States* (Burlington, VT: Free Press Printing, 1914), 176.

19. *Syracuse Herald*, February 24, 1927. The story first appeared when Feland was sent to Nicaragua and was repeated a year later in several other New York newspapers, such as the *Geneva (NY) Daily Times*, January 13, 1928, and the *Brooklyn Daily Eagle*, January 22, 1928.

20. For Feland at MIT, see Paris, "Hold Every Inch of Ground," 2. The growth of MIT under President Walker is detailed in Samuel C. Prescott, *When MIT Was Boston Tech, 1861–1914* (Cambridge, MA: Technology Press, 1954), 107–27. The campus newspaper, *The Tech*, identified Feland as a Marine Corps first lieutenant on January 9, 1902; it noted Feland's receipt of a Distinguished Service Cross on January 18, 1919, and reported his return to Nicaragua on January 18, 1928.

21. *Kentucky New Era*, September 21, 1895. Featuring an octagonal tower and polygonal bays, the Queen Anne–style D. D. Bogard House is located at the corner of Lewis and Fourth Streets in Owensboro. Its successful nomination to the National Register of Historic Places can be found at http://pdfhost.focus.nps.gov/docs/NRHP/Text/80001503.pdf.

22. Robert Burch and Logan Feland, *"Southern Homes": A Collection of Designs for Residences of Modest Cost* (Owensboro, KY: Burch and Feland, Architects, 1897), introduction.

23. Judge Feland's resignation as collector was reported in *New York Times*, June 9, 1893. Smith, *History of the Anti–Separate Coach Movement in Kentucky*, summarizes John Feland Jr.'s early career (165–66) and covers *W. H. Anderson v. Louisville and Nashville Railroad Company.*

24. For contemporary coverage of the filing of the suit, see "Separate Coach Law," *Breckenridge News* (Cloverport, KY), November 8, 1893. Results of the trial were reported in *New York Times*, February 5, 1895; the *Earlington (KY) Bee*, February 7 and June 7, 1895; and the *Hartford (KY) Herald*, February 13, 1895. The *New York Times* noted that Judge Barr "found for the plaintiff in the sum of 1 cent" and predicted that the case would be taken to the U.S. Supreme Court. For more on the separate coach issue in Kentucky, see Anne E. Marshall, "Kentucky's Separate Coach Law and African American Response, 1892–1900," *Register of the Kentucky Historical Society* 98 (Summer 2000): 241–59. The case is put in the larger context of discrimination in Kentucky in George C. Wright, *Life behind a Veil: Blacks in Louisville, Kentucky, 1865–1930* (Baton Rouge: Louisiana State University Press, 1985), 63–65.

25. Judge Feland's return to Hopkinsville was announced in *Kentucky New Era*, July 23, 1895. Logan Feland's appearance at his sister Mary's wedding was reported

in the *Owensboro Daily Messenger*, September 26, 1894, and in *Kentucky New Era*, September 27, 1894.

26. Feland's raising of a state militia company was reported in *Kentucky New Era*, June 2, 1897. His move to New York City was reported in the *Hopkinsville Kentuckian*, September 24, 1897.

2. Spanish-American War Service

1. The best general account of the rise of U.S. diplomacy before the Spanish-American War is George Herring's magisterial volume in the Oxford History of the United States series: *From Colony to Superpower: U.S. Foreign Relations since 1776* (New York: Oxford University Press, 2008); see especially chap. 8, "The War of 1898, the New Empire, and the Dawn of the American Century, 1893–1901" (299–336). The United States had pressed Britain to accept arbitration over the Venezuela–British Guiana boundary. This "elevated the Monroe Doctrine to near holy writ at home and marked the end of British efforts to contest U.S. preeminence in the Caribbean" (ibid., 308).

2. Ibid., 311.

3. For the sequence of events leading to the declaration of war against Spain, see Ivan Musicant, *Empire by Default: The Spanish-American War and the Dawn of the New Century* (New York: Henry Holt, 1998), 78–190. Standard works on the Spanish-American War include Philip Foner, *The Spanish-Cuban-American War and the Birth of American Imperialism, 1898–1902*, 2 vols. (New York: Monthly Review Press, 1972), and David Trask, *The War with Spain in 1898* (New York: Macmillan, 1981).

4. For excellent coverage of U.S. military unpreparedness and the army's efforts to ramp up for the war, see Graham A. Cosmas, *An Army for Empire: The United States Army in the Spanish-American War* (College Station: Texas A&M Press, 1994).

5. For a brief history of Kentucky's wartime regiments, see Kentucky Department of Military Affairs, *Kentucky State Guard in the Spanish-American War, 1898–1899* (Frankfort: Kentucky Department of Military Affairs, 1988).

6. Tucker is quoted in MIT's *Technology Review* 33 (1930–1931): 167.

7. "Captain Feland," *Owensboro Daily Messenger*, April 24, 1898.

8. *Owensboro Daily Messenger*, April 24, 1898.

9. "Soldier Boys," *Owensboro Daily Messenger*, April 26, 1898.

10. See Cosmas, *Army for Empire*, 1–132, for negotiations and decision-making on preparations for the war. Feland's expectations were reported in the *Owensboro Daily Messenger*, April 26, 1898.

11. *Owensboro Daily Messenger*, April 27, 28, 29, and 30 and May 1, 3, and 5, 1898.

12. *Owensboro Daily Messenger*, May 6 and 7, 1898.

13. *Owensboro Daily Messenger*, May 11, 1898. See also the May 8, 1898, edition for a description of Company H's departure.

14. *Owensboro Daily Messenger*, May 20, 1898. See also the May 15, 17, 18, and 19, 1898, editions for more details about Company H at Camp Collier.

15. *Hopkinsville Daily Kentuckian*, April 29 and 30 and May 10 and 20, 1898.

16. *Hopkinsville Daily Kentuckian*, May 21, 1898. Writing from Camp Collier to his mother, the Third Regiment's chaplain, Frank Thomas, lamented John Feland's dismissal: "It is likely I will go to Frankfort this afternoon to intercede with Gov. Bradley in behalf of Capt. John Feland, Jr. He has been acting very badly since coming here. Personally he deserves the surest censure, but I feel very sorry for his company, Mr. Latham, for whom it is named, and the town of Hopkinsville. However I shall be guided by what the staff thinks of the matter. What infinite harm one man can do by getting drunk and failing to perform his duties! Do not speak of these things outside of the family." Frank Thomas to Mrs. L. W. Thomas, May 20, 1898, folder 1, box 3, Thomas Collection (MSS 31), Manuscripts and Folklife Archives, Department of Library Special Collections, Western Kentucky University, Bowling Green.

17. John Feland's accounting of expenditures was reported in the *Hopkinsville Daily Kentuckian*, June 2, 1898. See also *Owensboro Daily Messenger*, May 21, 22, 24, 26, and 27, 1898.

18. Logan Feland's visit home was reported in the *Hopkinsville Daily Kentuckian*, May 27, 1898.

19. For the Battle of Manila Bay, see Musicant, *Empire by Default*, 191–234.

20. For Company F's move to Chickamauga, see *Owensboro Daily Messenger*, June 2 and 3, 1898.

21. Cosmas, *Army for Empire*, 165. For a larger picture of army preparation, see ibid., 80–101. A good description of Camp Thomas can be found in Gregory Dean Chapman, "Army Life at Camp Thomas, Georgia during the Spanish-American War," *Georgia Historical Quarterly* 70, no. 4 (Winter 1896): 633–56.

22. Cosmas, *Army for Empire*, 167.

23. *Owensboro Daily Messenger*, June 16, 1898. For additional reports of conditions, see the June 8, 9, and 14, 1898, editions of the *Messenger* and Chapman, "Army Life at Camp Thomas," 641–43.

24. The *Owensboro Daily Messenger*, June 22, 1898, reported that Feland was the regimental engineer in charge of laying out the new camp.

25. Chapman, "Army Life at Camp Thomas," 644–49.

26. For coverage of the landing at Guantanamo Bay to the capitulation of Manila, see Musicant, *Empire by Default*, 347–585. Efforts to bring about peace are covered in ibid., 586–630.

27. See George B. Bowers, *History of the 160th Ind. Vol. Infantry in the Spanish-American War, with Biographies of Officers and Enlisted Men and Rosters of the Companies* (Fort Wayne, IN: Archer Printing, 1900), 24–25. For most of the war, Bowers's 160th Indiana Volunteers served in tandem with the Third Kentucky Regiment. According to Bowers, the unsanitary conditions at Camp Grant, along with the bad food, which consisted of "hard-tack and bacon or corned beef," caused a lot of illness. The alleged bad meat served to soldiers during the war was one of the main subjects of investigation by the postwar Dodge Commission and eventually by a military

court of inquiry. The "beef controversy" proved somewhat overblown, but as Cosmas asserts: "The Army itself was the chief victim of the beef controversy. The quarrel completed the fragmentation of the high command" (*Army for Empire*, 295). The controversy embittered relations among the commanding general of the army, Major General Nelson Miles; Secretary of the Army Russell Alger; Commissary General Charles Egan; and President McKinley. See Cosmas, *Army for Empire*, 284–96, for the work of the Dodge Commission and the army board of inquiry.

28. *Owensboro Daily Messenger*, August 3, 5, and 7, 1898. For more information on conditions at Camp Thomas, see Cosmas, *Army for Empire*, 267–68.

29. Cosmas, *Army for Empire*, 171. Despite the many problems in "organization, officering, and equipment," Cosmas states that the preparation of 275,000 men in three months "constituted a remarkable achievement for the War Department."

30. *Owensboro Daily Messenger*, August 24, 1898. See also the August 8, 1898, edition for a report from Newport News.

31. Cosmas, *Army for Empire*, 269.

32. "Our Tin Soldier and What He Thinks," *Owensboro Daily Messenger*, September 1, 1898.

33. *Owensboro Daily Messenger*, September 10, 13, and 17, 1898.

34. *Owensboro Daily Messenger*, September 13, 1898. See also *Lexington Morning Herald*, September 19 and October 18 and 19, 1898, and Bowers, *History of the 160th Ind. Vol. Infantry*, 28. The Queen's Jubilee salute involved 400 men, including Company F. They were "drawn up in the necessary formation and fired 15 rounds with blank cartridges. Twelve of the rounds were fired from right to left by file and three by volley. It was certainly a beautiful sight—one almost continuous line of flame." *Lexington Morning Herald*, October 19, 1898.

35. Cosmas, *Army for Empire*, 299–304. For more on Camp Conrad, see Bowers, *History of the 160th Ind. Vol. Infantry*, 32–37.

36. *Columbus Enquirer-Sun*, January 7, 1899. The death of John Feland Sr. was reported in the *Earlington Bee* and the *Columbus Enquirer-Sun* on January 12, 1899. Significant dates in Feland's Company F service are included in the muster rolls in Kentucky Department of Military Affairs, *Kentucky State Guard*, 603.

37. For the assignments of Company F and Feland, see Kentucky Department of Military Affairs, *Kentucky State Guard*, 51–52, 603. The *Louisville Courier-Journal* quote was reprinted in the *Owensboro Daily Messenger*, March 5, 1898.

38. *Owensboro Daily Messenger*, April 1 and 6 and May 21, 1899.

39. *Owensboro Daily Messenger*, May 17, 18, and 19, 1899.

40. *Hopkinsville Kentuckian*, May 26, 1899; *Owensboro Daily Messenger*, May 27, 1899.

41. *Hopkinsville Kentuckian*, June 20, 1899. In fact, 40 percent of applicants failed the medical examination. For notice of Feland's appointment to the volunteer army, see the *Frankfort Roundabout*, July 15, 1899. Evidence of Deboe's and Evans's support of Feland's Marine Corps appointment can be found in Assistant Secretary of the Navy Charles H. Allen to William Deboe, May 15, 1899, and Allen to Walter

Evans, May 17, 1899, file 3917-335, box 30, RG 80, General Records of the Department of the Navy, 1798–1947, NARA, acknowledging receipt of their letters to the president on Feland's behalf. In this file, Allen also acknowledged, on May 8, 1899, receipt of Feland's application for a Marine Corps commission.

42. William Deboe to SECNAV John D. Long, June 17, 1899; William Lindsay to the President, June 17, 1899; Austin Bell, M.D., to Logan Feland, June 12, 1899; telegram from E. T. Franks to SECNAV, June 15, 1899; telegram from H. D. Allen to SECNAV, June 24, 1899, file 3917-335, box 30, RG 80, NARA.

43. *Hopkinsville Kentuckian*, June 30, 1899.

44. Peter Karsten, *The Naval Aristocracy: The Golden Age of Annapolis and the Emergence of Modern American Navalism* (New York: Free Press, 1972), 3–50.

45. Hans Schmidt, *Maverick Marine: General Smedley D. Butler and the Contradictions of American Military History* (Lexington: University Press of Kentucky, 1987), 6–10.

46. A brief biography of James Carson Breckinridge can be found at http://www.tecom.usmc.mil/mcu/mcrcweb/Archive/PersonalPapers/breckinridge/breckinridge.htm. For a tribute by his sister, Mary Breckinridge, see *Quarterly Bulletin of the Frontier Nursing Service* 17, no. 4 (Spring 1942). Mary Breckinridge founded the Frontier Nursing Service, which provided nursing and midwifery care throughout eastern Kentucky. For more on the famous Breckinridge family, see James Klotter, *The Breckinridges of Kentucky* (Lexington: University Press of Kentucky, 1986). The James Carson Breckinridge Library at the General Alfred M. Gray Marine Corps Research Center at Quantico, Virginia, is a tribute to Breckinridge's support of Marine Corps education.

47. The list of Marine Corps first and second lieutenants appointed in 1899 can be found in *Army and Navy Journal* 37, no. 17 (December 23, 1899): 408.

48. See one of the first histories of the Marine Corps: Willis John Abbot, *Soldiers of the Sea: The Story of the United States Marine Corps* (New York: Dodd, Mead, 1918), 4. Abbot asserts: "It had long been the practice of men prominent in American public service, military, naval or political, who had sons who were wild, and had no liking for the curriculum of West Point or Annapolis, to get these youths commissions in the Marine Corps. As a result there sprung up a cynical reading of the official designation of that organization—U.S.M.C., 'Useless Sons Made Comfortable.'" The phrase also appeared in the Marine Corps's *Recruiters' Bulletin* 3, no. 5 (March 1917): 18.

49. Jack Shulimson, Wanda Renfrow, David Kelly, and Evelyn Englander, eds., *Marines in the Spanish-American War, 1895–1899: Anthology and Annotated Bibliography* (Washington, DC: History and Museums Division, Headquarters, U.S. Marine Corps, 1998); this is the first sentence in the editors' introduction.

50. Edwin Simmons, "The Spanish-American War," in Shulimson et al., *Marines in the Spanish-American War*, 1–3.

51. Detailed accounts of Marine activity during the war can be found in Shulimson et al., *Marines in the Spanish-American War*: see especially David Kelly, "Marines in the Spanish-American War: A Brief History"; Jack Shulimson, "Marines

in the Spanish-American War"; Trevor Plante and James Holden-Rhodes, "Crucible of the Corps"; and Trevor Plante, "'New Glory to Its Already Gallant Record': The First Marine Battalion in the Spanish-American War."

52. For an examination of Marine Corps publicity and striving for identity, see Heather Pace Marshall, "It Means Something These Days to Be a Marine: Image, Identity, and Mission in the Marine Corps, 1861–1918" (PhD diss., Duke University, 2010), dukespace.lib.duke.edu/dspace/bitstream/handle/10161/3040/D_Marshall_Heather_a_201008.pdf?sequence=1. With regard to the importance of Guantanamo, Allan Millett concludes that, "compared with the fighting soon to follow in the Army's campaign against Santiago, the action at Guantanamo Bay was a minor skirmish of no consequence to the course of the war, but it took on incalculable importance for the Marine Corps" (Allan Millett, "The Spanish-American War," in Shulimson et al., *Marines in the Spanish-American War*, 35). In contrast, James Holden-Rhodes concludes, "In fact, Guantanamo Bay was the linch-pin to the entire invasion of Cuba, and the ultimate capitulation of the Spanish government" ("Crucible of the Corps," 76).

53. Herring, *From Colony to Superpower*, 336. For U.S. diplomacy roughly corresponding to the period of Feland's career in the Marine Corps, see ibid., 299–483.

3. Professional and Personal Milestones, 1899–1907

1. Allan Millett, *Semper Fidelis: The History of the United States Marine Corps*, rev. ed. (New York: Free Press, 1991), 134–35.

2. See Brig. Gen. Dion Williams, "The Education of a Marine Corps Officer," *Marine Corps Gazette* 18, no. 1 (May 1933): 16–26. For the establishment of the School of Application, see Jack Shulimson, "Daniel Pratt Mannix and the Establishment of the Marine Corps School of Application, 1889–1894," *Journal of Military History* 55, no. 4 (October 1991): 469–86.

3. Details of Dewey's parade and the Arlington sesquicentennial parade can be found in "Report of the Commandant of the United States Marine Corps," in *Annual Reports of the Department of the Navy for the Year 1900* (Washington, DC: Government Printing Office, 1900), 1094–95; cited hereafter as "Commandant's Report," with the appropriate year.

4. For a general history of the United States in the Philippines, see Stanley Karnow, *In Our Image: America's Empire in the Philippines* (New York: Ballantine Books, 1989), especially 78–175. The standard work on the initial conflict between the Americans and the Filipinos is Brian Linn, *The Philippine War, 1899–1902* (Lawrence: University Press of Kansas, 2000). For details of the Marine Corps in the Philippines, see Robert Heinl, *Soldiers of the Sea: The United States Marine Corps, 1775–1962*, 2nd ed. (Baltimore: Nautical and Aviation Publishing Company of America, 1991), 119–27, and Clyde Metcalf, *A History of the United States Marine Corps* (New York: G. P. Putnam's Sons, 1939), 266–71.

5. "Commandant's Report," 1900, 1103–9. See also Millett, *Semper Fidelis*, 150–53.

6. Feland Fitness Report, July 22–October 31, 1899, Logan Feland file, box 188: Feineman, Wilbur W., thru Fellis, James, entry 62, Proceedings of the Naval and Marine Examining Boards, ca. 1928–1941, RG 125, Records of the Office of the Judge Advocate General (Navy), NARA.

7. Millett, *Semper Fidelis*, 153. For a short biography of Waller, see Anne Cipriano Venzon, *Leaders of Men: Ten Marines Who Changed the Corps* (Lanham, MD: Scarecrow Press, 2008), 39–61.

8. Frederick Wise, as told to Meigs O. Frost, *A Marine Tells It to You* (New York: J. H. Sears, 1929), 9. See Venzon, *Leaders of Men*, for short biographies of Wise (193–215) and Bearss (171–92). See also George B. Clark, *Hiram Iddings Bearss, U.S. Marine Corps: Biography of a World War I Hero* (Jefferson, NC: McFarland, 2005).

9. Wise, *A Marine Tells It to You*, 5. James Carson Breckinridge concurred about conditions on the *Solace*. In describing the trip from the West Coast to Hawaii, Breckinridge wrote: "The Solace is a nasty craft in bad weather, and we had bad weather for six days." Noting that most of the men got seasick, Breckinridge humorously concluded: "The Solace would roll and pitch in a dry dock I am sure." See Breckinridge to his mother, November 21, 1899, folder 8: January 17 to December 27, 1899, box 4: Correspondence-Personal-Family 1889–1902, Papers of James Carson Breckinridge, MCA.

10. *Kentucky New Era*, February 2, 1900. The stopover in Hawaii is covered in "Commandant's Report," 1900, 1110.

11. Stephen Crane, "Marines Signaling under Fire at Guantanamo," *McClure's* 12, no. 4 (February 1899): 332–36. For Draper's raising of the flag, see Trevor K. Plante, "'New Glory to Its Already Gallant Record': The First Marine Battalion in the Spanish-American War," in *Marines in the Spanish-American War, 1895–1899: Anthology and Annotated Bibliography*, ed. Jack Shulimson, Wanda Renfrow, David Kelly, and Evelyn Englander (Washington, DC: History and Museums Division, Headquarters, U.S. Marine Corps, 1998), 82, 94 (photograph). In an August 26, 1898, report to Marine Corps Commandant Heywood, Colonel Robert Huntington praised Draper for his "untiring" assistance, performance of his duties with "zeal and discretion," and his conduct "marked by imperturbable coolness and courage." Consequently, Huntington recommended that Draper be "brevetted captain for his services" (ibid., 121). For more on "Handsome Jack" Myers, see Venzon, *Leaders of Men*, 105–24; for Feland's fellow lieutenant at Olongapo, George Thorpe, see ibid., 124–45.

12. See "Commandant's Report," 1900, 1114–15, for a summary of Marine Corps activities in the Olongapo area. For Draper's February 10, 1900, report on activities and his March 14, 1900, report praising Feland, see ibid., 1143–44 and 1145–46, respectively. See also Metcalf, *History of the U.S. Marine Corps*, 269–70, for a summary.

13. For the U.S. policy of "benevolent assimilation," see George Herring, *From Colony to Superpower: U.S. Foreign Relations since 1776* (New York: Oxford University Press, 2008), 326. Pacification efforts are reflected in Draper's report of February 10, 1900, in "Commandant's Report," 1900, 1144. See "Military Record of First

Lieutenant Logan Feland, U.S.M.C.," June 13, 1903, Feland file, RG 125, NARA, for Feland's assignments.

14. Draper's death was reported in *New York Times*, September 21, 1901. Feland's role in Royall Draper's wedding was reported in *Washington Post*, June 7, 1925.

15. Feland Fitness Report, January 1–March 31, 1901, Feland file, RG 125, NARA.

16. For the incident at Samar, see Robert Asprey, "Waller of Samar—Part I," *Marine Corps Gazette* 45, no. 5 (May 1961): 36–41, and "Waller of Samar—Part II," *Marine Corps Gazette* 45, no. 6 (June 1961): 44–48. See also Joel Thacker, *Stand, Gentlemen, He Served on Samar!* (Washington, DC: Marine Corps Headquarters, 1945); Millett, *Semper Fidelis*, 152–55; Metcalf, *History of the U.S. Marine Corps*, 270–79; and Heinl, *Soldiers of the Sea*, 123–27.

17. Linn, *Philippine War*, 207; the exception was the incident at Samar.

18. Ginger M. Doyel, "Halligan Hall: Home to Marines and Midshipmen," *Shipmate* 66, no. 9 (November–December 2003): 17. See also "Marine Barracks: A Fine Building at Annapolis Nearing Completion," *Baltimore Sun*, December 3, 1902.

19. George C. Reid to Logan Feland, August 12, 1902, Feland file, RG 125, NARA. Reid was the first Marine appointed to the Navy's new General Board, which would critically examine the Marine Corps's role in the early 1900s. Feland's service in overseeing construction of the Marine Barracks and firing range at Annapolis was recognized in "Commandant's Report," 1902, 956.

20. See "Record of Proceedings of a Marine Examining Board Convened at the Marine Barracks, Washington, D.C., in the Case of First Lieutenant Logan Feland, U.S. Marine Corps, July 15, 1903," Feland file, RG 125, NARA, for the three-page report on the examination, as well as his test scores. See "Military History of Brigadier Logan Feland," Feland file, HRB, MCHD, for the date of his captaincy. For short biographies of Biddle and Neville, see Allan Millett and Jack Shulimson, *Commandants of the Marine Corps* (Annapolis, MD: Naval Institute Press, 2004), 163–74 and 214–24, respectively.

21. For the Marine Corps in Panama, see Panama file, Geographical Files, HRB, MCHD. See also Danny J. Crawford, "Corps Has Long History in Protecting American Interests in Panama," *Marines Magazine*, March 1990, 27–28. Roosevelt's policies and actions are discussed in Henry J. Hendrix II, "TR's Plan to Invade Colombia," *Naval History* 20, no. 6 (December 2006): 36–42.

22. Hendrix, "TR's Plan to Invade Colombia," 37.

23. Panama file, HRB, MCHD, includes a typewritten copy of an unidentified work that gives many specifics of the 1903–1904 Panama expedition.

24. Hendrix, "TR's Plan to Invade Colombia," 40.

25. See "Military History of Brigadier General Logan Feland," Feland file, HRB, MCHD, for the dates of Feland's service in the Caribbean.

26. The photograph of Waller's officers, titled "All Quiet along the Chagres," appeared in *Marine Corps Gazette* 17, no. 4 (February 1933): 49.

27. See Hans Schmidt, *Maverick Marine: General Smedley D. Butler and the Con-

traditions of American Military History (Lexington: University Press of Kentucky, 1987). See also Merrill Bartlett, "Old Gimlet Eye," *Proceedings of the U.S. Naval Institute* 112, no. 11 (November 1986): 64–72. For a newer biography that places more emphasis on Butler's later years, see Mark Strecker, *Smedley Butler, USMC: A Biography* (Jefferson, NC: McFarland, 2011).

28. See Gerald C. Thomas Jr., "A Warrior-Scholar in the World War: Robert Henry Dunlap," *Marine Corps Gazette* 82, no. 1 (January 1998): 88–89, and Leo Daugherty III, *Pioneers of Amphibious Warfare, 1898–1945: Profiles of Fourteen American Military Strategists* (Jefferson, NC: McFarland, 2009), 194–212. Daugherty describes Dunlap as "the most important Marine officer to serve during the interwar period directly connected with the refinement of amphibious assault in the Marine Corps" (194).

29. Coyle's wedding was reported in *Philadelphia Record* and *New York Tribune*, December 22, 1904; Dunlap's in *Washington Post*, January 13, 1905; Jolly's in *Philadelphia Inquirer*, January 26, 1905; and Butler's in *New York Times*, July 1, 1905.

30. Feland is listed as an instructor in the 1903–1904 and 1905–1906 editions of the *Annual Register of the United States Naval Academy* (Washington, DC: Government Printing Office, 1903, 1905), 18, 19.

31. For the School of Application, see Clyde Metcalf, "A History of the Education of Marine Officers," *Marine Corps Gazette* 20, no. 2 (May 1936): 15–19, 49–54. See *Infantry Journal* 2, no. 4 (April 1906): 204, which lists Feland as a new subscriber.

32. See C. E. Waterman, "The United States Marine Corps School of Application," *Army and Navy Life and the United Service* 10, no. 6 (June 1907): 605–6.

33. The Gardener trial was reported in *New York Times*, March 25, 1905; the *Times* spelled his name "Gardiner." Gardener eventually became a major. For Draper's stint as judge advocate, see *New York Times*, September 1, 1895; the famous Captain Alfred Thayer Mahan was a member of that court.

34. For Feland's posting to Narragansett, see "Military History of Brigadier General Logan Feland," Feland file, HRB, MCHD.

35. *Baltimore Sun*, November 3 and 5, 1905.

36. Plans for the fleet review were reported in *New York Times*, August 24, 1906, and a lengthy account of the event appeared in the September 4, 1906, edition.

37. For the Cuban expedition of 1906, see Cuba file, Geographical Files, HRB, MCHD. See also Metcalf, *History of the U.S. Marine Corps*, 316–24.

38. Allan Millett, *The Politics of Intervention: The Military Occupation of Cuba, 1906–1909* (Columbus: Ohio State University Press, 1968), 62.

39. *New York Times*, October 5, 1906.

40. *New York Times*, October 7, 8, 10, and 15, 1906.

41. *New York Times*, October 9, 1906.

42. Metcalf, *History of the U.S. Marine Corps*, 321.

43. William Inglis, "How the 'Warlike' Cubans Gave Up Their Arms," *Harper's Weekly*, November 3, 1906, 1566. The *Syracuse (NY) Post Standard* picked up on the *Harper's* story in a November 26 article titled "The Smiling Marine in Cuba." The

Post Standard described Feland as a "tall, dark, good-natured youth" and concluded, "Our 'long, lean, agile, hardy, ever-ready sea soldiers,' have stopped all the fighting by merely standing by and grinning in the most friendly way."

44. *New York Times*, November 27, 1906. Feland's dates of service in Cuba can be found in Feland file, HRB, MCHD.

45. See Feland file, RG 125, NARA.

46. *Washington Post*, February 14, 1907. See also *Washington Times*, February 14, 1907, and *Washington Herald*, February 15, 1907.

47. *New York Times*, April 10, 1906.

48. William Alexander Taylor, *Centennial History of Columbus and Franklin County, Ohio* (Chicago: S. J. Clarke, 1909), 1:830–31.

49. *Army and Navy Journal*, February 23, 1907; *Hopkinsville Kentuckian*, February 16, 1907. Other details are from a copy of the marriage certificate in the author's possession. A copy of Katherine Feland's death certificate (in the author's possession) gives her birth date as February 14, 1875.

50. Gus E. Paris, "Hold Every Inch of Ground," unpublished manuscript, 4, MCA.

51. Examples of Katherine's musical appearances can be found in *New York Daily Tribune*, March 15, 1905, and February 16, 1906, and *New York Sun*, December 3, 1905.

4. Shuttling between the States and the Caribbean, 1907–1913

1. See Amy Waters Yarsinske, *Jamestown Exposition: American Imperialism on Parade*, 2 vols. (Mount Pleasant, SC: Arcadia Publishing, 1999).

2. See *New York Times*, April 26 and 27, 1907, for details of the opening of the Jamestown Exposition, and *Lewiston (ME) Evening Journal*, April 23, 1907, for information about the Atlantic Fleet. The *Minnesota*'s steam launch accident was reported in *New York Times*, June 12, 13, and 14, 1907, and *Pittsburgh Press*, June 15, 1907. Details of the *Minnesota*'s activities during this period can be found in "Log Book of the U.S.S. *Minnesota*, First Rate, Commanded by Captain John Hubbard, U.S. Navy, Attached to Atlantic Squadron, Commencing March, 1907, at Norfolk, Virginia and Ending August, 1907, at New York," vol. 52, RG 24, Records of the Bureau of Naval Personnel, NARA; cited hereafter as *Minnesota* log. For example, the log entry for May 26, 1907, described the day as "overcast and cloudy," with "light airs," and it noted that a deserter had been sentenced to "solitary confinement in double irons on bread and water for 15 days"; it also reported that Captain Feland, USMC, had returned from leave. The steam launch accident was reported in the entry for June 11, 1907.

3. *Lewiston (ME) Evening Journal*, October 1, 1907. The log entry dated September 29, 1907, stated that, in a "fresh gale," seaman Harris Carroll "fell overboard while engaged in securing of port shutters. Efforts to save him were unsuccessful." *Minnesota* log, August 21–December 19, 1907, vol. 53, RG 24, NARA.

4. James Reckner, *Teddy Roosevelt's Great White Fleet* (Annapolis, MD: Naval Institute Press, 1988), x.

5. *New York Times*, December 11, 12, 15, and 17, 1907. See also *New York Daily Tribune*, December 8, 15, and 16, 1907.

6. Details of the Great White Fleet's cruise come mainly from the contemporary accounts of Robert Dorsey Jones, *With the American Fleet from the Atlantic to the Pacific* (Seattle: Harrison, 1909), and Franklin Matthews, *With the Battlefleet: Cruise of the Sixteen Battleships of the United States Atlantic Fleet from Hampton Roads to the Golden Gate, December 1907–May 1908* (New York: B. W. Huebsch, 1908). Jones accompanied the fleet on the *Vermont*, while Matthews, a prominent national journalist, sailed on the *Louisiana*.

7. See Jones, *With the American Fleet*, 46–58, for an account of the visit to Rio de Janeiro. See Reckner, *Teddy Roosevelt's Great White Fleet*, 61–75, for a thorough discussion of criticisms about battleship design and Reuterdahl's role in publicizing the deficiencies.

8. See Jones, *With the American Fleet*, 60–61; Reckner, *Teddy Roosevelt's Great White Fleet*, 38–42.

9. Reckner, *Teddy Roosevelt's Great White Fleet*, 47.

10. Acting Chief of the Bureau of Navigation N. R. Usher to Feland, July 25, 1908, Feland file, RG 125, NARA. See also Marine Corps Assistant Adjutant and Inspector, Lt. Colonel H. C. Haines to Feland, August 4, 1908, ibid., congratulating Feland.

11. *San Francisco Call*, May 5, 1908.

12. According to the *Morning Oregonian*, July 5, 1908, the Felands stayed at the Portland Hotel. Captain Feland's assignment to the *Montana* and Katherine Feland's trip to France were reported in *Washington Post*, August 9, 1908. Katherine Feland was on the passenger list (accessed on Ancestry.com) for the SS *Merion* leaving Liverpool, England, on November 25, 1908. See also "Military Biography of Brigadier General Logan Feland," Feland file, HRB, MCHD.

13. See U.S. Congress, House Committee on Naval Affairs, *Hearings on the Status of the U.S. Marine Corps, Hearings before the Subcommittee on Naval Academy and Marine Corps, Committee on Naval Affairs, House of Representatives, the Status of the Marine Corps, 1909* (Washington, DC: Government Printing Office, 1909), 249–52, for Feland's testimony.

14. For the effort to remove Marines from ships, see Robert Heinl, *Soldiers of the Sea: The United States Marine Corps, 1775–1962*, 2nd ed. (Baltimore: Nautical and Aviation Publishing Company of America, 1991), 153–57, and Allan Millett, *Semper Fidelis: The History of the United States Marine Corps*, rev. ed. (New York: Free Press, 1991), 138–44.

15. Millett, *Semper Fidelis*, 144.

16. Feland's assignment to New London was reported in *Washington Post*, July 3, 1910, and *Baltimore American*, July 8, 1910. See also "Military Biography of Brigadier General Logan Feland." For the development of the advanced base concept, see "The Creation of the Advanced Base Force, 1900–1916," in Millett, *Semper Fidelis*, 267–86.

17. Major Dion Williams, "Report on Men, Materials and Drill Required for Establishing a Naval Advance Base," prepared for the Office of Naval Intelligence, November 2, 1909, HAF folder 769, Historical Amphibious Files Collection, box 42A, MCA; Major John Russell, "General Principles Governing the Selection and Establishment of Advanced Naval Base and the Composition of an Advanced Base Outfit," ibid., HAF folder 768. For more on Williams, see Leo Daugherty III, *Pioneers of Amphibious Warfare, 1898–1945: Profiles of Fourteen American Military Strategists* (Jefferson, NC: McFarland, 2009), 123–33; for more on Russell, who became Marine Corps Commandant in 1934, see Allan Millett and Jack Shulimson, *Commandants of the Marine Corps* (Annapolis, MD: Naval Institute Press, 2004), 234–52.

18. Millett, *Semper Fidelis*, 274–77. Initially, the Advanced Base School was going to be located at Port Royal, South Carolina, where the Marine Corps had transferred the School of Application for the instruction of new lieutenants. The school would have been under the overall command of the head of the Port Royal base, Colonel Eli K. Cole. See *Washington Post*, May 29, 1910.

19. For the Felands' social life, see *New London (CT) Day*, October 14, 1910, and February 27, 1911.

20. Clyde Metcalf, "A History of the Education of Marine Officers," *Marine Corps Gazette* 20, no. 2 (May 1936): 47. For more on Captain Ellis, see Dirk A. Ballendorf and Merrill L. Bartlett, *Pete Ellis: An Amphibious Warfare Prophet: 1880–1923* (Annapolis, MD: Naval Institute Press, 1997). Ellis would become more prominent in advanced base planning after he returned from the Philippines and attended the Naval War College in 1911, where he wrote papers about the advanced base concept. Ellis joined the Advanced Base Force in Philadelphia in the fall of 1913. He would serve under Feland after World War I, during which he wrote a seminal study of the need for advanced bases in the Pacific.

21. See "Amphibious Operations in the 21st Century," March 18, 2009, http://www.quantico.usmc.mil/MCBQ%20PAO%20Press%20Releases/090430%20CDI%20Docs/CDI_AmphibOps21stCent.pdf.

22. Examples of Feland's work as adjutant can be found in "Cuba 1911" folder, box 2, entry 43, RG 127, NARA. For Barnett's ratings of Feland's performance, see "Fitness Report from April 1, 1911 to June 22, 1911," Feland file, RG 125, NARA.

23. Gilson's pending trial and Feland's appointment as judge advocate were reported in *Washington Post*, May 7, 1911. The charges against Gilson and the trial transcript can be found in "Case of Captain Robert M. Gilson, U.S.M.C.," file 23815, box 94, entry 27, RG 125, NARA. For Gilson's service in Nicaragua under Butler, see Edwin N. McClellan, "American Marines in Nicaragua," *Marine Corps Gazette* 6, no. 1 (March 1921): 48–65.

24. "Case of Captain Robert M. Gilson, U.S.M.C."

25. Ibid. Gilson retired as a captain on October 29, 1903; see "Commandant's Report," 1904, 1201. For more about Captain Hughes, see Merrill Bartlett, "The Spirited Saga of 'Johnny the Hard,'" *Naval History* 21, no. 3 (June 2007): 54–61.

Hughes himself would come into conflict with Major Butler in 1912, after a fistfight with another officer. He would, however, go on to receive a Medal of Honor for his action at the landing at Vera Cruz in 1914, and he would serve with distinction during World War I, earning a Navy Cross, two Silver Stars, and two Croix de Guerres before receiving a disability discharge after the war.

26. Logan Feland to Smedley Butler, June 28, 1911, folder 6: Official Correspondence 1911, box 9, Smedley Darlington Butler Collection, MCA.

27. "Military Biography of Brigadier General Logan Feland."

28. Heinl, *Soldiers of the Sea*, 161.

29. "Military Biography of Brigadier General Logan Feland."

30. Dana G. Munro, *Intervention and Dollar Diplomacy in the Caribbean, 1900–1921* (Princeton, NJ: Princeton University Press, 1964), 469. Munro's analysis was based on his dozen years of State Department service in the Caribbean and in Central and Latin America, where he was special envoy to Haiti, chargé d'affaires in Nicaragua, consul in Chile, and head of the State Department's Latin American Division. In 1932 he became a professor at Princeton, where he taught until his retirement in 1961. He was chargé in Managua, Nicaragua, when Feland commanded Marines there in the late 1920s.

31. Merrill Bartlett, "Col Lincoln Karmany and Political Correctness, 1913," *Marine Corps Gazette* 82, no. 12 (December 1998): 47–49. Bartlett notes that when Commandant William F. Biddle retired in 1913, he favored Karmany as his successor. However, the straitlaced secretary of the navy, Josephus Daniels, rejected Karmany, who was not only a hard drinker but also divorced, having left his first wife for a younger woman.

32. Cuba file, Geographical Files, HRB, MCHD.

33. Major John Gray, "Recollections of the 1912 Cuban Expedition," *Marine Corps Gazette* 17, no. 1 (May 1932): 45–48.

34. For the Second Provisional Regiment's brief duty in Santo Domingo, see Clyde Metcalf, *A History of the United States Marine Corps* (New York: G. P. Putnam's Sons, 1939), 340; Munro, *Intervention and Dollar Diplomacy*, 259–68; Frank E. Evans, "The Marines Have Landed," *Marine Corps Gazette* 2, no. 3 (September 1917): 218.

35. Alan Knight, *The Mexican Revolution*, 2 vols. (Cambridge: Cambridge University Press, 1986), 2:11.

36. *New York Times*, February 18, 1913; *Baltimore Sun*, February 18, 1913.

37. "The Marine Corps Association, Its Formation and Objects," *Marine Corps Gazette* 1, no. 1 (March 1916): 73.

38. Ibid. The "Rifleman's Friend" was sold by the George S. Gethen Company of Philadelphia. Both Bogan and Feland would go on to write articles for the *Gazette*.

39. Heinl, *Soldiers of the Sea*, 150–51. The Marine Corps continues to award a Lauchheimer Trophy for top scores in combination rifle and pistol shooting.

40. L. W. T. Waller to Smedley Butler, July 19, 1911, folder 10, box 4, Butler Collection, MCA.

5. Prewar Postings, 1913–1917

1. Allan Millett, *Semper Fidelis: The History of the United States Marine Corps*, rev. ed. (New York: Free Press, 1991), 278. Note that Fullam's official title was "aid for inspections," and Marine Corps documents use the terms *advance* and *advanced* interchangeably to refer to the school, force, and brigade.

2. Ibid., 278–81.

3. Graham Cosmas and Jack Shulimson, "The Culebra Maneuver and the Formation of the U.S. Marine Corps' Advanced Base Force, 1913–1914," in *Changing Interpretations and New Sources in Naval History: Papers from the Third United States Naval Academy Symposium*, ed. Robert William Love Jr. (New York: Garland Press, 1980), 297–300.

4. Frederick Wise, as told to Meigs O. Frost, *A Marine Tells It to You* (New York: J. H. Sears, 1929), 119.

5. For a very good explanation of the use of mines in advanced base work, see Julian C. Smith, "Advanced Base Mines and Mining," *Marine Corps Gazette* 4, no. 3 (September 1919): 221–31. Smith believed that the "work connected with mining" was "undoubtedly the most important feature of Advanced Base work, and must ever be the main line of defense against a naval attack." Having entered the Marine Corps in 1909, Smith served for thirty-seven years. As a major general, he commanded Marines in the bloody battle on Tarawa in 1943.

6. Cosmas and Shulimson, " Culebra Maneuver," 300–304.

7. See Company Commander, Company C, to Commanding Officer, First Advance Base Brigade, VIA Commanding Officer, First Regiment, "Report of Work of Mine Company, December 19, 1913 to January 24, 1914," January 27, 1914; Logan Feland to Commanding Officer, First Advance Base Regiment, "Report of Work, January 23rd, 1914 to February 8, 1914," February 12, 1914; Logan Feland, "Report on Mine Practice, February 6, 1914," February 13, 1914; and Colonel Charles Long to Brigade Commander Colonel George Barnett, "Target and Mine Practice and Reembarkation of First Regiment, January 24 to February 8, 1914," February 12, 1914, all in folder 1, file 1975-80-20, box 236, entry 18, RG 127, NARA.

8. Millett, *Semper Fidelis*, 276.

9. Brian McAllister Linn, "William Phillips Biddle, 1911–1914," in Allan Millett and Jack Shulimson, *Commandants of the Marine Corps* (Annapolis, MD: Naval Institute Press, 2004), 173.

10. See Millett and Shulimson, *Commandants of the Marine Corps*, 163–73 and 174–93, for short biographies of Biddle and Barnett, respectively. See also Merrill Bartlett, "The Road to Eighth and Eye," *Proceedings of the U.S. Naval Institute* 114, no. 11 (November 1988): 74–76, for the candidates' maneuverings for the Commandant's position.

11. See Millett and Shulimson, *Commandants of the Marine Corps*, 178–81, for Barnett's Marine Corps service and his courtship of and marriage to Lelia Montague Gordon. See Merrill Bartlett, "Secretary of the Navy Josephus Daniels and the

Marine Corps, 1913–1921," in *New Interpretations in Naval History: Selected Papers from the Eighth Naval History Symposium*, ed. William B. Cogar (Annapolis, MD: Naval Institute Press, 1989), 199, which describes the social tension between Daniels and the Barnetts.

12. Feland file, HRB, MCHD. See also Garland Fay to Captain Logan Feland, "Detail on General Court-Martial Duty," February 21, 1914; radiogram from John Lejeune, March 11, 1914, requesting leave for Feland and Bearss; and radiogram from Major General Commandant Barnett, March 12, 1914, denying that request, all in Logan Feland file, NPRC. This NPRC file consists primarily of Feland's travel orders.

13. For origins of the crisis in Mexico and subsequent events, with a focus on diplomacy, see Robert Quirk, *An Affair of Honor: Woodrow Wilson and the Occupation of Veracruz* (Lexington: University of Kentucky Press, 1962). See also Alan Knight, *The Mexican Revolution*, 2 vols. (Cambridge: Cambridge University Press, 1986), 2:150–62. For the Marine Corps's role at Vera Cruz, covering almost exclusively the first day of operations, see Jack Sweetman, *The Landing at Veracruz, 1914: The First Complete Chronicle of a Strange Encounter in April, 1914, When the United States Navy Captured and Occupied the City of Veracruz, Mexico* (Annapolis, MD: Naval Institute Press, 1968). See also J. H. Alexander, "Roots of Deployment—Vera Cruz, 1914," *Marine Corps Gazette* 66, no. 11 (November 1982): 71–79.

14. "Old Timers' Corner: Eighteen Years After," *Leatherneck* 15, no. 2 (February 1932): 48.

15. The Second Battalion's landing time and orders can be found in Robert Dunlap to Brigade Commander, "Report of Operations of Second Battalion, First Regiment Marine Brigade, since Time of Landing at Vera Cruz, Mexico, to and including April 25, 1914," May 6, 1914; see also Feland's terse three-paragraph after-action report: Logan Feland to Brigade Adjutant, "Report of Operations, April 22nd to April 28th, 1914," May 4, 1914, both in Vera Cruz file, Geographical Files, HRB, MCHD.

16. Feland file, HRB, MCHD. See also Major General Commandant to Captain Logan Feland, "Revocation of Leave of Absence," November 24, 1914, Feland file, NPRC.

17. Feland's mine patent application can be found at www.google.com/patents?id=xvhkAAAAEBAJ&printsec=claims&zoom=4#v=onepage&q&f=false. On the application, Feland stated that he was a resident of Hopkinsville, Kentucky.

18. Maneuvers were reported in *Philadelphia Evening Public Ledger*, April 13, 1915. See Major General Commandant to Captain Logan Feland, "Lecture at the Coast Artillery School," August 12, 1915, and "Orders to Temporary Duty at Newport, R.I.," September 11, 1915; Secr. of the Navy to Comdr. T. C. Fenton, USN, Rtd., October 18, 1915, naming Feland as a general court-martial board member; and Major General Commandant to Captain Logan Feland, "Detail on Marine Examining Board," July 25, 1916, all in Feland file, NPRC.

19. See Captain Logan Feland to Major General Commandant, "Change of

Address while on Leave," September 5, 1916, Feland file, NPRC, in which Feland noted that his address during his monthlong leave would be "Rockbound Camp" in Glen Eyre. The camp, run by "Mrs. A. W. LeRoy, Prop.," advertised in a September 1916 *Field and Stream* directory that it offered "bass, pike, and pickerel fishing."

20. See *Philadelphia Inquirer*, April 19, June 14 and 17, December 15, 1914, and January 3, 1915.

21. The United States' slow advance into the war is examined in Justus D. Doenecke, *Nothing Less than War: A New History of America's Entry into World War I* (Lexington: University Press of Kentucky, 2011).

22. The history of the military training camp movement is covered in John Garry Clifford, *The Citizen Soldiers: The Plattsburg Training Camp Movement, 1913–1920* (Lexington: University Press of Kentucky, 1972).

23. *New York Times*, May 28, 1948. See also Cordelia Drexel Biddle, as told to Kyle Crichton, *My Philadelphia Father* (Garden City, NY: Doubleday, 1955). This book, by A. J. Drexel Biddle's daughter, became the basis for a Broadway play titled *The Happiest Millionaire*, starring Walter Pidgeon, and then a Walt Disney movie of the same name, starring Fred MacMurray. See also Robert Asprey, "The King of Kill," *Marine Corps Gazette* 51, no. 5 (May 1967): 31–35, for Biddle's Marine Corps activities.

24. The Felands were included among the "prominent Philadelphians" mentioned in "Society Views Drills at Biddle Bible Class," *Philadelphia Inquirer*, October 31, 1915. See *Philadelphia Inquirer*, October 23 and November 14 and 15, 1915, for more about the camp training, and the November 28, 1915, edition for the dinner for the Barnetts. See also Philadelphia War History Committee, *Philadelphia in the World War* (New York: Wynkoop Hollenbeck Crawford, 1922), 78–83.

25. "Unpreparedness Criminal Folly, Declares Maxim," *Philadelphia Inquirer*, February 4, 1916.

26. *Philadelphia Inquirer*, April 17, 1916.

27. Clifford, *Citizen Soldiers*, 152–92.

28. See Biddle, *My Philadelphia Father*, 149–50, for Biddle's attempts to work with army officials. According to Marine Corps legend, Tun Tavern was the birthplace of the Corps; the first colonial Marines were supposedly recruited there in 1775 by Captain Samuel Nichols, the first commissioned Marine officer. See Jack Keefe, "Philadelphia and the Marines," *Marine Corps Gazette* 8, no. 18 (May 2, 1925): 1–2.

29. See David J. Bettez, "The Marine Corps Prepares for War: The Philadelphia Military Training Camp," *Leatherneck* 92, no. 10 (October 2009): 48–51. See also Clarence Proctor, "Ten Years Ago," *Leatherneck* 9, no. 10 (July 1926): 22–23. Proctor noted that the camp had a band and that "several of the most expert drill masters of the Corps at that time handled the course of instruction at the camp."

30. *Philadelphia Inquirer*, July 24, 1916. Captain Earl "Pete" Ellis would become one of the Marine Corps's most enigmatic characters. Brilliant but troubled, Ellis would later serve as Feland's intelligence officer when the Kentuckian commanded Marines in Santo Domingo in 1920, and he would report to Feland at Headquarters

Marine Corps when he arrived to head the new Division of Operations and Training. Ellis would subsequently prepare a famous report anticipating war with Japan in
the Pacific. For a detailed biography, see Dirk A. Ballendorf and Merrill L. Bartlett,
Pete Ellis: An Amphibious Warfare Prophet, 1880–1923 (Annapolis, MD: Naval Institute Press, 1997).

31. See *Philadelphia Inquirer*, July 9 and 22, 1916.

32. *Philadelphia Inquirer*, August 21, 25, and 28, 1916. See also "Commandant's Report," 1916, 767, in which Barnett notes that he had "inspected the camp
at its opening and at its close, and found that the results achieved were extremely
satisfactory."

33. Corporal James Wisner, "The Reserve Camp at Lansdowne," *Marines Magazine* 1, no. 9 (September 1916): 13. Commandant Barnett also thought the camp
had gone well, and he asked Feland to "express to the officers and men concerned
the approbation of the Major General Commandant for the manner in which this
important duty was performed." Major General Commandant to Captain Logan
Feland, September 8, 1916, Feland file, RG 125, NARA.

34. For a contemporary view of A. J. Drexel Biddle and his contributions to the
Marine Corps, see James N. Wright, "On the Art of Hand to Hand: An Interview
with Col. A. J. Drexel Biddle, USMCR," *Leatherneck* (April 1940): 21–22, and Corporal Paul Hicks, "Fabulous Fighter," *Leatherneck* 31, no. 9 (September 1948): 16.

35. Examining Board Report, July 13, 1916, Feland file, RG 125, NARA.

36. Katherine Feland's tea for Lelia Barnett was reported in *Philadelphia Inquirer*,
November 27, 1916. The Barnetts' party was reported in *Washington Post*, January
5, 1917.

37. L. W. T. Waller to John Lejeune, October 13, 1915, microfilm reel 3, Lejeune
Papers, MD, LOC. The reason for Feland's cool attitude toward Waller remains a
mystery. For the Lauchheimer-Biddle clash, see Wayne Wiegand, "The Lauchheimer
Controversy: A Case of Group Pressure during the Taft Administration," *Military
Affairs* 40, no. 2 (April 1976): 54–59.

38. For news of the interned German cruisers, see *New York Times*, October
2, 1916, and *Philadelphia Inquirer*, March 27, 1917. Feland's administrative duty
assignments can be found in Major General Commandant to Major Logan Feland,
"Orders to Inspect," March 13, 1917, and "Orders to Temporary Duty at Rodington,
Pa.," April 7, 1917, Feland file, NPRC. For details about the armored car Feland was
sent to inspect, see "The King Armored Motor Car Proves Its Worth," *Marines Magazine* 1, no. 9 (September 1916): 62–64. This article noted that Captains Earl Ellis
and Seth Williams had taken the armored car on an endurance run between Philadelphia and Washington, where it proved to be quick and stable. See also Frank Evans,
"Motor Transportation in the Marine Corps," *Marine Corps Gazette* 2, no. 1 (March
1917): 1–12. An example of the King armored car is on display at the National
Museum of the Marine Corps in Quantico, Virginia.

39. See Officer in Charge, Planning Section [Wendell Neville] to Major General
Commandant, "Training and Preparedness for War," March 15, 1920, enclosure 2,

file 2515-20, War Preparations; Henry Roosevelt to the Major General Commandant, "Report of Observations Made in Europe," October 27, 1914; and "Memorandum for the Secretary of the Navy," October 21, 1915, all in file 2515-10, box 389, entry 18, RG 128, NARA.

40. Commandant to Feland, "Orders to Temporary Duty at Rodington, Pa."

41. Millett, *Semper Fidelis*, 287–90.

42. "Orders to Temporary Foreign Expeditionary Shore Service," May 22, 1917, Feland file, NPRC.

43. "Marine Examining Board Record," May 21, 1917, Feland file, RG 125, NARA.

6. World War I through Belleau Wood

1. For a list of Pershing's party, see *New York Times*, June 9, 1917. Actually, their departure remained relatively unknown to the public, as noted in *New York Times*, June 7, 1917. The men who would constitute Pershing's staff are covered in James J. Cooke, *Pershing and His Generals: Command and Staff in the AEF* (Westport, CT: Praeger, 1997).

2. James G. Harbord, *Leaves from a War Diary* (New York: Dodd, Mead, 1925), 6. For more on Harbord, see Brian Fisher Neumann, "Pershing's Right Hand: General James G. Harbord and the American Expeditionary Forces in the First World War" (PhD diss., Texas A&M University, 2006), repository.tamu.edu/bitstream/handle/1969.1/4424/etd-tamu-2006B-HIST-Neumann.pdf;jsessionid=747C233A699C73436004AD0DC176B617?sequence=1.

3. A brief account of the *Baltic*'s voyage can be found in Martin Blumenson, *The Patton Papers, 1885–1940* (Boston: Houghton Mifflin, 1972), 390–97. See also the account by Charles H. Grasty (former editor of the *Baltimore Sun* and special correspondent), *New York Times*, June 9, 1917.

4. Blumenson, *Patton Papers*, 392–97.

5. Charles Doyen file, Biographical Files, HRB, MCHD.

6. For more on the Fifth Regiment's preparations and travel to France, see Ronald J. Brown, *A Few Good Men: The Story of the Fighting Fifth Marines* (Novato, CA: Presidio Press, 2001), 9–16.

7. See Edwin Simmons and Joseph Alexander, *Through the Wheat: The U.S. Marines in World War I* (Annapolis, MD: Naval Institute Press, 2008), 13–17, 51–53. For firsthand accounts written by Marines, see Carl Andrew Brannen, *Over There: A Marine in the Great War* (College Station: Texas A&M University Press, 1996); Elton Mackin, *Suddenly We Didn't Want to Die: Memoirs of a World War I Marine* (Novato, CA: Presidio Press, 1993); George Clark, ed., *His Time in Hell. A Texas Marine in France: The World War I Memoir of Warren R. Jackson* (Novato, CA: Presidio Press, 2001); Louis C. Linn, Laura Jane Linn Wright, and B. J. Omanson, eds., *At Belleau Wood with Rifle and Sketchpad: Memoir of a United States Marine in World War I* (Jefferson, NC: McFarland, 2012); and Don V. Paradis and Peter F. Owen, eds., *The World War I Memoirs of Don V. Paradis, Gunnery Sergeant, USMC*, Marine Corps Historical Branch oral history available at lulu.com.

8. See Edwin N. McClellan, "The Fourth Brigade of Marines in the Training Areas and the Operations in the Verdun Sector," *Marine Corps Gazette* 5, no. 1 (March 1920): 81–110.

9. "Synopsis of Record of Brigadier General Logan Feland, U.S. Marine Corps, during World War," Feland file, HRB, MCHD.

10. Annette D. Amerman of the Marine Corps History Division explains that Marine regiments were "initially designated by number with the addition 'Regiment of Marines' or simply additionally 'Regiment' in an attempt to distinguish them from their Army counterparts." As time passed, they simply became "Marines," such as the Fifth Marines. Hence the various regimental designations in the text. The Fourth Brigade of Marines was simply known as the Marine Brigade when referring to World War I. Annette D. Amerman, "Marine Corps First World War Order of Battle: Anthology and Annotated Bibliography" (work in progress; copy in the author's possession).

11. Simmons and Alexander, *Through the Wheat*, 18–65; McClellan, "Fourth Brigade of Marines," 85–89. See also "Synopsis of Record of Brigadier General Logan Feland."

12. McClellan, "Fourth Brigade of Marines," 89–97. See also Simmons and Alexander, *Through the Wheat*, 66–80.

13. McClellan, "Fourth Brigade of Marines," 98–109. Brigadier General Doyen died of influenza in October 1918 and was buried in Arlington National Cemetery.

14. For the larger context of military affairs on all fronts, see John Keegan, *The First World War* (New York: Knopf, 1998). A renowned British historian, Keegan believed that "the best American units belonged to the Marine Corps" (352), which was "the most professional element of the doughboy army" (407). For a focus on the American Expeditionary Force and the U.S. contribution to the war effort in Europe, see Edward M. Coffman, *The War to End All Wars: The American Military Experience in World War I* (New York: Oxford University Press, 1968).

15. Logan Feland, "Retreat, Hell," *Marine Corps Gazette* 6, no. 3 (September 1921): 289–91. See also Frederick Wise, as told to Meigs O. Frost, *A Marine Tells It to You* (New York: J. H. Sears, 1929), 202. For Fourth Brigade activities before June 1, 1918, see Edwin McClellan, "Operations of the Fourth Brigade of Marines in the Aisne Defensive," *Marine Corps Gazette* 5, no. 2 (June 1920): 182–202, and Simmons and Alexander, *Through the Wheat*, 81–88.

16. See Aaron O'Connell, *Underdogs: The Making of the Modern Marine Corps* (Cambridge, MA: Harvard University Press, 2012), 10, 286n24, for a discussion of the "Devil Dog," or *Teufel Hunden*, appellation. According to O'Connell, although the phrase was used by a German newspaper in 1918 to describe Marine Corps combatants, it was actually created by Americans, having appeared in U.S. newspapers as early as April 1918, before the Marines had substantial combat experience at Belleau Wood. In any case, the Corps has long relished the phrase, creating a famous World War I recruiting poster that featured a Marine Corps bulldog chasing a *pickelhaube* helmet–wearing dachshund. For O'Connell, the Devil Dog mythology was

part of a Marine Corps story that "privileged the collective over the individual, venerated sacrifice and suffering, and spoke often of their service's unique sense of community" (9).

17. Ernst Otto, "The Battles for the Possession of Belleau Woods, June 1918," *Proceedings of the U.S. Naval Institute* 54, no. 11 (November 1928): 941.

18. Robert Asprey, *At Belleau Wood* (1965; reprint, Denton: University of North Texas Press, 1996), 118.

19. Simmons and Alexander, *Through the Wheat*, 100. The Battle of Belleau Wood still serves as a prime example of the Marine Corps's "venerated sacrifice and suffering" mentioned in O'Connell, *Underdogs*, 9.

20. Asprey, *At Belleau Wood*, 139. See also "Interview with Lt. Col. J. H. Turrill (U.S.M.C.), Hdqrs. 2nd Division," December 11, 1918, box 17, entry NN3-127-97-002, RG 127, NARA.

21. War Diary of the Fourth Brigade, June 6, 1918, container 31, James Harbord Papers, MD, LOC. For Hamilton's actions, see Asprey, *At Belleau Wood*, 145–49, and Mark Mortensen, *George W. Hamilton, USMC: America's Greatest World War I Hero* (Jefferson, NC: McFarland, 2011). Hamilton would later become one of Feland's most trusted wartime commanders and considered the Kentuckian a good friend. Hoffman, whose real name was Ernst Janson, enlisted in the Marine Corps four different times, including before and after the war, and retired in 1926 as a sergeant major. For more on Hoffman, see the Marine Corps History Division website: www.tecom.usmc.mil/HD/Whos_Who/Janson_EA.htm. For more on the attack on Hill 142 and subsequent attacks on Belleau Wood, see Edwin McClellan, "Capture of Hill 142, Battle of Belleau Wood, and Capture of Bouresches," *Marine Corps Gazette* 5, no. 3 (September 1920): 277–313. According to McClellan, Hill 142 was the first of seven main attacks in the Battle of Belleau Wood. McClellan was appointed the first official historian of the Marine Corps in 1919 and served under Feland in Nicaragua in 1928–1929.

22. Asprey, *At Belleau Wood*, 157–93.

23. Ibid., 194–96; Brown, *A Few Good Men*, 37. See also War Diary of the Fourth Brigade, June 6 and 7, 1918.

24. Asprey, *At Belleau Wood*, 204.

25. Feland file, HRB, MCHD.

26. Asprey, *At Belleau Wood*, 197–202; Wise, *A Marine Tells It to You*, 209. For the timing of the hookup between Wise and Feland, see War Diary of the Fourth Brigade, June 6, 1918, container 31, Harbord Papers, MD, LOC.

27. Asprey, *At Belleau Wood*, 204–14, 233–49.

28. Ibid., 250–73; McClellan, "Capture of Hill 142," 304–7.

29. *New York Sun*, June 15, 1918.

30. "A Brief History of the Fifth Regiment," 25, file: Fifth Marine Regiment (3), Unit Files, HRB, MCHD.

31. Asprey, *At Belleau Wood*, 273–85; McClellan, "Capture of Hill 142," 307–9.

32. Logan Feland, "Memoranda for Historical Section, Second Division, Feb-

ruary 21, 1930," and "Memorandum for Captain Thomason," box 17, entry NN3-127-97-002, RG 127, NARA. See also Harbord to Feland, July 28, 1924, file F, Harbord Papers, NYHS, in which Harbord reaffirms that he appointed Feland commander in Belleau Wood on the morning of June 14, 1918. After the war Feland and Harbord remained friends and communicated until Feland's death in 1936.

33. Feland, "Memoranda for Historical Section, Second Division, February 21, 1930," and "Memorandum for Captain Thomason." See David Ulbrich, *Preparing for Victory: Thomas Holcomb and the Making of the Modern Marine Corps, 1936–1943* (Annapolis, MD: Naval Institute Press, 2011), 20–23, for Holcomb's role at Belleau Wood.

34. Asprey, *At Belleau Wood*, 287–92; McClellan, "Capture of Hill 142," 309–13.

35. Wise, *A Marine Tells It to You*, 235. See also Asprey, *At Belleau Wood*, 287–93. Feland's plan of attack can be found in Feland to C.O. 5th Regt., June 14, 1918, no. 1, reproduced in box 17, entry NN3-127-97-002, RG 127, NARA.

36. Feland to C.O. 5th Regt., June 14, 1918.

37. Feland to C.O. 1st Bn. 5th Regt., June 14, 1918, box 17, entry NN3-127-97-002, RG 127, NARA.

38. Feland to C.O. 5th Regt., June 15, 1918, box 17, entry NN3-127-97-002, RG 127, NARA. Mathews is quoted in Asprey, *At Belleau Wood*, 295, from personal correspondence between Mathews and Asprey (302n17).

39. Asprey, *At Belleau Wood*, 300. See also Edwin McClellan, "The Battle of Belleau Wood," *Marine Corps Gazette* 5, no. 4 (December 1920): 370–404.

40. Feland, "Memoranda for Historical Section, Second Division, February 21, 1930," and "Memorandum for Captain Thomason."

41. Asprey, *At Belleau Wood*, 305–22.

42. See Coffman, *War to End All Wars*, 214: "The news coverage that the Marines got that month [June 1918] would rankle solders for 30 years." Coffman also addresses the subsequent criticism about the necessity of the battle: "Some military analysts would say that the Marines should have ignored the wood; that artillery could have neutralized it with a heavy gas barrage; that infantry should have bypassed it and forced the withdrawal of defenders by isolation; that as a military objective it was of little value—certainly not worth the cost that Marines and some soldiers (from the Second Engineer and Seventh Infantry Regiments) paid for it." Although historians might question whether it was the proper place and time and whether it was worth the cost, Coffman notes, "The fact remains that the officers and men of the Fourth Marine Brigade thought so in that summer month of fifty years ago."

43. Simmons and Alexander, *Through the Wheat*, 124–25.

44. "Major General Commandant B. H. Fuller, U.S.M.C., from J. D. Murray, Major, U.S.M.C. (Ret'd), Concord, Mass., 1932," manuscript, box 3, Ben H. Fuller Papers, MCA.

45. Harbord to the Secretary of War, April 24, 1924, file F, Harbord Papers, NYHS.

46. Feland's receipt of the Distinguished Service Cross was reported in *Washing-

ton Post, July 11, 1918, and *Hopkinsville Daily Kentuckian*, July 14, 1918. The citation can be found in Adjutant General, A.E.F., to Commanding General, Second Division, A.E.F., July 8, 1918, folder 1, Logan Feland Papers, MCA.

47. James G. Harbord, *The American Army in France, 1917–1919* (Boston: Little, Brown, 1936), 304.

7. From Soissons to the Return Home

1. See Edwin McClellan, "The Aisne-Marne Offensive," *Marine Corps Gazette* 6, no. 1 (March 1921): 70; Edwin Simmons, "Leathernecks at Soissons," *Naval History* 19, no. 6 (December 2005): 24.

2. See Simmons, "Leathernecks at Soissons," 24–33; James Nilo, "Attack on Soissons," *Leatherneck* 76, no. 7 (July 1993): 24–27; John Thomason Jr., "The Charge at Soissons," *Marine Corps Gazette* 53, no. 11 (November 1969): 60–69. Thomason's article, reprinted from his well-known collection of stories, *Fix Bayonets* (New York: Charles Scribner's Sons, 1926), gives a Marine Corps infantryman's point of view of the attack. Thomason, who achieved the rank of lieutenant colonel, stayed in the Marine Corps until he died in 1944. For more on Thomason, see George B. Clark, "Col John W. Thomason Jr., the 'Kipling of the Corps,'" *Leatherneck* 89, no. 8 (August 2006): 26–29.

3. Brady's description is from Craig Hamilton and Louise Corbin, eds., *Echoes from Over There* (New York: Soldiers' Publishing Company, 1919), 20. Brady also wrote about the march to Soissons in a retrospective on Feland published when the Kentuckian was commanding Marines in Nicaragua: "'Feland' Saved Allied Cause in War: Leader of Nicaragua Marines Took Vierzy," *New York Evening Journal*, July 20, 1927; copies are contained in box 302, entry 18, RG 127, NARA, and in Feland Scrapbook, Feland Papers, MCA. In *Echoes from Over There*, Brady misspelled Feland's last name as "Pheland," an error also made in a *New York Times* article about a postwar parade and in former secretary of war Henry Stimson's diary when he wrote about meeting Feland in Nicaragua in 1927. In the article in the *Evening Journal*, Brady got the spelling right.

4. Douglas V. Johnson II and Rolfe L. Hillman Jr., *Soissons 1918* (College Station: Texas A&M University Press, 1999), 62.

5. Ibid., 63.

6. Ronald J. Brown, *A Few Good Men: The Story of the Fighting Fifth Marines* (Novato, CA: Presidio Press, 2001), 54–56. For more on Cukela, see Edward A. Dieckmann Sr., "Louie Cukela," *Marine Corps Gazette* 45, no. 12 (December 1961): 34–39, and Allan C. Bevilacqua, "Next Time I Send Damn Fool I Go Myself," *Leatherneck* 89, no. 10 (October 2006): 52–54 (the title is a typical malapropism of the Croatian-born Cukela). Cukela retired as a major. For more on Sergeant Kocak, see Nilo, "Attack at Soissons," 26. Kocak died valiantly in October 1918 at the Battle of Blanc Mont Ridge, where he once again attacked a German machine gun position.

7. C.O. 2nd Bn., 5th Marines [Keyser] to C.O. 5th Marines [Feland], July 18,

1918, vol. 5, Records of the Second Division (Regular), container 30, James Harbord Papers, MD, LOC.

8. Thomason, "Charge at Soissons," 65. See also Nilo, "Attack at Soissons," 26.

9. Johnson and Hillman, *Soissons 1918*, 146. See also Simmons, "Leathernecks at Soissons," 33; Nilo, "Attack at Soissons," 27.

10. Commanding Officer 5th Regiment [Feland] to Commanding Officer 4th Brigade [Neville], July 30, 1918, vol. 7, Records of the Second Division (Regular), container 32, Harbord Papers, MD, LOC.

11. See "Synopsis of Record of Brigadier General Logan Feland, U.S. Marine Corps, during World War," folder 2, Feland Papers, MCA, for reference to the French awards, with later confirmation of these awards in folder 3. For his Army Distinguished Service Medal, see Adjutant General of the Army to Major General Commandant, United States Marine Corps, November 13, 1919, Feland file, RG 125, NARA. For his Navy Distinguished Service Medal commendation, see the letter from Secretary of the Navy Josephus Daniels, November 11, 1920, folder 4, Feland Papers, MCA.

12. Harbord to General Barnett, July 25, 1918, folder 3, Feland Papers, MCA.

13. Feland to the Secretary of the Navy, July 29, 1918, folder 1917–1926, Feland Papers, MCA.

14. Urey Woodson to Josephus Daniels, August 19, 1918, and Ollie James to Josephus Daniels, August 16, 1918, Feland file, RG 125, NARA.

15. Edwin McClellan, "In the Marbache Sector," *Marine Corps Gazette* 6, no. 3 (September 1921): 253–56; Julius Turrill file, Biographical Files, HRB, MCHD.

16. Edwin McClellan, "The St. Mihiel Offensive," *Marine Corps Gazette* 6, no. 4 (December 1921): 375–76; Brown, *A Few Good Men*, 49–61.

17. McClellan, "The St. Mihiel Offensive," 397; Brown, *A Few Good Men*, 61–64; James Nilo, "The Battle of St. Mihiel," *Leatherneck* 76, no. 9 (September 1993): 12–17.

18. For an overall history of the Meuse-Argonne offensive, see Edward Lengel, *To Conquer Hell: The Meuse-Argonne, 1918* (New York: Henry Holt, 2008).

19. For the Battle of Blanc Mont Ridge, see Edwin McClellan, "The Battle of Blanc Mont Ridge," *Marine Corps Gazette* 7, no. 1 (March 1922): 1–21, and "The Battle of Blanc Mont Ridge (continued)," *Marine Corps Gazette* 7, no. 2 (June 1922): 206–11; James R. Nilo, "The Battle of Blanc Mont," *Leatherneck* 76, no. 10 (October 1993): 10–15; Allan Bevilacqua, "The Battle of Blanc Mont Ridge," *Leatherneck* 83, no. 11 (November 2000): 26–31; Edwin Simmons, "With the Marines at Blanc Mont," *Marine Corps Gazette* 77, no. 11 (November 1993): 34–43. See also Brown, *A Few Good Men*, 64–70, for a focus on Feland's Fifth Regiment.

20. Brown, *A Few Good Men*, 65–66.

21. Edwin Simmons and Joseph Alexander, *Through the Wheat: The U.S. Marines in World War I* (Annapolis, MD: Naval Institute Press, 2008), 211.

22. C.O. 1st Bn. to C.O. 5th Regt., October 5, 1918, vol. 5, Records of the Second Division (Regular), container 30, Harbord Papers, MD, LOC.

23. See telephone message from Slap 1 [Feland] at 9:05 a.m., October 5, 1918,

Ellis report to Second Division at 9:15 a.m., October 5, 1918, and General Lejeune to Feland at 9:25 a.m., October 5, 1918, vol. 5, Records of the Second Division (Regular), container 30, Harbord Papers, MD, LOC.

24. Brown, *A Few Good Men*, 67–69.

25. See Feland's undated confidential memorandum to C.O.s 1st Bn., 2nd Bn., 3rd Bn., H.Q. Co. and Supply Co., box 20, entry NN3-127-97-002, RG 127, NARA.

26. Report of Major George Hamilton, October 4, 1918, certified on October 11, 1918, Robert Messersmith file, Biographical Files, HRB, MCHD.

27. "Military Record of Robert Eugene Messersmith, Major, U.S. Marine Corps," Messersmith file, HRB, MCHD.

28. Lieutenant Colonel J. S. Turrill, 5th Marines, to Commanding Officer, 5th Marines, October 24, 1918, Messersmith file, HRB, MCHD; emphasis in the original.

29. Feland to Commanding General Second Division via Commanding General 4th Brigade, 1st Indorsement to Turrill report of October 24, 1918, October 26, 1918, Messersmith file, HRB, MCHD.

30. Commanding General, 2nd Division, to Commander in Chief, A.E.F., "Promotion of Officers of the U.S. Marine Corps," October 16, 1918, folder 3, Feland Papers, MCA.

31. For more on armistice initiatives, see Edward M. Coffman, *The War to End All Wars: The American Military Experience in World War I* (New York: Oxford University Press, 1968), 341–43. Coffman notes that AEF commander Pershing favored unconditional surrender by the Germans, while President Wilson favored an armistice based on his Fourteen Points. According to Coffman, when the Germans sent an armistice delegation across French lines on the night of November 7, "a misinformed public celebrated the false armistice, but the war continued." Journalist Roy Howard received erroneous confirmation from Admiral Henry Wilson at Brest that the armistice had been signed, and he sent word to the United Press office in New York, which disseminated the good news across the country. See Nicholas Best, *The Greatest Day in History* (New York: Public Affairs, 2008), 69–73. In Feland's native Kentucky, the *Bowling Green Times-Journal* reported on November 7, 1918, "Pandemonium Breaks Loose," as people prematurely celebrated the armistice.

32. Simmons and Alexander, *Through the Wheat*, 219–33; Brown, *A Few Good Men*, 70–75.

33. Feland's note to Hamilton is reproduced in Jennifer Gooding, "Collection Adds Medals, Papers of WWI Hero," *Fortitudine* 18, no. 3 (Winter 1988–1989): 8. A photograph of the note is also contained in Chas. A. Hamilton to William Eddy, May 25, 1941, folder 14, box 10, William Alfred Eddy Collection, Seely Mudd Manuscript Library, Princeton University, in which George Hamilton's father claims that his son did not receive the note until 12:00 p.m. Badly wounded at Belleau Wood, Eddy served as Buck Neville's brigade intelligence officer until he became ill with pneumonia and was finally discharged. Eddy later became a noted Middle East expert

and served as president of Hobart College. He rejoined the Marines in World War II and served as envoy extraordinary and minister plenipotentiary to Saudi Arabia.

34. For the last night of the war, see Rolfe L. Hillman Jr., "Crossing the Meuse," *Marine Corps Gazette* 72, no. 11 (November 1988): 68–73; James R. Nilo, "World War I: 75 Years Ago: The Last Night of the War," *Leatherneck* 76, no. 11 (November 1993): 16–23. Samuel Cumming's brief account of the last day of the war can be found in the Samuel Cumming Collection, MCA. For more on Hamilton in the final days of the war, see Mark Mortensen, *George W. Hamilton, USMC: America's Greatest World War I Hero* (Jefferson, NC: McFarland, 2011), 154–69; Ronald J. Brown, "George Wallis Hamilton: The Forgotten Hero of World War I," *Leatherneck* 86, no. 11 (November 2003): 46–51. The larger context of the last day of the war is covered in Joseph Persico, *Eleventh Month, Eleventh Day, Eleventh Hour: Armistice Day, 1918. World War I and Its Violent Climax* (New York: Random House, 2004).

35. William Mathews to Robert Asprey, February 21, 1964, file Mathews, W. R., 1962–66, box 8, Robert Asprey Collection, Howard Gotlieb Archival Research Center, Boston University.

36. Material on the Fifth Regiment's march to the Rhineland can be found in "A Brief History of the Fifth Regiment U.S. Marines during the World War," 5th Regiment file, Unit Files, HRB, MCHD. See also Rolfe L. Hillman Jr., "Marines in the Rhineland, 1918–1919," *Naval History* 3, no. 3 (Summer 1989): 11–15.

37. Frederick Wise, as told to Meigs O. Frost, *A Marine Tells It to You* (New York: J. H. Sears, 1929), 294–95.

38. See Hans Schmidt, *Maverick Marine: General Smedley D. Butler and the Contradictions of American Military History* (Lexington: University Press of Kentucky, 1987), 96–109. Butler did an outstanding job improving conditions at Camp Pontanezen, attacking problems with his usual verve. He was known to shoulder duckboards himself and lay them across the ground to deal with the muddy conditions—hence his nickname "General Duckboard." Because of his enmity toward Barnett, Butler urged his father, a congressman, to defeat legislation that would have made the Marine Corps Commandant a lieutenant general.

39. *Kentucky New Era*, March 14, 1919. See *Register of the Commissioned and Warrant Officers of the United States Navy and Marine Corps and Reserve Officers on Active Duty* (Washington, DC: Government Printing Office, 1920), 308, for Feland's place on the Marine Corps lineal list.

40. "Military History of Brigadier General Logan Feland," Feland file, HRB, MCHD.

41. "A Brief History of the Fifth Regiment U.S. Marines during the World War."

42. See E. David Cronen, ed., *Cabinet Diaries of Josephus Daniels, 1913–1921* (Lincoln: University of Nebraska Press, 1963), 301–2. Daniels's trip to Germany was reported in the Second Division's periodical: *Indian* 1, no. 2 (April 29, 1919): 1–2.

43. Harry B. Field and Henry G. James, *Over the Top with the 18th Co., 5th Regt., U.S. Marines: A History* (Germany: n.p., 1919), 45–46.

8. The Dominican Republic, 1920

1. Feland's arrival in New Jersey was reported in *New York Times*, May 14, 1919. At one point, Katherine Feland had attempted to join her husband in Europe; see Feland file, NPRC. Philadelphia attorney John Bell wrote to Senator Penrose for assistance in getting passports for Mrs. Feland and for Mrs. A. J. Drexel Biddle, but there is no evidence that they were forthcoming. The remembrance of Belleau Wood was noted in *Washington Post*, June 4, 1919.

2. A copy of the deed for the land can be found in the Pike County Deed Office, Milford, Pennsylvania. The area became known as "Little Norway" after "a group of 20 Norwegian families from Brooklyn formed the Norwegian American Colony Association in 1902. They each contributed $200 toward the purchase of a tract of land at Rowland where they organized their own commune." Although the commune's sawmill and stone quarry eventually failed, several families stayed in the area, and their descendants are still there, active in the Sons of Norway Lodge. *Honesdale (PA) Wayne Independent*, September 22, 2008.

3. Katherine Feland's appearance at the Methodist centenary was reported in *Breckenridge News, Cloverport (KY)*, June 4, 1919. Logan Feland's visit to Owensboro was reported in *Owensboro Daily Messenger*, June 15, 25, and 26, 1919.

4. Dispatch, July 23, 1919, ordering Feland to report to "temporary duty Office Chief Naval Operations," Feland file, NPRC. For the duties of the Office of the Chief of Naval Operations, see *Official Congressional Directory* (Washington, DC: Government Printing Office, 1919), 325–31.

5. See John H. Maurer, "Fuel and the Battle Fleet: Coal, Oil, and American Naval Strategy, 1898–1925," *Naval War College Review* 34 (November–December 1981): 60–77; Annette Amerman, "Over Here! Marines in Texas during World War I," *Fortitudine* 33, no. 2 (2008): 7–8.

6. "Mexico—Tampico Tuxpam Oil Region—The Feland Plan—August 29, 1919," box 1, War Plans 1915–1920, entry 39D, Division of Plans and Policies War Plans, 1945, RG 127, NARA.

7. Ellis's travels to Mexico are covered in Dirk A. Ballendorf and Merrill L. Bartlett, *Pete Ellis: An Amphibious Warfare Prophet, 1880–1923* (Annapolis, MD: Naval Institute Press, 1997), 101–2. See "Mexico—Tampico-Tuxpam Oil Region—Ellis Plan—Summer 1919," box 1, War Plans 1915–1920, entry 39D, Division of Plans and Policies War Plans, 1945, RG 127, NARA; "Complete Plans of Operation against the Tampico-Tuxpam Oil Fields and Vera Cruz Prepared by Staff of the 4th Brigade U.S. Marines September 1920," box 2, War Plans 1919–1921, entry 39D, Division of Plans and Policies War Plans, 1945, RG 127, NARA.

8. "New York Greets Valorous Second," *Recruiters' Bulletin* 5, no. 7 (August 1919): 10. In the article, Feland's name is spelled "Phelan," a common error. See also *New York Times*, August 9, 1919. For articles on both the New York City and Washington, D.C., parades, see Ralph Keyser Collection, MCA.

9. Robert Heinl, *Soldiers of the Sea: The United States Marine Corps, 1775–1962*, 2nd ed. (Baltimore: Nautical and Aviation Publishing Company of America, 1991), 228.

10. For the reduction in the Marine Corps and the difficulties in deciding which officers to retain at rank, see R. H. Williams, "Those Controversial Boards," *Marine Corps Gazette* 66, no. 11 (November 1982): 91–96. The tension at Headquarters Marine Corps was noted in Charles Lyman to Joseph Pendleton, October 24, 1919, folder 4: October to December 1919, box 4, Joseph Pendleton Collection, MCA. For speculation on officer appointments, see *Washington Post*, August 24 and September 28, 1919.

11. Major General Commandant to Brigadier General Logan Feland, October 23, 1919, Feland file, NPRC. On October 8, 1919, the "Society" section of the *Washington Post* reported that the Felands were en route to Santo Domingo. A copy of Feland's passport application can be found on Ancestry.com; he indicated that his permanent residence was Hopkinsville, Kentucky, and stated that he had never had a passport before.

12. The background leading up to the landing of Wise's Marines is covered in Stephen Fuller and Graham Cosmas, *Marines in the Dominican Republic, 1916–1924* (Washington, DC: History and Museums Division, Headquarters, U.S. Marine Corps, 1974), 1–7. The events and circumstances leading up to intervention in the Dominican Republic in 1916 are examined in Bruce Calder, *The Impact of Intervention: The Dominican Republic during the U.S. Occupation of 1916–1924* (Austin: University of Texas Press, 1984), 1–35. See also Ellen Davies Tillman, "Imperialism Revised: Military, Society, and U.S. Occupation in the Dominican Republic, 1880–1924" (PhD diss., University of Illinois at Urbana-Champaign, 2010), which is based on extensive research in Marine Corps and Dominican archives. See also Valentina Peguero, *The Militarization of Culture in the Dominican Republic, from the Captains General to General Trujillo* (Lincoln: University of Nebraska Press, 2004), 27–43. The Marine Corps's occupation of Hispaniola is placed in a larger context in Lester Langley, *The Banana Wars: United States Intervention in the Caribbean, 1898–1934*, rev. ed. (Lexington: University Press of Kentucky, 1985), 111–58.

13. Calder, *Impact of Intervention*, 54–62; Fuller and Cosmas, *Marines in the Dominican Republic*, 26–29.

14. Calder, *Impact of Intervention*, 32–90.

15. Fuller and Cosmas, *Marines in the Dominican Republic*, 26–29. Comments regarding Snowden's aloofness toward the Dominicans can be found in Sumner Welles, *Naboth's Vineyard: The Dominican Republic, 1844–1924*, 2 vols. (New York: Payson and Clarke, 1928), 2:818–20. Welles served as head of the State Department's Latin American Division and as U.S. commissioner to the Dominican Republic from 1925 to 1928.

16. Calder, *Impact of Intervention*, 115–59.

17. Fuller and Cosmas, *Marines in the Dominican Republic*, 28–29. See also Clyde Metcalf, *A History of the United States Marine Corps* (New York: G. P. Putnam's Sons, 1939), 357–66.

18. James Carson Breckinridge to his mother, March 19, 1919, box 5, Correspondence-Personal-Family 1903–1920, folder 15, January 12 to December 30,

1919, Breckinridge Papers, MCA. Despite the heavy responsibilities, Breckinridge admitted, "This is the best job in the world." He was not fond of administrative duties, however: "I sit in the office and sweat and swear, while the lads go out and have a lot of fun. I do not like this Colonel business." Breckinridge to his mother, March 31, 1919, ibid.

19. See, for example, Ethan Harding, "Civil-Military Operations," *Marine Corps Gazette* 95, no. 8 (August 1911): 18–22, in which the author notes that regardless of what such operations are called (e.g., military operations other than war, nonkinetic techniques of pacification), "the abilities required to achieve success in civil-military operations (CMO) are typically counterintuitive to the skills valued by Marines" (18).

20. James Carson Breckinridge to his mother, April 20, 1920, box 5, folder 16, January 17 to December 11, 1920, Breckinridge Papers, MCA.

21. Brigade Commander to Major General Commandant, "Brigade Diary, January 11 to January 17, 1920," file Dominican Republic–Santo Domingo 1920, Geographical Files, HRB, MCHD.

22. Military Governor of Santo Domingo to Chief of Naval Operations, "Strength of Brigade," January 17, 1920, and "Increase in Marine Force in Santo Domingo," February 14, 1920, file 6, box 757, entry 520 WA-7, RG 45, NARA.

23. Metcalf, *History of the U.S. Marine Corps*, 525. See also Heinl, *Soldiers of the Sea*, 228. Hamilton's indecision is noted in Mark Mortensen, *George W. Hamilton, USMC: America's Greatest World War I Hero* (Jefferson, NC: McFarland, 2011), 219–25.

24. Brigade General Order No. 1, 1920, file D-32, and "Report of Operations, Second Provisional Brigade, U.S. Marines, June 19–July 17, 1920," July 31, 1920, file D-46, box 8, entry 38, RG 127, NARA; Feland to Barnett, May 20, 1920, folder 19, George Barnett Papers, MCA.

25. Ellis's report can be found in "Summary of Intelligence," June 1–August 1, 1920, file D-29, box 8, entry 38, RG 127, NARA.

26. "Increase in Marine Forces in Santo Domingo," July 2, 1920, and Chief of Naval Operations to Military Governor of Santo Domingo, "Increase in Marine Forces in Santo Domingo," July 21, 1920, file 6, box 757, entry 520 WA-7, RG 45, NARA.

27. "Quarterly Reports of Military Governor of Santo Domingo for 1920," file 4, box 760, entry 520 WA-7, RG 45, NARA. This file contains most of the executive orders produced by Feland, some in English and some in Spanish.

28. "Report of Operations, Second Provisional Brigade, U.S. Marines, 19 June–17 July 1920," July 31, 1920, file D-46, Dominican Republic, box 8, Cuba to the Dominican Republic, entry 38, Commandant's Office, General Correspondence, Operations and Training Division, Intelligence Section, 1915–1934, RG 127, NARA. See also similar reports filed on September 4, 1920 (covering July 17–September 1, 1920), and October 14, 1920 (covering September 1–30, 1920), ibid.

29. Commanding General to Major General Commandant, "Report of Activities

of the Second Brigade, U.S. Marines, for the Year Ending June 30, 1920," folder 2nd Brigade Reports, box 2, entry 243, Santo Domingo, RG 127, NARA.

30. Feland to SECNAV Josephus Daniels, July 29, 1920, file 5, box 5, entry 78, Miscellaneous Letters Sent and Reports, 1914 to 1924, RG 38, Records of the Office of Naval Operations, NARA.

31. Hans Schmidt, *Maverick Marine: General Smedley D. Butler and the Contradictions of American Military History* (Lexington: University Press of Kentucky, 1987), 99; Butler's role in World War I is described in chap. 8.

32. Merrill Bartlett, "Ouster of a Commandant," *Proceedings of the U.S. Naval Institute* 106, no. 11 (November 1980): 65–72; Schmidt, *Maverick Marine*, 110–28.

33. Merrill Bartlett, *Lejeune: A Marine's Life, 1867–1942* (Annapolis, MD: Naval Institute Press, 1991), 146–71.

34. Feland to Julian Smith, May 3, 1920, folder 17, box 11, Julian Smith Collection, MCA. See also Commanding General [Feland] to Major General Commandant [Lejeune], "Plan for the Concentration and Reorganization of the Second Brigade for Expeditionary Service outside Santo Domingo," August 12, 1920, folder 164, box 3, 146 China to 174 Dominican Republic, entry 38A, RG 127, NARA. Lejeune approved the plan; see Lejeune to Feland, August 31, 1920, ibid.

35. For an article on Feland's visit to Santiago, see *Fourth Regiment News*, September 1, 1920, folder: Newspaper Clippings, box 8, Lejeune Papers, MCA.

36. Oral history of Lieutenant General Edward A. Craig, U.S. Marine Corps (retired), conducted by Major L. E. Tatum, 27–28; copy available in MCA. Among other duties, Craig commanded the Ninth Marine Regiment at Guadalcanal in 1943, planned and participated in the Battle of Iwo Jima, and commanded Marines at Pusan, Korea, in 1950. He retired in 1951.

37. Commanding Officer, First Division, Squadron D, Marine Aviation Force, to Chief of Naval Operations, October 9, 1920, file Santo Domingo 1920, HRB, MCHD.

38. Commanding General to Military Governor, "Appointment of Colonel J. C. Breckinridge as Commandant, Guardia Nacional Dominicana," September 28, 1920, folder 3: Military Correspondence from 18 March 1920 to 2 November 1921, box 3, Breckinridge Papers, MCA.

39. "Report of Operations, Second Provisional Brigade, U.S. Marines, September 1–September 30, 1920," October 14, 1920, file D-46, box 8, entry 38, RG 127, NARA.

40. For Lejeune's report on the trip to Hispaniola, see Major General Commandant to the Secretary of the Navy, "Report of the Military Situation in Haiti," October 5, 1920, folder 12, box 2, Lejeune Papers, MCA. An outline of Lejeune's trip is included in a letter to his sister Augustine, February 25, 1920, folder 20, box 5, Lejeune Papers, MCA.

41. Calder, *Impact of Intervention*, 183–237; Tillman, "Imperialism Revised," 293–431; Fuller and Cosmas, *Marines in the Dominican Republic*, 61–69.

42. The Military Governor of Santo Domingo to the Secretary of the Navy, "Rec-

ommending Brigadier General Logan Feland, U.S. Marine Corps, for Appointment to Rank of Major General in the U.S. Marine Corps," September 29, 1920, folder 4, Feland Papers, MCA.

43. Logan Feland, "The Division of Operations and Training, Headquarters, U.S. Marine Corps," *Marine Corps Gazette* 7, no. 1 (March 1922): 41–45.

9. Headquarters Marine Corps

1. See Merrill Bartlett's chapter on Lejeune in Allan Millett and Jack Shulimson, *Commandants of the Marine Corps* (Annapolis, MD: Naval Institute Press, 2004), 201.

2. Minutes of Commandant Lejeune's weekly staff meetings for the better part of two years can be found in file 1395, box 84, entry 18, RG 127, NARA.

3. "Record of Weekly Conference Held in Office of Major General Commandant, Tuesday, December 14, 1920, file 1395, box 84, entry 18, RG 127, NARA.

4. Brigadier General Logan Feland, U.S.M.C., to Major General Commandant, "Commendation," October 25, 1920, box 1, Earl Ellis Papers, MCA.

5. Dirk A. Ballendorf and Merrill L. Bartlett, *Pete Ellis: An Amphibious Warfare Prophet, 1880–1923* (Annapolis, MD: Naval Institute Press, 1997), 109–22.

6. Earl H. Ellis, Major, U.S. Marines, to the Major General Commandant, "Request for Intelligence Duty in South America and in the Pacific Ocean," August 20, 1920, box 55, entry 78, RG 38, NARA. Feland's comments are in the first endorsement.

7. Ellis's medical record dated April 9, 1921, can be found in Ellis file, HRB, MCHD.

8. Earl Ellis to Feland, June 19, 1922; Feland to John Ellis, January 6, 1923, folder 5, box 3, Earl Ellis Papers, MCA.

9. Ellis's final days are described in Ballendorf and Bartlett, *Pete Ellis*, 123–41.

10. Feland to John Ellis, May 11 [1923], folder 2, box 2, Ellis Papers, MCA.

11. Feland to Ralph Ellis, June 4, 1923, folder 1923, box 8, Ellis Papers, MCA.

12. Feland to Ralph Ellis, June 14, 1923, folder 13, box 3, Ellis Papers, MCA. See Feland to John Ellis, June 13, 1923, ibid., about the difficulty in obtaining Earl's stored goods. Feland wrote: "I could have gotten the goods without any trouble if the storage people had not read in the papers of Earl's death. I am very anxious to be of any further service, if possible, in this matter or in any other, and I hope you will not hesitate to call on me."

13. In Feland to John Ellis, June 21, 1923, he notes that he will send trunks and boxes "tomorrow" and adds: "Am glad I was able to arrange this for you and you must not hesitate to call on me for anything I can do." See also Ralph Ellis to John Lejeune, September 14, 1923, expressing thanks, and Ralph Ellis to Lynn Turner, September 14, 1923, referring to Lejeune and Feland as two of Earl's best friends, folder 13, box 3, Ellis Papers, MCA.

14. In an effort to "ensure the retention and dissemination of useful information which is not intended to become doctrine or to be published in Fleet Marine Force

manuals," the Marine Corps published Ellis's work in 1992. See U.S. Marine Corps, *Advanced Base Operations in Micronesia* (Washington, DC: Government Printing Office, 1992), i.

15. See Cunningham to E. B. Miller, January 22, 1931, folder 4, box 2, Alfred Cunningham Collection, MCA.

16. Cunningham's lunch with Feland is noted in Graham Cosmas, ed., *Marine Flyer in France: The Diary of Captain Alfred A. Cunningham, November 1917–February 1918* (Washington, DC: History and Museums Division, Headquarters, U.S. Marine Corps, 1974), 30.

17. For Turner's historic flight, see Edward C. Johnson, *Marine Corps Aviation: The Early Years, 1912–1940*, ed. Graham Cosmas (Washington, DC: History and Museums Division, Headquarters, U.S. Marine Corps, 1977), 47. The photograph of Feland and Turner appeared in *New York Times*, January 13, 1924.

18. Evans to Feland, July 16, 1923, folder 26, box 12, Butler Papers, MCA. Evans had sent a copy of the letter to General Butler for his information. Evans was the first editor of the *Marine Corps Gazette* and would write numerous articles for the publication. He retired from the Corps as a captain in 1905 but rejoined and served in the Sixth Regiment in World War I, received the Navy Cross for meritorious action at Belleau Wood, commanded the *Gendarmerie d'Haiti*, and retired as a brigadier general in 1940.

19. John M. Elliott, "The Longest Flight: Early Marine Aviators Make History," *Leatherneck* 91, no. 5 (May 2008): 54–59.

20. Ibid., 59. See also Logan Feland to Hugh Robinson, St. Louis Aeronautics Corporation, September 22, 1923, folder 1165-10, Aviation, box 11, General Correspondence, 1913–1932, RG 127, NARA; William F. Trimble, *Admiral William A. Moffett: Architect of Naval Aviation* (Washington, DC: Smithsonian Institution Press, 1994), 123.

21. Brigadier Logan Feland, U.S.M.C., to the Major General Commandant, "Request for Assignment to School for Observers," May 17, 1926, and Commanding General to Major General Commandant, "Termination of Flight Detail in the Case of Brigadier General Logan Feland, U.S.M.C.," June 15, 1926, folder 1917–1926, Feland Papers, MCA; Major General Commandant to the Commanding General, Marine Barracks, Quantico, VA, "Orders for Officers to Attend Aviation Observers Course," June 1, 1926, and Major General Commandant to Brigadier General Logan Feland, "Detail to Duty Involving Flying," June 9, 1926, Feland file, NPRC. For Feland's health problems, see his medical history dated September 9, 1929, Feland file, RG 125, NARA.

22. "General Feland Speaks at Armistice Day Celebration," *Leatherneck* 5, no. 58 (November 25, 1922): 1–2. For brief biographies of Admirals Watson and Rodman, who both had ships named after them, see *Dictionary of American Naval Fighting Ships* at the Naval History and Heritage Command website, www.history.navy.mil/danfs/index.html. See also Hugh Rodman, *Yarns of a Kentucky Admiral* (Indianapolis: Bobbs-Merrill, 1928).

23. See *Louisville Courier-Journal*, November 10, 11, and 12, 1922. Ellerbe Carter eventually became a brigadier general in the Kentucky National Guard and was well known for commanding troops during a 1939 United Mine Workers' strike in Harlan County. See Ellerbe Carter file, Military Records and Research Branch, Department of Military Affairs, Frankfort, KY.

24. *Washington Post*, October 19, 1924, reported Feland serving on the Kentucky Society's reception committee with Brandeis, McReynolds, Rodman, and Ernst. The Felands hosted Senator Ernst at a dinner in February 1922; see *Washington Post*, February 15, 1922. They also hosted a dinner for Major General and Mrs. Eli Cole in 1925, which the Eberles attended; see *North Adams (MA) Transcript*, November 25, 1925.

25. *Washington Post*, June 4, 1919.

26. *Washington Post*, February 13, 1921, and December 21, 1924.

27. For the Crittenton committee, see *Washington Post*, October 7, 1923; for the Belleau Wood memorial fund-raisers, see *Washington Post*, February 7, 1925, and November 20, 1921.

28. Marietta Andrews, *My Studio Window: Sketches of the Pageant of Washington Life* (New York: E. P. Dutton, 1928), 416–23.

29. *Historical Sketch, Constitution, and Register of the Military Order of the Carabao* (Washington, DC: W. F. Roberts, n.d.), 7–109; Ralph Ghormley, *The Military Order of the Carabao: Centennial History* (n.p.: Military Order of the Carabao, 2000), 2–16. Unlike the Order of the Dragon, the Military Order of the Carabao still exists.

30. Feland's presidency of the D.C. branch was reported in *Washington Post*, April 15, 1923.

31. Formation of the Military Order of the World War was noted in *New York Times*, September 10, 1920; Harries was quoted in *Spokane Daily Chronicle*, September 19, 1922. The order called for a military presence of 150,000 men, well above the planned 115,000; see *New York Times*, September 21, 1922. The order still exists today, but its name is now plural: Military Order of the World Wars.

32. The initial reunion was reported in *Baltimore Sun*, May 29, 1923. See *New York Times*, May 24, 1929, noting the formation of the actual Baltic Society four years previously.

33. For Harbord's post–World War I activities, see Brian Fisher Neumann, "Pershing's Right Hand: General James G. Harbord and the American Expeditionary Forces in the First World War" (PhD diss., Texas A&M University, 2006), 413–31. During the Armenian mission, Harbord's friend, Brigadier General Frank McCoy, served as his chief of staff. McCoy and Feland would both serve in Nicaragua in 1928.

34. See "Marine Officers to Present Portrait of General Harbord," *Leatherneck* 5, no. 21 (March 25, 1922): 1, and "Harbord Portrait Presented to Army and Navy Club," *Leatherneck* 8, no. 2 (June 1923): 110–24.

35. Logan Feland to James Harbord, September 24, 1923, file F, Harbord Papers, NYHS.

36. Major General James G. Harbord, U.S.A. Retired, to the Major General Commandant, U.S. Marine Corps, Washington, D.C., Attention of General J. A. Lejeune, "Promotion of Brigadier General Logan Feland," October 4, 1923, file F, Harbord Papers, NYHS. Harbord also sent Feland a copy of the letter.

37. Major General Commandant to Major General James G. Harbord, U.S. Army Retired, October 8, 1923, file F, Harbord Papers, NYHS.

38. Logan Feland to the Secretary of the Navy, "Rank in Grade," November 29, 1916, file 11123–11130, box 560, RG 80, NARA. With this memo, Feland provided more than twenty references, primarily to opinions of the U.S. attorney general and the U.S. Army judge advocate general. See also Major General Commandant [George Barnett] to Judge Advocate General, "Claim of Major Logan Feland re Rank in Grade," December 18, 1916, and Secretary of the Navy to Major Logan Feland, "Claim of Major Logan Feland, M.C. to Rank in Grade," December 20, 1916, ibid. Copies of Major Marix's paperwork requesting that he be placed on the lineal list ahead of James Carson Breckinridge can also be found in the file. Marix had been L. W. T. Waller's defense counsel at his trial for the Samar massacre. Marix eventually retired as a colonel; he founded the Military Officers Association of America in 1929 and was its first president.

39. Brigadier General Logan Feland, U.S.M.C., to the Secretary of the Navy, via the Major General Commandant, "Relative Rank," October 29, 1923, file 11120 (63)–11130 (106), box 561, RG 80, NARA.

40. Major General Commandant to the Secretary of the Navy, "Relative Rank of Brigadiers General with Same Date of Commission: Brig. Gen. Logan Feland, 29 Oct. 1923, Requests Decision re," October 30, 1923, ibid. Lejeune's conclusion about the intent to favor Butler can be found in Major General Commandant to the Secretary of the Navy, "Relative Rank of Brigadiers General with Same Date of Commission: Brig. Gen. Logan Feland, 29 Oct. 1923, Requests Decision re," December 8, 1923, file F, box 4, Butler Papers, MCA.

41. Judge Advocate General to Major General Commandant, U.S. Marine Corps, "Letter of Brigadier General Logan Feland to the Secretary of the Navy Dated October 29, 1923 and Endorsement to Thereon by Major General Commandant," March 3, 1924, file 11120 (63)–11130 (106), box 561, RG 80, NARA. The JAG at the time was Rear Admiral Julian L. Latimer, to whom Feland would report when he was commander of Marines in Nicaragua in 1927.

42. Harbord to the Secretary of War, April 24, 1924, file F, Harbord Papers, NYHS.

10. Assistant to the Commandant

1. Chief of Naval Operations to Major General Commandant, "Function of Marine Corps in War Plans," January 23, 1920, file 1920–1932, Plan Orange, box 3, entry 39D, RG 127, NARA. Coontz suggested that the East and West Coast Expeditionary Forces each contain 6,000 to 8,000 men.

2. Allan Millett, *Semper Fidelis: The History of the United States Marine Corps,*

rev. ed. (New York: Free Press, 1991), 326. For Millett's analysis of the Corps in the 1920s, see 319–43.

3. "Record of Weekly Conference Held in Office of Major General Commandant, Tuesday, December 14, 1920," file 1395, box 84, entry 18, RG 127, NARA.

4. Logan Feland, "Soldiers of the Navy," *Leatherneck* 7, no. 15 (April 3, 1924): 4. The *Leatherneck* editor in chief at the time was Colonel James Carson Breckinridge.

5. Millett, *Semper Fidelis*, 324. See also Merrill Bartlett, *Lejeune: A Marine's Life, 1867–1942* (Annapolis, MD: Naval Institute Press, 1991), 160–61.

6. Feland's leave orders and recision are in Feland file, NPRC.

7. Logan Feland, "Annex No. 1, to Letter of Instruction in re Duties of U.S. Marine Corps Detached Guard Companies on Duty Guarding U.S. Mail," November 13, 1921, and Major General Commandant to All Commanding Officers, U.S. Marine Corps Detached Guard Companies, "Miscellaneous Instructions," December 13, 1921, Mail Guard folder, HRB, MCHD. Although it was sent out under the Commandant's order, Feland signed the latter document. See also "The Mail Guard," *Marine Corps Gazette* 11, no. 4 (December 1926): 259–71; Robert W. Tallent, "The Great Mail Call," *Leatherneck* 38, no. 2 (February 1955): 44–47; and George Corney, "Crime and Postal History: Bring in the Marines!" *Marine Corps Gazette* 77, no. 10 (October 1993): 50–52.

8. Postmaster General Hubert Work to Major General Commandant, via the Secretary of the Navy, March 14, 1922, and Major General Commandant to Brigadier General Logan Feland, "Letter from the Postmaster General, Commending the Officers and Men Who Performed Duties in Connection with the Guarding of the United States Mails," April 3, 1922, folder 5, Feland Papers, MCA.

9. "Synopsis of Record Major General Feland since World War," folder 2, Feland Papers, MCA.

10. See Bartlett, *Lejeune*, 146–71, for Lejeune's tenure as Commandant. For the development of the Marine Corps in the 1920s, see Millett, *Semper Fidelis*, 319–31, and Clyde Metcalf, *A History of the United States Marine Corps* (New York: G. P. Putnam's Sons, 1939), 524–29.

11. See Heather Pace Marshall, "It Means Something These Days to Be a Marine: Image, Identity, and Mission in the Marine Corps, 1861–1918" (PhD diss., Duke University, 2010). An article about Rowell, accompanied by a photograph of him standing next to the poster along with artist Flagg, appeared in *Fortitudine* 7, no. 2 (Fall 1978): 12–15. For the significance of World War I recruiting posters, see Pearl James, ed., *Picture This: World War I Posters and Visual Culture* (Lincoln: University of Nebraska Press, 2009).

12. Hans Schmidt, *Maverick Marine: General Smedley D. Butler and the Contradictions of American Military History* (Lexington: University Press of Kentucky, 1987), 129–43.

13. See John H. Craige, "The 'Wilderness' Manoeuvres," *Marine Corps Gazette* 6, no. 4 (December 1921): 418–23; *New York Times*, October 2 and 3, 1921.

14. See John H Craige, "The Marines at Gettysburg," *Marine Corps Gazette* 7,

no. 3 (September 1922): 249–52; *Washington Post*, June 22 and 24, 1923; Mark Mortensen, *George W. Hamilton, USMC: America's Greatest World War I Hero* (Jefferson, NC: McFarland, 2011), 224–42; "Death of Captain Hamilton and Sergeant Martin Saddens Troops," *Leatherneck* 5, no. 35 (July 1, 1922): 1–2.

15. For Feland's letter to Hamilton, see Mortensen, *George W. Hamilton*, 219–20. According to Mortensen, Feland was one of Hamilton's closest friends in the Corps, along with Maurice Shearer.

16. See "Annual Field Exercises of the Marine Corps East Coast Expeditionary Force," *Marine Corps Gazette* 8, no. 3 (September 1923): 158–60; "Present Civil War Battle," *Leatherneck* 6, no. 38 (September 25, 1923): 2. The commander of Confederate forces at New Market, General John C. Breckinridge, was the grandfather of Feland's colleague James Carson Breckinridge.

17. Feland, memorandum for the Commandant, "Basic Plan, Fall Maneuvers, 1923," April 28, 1923, file 1975-70-12, box 255, entry 18, RG 127, NARA.

18. See "M.C.E.F. Enjoys Good Weather," *Leatherneck* 7, no. 37 (September 6, 1924): 2–3; "The Leathernecks Return Home," *Leatherneck* 7, no. 40 (September 27, 1924): 1; Dion Williams, "The Fall Exercises of the 1924 Marine Corps Expeditionary Force," *Marine Corps Gazette* 10, no. 1 (June 1925): 30–62.

19. Schmidt, *Maverick Marine*, 144–60.

20. See Leo Daugherty III, "Away All Boats: The Army-Navy Maneuvers of 1925," *Joint Forces Quarterly* 20 (Autumn–Winter 1998–1999): 107–13. For contemporary reports of the 1925 Oahu exercise, see Dion Williams, "Blue Marine Expeditionary Force," *Marine Corps Gazette* 10, no. 2 (September 1925): 76–88; E. A. Fellowes, "Marines Embark for Expeditionary Duty," *Leatherneck* 8, no. 12 (March 21, 1925): 1; "Blue Marine Expeditionary Force Arrives at Panama City," *Leatherneck* 8, no. 14 (April 4, 1925): 1; "Marines Stage Final Practice for Oahu Maneuver," *Leatherneck* 8, no. 17 (April 25, 1925): 1; "Marines Force Landing at Oahu but Technical Victor Is Still in Hands of the Critics," *Leatherneck* 8, no. 21 (May 23, 1925): 4.

21. Brigadier General Robert C. Kilmartin, USMC, oral history transcript, 74, MCA.

22. Daugherty, "Away All Boats," 113.

23. Feland's appointment to the East Coast Expeditionary Force was reported in *Washington Post*, June 28, 1925. The Felands' party for General Cole was reported in *Washington Post*, November 21, 1925.

24. Feland's attendance at the Fort Tilden test was reported in *New York Times*, August 18, 1925.

25. The Fort Meade aviation maneuvers are covered in "Aviation Force on Maneuvers at Camp Meade, Maryland," *Leatherneck* 8, no. 36 (September 25, 1925): 5. The artillery maneuvers are covered in H. W. Stone, "Field Exercises of the 10th Regiment at Camp Meade, Maryland," *Marine Corps Gazette* 10, no. 3 (December 1925): 157–60. The photo of the three officers being driven around by Colonel O. S. Eskridge, commander of Fort Meade, appeared in *New York Times*, September 13, 1925.

26. Alexander S. Williams, "The San Diego Marine Base," *Marine Corps Gazette*

11, no. 2 (June 1926): 82–86. Among many contemporary national articles covering the Butler-Williams imbroglio, see especially the following from the *New York Times*: "Gen. Butler Causes His Host's Arrest," March 11, 1926; "Rally to Defense of Col. Williams," March 12, 1926; "Butler Defends Arrest of Officer," March 13, 1926; "Col. Williams May Plead Guilty to Save Guests at Cocktail Party, Including Gen. Butler," March 26, 1926; "Officer Holds Butler Cannot Prove Charge," March 29, 1926; "Butler Emphatic in His Replies," April 13, 1926, detailing Butler's testimony at the court-martial; "Williams Sober, Officers Testify," April 14, 1926; "Williams Convicted by Court-Martial," April 20, 1926; "Transfers Williams to San Francisco," May 23, 1926; "Col. Williams Dies as Car Dives off San Francisco Pier," October 2, 1926; "Colonel Williams's Funeral," October 13, 1926, in which Feland, Robert Dunlap, and four other colonels were mentioned as honorary pallbearers. For a more recent analysis, see James W. Hammond, "Butler's Bouts with 'Illegal Substances,'" *Marine Corps Gazette* 66, no. 2 (February 1982): 51–57.

27. Secretary of the Navy to Marine Corps Commandant, "Marine Corps Postal Guards," October 19, 1926, Mail Guard file, HRB, MCHD. See also Tallent, "The Great Mail Call," 45; Corney, "Crime and Postal History," 50–52.

28. Clippings can be found in Feland Scrapbook, Feland Papers, MCA. The "Devil Dog" and "Shoot-to-Kill" comments were from a *St. Louis Globe-Democrat* article, labeled in the Scrapbook as being from the November 15, 1926, edition. Other articles were from newspapers in New Orleans, Atlanta, St. Paul, Washington, D.C., New York City, and elsewhere.

29. John Lejeune to Smedley Butler, February 21, 1927, in *My Dear Smedley: Personal Correspondence of John A. Lejeune to Smedley D. Butler, 1927–1928*, ed. Michael Miller (Washington, DC: Marine Corps Research Center, Archives Branch, 2002), 4.

30. Schmidt, *Maverick Marine*, 54.

31. Lejeune to Butler, February 7, 1927, in Miller, *My Dear Smedley*, 1.

32. Lejeune to Butler, February 21, 1927, ibid., 3.

33. Mrs. Reath's visit to France was reported in *Philadelphia Inquirer*, September 3, 1921. Feland's attendance at the American Legion post dinner was reported in *Philadelphia Inquirer*, November 21, 1920.

34. The Reaths' dinner party was reported in *Washington Post*, November 7, 1924. See also Theodore Reath to Smedley Butler, November 9, 1924, folder 13, Official Correspondence 1924, box 13, Butler Papers, MCA. In this letter, Reath noted that he held Feland in high regard both as a soldier and personally, given Feland's assistance in obtaining a posthumous Distinguished Service Cross for his son. Reath also assured Butler that he would always value Butler's work as "the soldier who has raised our police force out of the gutter of politics."

35. Feland to Harbord, May 17, 1924, file F, Harbord Papers, NYHS.

36. Harbord to Feland, May 19, 1924, file F, Harbord Papers, NYHS.

37. Feland's orders to report to the *Henderson* are found in Major General Commandant to Brigadier General Logan Feland, February 19, 1927, folder 1927–1933, Feland Papers, MCA. For newspaper accounts, see "Intervention by U.S. in Nicara-

gua Reported," *Washington Post*, February 20, 1927, and "Gen. Feland Heads Fighting Marines," *New York Times*, February 20, 1927. Folder 1927–1933 contains other letters regarding Feland's personal arrangements before leaving for Nicaragua; for instance, his letter to Thomas Turner, February 25, 1927, mentioned the storage of duck decoys. Feland also expressed the hope that, after finishing at the Army Air School, Turner would consider joining Feland in Nicaragua. Although he was not sure that an aviation officer of Turner's high rank (lieutenant colonel) would be warranted, Feland speculated that such personnel might be needed by June. Turner ended up going to China instead.

11. Nicaragua, 1927

1. Early intervention in Nicaragua is covered in Bernard C. Nalty, *The United States Marines in Nicaragua*, rev. ed. (Washington, DC: Headquarters, U.S. Marine Corps, 1962), 1–13. See also Allan Millett, *Semper Fidelis: The History of the United States Marine Corps*, rev. ed. (New York: Free Press, 1991), 236–44, and Clyde Metcalf, *A History of the United States Marine Corps* (New York: G. P. Putnam's Sons, 1939), 408–22. For the Marines in a larger context, see Neill Macauley, *The Sandino Affair* (1967; reprint, Durham, NC: Duke University Press, 1985), 19–29, and Lester Langley, *The Banana Wars: United States Intervention in the Caribbean, 1898–1934*, rev. ed. (Lexington: University Press of Kentucky, 1985), 175–84.

2. See "Borah Hits Policy of 'Mahogany, Oil,'" *New York Times*, February 21, 1927; Langley, *Banana Wars*, 183–84; William Kamman, *A Search for Stability: United States Diplomacy toward Nicaragua, 1925–1933* (Notre Dame, IN: University of Notre Dame Press, 1968), 1–81; "Stimson Will Make Nicaragua Inquiry," *New York Times*, April 8, 1927. See also Godfrey Hodgson, *The Colonel: The Life and Wars of Henry Stimson, 1867–1950* (New York: Knopf, 1990).

3. "Marines Off to Nicaragua after Review by Lejeune," *Washington Post*, February 24, 1927; "Items from the M.C.E.F. Aboard the Henderson," *Leatherneck* 10, no. 4 (April 1927): 33–34.

4. Latimer's arrival was reported in "Eberhardt Also Makes Denial," *New York Times*, March 13, 1927. Latimer's and Feland's committee service is covered in Manley R. Irwin, *Silent Strategists: Harding, Denby, and the U.S. Navy's Trans-Pacific Offensive, World War II* (Lanham, MD: University Press of America, 2008), 44–46.

5. Chief of Naval Operations to Commander Special Services Squadron, "Organization and Mission of Special Services Squadron," September 25, 1920, file 9-25-20 to 12-14-21, box 682, Special Services Squadron, RG 80, NARA. See also Richard Millett, "The State Department's Navy: A History of the Special Services Squadron, 1920–1940," *American Neptune* 25, no. 2 (April 1975): 118–38, and Donald Yerxa, "The Special Services Squadron and the Caribbean Region, 1920–1940: A Case Study in Naval Diplomacy," *Naval War College Review* 39, no. 4 (Autumn 1986): 60–72.

6. "Nicaraguan Bullets Riddle Marine Plane," *New York Times*, March 30, 1927.

7. Feland to Lejeune, March 21, 1927, Nicaragua film no. 1, HRB, MCHD.

8. Feland to Lejeune, April 4, 1927, Nicaragua film no. 1, HRB, MCHD.

9. Munro quoted in Richard Millett, *Guardians of the Dynasty: A History of the U.S. Created Guardia Nacional de Nicaragua and the Somoza Family* (Maryknoll, NY: Orbis Books, 1977), 41. Munro made these comments in a letter to Millett on February 14, 1965.

10. On Feland's recommendation, Breckinridge served as commander of the *Guardia Nacional Dominicana* starting on October 5, 1920, shortly before Feland left the country. Breckinridge's service record notes that on April 15, 1921, he requested reassignment after learning that he would be reporting to the Dominican Department of Interior and Police. He was dispatched from the Dominican Republic on April 20, 1921. See Breckinridge Chronology, box 1, Breckinridge Papers, MCA.

11. Hodgson, *The Colonel*, 112; Henry Lewis Stimson Diaries, 7:65 (microfilm edition, reel 1), Manuscripts and Archives, Yale University Library, New Haven, CT.

12. "Report of Mission to Nicaragua," reel 71, no. 504, Stimson Papers, Yale University Library. See also Macauley, *Sandino Affair*, 31–42.

13. Feland to Lejeune, April 22, 1927, Nicaragua film no. 1, HRB, MCHD.

14. Feland to Lejeune, May 15 and June 6, 1927, Nicaragua film no. 1, HRB, MCHD. See also Hans Schmidt, *The United States Occupation of Haiti, 1915–1934* (New Brunswick, NJ: Rutgers University Press, 1995).

15. Feland to Julian Brown, May 10, 1927, Nicaragua film no. 4, HRB, MCHD.

16. Henry Stimson to Curtis Wilbur, May 25, 1927, reel 71, no. 543, Stimson Papers, Yale University Library.

17. Katherine MacVeagh to Mabel White Simpson, May 18, 1927, reel 71, nos. 476–77, Stimson Papers, Yale University Library.

18. Minister in Nicaragua (Eberhardt) to the Secretary of State, May 26, 1927, in *FRUS, 1927*, 3:349.

19. Stimson to Feland, June 22, 1927, and Feland to Stimson, July 10, 1927, reel 71, nos. 761–62 and 948–49, Stimson Papers, Yale University Library. Feland also wrote to Lejeune, describing himself as "delighted that you are sending Colonel Beadle to take command of the Guardia. There is no more important work to be done for this country than the upbuilding of a thoroughly good Constabulary, and it seems to me that Beadle is exactly the right man to do it." Feland to Lejeune, June 12, 1927, Nicaragua film no. 1, HRB, MCHD.

20. See Glendell L. Fitzgerald, "Combat Reports of Operations in Nicaragua," *Marine Corps Gazette* 13, no. 4 (December 1928): 241–47, for after-action reports from two men in Buchanan's command: Second Lieutenant C. J. Chappell and Sergeant Glendell Fitzgerald. The deaths of the two leathernecks were reported in "Two Marines Slain in Nicaragua Fight," *New York Times*, May 17, 1927, and "Killed in Action in Nicaragua, May 16, 1927," *Leatherneck* 10, no. 7 (July 1927): 17. See also Dion Williams, "Captain Richard Bell Buchanan, U.S. Marine Corps," *Marine Corps Gazette* 12, no. 2 (June 1927): 72, and "Marines Received Navy Awards for Distinguished Service in Nicaragua," *Leatherneck* 11, no. 1 (January 1928): 15. A 1917 graduate of the University of Illinois, Buchanan had pledged the same fraternity as

Feland: Sigma Alpha Epsilon. At one time there was a bronze plaque at the fraternity house inscribed as follows: "His commanding officer, Brigadier General Logan Feland, said of him, 'I am glad to state this Marine detachment, under most difficult circumstances and although outnumbered ten to one, has upheld the reputation of the Marine Corps. Captain Buchanan and his detachment showed bravery of the highest order.'"

21. Macauley, *Sandino Affair*, 46–47. Cabulla's shooting by Richards was reported in "Nicaraguan Chief Killed by Marine," *New York Times*, May 28, 1927, and "Protection of American Interests," *Marine Corps Gazette* 12, no. 3 (September 1927): 178–79.

22. See Macauley, *Sandino Affair*, 65; Feland to Lejeune, May 24, 1927, Nicaragua film no. 1, HRB, MCHD. For more on Sandino, see Joseph O. Baylen, "Sandino: Patriot or Bandit?" *Hispanic American Historical Review* 31, no. 3 (August 1951): 394–419.

23. Pierce's mission is covered in Edwin North McClellan, "He Remembered His Mission," *Marine Corps Gazette* 15, no. 3 (November 1930): 30–32, 51–52. This article was illustrated by the "Kipling of the Corps," John Thomason.

24. Feland to Lejeune, June 6, 1927, Nicaragua film no. 1, HRB, MCHD.

25. Edwin North McClellan, "The Nueva Segovia Expedition," *Marine Corps Gazette* 15, no. 5 (May 1931): 21. See also Minister in Nicaragua (Eberhardt) to the Secretary of State, June 20, 1927, in *FRUS, 1927*, 3:439, noting Butters's appeal.

26. Feland to Lejeune, May 24, 1927, Nicaragua film no. 1, HRB, MCHD.

27. Ibid. See Cutts's obituary, *New York Times*, November 25, 1934; South's obituary, *New York Times*, January 30, 1931; Dunlap and Beadle files, HRB, MCHD; "General McDougal to Major General" and "Selected for Major General, U.S.M.C.," *Leatherneck* 23, no. 3 (September 1939): 10, 41.

28. Feland to Lejeune, June 12, 1927, Nicaragua film no. 1, HRB, MCHD.

29. Commander, Special Services Squadron to Major General Commandant, U.S. Marine Corps, "Commendation of Brig. Gen. Logan Feland, USMC," July 8, 1927, and Secretary of the Navy Curtis Wilbur to Brigadier General Logan Feland, October 22, 1927, informing Feland of his DSM Star, folder 6, Feland Papers, MCA.

30. Feland to Lejeune, May 15, June 6 and 12, and July 15, 1927, Nicaragua film no. 1, HRB, MCHD.

31. McClellan, "Nueva Segovia Expedition," 22–23. See also Millett, *Guardians of the Dynasty*, 61–66.

32. Feland quoted in McClellan, "Nueva Segovia Expedition," 22.

33. McClellan, "Nueva Segovia Expedition," 23.

34. The *New York Times* reported Hatfield's letter to Sandino and Sandino's refusal in "Ultimatum Sent to Nicaraguan Rebel," July 13, 1927, and "Nicaraguan Rebel Defiant," July 17, 1927. The Battle of Ocotal was reported in "Will Fight until We Die, Marine Major Tells Rebel," *Leatherneck* 10, no. 8 (August 1927): 22, and *New York Times*, July 18, 19, and 20, 1927; it is thoroughly covered in Macauley, *Sandino Affair*, 62–82.

35. Rowell's attack is covered in "The Aerial Rescue of Ocotal," *Leatherneck* 10, no. 10 (October 1927): 9–11, 48. Rowell's own account can be found in his Army War College lecture presented on January 12, 1929, "Experiences with the Air Service in Minor Warfare," Ross Rowell Collection, MCA. Rowell recalled Feland's analysis of the hopeless situation in Ocotal and his "very general directive" in "Interview with Major General Ross E. Rowell, USMC, on the Origin and Early Use of Dive-Bombing Tactics Held in Aviation History Unit-24 October 1946," Aviation File No. 1, Nicaragua Geographical Files, HRB, MCHD. See also John M. Elliott, "Marine Aviation in Nicaragua: A Time of Pioneering," *Leatherneck* 92, no. 9 (September 2009): 20–23, and Wray R. Johnson, "Airpower and Restraint in Small Wars: Marine Corps Aviation in the Second Nicaraguan Campaign, 1927–33," *Aerospace Power Journal* 15 (Fall 2001), http://www.airpower.maxwell.af.mil/airchronicles/apj/apj01/fa101/johnson .html. For more on "Rusty" Rowell, see "LtGen Ross E. Rowell: Marine of Many Talents," *Fortitudine* 7, no. 2 (Fall 1978): 12–15, and Edwin H. Simmons, "Ross Rowell: Aviator with a Flair," *Marine Corps Gazette* 69, no. 5 (May 1985): 82–91. Rowell was the dashing officer depicted on a famous World War I recruiting poster by James Montgomery Flagg.

36. Feland to Hatfield, July 17, 1927, Gilbert Hatfield Collection, MCA.

37. See Diaz to Feland, August 7, 1927, Brigade Order No. 29, August 10, 1927, Feland to Lejeune, August 10, 1928, and Major General Commandant to Captain Hatfield, December 30, 1928, announcing Hatfield's Navy Cross, Gilbert Hatfield Collection, MCA. See also Rowell's citation for the Distinguished Flying Cross, November 15, 1927, in Rowell file, HRB, MCHD.

38. "Scores Nicaragua Policy," *New York Times*, July 23, 1927.

39. Minister in Nicaragua (Eberhardt) to the Secretary of the State, July 20, 1927, in *FRUS, 1927*, 3:441.

40. For Sellers's report, see COMSPERON to CNO, July 25, 1927, folder 1, box 5, David Foote Sellers Papers, MD, LOC.

41. For Feland's policy, see Edwin North McClellan, "The Nueva Segovia Expedition (Part 2)," *Marine Corps Gazette* 16, no. 2 (August 1931): 11.

42. "Gen. Feland Offers Nicaraguan Amnesty," *Washington Post*, August 13, 1927; "Gen. Logan Feland Leaves Nicaragua for Quantico Post," *Washington Post*, August 14, 1927. Lejeune's decision was reflected in his August 11, 1927, letter to Butler; see Michael Miller, ed., *My Dear Smedley: Personal Correspondence of John A. Lejeune to Smedley D. Butler, 1927–1928* (Washington, DC: Marine Corps Research Center, Archives Branch, 2002), 124.

43. See "Nicaraguans to Assume Police Role of Marines," *Washington Post*, August 21, 1927; "Nicaragua Now Orderly," *New York Times*, August 21, 1927; "Sees Need of Force Ended in Nicaragua," *New York Times*, August 28, 1927.

44. Intelligence Report 87, August 21, 1927, Nicaragua film no. 4, HRB, MCHD.

45. Beadle to Lejeune, September 1, 1927, Nicaragua film no. 1, HRB, MCHD.

12. Back to Nicaragua, 1928

1. Joseph O. Baylen, "Sandino: Patriot or Bandit?" *Hispanic American Historical Review* 31, no. 3 (August 1951): 404–7.

2. The downing of Thomas and Dowdell and the efforts to find them were reported in the following *New York Times* articles: "Kill or Wound 67 in Nicaragua Fight," October 19, 1927; "Air Patrols Seek Fliers in Nicaragua," October 20, 1927; "Rebellion Spreads in North Nicaragua," October 22, 1927; "Marine Fliers Slain Fighting to the End," November 9, 1927; "Deaths of Marine Fliers Confirmed," November 26, 1927. Marine Corps accounts include "Marine Flyers Die Fighting to the Last," *Leatherneck* 10, no. 12 (December 1927): 16; "The Death of Lieutenant Thomas and Sergeant Dowdell," *Leatherneck* 11, no. 1 (January 1928): 13; and E. H. Brainard, "The Marines Take Wings," *Leatherneck* 11, no. 8 (August 1928): 28. See also Neill Macauley, *The Sandino Affair* (1967; reprint, Durham, NC: Duke University Press, 1985), 93, which states that the men were captured, tried, and hung.

3. See Andrew J. Bacevich, *Diplomat in Khaki: Major General Frank Ross McCoy and American Foreign Policy, 1898–1949* (Lawrence: University Press of Kansas, 1989); the chapter on McCoy in Nicaragua first appeared as "The American Electoral Mission in Nicaragua, 1927–28," *Diplomatic History* 4, no. 3 (Summer 1980): 241–61.

4. "To Press Drive to Finish," *New York Times*, January 4, 1928; "1,000 Marines Ordered to Sail to Reinforce Men Now There," *Washington Post*, January 4, 1928; "Chief of Corps Is Stirred by Report Deserters Aid Sandino," *Washington Post*, January 7, 1928; "Quantico Marines Depart to Bring in Sandino Their Foe," *Washington Post*, January 7, 1928; "Gen. Lejeune Going to Nicaragua Field with Marine Units," *New York Times*, January 7, 1928; Secretary of State to the Minister in Honduras (Summerlin), January 3, 1928, in *FRUS, 1928*, 3:559–60.

5. Macauley, *Sandino Affair*, 90–104.

6. Commanding General to Major General Commandant, February 28, 1928, folder 2 of 3: 2nd Brigade, January 1927–May 31, 1928, box 251, entry 18, RG 127, NARA.

7. A copy of Sellers's letter to Sandino, "The Commander of the U.S. Special Services Squadron to General Sandino," can be found in *FRUS, 1928*, 3:562–63, as an enclosure to "The Chargé in Managua (Munro) to the Secretary of State," January 27, 1928, ibid., 561–62. Munro did not believe that Sandino would accept Sellers's offer.

8. "Nicaragua Force Gets Praise from Lejeune," *New York Times*, January 28, 1928; John A. Lejeune, "The Nicaraguan Situation," *Leatherneck* 11, no. 2 (February 1928): 10, 52.

9. Commanding General to Commander, Northern Area (CO, 11th Regiment) and Commander, Southern Area (CO, 5th Regiment), "Tactical Doctrine Governing Operations against Outlaws," February 13, 1928, file 150, Nicaragua, box 5, entry 204, RG 127, NARA.

10. For the section staff reports, see Major Harold Schmidt, "Memorandum from

B-2 to B-Ex.: Summary of B-2 Activities since 15 January, 1928," February 21, 1928; Major Oliver Floyd, B-3, Second Brigade, Marine Corps, to Commanding General, "Report of Operations and Training, Second Brigade, Marine Corps, from January 15, 1928 to February 21, 1928 (Both Dates Inclusive)," February 22, 1928; Lieutenant Colonel Charles Sanderson, "Activities of B-4 Section, 15 January to 20 February, 1928," February 20, 1928, all in file General Correspondence, 1927–March 1928, box 3, Sellers Papers, MD, LOC. See also Sellers to Feland, February 25, 1928, folder 2, box 6, Sellers Papers, MD, LOC.

11. Commander Special Services Squadron to Chief of Naval Operations, "Affairs in Nicaragua," February 27, 1928, vol. 6, box 5, Sellers Papers, MD, LOC.

12. The first six *Nation* articles by Beals were as follows: "With Sandino in Nicaragua: To the Nicaraguan Border," February 22, 1928; "On the Sandino Front," March 1, 1928; "On the Trail of Sandino," March 7, 1928; "Sandino Himself," March 14, 1928; "Send the Bill to Mr. Coolidge," March 21, 1928; "Sandino—Bandit or Patriot?" March 28, 1928. The article highly critical of the Marines was "This Is War, Gentlemen!" April 11, 1928, filed from Managua with a dateline of March 6, 1928. A copy of Sandino's reply to Sellers, delivered by Beals, is in *FRUS, 1928*, 3:569.

13. Carleton Beals, *Banana Gold* (Philadelphia: J. B. Lippincott, 1932), 306.

14. Harold Denny, "Sandino Territory Turns against Him," *New York Times*, February 28, 1928; Feland to Sellers, February 27, 1928, file General Correspondence 1927–March 1928, box 3, Sellers Papers, MD, LOC. A sergeant during World War I and later a World War II correspondent, Denny wrote about Nicaragua in *Dollars for Bullets: The Story of American Rule in Nicaragua* (New York: Dial Press, 1929).

15. Parker's visit to Ocotal was reported in Minister in Nicaragua (Eberhardt) to the Secretary of State, February 9, 1928, in *FRUS, 1928*, 3:565–66.

16. Sellers expressed his dismay over McCoy's intrusion into military matters in Commander Special Services Squadron to Chief of Naval Operations, "Affairs in Nicaragua," February 27, 1928, vol. 1, box 5, Sellers Papers, MD, LOC: "Just why an official, whose duty it is to supervise the presidential election, should conduct an investigation and report on the military situation is not apparent to the Squadron Commander, except for the fact that General McCoy's orders (which were written by himself, according to his own statement) direct him to do so."

17. Secretary of State Kellogg to General McCoy, March 3, 1928, box 79, Frank Ross McCoy Papers, MD, LOC. Although this letter was personal and confidential, it was decoded by Colonel Parker and typed by army captain Matthew Ridgway—the future general, commander of the Eighty-Second Airborne in World War II, and commander of UN troops during the Korean War.

18. General McCoy to Secretary of State Kellogg, March 5, 1928, box 79, McCoy Papers, MD, LOC.

19. Ibid.

20. See brigade B-2 journal reports, Nicaragua film no. 4, HRB, MCHD.

21. See Major Harry Schmidt, "Memorandum to All Units," February 7, 1928, Nicaragua film no. 11, and Schmidt's confidential B-2 report, February 19, 1928,

covering the week of February 5–12, 1928, Nicaragua film no. 4, HRB, MCHD. See also Harry Schmidt file, Biographical Files, HRB, MCHD.

22. COMSPERON to OPNAV, March 14 and 17, 1928, and Commander Special Services Squadron to Chief of Naval Operations, March 18, 1928, vol. 1, box 5, Sellers Papers, MD, LOC.

23. See Secretary of the Navy to Commander Special Services Squadron, "Instructions for Forces in Nicaragua," December 9, 1927, file 8-1-26 to 2-18-28, box 682, RG 80, NARA.

24. Feland to Sellers, March 22, 1928, file General Correspondence 1928, box 3, Sellers Papers, MD, LOC.

25. See Feland to Sellers, March 23, 1928, McCoy to Sellers, March 28, 1928, and Sellers to McCoy, March 29, 1928, all in ibid.

26. COMSPERON to OPNAV, March 19, 1925, vol. 1, box 5, Sellers Papers, MD, LOC.

27. Harold Denny, "Wipe out Sandino, Gen. Feland Orders," *New York Times*, March 15, 1928; Harold Denny, "Marine Units Prepare to 'Eliminate Rebels,'" *New York Times*, April 4, 1928. In the latter article, Denny quotes Feland as saying that the Marines would try to "clear up the situation before the rainy season begins," but "if that proves impossible, they will fight on, rainy season or no rainy season, until it is cleared up." See also Feland to Sellers, April 6, 1928, file General Correspondence 1928, box 3, Sellers Papers, MD, LOC, in which Feland notes that he talked to Denny to clarify the Marine Corps's position.

28. Secretary of State to the Minister in Nicaragua (Eberhardt), July 27, 1927, and Minister in Nicaragua (Eberhardt) to the Secretary of State, July 31, 1927, in *FRUS, 1927*, 3:442–44.

29. Feland's relationship with the Nicaraguan press is discussed briefly in a paper written a few years later by his intelligence officer, who was attending the U.S. Army Command and General Staff School at Fort Leavenworth, Kansas: see Harry Schmidt, "Operations of the Intelligence Section of the 2nd Brigade in Nicaragua, 1928–1929," cgsc.contentdm.oclc.org/cgi-bin/showfile.exe?CISOROOT=/p4013c0 1114&CISOPTR=1046&filename=1047.pdf.

30. Beals, "This Is War, Gentlemen!"

31. "Depicts Air Record of Nicaragua Force," *New York Times*, July 12, 1928.

32. See Schmidt, "Operations of the Intelligence Section," 8.

33. See Macauley, *Sandino Affair*, 105–25, for the Marine Corps's struggles against Sandino in early 1928. See also "Events in Nicaragua since February 28, 1928," *Marine Corps Gazette* 13, no. 2 (June 1928): 143–46.

34. For Howe's reports on his conversations with Beadle and Feland, see McCoy to Kellogg, April 17, 1928, file 817.00/5655, RG 59, NARA-CP, containing "Memorandum of Talk with General Elias R. Beadle," April 12, 1928, and "Interview with General Feland," April 13, 1928. Admiral Sellers forwarded copies of Howe's reports to the CNO, but with this caveat: "the Squadron Commander deems it proper to state that in evaluating a report of this kind it must be remembered that a report

on the military situation in Nicaragua by a civilian, based on an interview with the military commander in the field, must, of necessity, be of only superficial value. The Squadron Commander has therefore made no attempt to analyze or comment upon any of the statements made by Mr. Howe, inasmuch as full, detailed reports of military operations in Nicaragua are on file in the Department." Commander Special Services Squadron to Chief of Naval Operations, "Report of Military Situation in Nicaragua by General McCoy," May 13, 1928, folder General Correspondence 1928, box 1, Sellers Papers, MD, LOC.

35. McCoy's outburst was reported in Commanding General to Commander Special Services Squadron, "Conference at Legation of the United States of America, Managua, Nicaragua, April 18th, 1928," April 19, 1928, folder 1, box 6, Sellers Papers, MD, LOC.

36. Ibid.

37. Sellers to Feland, April 20, 1928, file 3, box 6, Sellers Papers, MD, LOC.

38. Secret first endorsement, April 29, 1928, folder 1, box 6, Sellers Papers, MD, LOC. This was a follow-up to a previous COMSPERON message to the Navy Department reporting Feland's contretemps with McCoy. Sellers wrote that Feland had "displayed an enormous amount of patience and tact" with McCoy; see Sellers to Feland, May 2, 1928, file 3, box 6, Sellers Papers, MD, LOC. For Feland's response, see Feland to Sellers, May 7, 1928, file General Correspondence 1928, box 3, Sellers Papers, MD, LOC.

39. Feland to Lejeune, May 19, 1928, Nicaragua film no. 1, HRB, MCHD.

40. For Feland's orders, see Harold Denny, "Our Marines Must Guard Nicaraguans," *New York Times*, June 1, 1928.

41. Roosevelt to Feland, September 1, 1928, quoted in Frank Freidel, *Franklin D. Roosevelt: The Ordeal* (Boston: Little, Brown, 1954), 236.

42. For Feland and Eberhardt's concerns, see "Hint 'Medical' Fund Buys Sandino Arms," *New York Times*, June 6, 1928. For the All-America Anti-Imperialist League's denial, see "Denies Charges of Feland," *New York Times*, June 7, 1928.

43. Minister in Nicaragua (Eberhardt) to the Secretary of State, May 31, 1928, in *FRUS, 1928*, 3:577; in this letter, Eberhardt notes that Feland considered the Masaya incident "unimportant from a military point of view." Feland's comments about Chamorro and the press are in Feland to Sellers, June 7 and 12, 1928, file General Correspondence 1928, box 3, Sellers Papers, MD, LOC. The newspaper articles Feland sent to Sellers included the following: "General Feland's Statements to the Journalists," from the Liberal *Diario Moderno*, June 3, 1928; "The Vision of Silence," from the Liberal *El Commercio*, June 5, 1928; and "General Feland Is Right," from the Conservative *La Prensa*, June 6, 1928.

44. "Feland Goes to Bluefields," *New York Times*, June 26, 1928.

45. Edson wrote extensively about his riverine trips in Merritt A. Edson, "The Coco Patrol," *Marine Corps Gazette* 19, no. 3 (August 1936): 18–23, 38–48; 20, no. 4 (November 1936): 40–41, 60–72; and 21, no. 1 (February 1937): 35–43, 57–63 (the exchange between Feland and Edson is in the February 1937 issue, p. 35). See

also Jon T. Hoffman, *Once a Legend: "Red Mike" Edson of the Marine Raiders* (Novato, CA: Presidio Press, 1994).

46. For a different analysis of the Coco Patrol focusing on the "ethnic and political" aspects, see David C. Brooks, "U.S. Marines, Miskitos and the Hunt for Sandino: The Rio Coco Patrol in 1928," *Journal of Latin American Studies* 21, no. 2 (May 1989): 311–42.

47. COMSPERON to OPNAV, July 19, 1928, and a follow-up report, Commander Special Services Squadron to Chief of Naval Operations, "Affairs in Nicaragua," July 21, 1928, vol. 1, box 5, Sellers Papers, MD, LOC.

48. Feland expressed his wariness about *Guardia* changes in Feland to Sellers, July 26, 1928, file General Correspondence 1928, box 3, Sellers Papers, MD, LOC.

49. Feland to Utley, August 28, 1928, file 922, entry 221, RG 127, NARA.

50. See "Navy Cross Given to Seven Marines," *New York Times*, August 7, 1928; "Marine Wins Navy Cross," *New York Times*, August 20, 1928. Several copies of a March 1929 wire service article and a photograph of Feland shaking hands with Corporal Lester can be found in the Feland Scrapbook, Feland Papers, MCA. The article appeared in many Kentucky newspapers, ranging from the *Princeton Leader* to the *Lexington Leader*. A copy of Feland's birthday dinner menu, signed by his chief officers, can also be found in the Feland Scrapbook.

51. McCoy to the Secretary of State, August 2, 1928, folder 3, box 6, Sellers Papers, MD, LOC.

52. R. C. B. [Randolph Carter Berkeley], "Memorandum for General Feland," July 8, 1928, file 150, Nicaragua, box 5, entry 204, RG 127, NARA. Berkeley received the Medal of Honor for his actions at Vera Cruz in 1914 and the Navy Cross for his service in Nicaragua; he retired as a major general in 1939. Berkeley file, HRB, MCHD.

53. Logan Feland to James Harbord, August 4, 1928, file F, Harbord Papers, NYHS. For a short biography of Cyrus Radford, see Charles Mayfield Meacham, *A History of Christian County Kentucky from Oxcart to Airplane* (Nashville, TN: Marshall and Bruce, 1930), 192–93. Radford became Marine Corps quartermaster in 1929 and retired as a brigadier general later that year. Feland was right in surmising that Butler and Radford were close friends of Lejeune's. In a letter to Butler, Lejeune revealed that Radford and his wife had just spent the night with the Lejeunes and noted that "Cyrus is the same fine fellow he always has been and a most loyal friend of mine and yours." He later wrote that Radford was "chock full of wisdom and good will." Michael Miller, ed., *My Dear Smedley: Personal Correspondence of John A. Lejeune to Smedley D. Butler, 1927–1928* (Washington, DC: Marine Corps Research Center, Archives Branch, 2002), 234, 274.

54. Feland to Harbord, August 4, 1928.

55. Harbord to Feland, August 22 and September 23, 1928, file F, Harbord Papers, NYHS.

56. Lejeune's transfer plan was outlined in his letter to Butler on May 11, 1928, in Miller, *My Dear Smedley*, 254. See "Notables at Funeral of Thomas S. Butler," *New*

York Times, May 30, 1928. For more on Thomas Butler and his significance to the Marine Corps, see J. C. Fegan, "Thomas S. Butler," *Marine Corps Gazette* 13, no. 2 (June 1928): 89–90, and "Marine Corps Loses Sincere Friend in Death of the Honorable Thomas S. Butler," *Leatherneck* 11, no. 7 (July 1928): 7.

57. Brigade Memorandum No. 23, "General Clean Up Week," September 30, 1928, and Berkeley memorandum to Commanding Officers, Northern, Southern, Western, and Eastern Areas, September 30, 1928, Nicaragua film no. 1, HRB, MCHD.

58. See Edwin McClellan file, Biographical Files, HRB, MCHD, for his service history. His appointment as chief of the Photographic Party can be found in Commanding General to Edwin McClellan, October 19, 1928, folder: McClellan Diary October 1 to November 15, 1928, box 16, Edwin North McClellan Collection, MCA.

59. Logan Feland to Joseph Pendleton, August 17, 1920, folder 10: August 1920, and Pendleton to Feland, September 7, 1920, folder 11: September 1920, Pendleton Papers, MCA.

60. For McClellan's comments, see his unsent letter to "Guy," October 31, 1928, folder: McClellan Diary October 1 to November 15, 1928, box 16, McClellan Papers, MCA.

61. Brigade Memorandum No. 21, October 9, 1928, Nicaragua film no. 1, and Brigade Order No. 69, Nicaragua film no. 11, HRB, MCHD. For Mattis's memo, "Commanding General to All Hands," sent to the Marine Corps First Division in March 2003, on the eve of the invasion of Iraq, see Bing West and Major General Ray Smith, USMC (Ret.), *The March Up: Taking Baghdad with the 1st Marine Division* (New York: Bantam, 2004), xvi.

13. Postelection Nicaragua, 1929

1. For Feland's deer hunting, see Edwin North McClellan, "Supervising Nicaraguan Elections, 1928," *Proceedings of the U.S. Naval Institute* 59, no. 1 (January 1933): 37. McClellan noted that while Feland went hunting, his chief of staff Randolph Berkeley and other staff members went golfing. McClellan believed that this was "as it should be," given their proper preparation for the election; see his diary entry for Saturday, November 3, 1928, folder: McClellan Diary October 1 to November 15, 1928, box 16, McClellan Papers, MCA. For Riseley's reminiscences, see James P. Riseley Jr., *Uncle Jim: Recollections of Lt. Gen. James P. Riseley, United States Marine Corps (Ret.)* (Roswell, NM: James P. Riseley, 1991), 20.

2. McClellan to Craige, November 5, 1928, folder: McClellan Diary October 1 to November 15, 1928; McClellan to Fegan and Craige, November 16, 1928, and Craige to McClellan, November 22, 1928, folder: McClellan Diary November 15 through December 1928, box 16, McClellan Papers, MCA. Craige had served as Lejeune's aide-de-camp in the early 1920s. Craige, Lejeune, and Lejeune's other aide, Lem Shepherd, would meet at 7:00 each morning at the Commandant's house at "Eighth and Eye" to go riding. See Merrill Bartlett, *Lejeune: A Marine's Life, 1867–1942* (Annapolis, MD: Naval Institute Press, 1991), 157.

3. Brigade Memorandum No. 28, November 9, 1928, file N-87.5, box 30 N-87-90 Nicaragua, entry 38, RG 127, NARA.

4. Major John A. Gray to Brigade Commander, "Suggestions and Recommendations," March 20, 1929, file N-87.5, box 30 N-87-90 Nicaragua, entry 38, RG 127, NARA: John Gray, "A Plea for the Revision of the Field Officers' Course," *Marine Corps Gazette* 15, no. 4 (February 1931): 64.

5. Commander, Eastern Area, Nicaragua [Utley] to the Commanding General, 2nd Brigade, March 27, 1929, file N-87.5, box 30 N-87-90 Nicaragua, entry 38, RG 127, NARA. Feland appreciated Utley's work in the Eastern District and recommended the major for the Distinguished Service Medal (DSM). Feland noted that Utley had been "thrown on his own responsibility to an extraordinary degree on account of the inaccessibility of this area from Brigade Headquarters and the rest of the country. All decisions as to operations, distribution of troops and their supply devolved upon him. His duty was performed with such energy, understanding and zeal as to plainly warrant the statement that he greatly distinguished himself in duties of the highest importance." Feland to Lejeune via Sellers, May 14, 1929, folder 75, box 4, RG 127, NARA. Utley finally got his DSM in 1932. For Utley's difficulties and Feland's intercession, see Hoffman, *Once a Legend*, 96.

6. Colonel R. H. Dunlap to the Commanding General, March 23, 1929, file N-87.5, box 30 N-87-90 Nicaragua, entry 38, RG 127, NARA.

7. The Marine Corps's efforts to create a "bush war" or "small war" doctrine are covered in Keith A. Bickel, *Mars Learning: The Marine Corps' Development of Small Wars Doctrine, 1915–1940* (Boulder, CO: Westview Press, 2001). For more on the growth of Marine Corps schools during the critical period of the early 1930s, see Donald F. Bittner, *Curriculum Evolution: Marine Corps Command and Staff College, 1920–1988* (Washington, DC: History and Museums Division, Headquarters, U.S. Marine Corps, 1988). The vital role of James Carson Breckinridge in Marine Corps education is covered in Troy R. Elkins, "A Creditable Position: James Carson Breckinridge and the Development of the Marine Corps Schools" (MA thesis, Kansas State University, 2011), http://krex.k-state.edu/dspace/bitstream/handle/2097/13160/TroyElkins2011.pdf?sequence=5.

8. McCoy to Feland, November 10, 1928, folder 7, Feland Papers, MCA.

9. A copy of Johnston's memo, dated November 10, 1928, can be found in vol. 7, box 5, Sellers Papers, MD, LOC. Feland forwarded the memo to Sellers on November 12, 1928. For Feland's opinion of McCoy, see Commanding General to the Commander, Special Services Squadron, n.d., folder 1, box 6, Sellers Papers, MD, LOC.

10. Commander Special Services Squadron to Chief of Naval Operations, November 17, 1928, vol. 7, box 5, Sellers Papers, MD, LOC.

11. McCoy's focus on Sandino was reported in ibid. For the Marine Corps analysis of the military situation, see intelligence officer Harry Schmidt's "Memo for Commanding Officer," November 19, 1928, and Feland's "Memorandum," November

20, 1928, and "An Estimate of the Situation with Decision as to the Distribution of the Second Brigade in Nicaragua after the Withdrawal of the Battle Fleet and Scouting Fleet Marines," November 23, 1928, file General Correspondence 1928, box 3, Sellers Papers, MD, LOC.

12. McClellan to Lejeune, December 3, 1928, folder: McClellan Diary November 15 through December 1928, box 16, McClellan Papers, MCA. John Craige wrote to thank McClellan for pointing out to Lejeune that, when it came to publicity, "the Marine Corps is still using a bow and arrow while the Army has got itself a Big Bertha [German cannon]." Craige to McClellan, February 2, 1929, file: Personal Papers, Correspondence, Nicaragua, January–February 1929, box 17, McClellan Papers, MCA.

13. McClellan diary entries for Tuesday, January 15, 1929, and Monday, January 21, 1929, file: Personal Papers, Correspondence, Nicaragua, January–February 1929, box 17, McClellan Papers, MCA.

14. McClellan diary entry for Friday, March 22, 1929, file: Personal Papers, Correspondence, Nicaragua, March to May 1929, box 17, McClellan Papers, MCA.

15. McClellan diary entry for Tuesday, March 26, 1929, ibid.

16. Brigade Memorandum No. 31, December 17, 1928, Nicaragua film no. 1, HRB, MCHD.

17. For Moncada's idea about a military adviser, see COMSPERON to OPNAV, November 20, 1928, file 4, box 6, Sellers Papers, MD, LOC. See also Moncada to Sellers, December 29, 1928, file 4, box 6, Sellers Papers, MD, LOC; Feland to Lejeune, January 3, 1929, folder 28, box 2, Lejeune Papers, MCA.

18. Feland to Lejeune, January 3, 1929.

19. Moncada to Sellers, December 29, 1928, and Commander Special Services Squadron to the Chief of Naval Operations, "Request for Services of Brigadier General Logan Feland, U.S. Marine Corps, by the President of Nicaragua," January 3, 1929, file 4, box 6, Sellers Papers, MD, LOC.

20. Feland's use of Sandino's family in an effort to end hostilities is recorded in Neill Macauley, *The Sandino Affair* (1967; reprint, Durham, NC: Duke University Press, 1985), 131–33. Sellers's letter to Sandino is in vol. 7, box 5, Sellers Papers, MD, LOC.

21. A copy of the Wide World Photos picture can be found in Feland Scrapbook, Feland Papers, MCA. Admiral Sellers reported on the visit in Commander Special Services Squadron to Chief of Naval Operations, "Affairs in Nicaragua," December 4, 1928, vol. 2, box 5, Sellers Papers, MD, LOC. For more on Hoover's tour, see Alexander Deconde, "Herbert Hoover's Good Will Tour," *Historian* 12, no. 2 (March 1950): 167–81.

22. Feland to Sellers, December 4 and 16, 1928, file General Correspondence 1928, box 3, Sellers Papers, MD, LOC.

23. Feland to Sellers, December 16, 1928.

24. Feland apprised Sellers of the House of Deputies' action in a radio dispatch, December 30, 1928, vol. 2, box 5, Sellers Papers, MD, LOC. Eberhardt's comments

are from Minister in Nicaragua (Eberhardt) to the Secretary of State, January 7, 1929, in *FRUS, 1929*, 3:642.

25. Sellers to Munro, January 4, 1929, file General Correspondence 1929–1932, box 3, Sellers Papers, MD, LOC.

26. Munro to White, November 3, 1928, and White to Eberhardt, December 6, 1928, 817.1051/231 and 234, Nicaragua, microfilm roll 63, RG 59, NARA-CP.

27. Munro to White, April 6, 1929, 817.77/212, microfilm roll 100, RG 59, NARA-CP. Moncada, Feland, and Challacombe had certainly become good acquaintances by Thanksgiving, when Moncada gave a dinner for Feland. A picture of the event shows the three men with the young, upcoming Anastasio Somoza, who would hold several positions in the Moncada government, including head of the *Guardia*, and would eventually become Nicaraguan president. See file Various Photographs, Feland Papers, MCA.

28. The controversy over French's proposed appointment was noted in Eberhardt to Secretary of State, April 4, 1929, Stimson to American Legation Managua, April 4, 1929, White to Secretary Stimson, April 5, 1929, Munro to White, April 6, 1929, and Minister Mark Hanna in Managua to Secretary of State, June 7, 1929, 817.77/212, microfilm roll 100, RG 59, NARA-CP.

29. Eberhardt to the Secretary of State, January 22, 1929, 817.051/238, microfilm roll 63, RG 59, NARA-CP; Commanding General, 2nd Brigade, U.S.M.C., to Marine Corps Headquarters, Washington, D.C., with info to Commander, Special Services Squadron, January 15, 1929 (Feland's request for a brigade-supervised audit), Commanding General, 2nd Brigade, U.S.M.C, to Marine Corps Headquarters, Washington, D.C., with info to Commander, Special Services Squadron, January 22, 1929, and Commanding General, 2nd Brigade, U.S.M.C., to Commander, Special Services Squadron, January 26, 1929, (recommending that Beadle be relieved but retained in Nicaragua), file 4, box 6, Sellers Papers, MD, LOC.

30. See Commanding Officer, Nicaraguan National Guard Detachment, to Marine Corps Headquarters, Washington, D.C., with info to Commander, Special Services Squadron, January 22, 1929, (Beadle's request that the adjutant and inspector be sent to Nicaragua), and Commander, Special Services Squadron, to Commanding General, 2nd Brigade, U.S.M.C., with info to the Chief of Naval Operations and Marine Corps Headquarters, January 24, 1929, (Sellers's order to carry out the audit), file 4, box 6, Sellers Papers, MD, LOC.

31. Feland to Lejeune, January 18, 1929, Nicaragua film no. 1, HRB, MCHD. For more on the Feland-Beadle disagreement over the *Voluntarios*, see Richard Millett, *Guardians of the Dynasty: A History of the U.S. Created Guardia Nacional de Nicaragua and the Somoza Family* (Maryknoll, NY: Orbis Books, 1977), 89. For more on the *Voluntarios* and their subsequent engagements, see Herman H. Hanneken, "A Discussion of the *Voluntario* Troops in Nicaragua," *Marine Corps Gazette* 26, no. 4 (November 1942): 120, 247–66. Hanneken began his Marine Corps career as an enlisted man, received a Medal of Honor for killing Haitian rebel leader Charlemagne Péralte in a bold raid, and was eventually promoted in retirement to briga-

dier general. He led the combined Marine and *Voluntario* patrols with General Juan Escamilla.

32. Feland to Lejeune, January 18, 1929; Minister in Nicaragua (Eberhardt) to Secretary of State, January 3 and 9, 1929, and Secretary of State to Minister in Nicaragua (Eberhardt), January 15, 1929, in *FRUS, 1929*, 3:549–51. In his January 18 letter, Feland told Lejeune that the imposition of martial law would "have even more effect than the actual operations of the columns in the field."

33. Kellogg to American Legation Managua, January 30, 1929, Eberhardt to the Secretary of State, January 31 and February 1, 1929, 817.051/238, 244, and 246, microfilm roll 63, RG 59, NARA-CP. See also Marine Corps Headquarters, Washington, to Commander, Special Services Squadron, January 31, 1929, and Commander, Special Services Squadron, to Commanding General, 2nd Brigade, U.S.M.C., February 1, 1929, file 4, box 6, Sellers Papers, MD, LOC.

34. Secretary of State to the Minister in Nicaragua (Eberhardt), February 2, 1929, in *FRUS, 1929*, 3:644.

35. See Commander, Special Services Squadron, to Chief of Naval Operations, with info to Marine Corps Headquarters, Washington, January 24, 1929 (cancellation of the Havana trip), and COMSPERON to OPNAV, February 6, 1929 (Feland's retention), file 4, box 6, Sellers Papers, MD, LOC.

36. See Sellers to Feland and Sellers to Beadle, February 10, 1929, and Feland to Sellers, February 12, 1929, file General Correspondence 1929–1932, box 3, Sellers Papers, MD, LOC.

37. Brigade Memorandum No. 5, February 6, 1929, Nicaragua film no. 1, HRB, MCHD.

38. Commander Special Services Squadron to the Chief of Naval Operations, "Affairs in Nicaragua," February 14, 1929, and Sellers to Hughes, February 16, 1929, vol. 2, box 5, Sellers Papers, MD, LOC.

39. See "Disinclination of the United States to Consent to Amendments to the Guardia Nacional Agreement," in *FRUS, 1929*, 3:606–61; Minister in Nicaragua (Eberhardt) to the Secretary of State, January 26 and February 9, 1929, ibid., 609, 613–14.

40. COMSPERON to OPNAV, with info to COMSECBRIG, February 21, 1929, and COMSECBRIG to COMSPERON, February 26, 1929, folder 4, box 6, Sellers Papers, MD, LOC.

41. Sellers to Feland, February 27, 1929, file General Correspondence 1929–1932, box 3, Sellers Papers, MD, LOC.

42. Press releases about the two parties can be found in file: Personal Papers, Correspondence, Nicaragua, March to May 1929, box 17, McClellan Papers, MCA.

43. For Wheeler's visit, see McClellan's diary entry for March 22, 1929, file: Personal Papers, Correspondence, Nicaragua, March to May 1929, box 17, McClellan Papers, MCA. Wheeler's comment about the Marines was reported in *New York Times*, March 22, 1929. He opposed the building of a Nicaraguan canal, preferring that the money be spent elsewhere.

44. For Feland's surprise notification of his imminent departure, see McClellan to daughter Anne, March 24, 1929, file: Personal Papers, Correspondence, Nicaragua, March to May 1929, box 17, McClellan Papers, MCA. A few days earlier, McClellan still believed Feland would be leaving around April 20; see McClellan to Craige, March 20, 1929, ibid.

45. See Chief of Naval Operation to Commander Special Services Squadron, "Retention of General Feland on Duty in Nicaragua," March 7, 1929, in which Hughes noted that "the matter of retaining General Feland in Nicaragua was taken up in conference and the Major General Commandant was directed to comply with your [Sellers's] recommendation." Feland relinquishing command to Dunlap was reflected in Brigade Memorandum No. 12, March 26, 1929, Nicaragua film no. 1, HRB, MCHD. Pictures of the Felands at the airfield can be found in Feland Scrapbook, Feland Papers, MCA.

46. Sandino's last days are covered in Macauley, *Sandino Affair*, 242–56.

47. For Beadle's service, see Elias Beadle file, Biographical Files, HRB, MCHD.

48. "Gen. Feland Returns from Nicaragua Duty," *New York Times*, April 8, 1929.

49. "Discussion of Situation in Nicaragua," April 9, 1929, Countries Files, Mexico to Nicaragua General, Nicaragua General 1929, box 16, Francis White Papers, Herbert Hoover Presidential Library, West Branch, IA.

50. "Moncada Praises American Marines," *New York Times*, April 20, 1929.

51. "Friend of Justice," *Leatherneck* 12, no. 5 (May 1929): 16–17, translating an article appearing in Managua's *Diario Moderno* on April 2, 1929. For Feland's third DSM, see Secretary of the Navy C. F. Adam to Brigadier General Feland, July 17, 1929, folder 7, Feland Papers, MCA. See also "General Feland Honored," *New York Times*, July 20, 1929.

14. Returning Home

1. Merrill Bartlett, *Lejeune: A Marine's Life, 1867–1942* (Annapolis, MD: Naval Institute Press, 1991), 168–74.

2. Feland to Harbord, March 22, 1929, file F, Harbord Papers, NYHS.

3. For comments about working with Lejeune and Neville, see McClellan diary entry for Monday, March 11, 1929, file: Personal Papers, Correspondence, Nicaragua, March to May 1929, box 17, McClellan Papers, MCA.

4. Feland's probable posting to Parris Island was reflected in McClellan diary entry for Friday, March 15, 1929, file: Personal Papers, Correspondence, Nicaragua, March to May 1929, box 17, McClellan Papers, MCA. The Second Brigade quartermaster, Charles Sanderson, was afraid to ask Feland when he wanted his Cadillac moved to Parris Island. McClellan predicted that if Sanderson posed the question, "there will be a deep blue silence."

5. Feland's appointment was reported in "Marine Corps Orders," *New York Times*, July 11, 1929, and "Brig. Gen. Feland Ordered to Pacific," *Washington Post*, July 9, 1929. The latter article also speculated that Butler would receive the major

general slot vacated by Cole, while Feland would probably be promoted when Lejeune officially retired in November.

6. For general officer assignments, see *Navy Register* (Washington, DC: Government Printing Office, 1929–1931).

7. For more on Butler's speech and the resulting inquiry, see Hans Schmidt, *Maverick Marine: General Smedley D. Butler and the Contradictions of American Military History* (Lexington: University Press of Kentucky, 1987), 204–5.

8. Feland's retort can be found in an undated, unattributed newspaper article in Feland Scrapbook, Feland Papers, MCA. A picture of Feland standing in full dress uniform, with Wilbur sitting and looking up at him, accompanied the article.

9. Neville to Lejeune, April 12, 1930, reel 4, Lejeune Papers, MD, LOC.

10. Requa's April 15, 1929, letter and his note to Lawrence Ritchey, May 27, 1929, can be found in file Navy–Marine Corps 1929 to July 1930, box 36, Presidential Papers Cabinet Offices, Herbert Hoover Presidential Library, West Branch, IA. Secretary Adams wrote to President Hoover on September 4, 1929, noting that Commandant Neville had recommended the promotion of Smedley Butler and Logan Feland to major general, with Robert Dunlap to fill Feland's brigadier general slot, which the president approved.

11. See Lawrence Ritchey to Acting Secretary of the Navy Ernest Lee Jahncke, April 12, 1930, in which Ritchey forwarded Feland's letter to Jahncke, which Requa had sent to Ritchey. (Jahncke was actually assistant, not acting, secretary of the navy, starting on April 1, 1929.) Ritchey sent Jahncke another letter from Requa regarding Feland on April 23, 1930. For Feland's late June analysis of the situation, see Feland to Requa, June 27, 1930, which Requa forwarded to Ritchey on June 28, 1930. See also copy of Requa telegram on White House letterhead, July 9, 1930. All are contained in file Navy–Marine Corps 1929 to July 1930, box 36, Presidential Papers Cabinet Offices, Hoover Library.

12. For more on Neville, see Allan Millett and Jack Shulimson, *Commandants of the Marine Corps* (Annapolis, MD: Naval Institute Press, 2004), 214–23. For speculation about Neville's possible successors, see the *Washington Post*, July 10, 13, and 14, 1930. On July 20, 1930, the *Washington Post* pictured and profiled the four main candidates in an article titled "Marine Corps Stirred over Choice of Chief: Quartet of Candidates May Include Neville Successor."

13. Telegram from Feland to Harbord, July 27, 1930, file F, Harbord Papers, NYHS.

14. Telegram from Harbord to George Akerson, July 28, 1930 (Akerson was the first White House press secretary); Harbord to President Hoover, July 28, 1930; and telegram from Harbord to Feland, July 28, 1930 (acknowledging that he had sent a telegram and letter to Hoover and adding, "I am sorry you [Feland] did not ask me immediately after General Neville's death"), all in file F, Harbord Papers, NYHS.

15. Telegrams from Harbord to General Frank McCoy and to Colonel J. C. O'Laughlin, July 28, 1930; Harbord to Feland, July 29, 1930, all in file F, Harbord Papers, NYHS.

16. Telegram from Feland to Harbord, August 4, 1930; Harbord to Secretary of

the Navy Charles Adams, August 4, 1930; and Adams to Harbord, August 7, 1930, all in file F, Harbord Papers, NYHS. See "MacArthur Named Chief of Army Staff," *New York Times*, August 6, 1930, which also reported Fuller's appointment as Commandant. For the full story of the selection of the Marine Corps Commandant in 1930, see Merrill Bartlett, "The Inside Track to Commandant," *Proceedings of the U.S. Naval Institute* 121, no. 1 (January 1995): 58–63.

17. Butler to Thomas Holcomb, July 17, 1930, folder 13: Personal Correspondence June–August 1930, box 8, Butler Papers, MCA.

18. Dirk A. Ballendorf and Merrill L. Bartlett, *Pete Ellis: An Amphibious Warfare Prophet, 1880–1923* (Annapolis, MD: Naval Institute Press, 1997), 146.

19. Feland's medical history can be found in Feland File, RG 125, NARA. He remained in reasonably good health throughout most of his career, with the exception of suffering malaria-like symptoms in Nicaragua. Just before leaving for Nicaragua in January 1928 he had undergone a medical examination and received a clean bill of health.

20. C. R. Train, Memorandum for the President, "In re Appointment Major General Commandant for the Marine Corps," file Navy–Marine Corps 1929 to July 1930, box 36, Presidential Papers Cabinet Offices, Hoover Library.

21. Feland to Harbord, August 22, 1930, file F, Harbord Papers, NYHS. In "Inside Track to the Commandant," Bartlett takes issue with Feland's assessment of Fuller: "The officer whom Feland considered 'worthless' proved to be better than expected at the helm of the Marine Corps" (62). Bartlett underscores this theme in his article "Ben Hebard Fuller and the Genesis of a Modern United States Marine Corps, 1891–1934," *Journal of Military History* 69 (January 2005): 73–91. Bartlett also points out that in 1922 Feland had described Fuller as "an officer of executive ability, poise, and sound judgment" (Millett and Shulimson, *Commandants of the Marine Corps*, 503n8).

22. "2nd Division Memorial Fund," *Leatherneck* 9, no. 14 (November 1926): 17.

23. Feland to Harbord, September 19, 1930, file F, Harbord Papers, NYHS.

24. Ibid.

25. Harbord to Feland, September 21, 1930, file F, Harbord Papers, NYHS.

26. Feland to Smith, May 3, 1920, folder 17, Correspondence February–October 1920, box 11, Julian Smith Collection, MCA; Julian Smith oral history transcript, 25, MCA.

27. Owen E. Jensen, "307th Reserve Company Entrains under Last Minute Orders for Annual Summer Camp at San Diego," *Leatherneck* 13, no. 10 (October 1930): 25–26.

28. Frank X. Lambert et al., "Marine Corps League News," *Leatherneck* 14, no. 2 (February 1931): 52.

29. Dion Williams, "In Memoriam Brigadier General Robert Henry Dunlap, U.S.M.C.," *Marine Corps Gazette* 16, no. 2 (August 1931): 4–7.

30. For Turner's death, see "The Chief Passes," *Leatherneck* 14, no. 12 (December 1931): 13, and "Arlington Burial for Two Officers," *New York Times*, November

4, 1931. Ross Rowell, promoted to lieutenant colonel, succeeded Turner as chief of Marine Corps aviation.

31. For Lay's death, see "Colonel H. R. Lay Dies in San Diego," *Leatherneck* 15, no. 9 (September 1932): 20, and "Col. H. R. Lay Dead; Won Honors in War," *New York Times*, July 28, 1932. See also Feland to Harbord, July 27, 1932, and Harbord to Feland, August 1, 1932, file F, Harbord Papers, NYHS, in which Harbord noted that Lay was the first of his old Marine Brigade staff to die. Harbord "was inclined to believe Harry more or less made a mess of his life in the years after the War, from what I have heard, but he was a good officer just the same, and I am sorry he is gone."

32. "Hosts to General Feland," *Leatherneck* 15, no. 6 (June 1932): 13.

33. Milly Bennett, "Sandino—Rebel with a Double," unidentified newspaper clipping, n.d., Feland Scrapbook, Feland Papers, MCA. This two-page article referred to Feland as the head of the Marine Corps Department of the Pacific. Milly Bennett was the pseudonym of Mildred Jacqueline Bremler. She had previously spent time reporting from China and in 1931 would go to Moscow for five years, after which she traveled to Spain to report on the Spanish Civil War.

34. See Beals to Feland, July 15, 1930, and Feland to the Secretary of the Navy via the Major General Commandant, September 8, 1930, file 1240-3, Awards July 1927–October 1933, box 35, entry 18, RG 127, NARA. Additional letters, including Feland to Beals, June 17, 1930, Beals to Feland, June 27, 1930, Feland to Beals, July 10, 1930, and Beals to Feland, n.d., can be found in folder 2, box 170, Carleton Beals Collection, Howard Gotlieb Archival Research Center, Boston University.

35. Schmidt to Feland, June 9, 1933, and Floyd to Feland, March 18, 1933, folder 9, Feland Papers, MCA.

15. Retirement

1. See Brian Bruce, "Thomas Boyd: Jazz Age Author and Editor," *Minnesota History* 56, no. 1 (Spring 1998): 2–17, and Brian Bruce, *Thomas Boyd: Lost Author of the "Lost Generation"* (Akron, OH: University of Akron Press, 2006). Although Boyd's book sold reasonably well, it was soon eclipsed by other U.S. writers such as John Dos Passos and Ernest Hemingway. In 1978, however, Southern Illinois University Press reissued *Through the Wheat* with an afterword by noted author James Dickey; the University of Nebraska Press published a 2000 edition with a foreword by the director of Marine Corps history, Edwin Simmons.

2. For more on Stallings and Thomason, see Rolfe L. Hillman, "Fighters and Writers," *Marine Corps Gazette* 72, no. 11 (November 1988): 90–98.

3. For Feland's comments about Boyd's book and their attempt at collaboration, see Bruce, *Thomas Boyd: Lost Author*, 56, 123–29.

4. Feland to Harbord, August 27, 1931, and January 28, 1933, file F, Harbord Papers, NYHS.

5. Melville A. Shauer to Feland, January 28, 1933, file Letters 1931–1933, A. B. Miller Papers, MCA.

6. "W. S. Van Dyke Commissioned in Reserve," *Leatherneck* 17, no. 5 (May 1934): 35. Major A. B. Miller administered the commissioning oath.

7. W. S. Van Dyke to Logan Feland, May 18, 1933, folder 9, Feland Papers, MCA. See also Feland to Miller, June 6, 1933, ibid., in which he noted that it would be impossible to insert romance into the film "if the picture is to be a true showing of what took place at the front." In W. S. Van Dyke to A. B. Miller, June 13, 1933, ibid., the director mentioned Academy Award–winning scriptwriter Frances Marion as someone who might be able to inject some romance into the script; Van Dyke also cautioned against using an agent, who "might only steal the cream and the best ideas, and sell them as originals." In 1937 the Marine Corps magazine reprinted a Van Dyke article from the *Hollywood Reporter* titled "The Motion Picture Industry in the Next War," *Leatherneck* 21, no. 1 (February 1937): 44. Van Dyke foresaw that industry cameramen not only would record the entire history of the next war but also would be helpful in preparing training films. Sound engineers would be able to use new sound technology to detect enemy planes, and set designers could use their talents in camouflage and to "create other illusions to deceive the enemy."

8. "Commonwealth Club of California, Section on International Relations, Minutes of November 26, 1930," typescript, Feland Scrapbook, Feland Papers, MCA.

9. Logan Feland, "Central America," *Los Angeles Times*, January 14, 1931.

10. Henry Lewis Stimson diaries, December 19, 1930, reel 2, frames 582 and 583, Yale University Library.

11. Harbord to McCoy, June 22, 1931, and McCoy to Harbord, June 23, 1931, file F, Harbord Papers, NYHS.

12. Harbord to Feland, June 30, 1931; Feland to Harbord, July 7, 1931; telegram from Feland to Harbord, July 30, 1931; Harbord to McCoy, July 31, 1931; and Feland to Harbord, August 3, 1931, all in file F, Harbord Papers, NYHS.

13. McCoy to Harbord, August 8, 1931, file F, Harbord Papers, NYHS.

14. Harbord to Feland, August 10, 1931, and Feland to Harbord, August 27, 1931, file F, Harbord Papers, NYHS. Woodward's appointment is noted in Earl B. Hardy, "Supervision of Nicaraguan Elections," *Leatherneck* 15, no. 4 (April 1932): 7–9, 58. Staff Sergeant Hardy served on the Nicaraguan Electoral Commissions of 1928, 1930, and 1932.

15. Feland to Harbord, February 10, 1932, and January 28, 1933, file F, Harbord Papers, NYHS. In his letter asking RCA Victor president J. R. McDonough to supply Feland with a radio at a discount, Harbord noted: "This is the boy who really did most of the fighting that was done in the Belleau Wood. He has never had quite the recognition from his own Corps that he should have had. He is retiring with a little bitterness in his heart, and I would like to cheer him up a little with a discount, if you can do it." Harbord to McDonough, February 1, 1933, ibid.

16. Feland to Harbord, January 7, 1932; Harbord to Feland, January 19, 1932 (in which Harbord noted that the newspapers were wrong: the American Legion had not taken any position on the thirty-hour workweek); and Feland to Harbord, February 10, 1932, all in file F, Harbord Papers, NYHS.

17. Marion Humphrey to Feland, August 18, 1933, folder 9, Feland Papers, MCA. The other letters mentioned are also in folder 9.

18. Henry Larsen to Feland, March 21, 1933, folder 9, Feland Papers, MCA.

19. "Marine Officers Promoted," *Leatherneck* 17, no. 8 (August 1934): 1.

20. "Marine Officers Will Be Shifted," *Leatherneck* 15, no. 12 (December 1932): 37; "General Feland Decorates Marines at Philly," *Leatherneck* 16, no. 6 (June 1933): 24–25.

21. "Gen. Feland, Marines Hero, Retires Sept. 1," *Washington Post*, August 27, 1933; "Maj. Gen. Logan Feland Retires after 34 Years with Marines," *Louisville Courier-Journal*, August 27, 1933; Associated Press, *Lima (OH) News*, July 19, 1933.

22. Harbord to Feland, September 11, 1933, file F, Harbord Papers, NYHS.

23. John Calahan to Feland, September 4, 1933, folder 9, Feland Papers, MCA. This was probably the "Callahan" mentioned in "Old Timers' Corner: Eighteen Years After," *Leatherneck* 15, no. 2 (February 1932): 48. The article referred to Callahan as a man of "gigantic size" who "could lift mine anchors with ease."

24. Harbord to Feland, May 8, 1934, file F, Harbord Papers, NYHS.

25. Hans Schmidt, *Maverick Marine: General Smedley D. Butler and the Contradictions of American Military History* (Lexington: University Press of Kentucky, 1987), 208–13. For the list of proposed court-martial members, see Smedley Butler to his "Aunt Bell," January 30, 1931, folder 15: Personal Correspondence 1931, box 8, Butler Papers, MCA. Butler had received the list from Commandant Ben Fuller.

26. For a copy of the committee's letter, see "Memorial Planned for Major General George Barnett," *Leatherneck* 16, no. 6 (June 1933): 30–31. See also "The George Barnett Memorial," *Marine Corps Gazette* 18, no. 1 (May 1933): 5, and "Barnett Memorial Tablet Unveiled," *Leatherneck* 17, no. 7 (July 1934): 26.

27. For the Baltic Society reunion, see "A.E.F. 'G.H.Q.' in Reunion," *New York Times*, May 29, 1934. See also Feland to Harbord, May 6, [1934], file F, Harbord Papers, NYHS, in which Feland asked Harbord about visiting Radio City Music Hall as Harbord's guest. In that letter, written from Columbus, Feland noted that he "did not know it was feasible in this life for a man to be as happy as I am now." In his reply on May 8, 1934, Harbord expressed his delight that Feland would be attending both the Baltic Society and the Second Division Association reunions and assured him there would "be no difficulty about seeing Radio City." He also noted his surprise that Feland was living in Columbus and said he hoped Feland had not left Pennsylvania "on account of Smedley."

28. For the Second Division reunion, see the following *New York Times* articles: "2d Division Veterans to Be Fleet Guests," June 2, 1934; "2d Division Veterans to Meet Thursday," June 3, 1934; "Sergeant Is Hero at Veteran Dinner," June 10, 1934.

29. "Second Division Shrine Marked," *Marine Corps Gazette* 19, no. 3 (August 1935): 34, 62.

30. Lejeune to Feland, May 31 and July 10, 1935, reel 6, Lejeune Papers, MD, LOC. Lejeune's fall and subsequent poor health are covered in Merrill Bartlett, *Lejeune: A Marine's Life, 1867–1942* (Annapolis, MD: Naval Institute Press, 1991), 181.

31. *Indian Head* 10, no. 9 (September 1935): 3.

32. Frank Mason to Feland, November 18, 1935; Feland to Harbord, November 20, 1935; and Harbord to Feland, November 29, 1935, all in file F, Harbord Papers, NYHS.

33. *Ohio State Journal,* July 5, 1934. See also Daniel Earhart to Feland, July 5, 1934, folder 10, Feland Papers, MCA, thanking Feland for speaking at the National Defense Day celebration.

34. *Ohio State Journal,* October 29, 1935.

35. Carleton Beals, *Glass Houses: Ten Years of Free-Lancing* (Philadelphia: J. B. Lippincott, 1938), 296. According to Beals, Feland was glad that President Roosevelt had not intervened in Cuba, dismissing the notion that American mine and plantation owners had needed protection there. In Nicaragua, Feland claimed, Americans were "always bleating for protection they didn't need" (ibid., 298).

36. Carleton Beals, *Great Guerrilla Warriors* (Englewood Cliffs, NJ: Prentice-Hall, 1970), 94.

37. Frederick Palmer, "Pershing Pays the Check," *American Legion Monthly* 21, no. 2 (August 1936): 49.

38. "Logan Feland, War Hero, Dies in Columbus, O.," *Washington Post,* July 18, 1936; "2d Division Veterans Dedicate Monument to Honor War Dead," *Washington Post,* July 19, 1936; "Gen. Feland Burial Is Set Tomorrow," *Washington Post,* July 21, 1936; "Gen. Logan Feland of Marines Dead," *New York Times,* July 18, 1936; "General Feland Is Buried in Washington," *Washington Times,* July 22, 1936. See telegram to F. P. Guthrie, District Manager, RCA, Washington, July 17, 1936, file F, Harbord Papers, NYHS, stating: "Please forward the following to General Harbord Metropolitan Club Washington quote the following from Mrs. Logan Feland Columbus Ohio Stop. General Feland Died Today Burial at Arlington Arrangements Not Completed." Guthrie forwarded the message to Harbord early the next morning. See also Harbord to Katherine Feland, July 23, 1936, ibid.

Epilogue

1. Newspaper articles on the launching of the USS *Feland* can be found in folder 12, and the event's program can be found in folder 14, Feland Papers, MCA. The launching was depicted in *Los Angeles Times,* November 12, 1942.

2. "Major General Logan Feland, USMC," February 27, 1953, Feland file, HRB, MCHD.

3. H. R. McMaster, "Adaptive Leadership: Harold G. 'Hal' Moore," in *The Art of Command: Military Leadership from George Washington to Colin Powell,* ed. Harry S. Laver and Jeffrey J. Matthews (Lexington: University Press of Kentucky, 2008), 209–11. Born in Bardstown, Kentucky, Moore received the Distinguished Service Cross, as did Feland. He eventually retired as an army lieutenant general.

4. Feland's subscription was mentioned in *Infantry Journal* 2, no. 4 (April 1906): 204.

5. Keith Bickel points out that "the Corps leadership of the 1930s—not know-

ing whether the future held more of the past or something entirely new—was able intellectually to hedge by encouraging and protecting competing subcultures." Keith A. Bickel, *Mars Learning: The Marine Corps' Development of Small Wars Doctrine, 1915–1940* (Boulder, CO: Westview Press, 2001), 248.

6. Lieutenant General Julian Smith, oral history transcript, 1973, 25, MCA.

7. Alfred Gray, foreword to Edgar F. Puryear Jr., *Marine Corps Generalship* (Washington, DC: National Defense University Press, 2009), xiii.

Selected Bibliography

Archival Sources

Boston University, Howard Gotlieb Archival Research Center
    Robert Asprey Collection
    Carleton Beals Collection
Detroit Public Library, Burton Historical Collection
    Papers of Edwin Denby
Herbert Hoover Presidential Library and Museum, West Branch, IA
    Presidential Papers
        Cabinet Office
        Foreign Affairs
        Secretary's File
    Papers of Francis White
Library of Congress, Washington, DC
    Papers of Merritt Edson
    Papers of James Harbord
    Papers of John A. Lejeune
    Papers of Frank McCoy
    Papers of David Foote Sellers
Massachusetts Institute of Technology, Boston, MA
    MIT Archives
    MIT Museum
Military Heritage Institute, Carlisle, PA
    Frederick H. Delano Papers
    Hugh Drum Papers and Diary
    Richard B. Millin Papers
    Matthew B. Ridgeway Papers
    World War I Survey
National Archives and Records Administration, College Park, MD
    Record Group 59: Department of State
National Archives and Records Administration, Washington, DC
    Record Group 24: Bureau of Naval Personnel

Record Group 38: Chief of Naval Operations
Record Group 45: Office of Naval Records and Library
Record Group 80: Department of the Navy
Record Group 125: Judge Advocate General (Navy)
Record Group 127: United States Marine Corps
National Personnel Records Center, St. Louis, MO
   Logan Feland File
New-York Historical Society, New York, NY
   Papers of James Harbord
Princeton University Mudd Manuscript Library, Princeton, NJ
   William Alfred Eddy Collection
   Dana Gardner Munro Collection
Franklin D. Roosevelt Presidential Library and Museum, Hyde Park, NY
   Assistant Secretary of the Navy Papers
   Family Papers
United States Marine Corps Archives and Special Collections, Alfred M. Gray
   Marine Corps Research Center, Quantico, VA
   Historical Amphibious Files
   Oral History Transcripts: Edward Craig, Robert Kilmartin, Julian Smith
   Papers of: Robert Asprey, George Barnett, Hiram Bearss, James Carson Breckin-
   ridge, Smedley Darlington Butler, Bailey Coffenberg, Samuel Cumming, Alfred
   Cunningham, Robert Denig, Robert Dunlap, Earl Ellis, Logan Feland, Ben
   Fuller, James Harbord, Robert Hogaboom, Ralph Stover Keyser, Carl S. Kus-
   ley Jr., John Archer Lejeune, Edwin McClellan, A. B. Miller, Wendell Neville,
   Joseph Pendleton, Ross Rowell, Julian Smith, Harold Snyder, Thomas Turner,
   Harold Utley, Littleton W. T. Waller, Frederick Wise
United States Marine Corps History Division, Historical Reference Branch, Quan-
   tico, VA
   Biographical Files: George Barnett, Elias Beadle, Hiram Bearss, Randolph
   Berkeley, Benjamin Berry, Anthony J. Drexel Biddle, James Carson Breckin-
   ridge, Julian Brown, Smedley Darlington Butler, Arthur Challacombe, John
   Craige, Alphonse DeCarre, Charles Doyen, Herbert Draper, Robert Dunlap,
   Earl Ellis, Logan Feland, Oliver Floyd, Ben Fuller, John Gray, Thomas Hol-
   comb, Marion Humphrey, Gilder Jackson, Ralph Stover Keyser, Henry Larsen,
   John Archer Lejeune, Louis Little, Charles Lyman, Henry Manney, William
   R. Mathews, Hugh Matthews, Edwin McClellan, Robert Messersmith, Clyde
   Metcalf, A. B. Miller, John T. Myers, Wendell Neville, Harold Pierce, Cyrus
   Radford, James Riseley, Keller Rockey, Ross Rowell, Charles Sanderson, Harry
   Schmidt, Maurice Shearer, George Shuler, Berton Sibley, Harold Snyder, John
   Thomason, Philip Torrey, Thomas Turner, Julius Turrill, Harold Utley, Alexan-
   der Williams, Richard Williams, Frederick Wise
   Geographical Files: Cuba, Nicaragua, Panama, Pennsylvania, Philippines, Santo
   Domingo, Vera Cruz

Nicaragua Microfilm
Subject Files: 5th Regiment, Mail Guard, School of Application, Schools (General), World War I Western Front
University of Arizona, Tucson, Libraries Special Collections
William R. Mathews Papers (MS 406)
Yale University Archives, New Haven, CT
Diaries of Henry Stimson
Letters of Henry Stimson

Secondary Sources

Abbot, Willis John. *Soldiers of the Sea: The Story of the United States Marine Corps.* New York: Dodd, Mead, 1918.

Alexander, J. H. "Roots of Deployment—Vera Cruz, 1914." *Marine Corps Gazette* 66, no. 11 (November 1982): 71–79.

Amerman, Annette. "Over Here! Marines in Texas during World War I." *Fortitudine* 33, no. 2 (2008): 7–8.

Andrews, Marietta. *My Studio Window: Sketches of the Pageant of Washington Life.* New York: E. P. Dutton, 1928.

Annual Register of the United States Naval Academy. Washington, DC: Government Printing Office, 1903, 1905.

Anonymous. "The Aerial Rescue of Ocotal." *Leatherneck* 10, no. 10 (October 1927): 9–11, 48.

———. "Annual Field Exercises of the Marine Corps East Coast Expeditionary Force." *Marine Corps Gazette* 8, no. 3 (September 1923): 158–60.

———. "Aviation Force on Maneuvers at Camp Meade, Maryland." *Leatherneck* 8, no. 36 (September 25, 1925): 5.

———. "Barnett Memorial Tablet Unveiled." *Leatherneck* 17, no. 7 (July 1934): 26.

———. "Blue Marine Expeditionary Force Arrives at Panama City." *Leatherneck* 8, no. 14 (April 4, 1925): 1.

———. "The Chief Passes." *Leatherneck* 14, no. 12 (December 1931): 13.

———. "Colonel H. R. Lay Dies in San Diego." *Leatherneck* 15, no. 9 (September 1932): 20.

———. "Death of Captain Hamilton and Sergeant Martin Saddens Troops." *Leatherneck* 5, no. 35 (July 1, 1922): 1–2.

———. "The Death of Lieutenant Thomas and Sergeant Dowell." *Leatherneck* 11, no. 1 (January 1928): 13.

———. "Events in Nicaragua since February 28, 1928." *Marine Corps Gazette* 13, no. 2 (June 1928): 143–46.

———. "Friend of Justice." *Leatherneck* 12, no. 5 (May 1929): 16–17.

———. "General Feland Decorates Marines at Philly." *Leatherneck* 16, no. 6 (June 1933): 24–25.

———. "General Feland Speaks at Armistice Day Celebration." *Leatherneck* 5, no. 58 (November 25, 1922): 1–2.

———. "General McDougal to Major General." *Leatherneck* 23, no. 3 (September 1939): 10, 41.

———. "The George Barnett Memorial." *Marine Corps Gazette* 18, no. 1 (May 1933): 5.

———. "Harbord Portrait Presented to Army and Navy Club." *Leatherneck* 8, no. 2 (June 1923): 110–24.

———. "Hosts to General Feland." *Leatherneck* 15, no. 6 (June 1932): 13.

———. "Items from the M.C.E.F. Aboard the Henderson." *Leatherneck* 10, no. 4 (April 1927): 33–34.

———. "Killed in Action in Nicaragua, May 16, 1927." *Leatherneck* 10, no. 7 (July 1927): 17.

———. "The King Armored Motor Car Proves Its Worth." *Marines Magazine* 1, no. 9 (September 1916): 62–64.

———. "The Leathernecks Return Home." *Leatherneck* 7, no. 40 (September 27, 1924): 1.

———. "LtGen Ross E. Rowell: Marine of Many Talents." *Fortitudine* 7, no. 2 (Fall 1978): 12–15.

———. "The Mail Guard." *Marine Corps Gazette* 11, no. 4 (December 1926): 259–71.

———. "The Marine Corps Association, Its Formation and Objects." *Marine Corps Gazette* 1, no. 1 (March 1916): 73.

———. "Marine Corps Loses Sincere Friend in Death of the Honorable Thomas S. Butler." *Leatherneck* 11, no. 7 (July 1928): 7.

———. "Marine Flyers Die Fighting to the Last." *Leatherneck* 10, no. 12 (December 1927): 16.

———. "Marine Officers to Present Portrait of General Harbord." *Leatherneck* 5, no. 21 (March 25, 1922): 1.

———. "Marine Officers Will Be Shifted." *Leatherneck* 15, no. 12 (December 1932): 37.

———. "Marines Force Landing at Oahu but Technical Victor Is Still in Hands of the Critics." *Leatherneck* 8, no. 21 (May 23, 1925): 4.

———. "Marines Received Navy Awards for Distinguished Service in Nicaragua." *Leatherneck* 11, no. 1 (January 1928): 15.

———. "Marines Stage Final Practice for Oahu Maneuver." *Leatherneck* 8, no. 17 (April 25, 1925): 1.

———. "M.C.E.F. Enjoys Good Weather." *Leatherneck* 7, no. 37 (September 6, 1924): 2–3.

———. "Memorial Planned for Major General George Barnett." *Leatherneck* 16, no. 6 (June 1933): 30–31.

———. "The Motion Picture Industry in the Next War." *Leatherneck* 21, no. 1 (February 1937): 44.

———. "New York Greets Valorous Second." *Recruiters' Bulletin* 5, no. 7 (August 1919): 10.

———. "Old Timers' Corner: Eighteen Years After." *Leatherneck* 15, no. 2 (February 1932): 48.

———. "Present Civil War Battle." *Leatherneck* 6, no. 38 (September 25, 1923): 2.

———. "Schools." *Marine Corps Gazette* 14, no. 8 (August 1931): 20.

———. "2nd Division Memorial Fund." *Leatherneck* 9, no. 14 (November 1926): 17.

———. "Second Division Shrine Marked." *Marine Corps Gazette* 19, no. 3 (August 1935): 34, 62.

Asprey, Robert. *At Belleau Wood.* 1965. Reprint, Denton: University of North Texas Press, 1996.

———. "The King of Kill." *Marine Corps Gazette* 51, no. 5 (May 1967): 31–35.

———. "Waller of Samar—Part I." *Marine Corps Gazette* 45, no. 5 (May 1961): 36–41.

———. "Waller of Samar—Part II." *Marine Corps Gazette* 45, no. 6 (June 1961): 44–48.

Bacevich, Andrew. "The American Electoral Mission in Nicaragua, 1927–28." *Diplomatic History* 4 (July 1980): 241–61.

———. *Diplomat in Khaki: Major General Frank Ross McCoy and American Foreign Policy, 1898–1949.* Lawrence: University Press of Kansas, 1989.

Ballendorf, Dirk A., and Merrill L. Bartlett. *Pete Ellis: An Amphibious Warfare Prophet, 1880–1923.* Annapolis, MD: Naval Institute Press, 1997.

Bartlett, Merrill. *Assault from the Sea: Essays on the History of Amphibious Warfare.* Annapolis, MD: Naval Institute Press, 1993.

———. "Ben Hebard Fuller and the Genesis of a Modern United States Marine Corps, 1891–1934." *Journal of Military History* 69 (January 2005): 73–91.

———. "Col Lincoln Karmany and Political Correctness, 1913." *Marine Corps Gazette* 82, no. 12 (December 1998): 47–49.

———. *George Barnett, 1859–1930: Register of His Personal Papers.* Washington, DC: History and Museums Division, Headquarters, U.S. Marine Corps, 1980.

———. "The Inside Track to Commandant." *Proceedings of the U.S. Naval Institute* 121, no. 1 (January 1995): 58–63.

———. *James Guthrie Harbord, 1866–1947: Register of His Personal Papers.* Washington, DC: History and Museums Division, Headquarters, U.S. Marine Corps, 1995.

———. *Lejeune: A Marine's Life, 1867–1942.* Annapolis, MD: Naval Institute Press, 1991.

———. "Old Gimlet Eye." *Proceedings of the U.S. Naval Institute* 112, no. 11 (November 1986): 64–72.

———. "Ouster of a Commandant." *Proceedings of the U.S. Naval Institute* 106, no. 11 (November 1980): 80–85.

———. "The Road to Eighth and Eye." *Proceedings of the U.S. Naval Institute* 114, no. 11 (November 1988): 74–76.

———. "Secretary of the Navy Josephus Daniels and the Marine Corps, 1913–

1921." In *New Interpretations in Naval History: Selected Papers from the Eighth Naval History Symposium*, edited by William B. Cogar, 190–208. Annapolis, MD: Naval Institute Press, 1989.

———. "The Spirited Saga of 'Johnny the Hard.'" *Naval History* 21, no. 3 (June 2007): 54–61.

———. *The U.S. Marine Corps: An Illustrated History*. Annapolis, MD: Naval Institute Press, 2001.

Battle, J. H., ed. *County of Todd, Kentucky. Historical and Biographical*. Chicago: F. A. Battey, 1884.

Baylen, Joseph O. "Sandino: Patriot or Bandit?" *Hispanic American Historical Review* 31, no. 3 (August 1951): 394–414.

Beals, Carleton. *Banana Gold*. Philadelphia: J. B. Lippincott, 1932.

———. *Glass Houses: Ten Years of Free-Lancing*. Philadelphia: J. B. Lippincott, 1938.

———. *Great Guerrilla Warriors*. Englewood Cliffs, NJ: Prentice-Hall, 1970.

Bettez, David J. "The Marine Corps Prepares for War: The Philadelphia Military Training Camp." *Leatherneck* 92, no. 10 (October 2009): 48–51.

Bevilacqua, Allan C. "The Battle of Blanc Mont Ridge." *Leatherneck* 83, no. 11 (November 2000): 26–31.

———. "Next Time I Send Damn Fool I Go Myself." *Leatherneck* 89, no. 10 (October 2006): 52–54.

Bickel, Keith A. *Mars Learning: The Marine Corps' Development of Small Wars Doctrine, 1915–1940*. Boulder, CO: Westview Press, 2001.

Biddle, Cordelia Drexel, as told to Kyle Crichton. *My Philadelphia Father*. Garden City, NY: Doubleday, 1955.

Bittner, Donald F. *Curriculum Evolution: Marine Corps Command and Staff College, 1920–1988*. Washington, DC: History and Museums Division, Headquarters, U.S. Marine Corps, 1988.

Blumenson, Martin. *The Patton Papers, 1885–1940*. Boston: Houghton Mifflin, 1972.

Bonk, David, and Peter Dennis. *Chateau Thierry & Belleau Wood 1918: The AEF's Baptism of Fire on the Marne*. Oxford: Osprey Publishing, 2007.

Bowers, George B. *History of the 160th Ind. Vol. Infantry in the Spanish-American War, with Biographies of Officers and Enlisted Men and Rosters of the Companies*. Fort Wayne, IN: Archer Printing, 1900.

Brainard, E. H. "The Marines Take Wings." *Leatherneck* 11, no. 8 (August 1928): 28.

Brannen, Carl Andrew. *Over There: A Marine in the Great War*. College Station: Texas A&M University Press, 1996.

Brooks, David C. "U.S. Marines, Miskitos and the Hunt for Sandino: The Rio Coco Patrol in 1928." *Journal of Latin American Studies* 21, no. 2 (May 1989): 311–42.

Brown, Ronald J. *A Few Good Men: The Story of the Fighting Fifth Marines*. Novato, CA: Presidio Press, 2001.

———. "George Wallis Hamilton: The Forgotten Hero of World War I." *Leatherneck* 86, no. 11 (November 2003): 46–51.

Bruce, Brian. "Thomas Boyd: Jazz Age Author and Editor." *Minnesota History* 56, no. 1 (Spring 1998): 2–17.

———. *Thomas Boyd: Lost Author of the "Lost Generation."* Akron, OH: University of Akron Press, 2006.

Burch, Robert, and Logan Feland. *"Southern Homes": A Collection of Designs for Residences of Moderate Cost.* Owensboro, KY: Burch and Feland, Architects, 1897.

Calder, Bruce. *The Impact of Intervention: The Dominican Republic during the U.S. Occupation of 1916–1924.* Austin: University of Texas Press, 1984.

Camp, Richard. *Leatherneck Legends: Conversations with the Marine Corps' Old Breed.* St. Paul, MN: Zenith Press, 2006.

Catlin, A. W. *With the Help of God and a Few Marines.* Garden City, NY: Doubleday, Page, 1919.

Chapman, Gregory Dean. "Army Life at Camp Thomas, Georgia during the Spanish-American War." *Georgia Historical Quarterly* 70, no. 4 (Winter 1896): 633–56.

Clark, George B. "Col John W. Thomason Jr., the 'Kipling of the Corps.'" *Leatherneck* 89, no. 8 (August 2006): 26–29.

———. *Devil Dogs: Fighting Marines of World War I.* Novato, CA: Presidio Press, 2000.

———. *Hiram Iddings Bearss, U.S. Marine Corps: Biography of a World War I Hero.* Jefferson, NC: McFarland, 2005.

———. *With the Old Corps in Nicaragua.* Novato, CA: Presidio Press, 2001.

———, ed. *His Time in Hell. A Texas Marine in France: The World War I Memoir of Warren R. Jackson.* Novato, CA: Presidio Press, 2001.

Clifford, John Garry. *The Citizen Soldiers: The Plattsburg Training Camp Movement, 1913–1920.* Lexington: University Press of Kentucky, 1972.

Clifford, Kenneth J. *Progress and Purpose: A Developmental History of the United States Marine Corps, 1900–1970.* Washington, DC: History and Museums Division, Headquarters, U.S. Marine Corps, 1973.

Coffman, Edward M. *The War to End All Wars: The American Military Experience in World War I.* New York: Oxford University Press, 1968.

Collins, Lewis, and Richard H. Collins. *History of Kentucky.* Rev. ed. Covington, KY: Collins and Company, 1878.

———. *History of Kentucky.* Rev. 2nd ed. Vol. 2. Frankfort, KY: Kentucky Historical Society, 1966.

Condit, Kenneth, John Johnstone, and Ella Nargele. *A Brief History of Headquarters Marine Corps Staff Organization.* Washington, DC: Historical Division, Headquarters, U.S. Marine Corps, 1971.

Cooke, James J. *Pershing and His Generals: Command and Staff in the AEF.* Westport, CT: Praeger, 1997.

Corney, George. "Crime and Postal History: Bring in the Marines!" *Marine Corps Gazette* 77, no. 10 (October 1993): 50–52.

Cosmas, Graham A. *An Army for Empire: The United States Army in the Spanish-American War.* College Station: Texas A&M Press, 1994.

———, ed. *Marine Flyer in France: The Diary of Captain Alfred A. Cunningham, November 1917–February 1918.* Washington, DC: History and Museums Division, Headquarters, U.S. Marine Corps, 1974.

Cosmas, Graham, and Jack Shulimson. "The Culebra Maneuver and the Formation of the U.S. Marine Corps' Advance Base Force, 1913–1914." In *Changing Interpretations and New Sources in Naval History: Papers from the Third United States Naval Academy History Symposium*, edited by Robert William Love Jr., 293–308. New York: Garland Publishing, 1980.

Craige, John H. "The Marines at Gettysburg." *Marine Corps Gazette* 7, no. 3 (September 1922): 249–52.

———. "The 'Wilderness' Manoeuvres." *Marine Corps Gazette* 6, no. 4 (December 1921): 418–23.

Crane, Stephen. "Marines Signaling under Fire at Guantanamo." *McClure's Magazine* 12, no. 4 (February 1899): 332–36.

Crawford, Danny J. "Corps Has Long History in Protecting American Interests in Panama." *Marines Magazine*, March 1990, 27–28.

Cronen, E. David, ed. *Cabinet Diaries of Josephus Daniels, 1913–1921.* Lincoln: University of Nebraska Press, 1963.

Current, Richard Nelson. *Secretary Stimson, a Study in Statecraft.* New Brunswick, NJ: Rutgers University Press, 1954.

Daugherty, Leo J., III. "Away All Boats: The Army-Navy Maneuvers of 1925." *Joint Forces Quarterly* (Autumn–Winter 1998–1999): 107–13.

———. *Pioneers of Amphibious Warfare, 1898–1945: Profiles of Fourteen American Military Strategists.* Jefferson, NC: McFarland, 2009.

Deconde, Alexander. "Herbert Hoover's Good Will Tour." *Historian* 12, no. 2 (March 1950): 167–81.

Denny, Harold. *Dollars for Bullets: The Story of American Rule in Nicaragua.* New York: Dial Press, 1929.

Dieckmann, Edward A., Sr. "Louie Cukela." *Marine Corps Gazette* 45, no. 12 (December 1961): 34–39.

Doenecke, Justus D. *Nothing Less than War: A New History of America's Entry into World War I.* Lexington: University Press of Kentucky, 2011.

Dollen, Charles. *Bibliography of the United States Marine Corps.* New York: Scarecrow Press, 1963.

Doyel, Ginger M. "Halligan Hall: Home to Marines and Midshipmen." *Shipmate* 66, no. 9 (November–December 2003): 17.

Edson, Merritt A. "The Coco Patrol." *Marine Corps Gazette* 19, no. 3 (August 1936): 18–23, 38–48.

———. "The Coco Patrol (Part 2)." *Marine Corps Gazette* 20, no. 4 (November 1936): 40–41, 60–72.

———. "The Coco Patrol (Part 3)." *Marine Corps Gazette* 21, no. 1 (February 1937): 35–43, 57–63.

Eisenhower, John S. D. *Intervention! The United States and the Mexican Revolution, 1913–1917.* New York: W. W. Norton, 1993.

Elkins, Troy R. "A Creditable Position: James Carson Breckinridge and the Development of the Marine Corps Schools." MA thesis, Kansas State University, 2011.

Elliott, John M. "The Longest Flight: Early Marine Aviators Make History." *Leatherneck* 91, no. 5 (May 2008): 54–59.

———. "Marine Aviation in Nicaragua: A Time of Pioneering." *Leatherneck* 92, no. 9 (September 2009): 20–23.

Evans, Frank E. "The Marines Have Landed." *Marine Corps Gazette* 2, no. 3 (September 1917): 218.

———. "Motor Transportation in the Marine Corps." *Marine Corps Gazette* 2, no. 1 (March 1917): 1–12.

Fegan, J. C. "Thomas S. Butler." *Marine Corps Gazette* 13, no. 2 (June 1928): 89–90.

Feland, Logan. "The Division of Operations and Training, Headquarters, U.S. Marine Corps." *Marine Corps Gazette* 7, no. 1 (March 1922): 41–45.

———. "Retreat, Hell." *Marine Corps Gazette* 6, no. 3 (September 1921): 289–91.

———. "Soldiers of the Navy." *Leatherneck* 7, no. 15 (April 3, 1924): 4.

Fellowes, E. A. "Marines Embark for Expeditionary Duty." *Leatherneck* 8, no. 12 (March 21, 1925): 1.

Field, Harry B., and Henry G. James. *Over the Top with the 18th Co., 5th Regt. U.S. Marines: A History.* Germany: n.p., 1919.

Fitzgerald, Glendell L. "Combat Reports of Operations in Nicaragua." *Marine Corps Gazette* 13, no. 4 (December 1928): 241–47.

Foner, Philip. *The Spanish-Cuban-American War and the Birth of American Imperialism, 1898–1902.* 2 vols. New York: Monthly Review Press, 1972.

Frank, Benis. *Marine Corps Oral History Collection Catalog.* Washington, DC: History and Museums Division, Headquarters, U.S. Marine Corps, 1979.

Freidel, Frank. *Franklin D. Roosevelt: The Ordeal.* Boston: Little, Brown, 1954.

Fuller, Stephen, and Graham Cosmas. *Marines in the Dominican Republic, 1916–1924.* Washington, DC: History and Museums Division, Headquarters, U.S. Marine Corps, 1974.

Ghormley, Ralph. *The Military Order of the Carabao: Centennial History.* N.p.: Military Order of the Carabao, 2000.

Gooding, Jennifer. "Collection Adds Medals, Papers of WWI Hero." *Fortitudine* 18, no. 3 (Winter 1988–1989): 8.

Gray, John. "A Plea for the Revision of the Field Officers' Course." *Marine Corps Gazette* 15, no. 4 (February 1931): 64.

———. "Recollections of the 1912 Cuban Expedition." *Marine Corps Gazette* 17, no. 1 (May 1932): 45–48.

Hamilton, Craig, and Louise Corbin, eds. *Echoes from Over There.* New York: Soldiers' Publishing Company, 1919.

Hammond, James W. "Butler's Bouts with 'Illegal Substances.'" *Marine Corps Gazette* 66, no. 2 (February 1982): 51–57.

Hanneken, Herman H. "A Discussion of the *Voluntario* Troops in Nicaragua." *Marine Corps Gazette* 26, no. 4 (November 1942): 120, 247–66.

Harbord, James. *The American Army in France 1917–1919.* Boston: Little, Brown, 1936.

———. *Leaves from a War Diary.* New York: Dodd, Mead, 1925.

Harding, Ethan. "Civil-Military Operations." *Marine Corps Gazette* 95, no. 8 (August 1911): 18–22.

Hardy, Earl B. "Supervision of Nicaraguan Elections." *Leatherneck* 15, no. 4 (April 1932): 7–9, 58.

Heinl, Robert. *Soldiers of the Sea: The United States Marine Corps, 1775–1962.* 2nd ed. Baltimore: Nautical and Aviation Publishing Company of America, 1991.

Hendrix, Henry J., II. "TR's Plan to Invade Colombia." *Naval History* 20 (December 2006): 36–42.

Herring, George. *From Colony to Superpower: U.S. Foreign Relations since 1776.* New York: Oxford University Press, 2008.

Hicks, Paul. "Fabulous Fighter." *Leatherneck* 31, no. 9 (September 1948): 16.

Hillman, Rolfe L., Jr. "Crossing the Meuse." *Marine Corps Gazette* 72, no. 11 (November 1988): 68–73.

———. "Fighters and Writers." *Marine Corps Gazette* 72, no. 11 (November 1988): 90–98.

———. "Marines in the Rhineland, 1918–1919." *Naval History* 3, no. 3 (Summer 1989): 11–15.

Historical Sketch, Constitution, and Register of the Military Order of the Carabao. Washington, DC: W. F. Roberts, n.d.

Hodgson, Godfrey. *The Colonel: The Life and Wars of Henry Stimson 1867–1950.* New York: Knopf, 1990.

Hoffman, Jon T. *Once a Legend: "Red Mike" Edson of the Marine Raiders.* Novato, CA: Presidio Press, 1994.

Inglis, William. "How the 'Warlike' Cubans Gave Up Their Arms." *Harper's Weekly,* November 3, 1906, 1564–66.

Irwin, Manley R. *Silent Strategists: Harding, Denby, and the U.S. Navy's Trans-Pacific Offensive, World War II.* Lanham, MD: University Press of America, 2008.

James, Larry. *The Feland Family, 1750–1979.* Neosho, MO: L. A. James, 1979.

James, Pearl, ed. *Picture This: World War I Posters and Visual Culture.* Lincoln: University of Nebraska Press, 2009.

Jensen, Owen E. "307th Reserve Company Entrains under Last Minute Orders for Annual Summer Camp at San Diego." *Leatherneck* 13, no. 10 (October 1930): 25–26.

Johnson, Douglas V., II, and Rolfe L. Hillman Jr. *Soissons 1918*. College Station: Texas A&M University Press, 1999.

Johnson, Lt. Col. Edward C., USMC. *Marine Corps Aviation: The Early Years, 1912–1940*. Edited by Graham Cosmas. Washington, DC: History and Museums Division, Headquarters, U.S. Marine Corps, 1977.

Johnson, Wray R. "Airpower and Restraint in Small Wars: Marine Corps Aviation in the Second Nicaraguan Campaign, 1927–33." *Aerospace Power Journal* 15 (Fall 2001). http://www.airpower.maxwell.af.mil/airchronicles/apj/apj01/fa101/johnson.html.

Jones, Robert Dorsey. *With the American Fleet from the Atlantic to the Pacific*. Seattle: Harrison, 1909.

Kamman, William. *A Search for Stability: United States Diplomacy toward Nicaragua, 1925–1933*. Notre Dame, IN: University of Notre Dame Press, 1968.

Karnow, Stanley. *In Our Image: America's Empire in the Philippines*. New York: Ballantine Books, 1989.

Karsten, Peter. *The Naval Aristocracy: The Golden Age of Annapolis and the Emergence of Modern American Navalism*. New York: Free Press, 1972.

Keefe, Jack. "Philadelphia and the Marines." *Marine Corps Gazette* 8, no. 18 (May 2, 1925): 1–2.

Keegan, John. *The First World War*. New York: Knopf, 1998.

Kentucky Department of Military Affairs. *Kentucky State Guard in the Spanish-American War, 1898–1899*. Frankfort: Kentucky Department of Military Affairs, 1988.

Kentucky Historical Society. *"A Splendid Little War": The Spanish American War and Kentucky*. Frankfort: Kentucky Historical Society, 1998.

Kleber, John E. *The Kentucky Encyclopedia*. Lexington: University Press of Kentucky, 1992.

Klotter, James. *The Breckinridges of Kentucky*. Lexington: University Press of Kentucky, 1986.

Knight, Alan. *The Mexican Revolution*. 2 vols. Cambridge: Cambridge University Press, 1986.

Lambert, Frank X., et al. "Marine Corps League News." *Leatherneck* 14, no. 2 (February 1931): 52.

Langley, Lester. *The Banana Wars: United States Intervention in the Caribbean, 1898–1934*. Rev. ed. Lexington: University Press of Kentucky, 1985.

Lejeune, John A. "The Nicaraguan Situation." *Leatherneck* 11, no. 2 (February 1928): 10, 52.

———. *Reminiscences of a Marine*. Philadelphia: Dorrance, 1930.

Leonard, John, and Fred Chitty. *The Story of the United States' Marines 1740–1919*. New York: n.p., 1919.

Levere, William Collin. *The History of Sigma Alpha Epsilon in the World War*. Menasha, WI: George Banta, 1928.

Lewis, Alfred Fayette. *History of Higher Education in Kentucky*. Washington, DC: Government Printing Office, 1899.

Link, Arthur, ed. *Papers of Woodrow Wilson*. Vol. 26, *August 2–December 23, 1920*. Princeton, NJ: Princeton University Press, 1992.

Linn, Brian McAllister. *The Philippine War, 1899–1902*. Lawrence: University Press of Kansas, 2000.

———. *The U.S. Army and Counterinsurgency in the Philippine War, 1899–1902*. Chapel Hill: University of North Carolina Press, 1989.

Linn, Louis C., Laura Jane Linn Wright, and B. J. Omanson, eds. *At Belleau Wood with Rifle and Sketchpad: Memoir of a United States Marine in World War I*. Jefferson, NC: McFarland, 2012.

Macauley, Neill. *The Sandino Affair*. 1967. Reprint, Durham, NC: Duke University Press, 1985.

Mackin, Elton. *Suddenly We Didn't Want to Die: Memoirs of a World War I Marine*. Novato, CA: Presidio Press, 1993.

MacPherson, R. T. *John H. Russell, Jr. 1872–1947: Register of His Personal Papers*. Washington, DC: History and Museums Division, Headquarters, U.S. Marine Corps, 1987.

Marshall, Anne E. "Kentucky's Separate Coach Law and African American Response, 1892–1900." *Register of the Kentucky Historical Society* 98 (Summer 2000): 241–59.

Marshall, Heather Pace. "It Means Something These Days to Be a Marine: Image, Identity, and Mission in the Marine Corps, 1861–1918." PhD diss., Duke University, 2010.

Matthews, Franklin. *With the Battlefleet: Cruise of the Sixteen Battleships of the United States Atlantic Fleet from Hampton Roads to the Golden Gate, December 1907–May 1908*. New York: B. W. Huebsch, 1908.

Maurer, John H. "Fuel and the Battle Fleet: Coal, Oil, and American Naval Strategy, 1898–1925." *Naval War College Review* 34 (November–December 1981): 60–77.

McClain, G. Lee. *Military History of Kentucky*. Frankfort, KY: State Journal, 1939.

McClellan, Edwin N. "The Aisne-Marne Offensive." *Marine Corps Gazette* 6, no. 1 (March 1921): 70.

———. "American Marines in Nicaragua." *Marine Corps Gazette* 6, no. 1 (March 1921): 48–65.

———. "The Battle of Belleau Wood." *Marine Corps Gazette* 5, no. 4 (December 1920): 370–404.

———. "The Battle of Blanc Mont Ridge." *Marine Corps Gazette* 7, no. 1 (March 1922): 1–21.

———. "The Battle of Blanc Mont Ridge (Continued)." *Marine Corps Gazette* 7, no. 2 (June 1922): 206–11.

———. "Capture of Hill 142, Battle of Belleau Wood, and Capture of Bouresches." *Marine Corps Gazette* 5, no. 3 (September 1920): 277–313.

———. "The Fourth Brigade of Marines in the Training Areas and the Operations in the Verdun Sector." *Marine Corps Gazette* 5, no. 1 (March 1920): 81–110.

———. "He Remembered His Mission." *Marine Corps Gazette* 15, no. 3 (November 1930): 30–32, 51–52.

———. "In the Marbache Sector." *Marine Corps Gazette* 6, no. 3 (September 1921): 253–56.

———. "The Nueva Segovia Expedition." *Marine Corps Gazette* 15, no. 5 (May 1931): 21.

———. "The Nueva Segovia Expedition (Part 2)." *Marine Corps Gazette* 16, no. 2 (August 1931): 11.

———. "Operations of the Fourth Brigade of Marines in the Aisne Defensive." *Marine Corps Gazette* 5, no. 2 (June 1920): 182–202.

———. "The St. Mihiel Offensive." *Marine Corps Gazette* 6, no. 4 (December 1921): 375–76.

———. "Supervising Nicaraguan Elections, 1928." *Proceedings of the U.S. Naval Institute* 59, no. 1 (January 1933): 37.

———. *The United States Marine Corps in the World War.* Washington, DC: Historical Branch, G-3 Division, Headquarters, U.S. Marine Corps, 1968.

McMaster, H. R. "Adaptive Leadership: Harold G. 'Hal' Moore." In *The Art of Command: Military Leadership from George Washington to Colin Powell*, edited by Harry S. Laver and Jeffrey J. Matthews, 209–230. Lexington: University Press of Kentucky, 2008.

Meacham, Charles Mayfield. *A History of Christian County Kentucky from Oxcart to Airplane.* Nashville, TN: Marshall and Bruce, 1930.

Metcalf, Clyde. "A History of the Education of Marine Officers." *Marine Corps Gazette* 20, no. 2 (May 1936): 15–19, 49–54.

———. *A History of the United States Marine Corps.* New York: G. P. Putnam's Sons, 1939.

Miller, Michael, ed. *My Dear Smedley: Personal Correspondence of John A. Lejeune to Smedley D. Butler, 1927–1928.* Washington, DC: Marine Corps Research Center, Archives Branch, 2002.

Millett, Allan. *The General: Robert L. Bullard and Officership in the United States Army, 1881–1925.* Westport, CT: Greenwood Press, 1975.

———. *In Many a Strife: General Gerald C. Thomas and the U.S. Marine Corps, 1917–1956.* Annapolis, MD: Naval Institute Press, 1993.

———. *The Politics of Intervention: The Military Occupation of Cuba, 1906–1909.* Columbus: Ohio State University Press, 1968.

———. *Semper Fidelis: The History of the United State Marine Corps.* Rev. ed. New York: Free Press, 1991.

Millett, Allan, and Jack Shulimson. *Commandants of the Marine Corps.* Annapolis, MD: Naval Institute Press, 2004.

Millett, Richard. *Guardians of the Dynasty: A History of the U.S. Created Guardia*

Nacional de Nicaragua and the Somoza Family. Maryknoll, NY: Orbis Books, 1977.

———. "The State Department's Navy: A History of the Special Services Squadron, 1920–1940." *American Neptune* 25, no. 2 (April 1975): 118–38.

Mortensen, Mark. *George W. Hamilton, USMC: America's Greatest World War I Hero*. Jefferson, NC: McFarland, 2011.

Munro, Dana. *The United States and the Caribbean Republics, 1921–1933*. Princeton, NJ: Princeton University Press, 1974.

Musicant, Ivan. *Empire by Default: The Spanish-American War and the Dawn of the New Century*. New York: Henry Holt, 1998.

Nalty, Bernard C. *The United States Marines in Nicaragua*. Rev. ed. Washington, DC: Headquarters, U.S. Marine Corps, 1962.

Nash, Howard P., Edward H. Virgin, and William Collin Levere. *The Sixth General Catalogue of Sigma Alpha Epsilon*. Evanston, IL: Sigma Alpha Epsilon, 1904.

Neumann, Brian Fisher. "Pershing's Right Hand: General James G. Harbord and the American Expeditionary Forces in the First World War." PhD diss., Texas A&M University, 2006.

Nilo, James. "Attack on Soissons." *Leatherneck* 76, no. 7 (July 1993): 24–27.

———. "The Battle of Blanc Mont." *Leatherneck* 76, no. 10 (October 1993): 10–15.

———. "The Battle of St. Mihiel." *Leatherneck* 76, no. 9 (September 1993): 12–17.

———. "World War I: 75 Years Ago: The Last Night of the War." *Leatherneck* 76, no. 11 (November 1993): 16–23.

O'Connell, Aaron. *Underdogs: The Making of the Modern Marine Corps*. Cambridge, MA: Harvard University Press, 2012.

Otto, Ernst. "The Battles for the Possession of Belleau Woods, June 1918." *Proceedings of the U.S. Naval Institute* 54, no. 11 (November 1928): 941.

Palmer, Frederick. "Pershing Pays the Check." *American Legion Monthly* 21, no. 2 (August 1936): 49.

Paradis, Don V., and Peter F. Owen, eds. *The World War I Memoirs of Don V. Paradis, Gunnery Sergeant, USMC*. Marine Corps Historical Branch oral history available at lulu.com.

Paris, Gus. "Hold Every Inch of Ground." Unpublished paper. Logan Feland Papers, Marine Corps Archive, Quantico, VA.

Peguero, Valentina. *The Militarization of Culture in the Dominican Republic, from the Captains General to General Trujillo*. Lincoln: University of Nebraska Press, 2004.

Perrin, William Henry. *County of Christian, Kentucky: Historical and Biographical*. Chicago: F. A. Battey, 1884.

———, ed. *Counties of Christian and Trigg, Kentucky: Historical and Biographical*. Chicago: F. A. Battey, 1884.

Persico, Joseph. *Eleventh Month, Eleventh Day, Eleventh Hour: Armistice Day, 1918. World War I and Its Violent Climax*. New York: Random House, 2004.

Philadelphia War History Committee. *Philadelphia in the World War*. New York: Wynkoop Hollenbeck Crawford, 1922.

Prescott, Samuel C. *When MIT Was Boston Tech, 1861–1914*. Cambridge, MA: Technology Press, 1954.

Proctor, Clarence. "Ten Years Ago." *Leatherneck* 9, no. 10 (July 1926): 22–23.

Puryear, Edgar F., Jr. *Marine Corps Generalship*. Washington, DC: National Defense University Press, 2009.

Queseda, Alejandro M. de. "The *Carte de Visite* of Cadet Logan Feland: The Making of a Marine Corps General." *Military Collector and Historian* 61, no. 3 (Fall 2009): 225–26.

Quirk, Robert. *An Affair of Honor: Woodrow Wilson and the Occupation of Veracruz*. Lexington: University of Kentucky Press, 1962.

Reckner, James. *Teddy Roosevelt's Great White Fleet*. Annapolis, MD: Naval Institute Press, 1988.

Reeves, Ira. *Military Education in the United States*. Burlington, VT: Free Press Printing, 1914.

Riseley, James P., Jr. *Uncle Jim: Recollections of Lt. Gen. James P. Riseley, United States Marine Corps (Ret.)*. Roswell, NM: James P. Riseley, 1991.

Rodman, Hugh. *Yarns of a Kentucky Admiral*. Indianapolis: Bobbs-Merrill, 1928.

Ross, Stephen T. *American War Plans, 1890–1939*. Portland, OR: Frank Cass, 2002.

Schmidt, Hans. *Maverick Marine: General Smedley D. Butler and the Contradictions of American Military History*. Lexington: University Press of Kentucky, 1987.

———. *The United States Occupation of Haiti, 1915–1934*. New Brunswick, NJ: Rutgers University Press, 1995.

Shulimson, Jack. "Daniel Pratt Mannix and the Establishment of the Marine Corps School of Application, 1889–1894." *Journal of Military History* 55, no. 4 (October 1991): 469–86.

———. *The Marine Corps Search for a Mission, 1880–1898*. Lawrence: University Press of Kansas, 1993.

Shulimson, Jack, Wanda Renfrow, David Kelly, and Evelyn Englander, eds. *Marines in the Spanish-American War, 1895–1899: Anthology and Annotated Bibliography*. Washington, DC: History and Museums Division, Headquarters, U.S. Marine Corps, 1998.

Simmons, Edwin. "Leathernecks at Soissons." *Naval History* 19, no. 6 (December 2005): 24.

———. "Ross Rowell: Aviator with a Flair." *Marine Corps Gazette* 69, no. 5 (May 1985): 82–91.

———. *The United States Marines: A History*. 3rd ed. Annapolis, MD: Naval Institute Press, 1998.

———. "With the Marines at Blanc Mont." *Marine Corps Gazette* 77, no. 11 (November 1993): 34–43.

Simmons, Edwin, and Joseph Alexander. *Through the Wheat: The U.S. Marines in World War I*. Annapolis, MD: Naval Institute Press, 2008.

Smith, Julian C. "Advanced Base Mines and Mining." *Marine Corps Gazette* 4, no. 3 (September 1919): 221–31.

Smith, Rev. S. E., ed. *History of the Anti–Separate Coach Movement of Kentucky: Containing Half-Tone Cuts and Biographical Sketches.* Evansville, IN: National Afro-American Journal and Directory, 1895.

Southard, Mary Young, and Ernest C. Miller. *Who's Who in Kentucky; A Biographical Assembly of Notable Kentuckians, 1936.* Louisville, KY: Standard Print Co., 1936.

Spaulding, Oliver, and John Wright. *The Second Division, American Expeditionary Force in France, 1917–1919.* New York: Historical Committee, Second Division Association, Hillman Press, 1937.

Speed, Thomas, R. M. Kelly, and Alfred Pirtle. *The Union Regiments of Kentucky.* Louisville, KY: Courier-Journal Job Printing Co., 1897.

Stallings, Laurence. *The Doughboys: The Story of the AEF, 1917–1918.* New York: Harper and Row, 1963.

Stone, H. W. "Field Exercises of the 10th Regiment at Camp Meade, Maryland." *Marine Corps Gazette* 10, no. 3 (December 1925): 157–60.

Strecker, Mark. *Smedley D. Butler, USMC: A Biography.* Jefferson, NC: McFarland, 2011.

Sweetman, Jack. *The Landing at Veracruz, 1914: The First Complete Chronicle of a Strange Encounter in April, 1914, When the United States Navy Captured and Occupied the City of Veracruz, Mexico.* Annapolis, MD: Naval Institute Press, 1968.

Tallent, Robert W. "The Great Mail Call." *Leatherneck* 38, no. 2 (February 1955): 44–47.

Taylor, William Alexander. *Centennial History of Columbus and Franklin County, Ohio.* Chicago: S. J. Clarke, 1909.

Thacker, Joel. *Stand, Gentlemen, He Served on Samar!* Washington, DC: U.S. Marine Corps Headquarters, 1945.

Thomas, Gerald C., Jr. "A Warrior-Scholar in the World War: Robert Henry Dunlap." *Marine Corps Gazette* 82, no. 1 (January 1998): 88–89.

Thomas, Lowell. *Old Gimlet Eye: Adventures of Smedley D. Butler.* New York: Farrar and Rinehart, 1933.

Thomason, John W., Jr. "The Charge at Soissons." *Marine Corps Gazette* 53, no. 11 (November 1969): 60–69.

———. *The Second Infantry Division in World War I: A History of the American Expeditionary Force Regulars, 1917–1919.* Edited by George Clark. Jefferson, NC: McFarland, 2011.

Thompson, Martha. *Feland and Singleton Families: Virginia, Kentucky, and Missouri.* Redding, CA: Martha Thompson, 1985.

Tillman, Ellen Davies. "Imperialism Revised: Military, Society, and U.S. Occupation in the Dominican Republic, 1880–1924." PhD diss., University of Illinois at Urbana-Champaign, 2010.

Trask, David. *The War with Spain in 1898*. New York: Macmillan, 1981.

Trimble, William F. *Admiral William A. Moffett: Architect of Naval Aviation*. Washington, DC: Smithsonian Institution Press, 1994.

Ulbrich, David. *Preparing for Victory: Thomas Holcomb and the Making of the Modern Marine Corps, 1936–1943*. Annapolis, MD: Naval Institute Press, 2011.

United States. *Official Congressional Directory*. Washington, DC: Government Printing Office, 1919.

———. *Official Register of the United States, Containing a List of Officers and Employees in the Civil, Military, and Naval Service*. Washington, DC: Government Printing Office, 1892.

———. *Register of the Commissioned and Warrant Officers of the United States Navy and Marine Corps*. Washington, DC: Government Printing Office, 1899–1933.

United States Congress. House Committee on Naval Affairs. *Hearings on the Status of the U.S. Marine Corps, Hearings before the Subcommittee on Naval Academy and Marine Corps, Committee on Naval Affairs, House of Representatives, the Status of the Marine Corps, 1909*. Washington, DC: Government Printing Office, 1909.

United States Department of State. *Foreign Relations of the United States, 1927*. Vol. 3. Washington, DC: Government Printing Office, 1942.

———. *Foreign Relations of the United States, 1928*. Vol. 3. Washington, DC: Government Printing Office, 1943.

———. *Foreign Relations of the United States, 1929*. Vol. 3. Washington, DC: Government Printing Office, 1943–1944.

United States Marine Corps. *Advanced Base Operations in Micronesia*. Washington, DC: Government Printing Office, 1992.

United States Navy Department. *Annual Reports of the Secretary of the Navy*. Washington, DC: Government Printing Office, 1898–1935.

Venzon, Anne Cipriano. *Leaders of Men: Ten Marines Who Changed the Corps*. Lanham, MD: Scarecrow Press, 2008.

———, ed. *From Whaleboats to Amphibious Warfare: Lt. Gen. "Howling Mad" Smith and the Marine Corps*. Westport, CT: Praeger, 1992.

———. *General Smedley Darlington Butler: The Letters of a Leatherneck, 1898–1931*. New York: Praeger, 1992.

Waterman, C. E. "The United States Marine Corps School of Application." *Army and Navy Life and the United Service* 10, no. 6 (June 1907): 605–6.

Welles, Sumner. *Naboth's Vineyard: The Dominican Republic, 1844–1924*. 2 vols. New York: Payson and Clarke, 1928.

West, Bing, and Major General Ray Smith, USMC (Ret.). *The March Up: Taking Baghdad with the 1st Marine Division*. New York: Bantam, 2004.

Wiegand, Wayne. "The Lauchheimer Controversy: A Case of Group Pressure during the Taft Administration." *Military Affairs* 40, no. 2 (April 1976): 54–59.

Williams, Alexander S. "The San Diego Marine Base." *Marine Corps Gazette* 11, no. 2 (June 1926): 82–86.

Williams, Dion. "Blue Marine Expeditionary Force." *Marine Corps Gazette* 10, no. 2 (September 1925): 76–88.

———. "Captain Richard Bell Buchanan, U.S. Marine Corps." *Marine Corps Gazette* 12, no. 2 (June 1927): 72.

———. "The Education of a Marine Corps Officer." *Marine Corps Gazette* 18, no. 1 (May 1933): 16–26.

———. "The Fall Exercises of the 1924 Marine Corps Expeditionary Force." *Marine Corps Gazette* 10, no. 1 (June 1925): 30–62.

———. "In Memoriam Brigadier General Robert Henry Dunlap, U.S.M.C." *Marine Corps Gazette* 16, no. 2 (August 1931): 4–7.

Williams, R. H. "Those Controversial Boards." *Marine Corps Gazette* 66, no. 11 (November 1982): 91–96.

Wise, Frederick, as told to Meigs O. Frost. *A Marine Tells It to You.* New York: J. H. Sears, 1929.

Wisner, James. "The Reserve Camp at Lansdowne." *Marines Magazine* 1, no. 9 (September 1916): 13.

Wood, Charles. *Marine Corps Personal Papers Collection Catalog.* Washington, DC: History and Museums Division, Headquarters, U.S. Marine Corps, 1980.

Wright, George C. *Life behind a Veil: Blacks in Louisville, Kentucky, 1865–1930.* Baton Rouge: Louisiana State University Press, 1985.

Wright, James N. "On the Art of Hand to Hand: An Interview with Col. A. J. Drexel Biddle, USMCR." *Leatherneck* (April 1940): 21–22.

Yarsinske, Amy Waters. *Jamestown Exposition: American Imperialism on Parade.* 2 vols. Mount Pleasant, SC: Arcadia Publishing, 1999.

Yerxa, Donald A. *Admirals and Empire: The United States Navy and the Caribbean, 1898–1945.* Columbia: University of South Carolina Press, 1991.

———. "The Special Services Squadron and the Caribbean Region, 1920–1940: A Case Study in Naval Diplomacy." *Naval War College Review* 39, no. 4 (Autumn 1986): 60–72.

Index

CPSIA information can be obtained at www.ICGtesting.com
Printed in the USA
BVOW04*1532070214

344196BV00002B/4/P